FONDATION HARDT

POUR L'ÉTUDE DE L'ANTIQUITÉ CLASSIQUE

ENTRETIENS

Tome XVII

ENNIUS

ENTRETIENS SUR L'ANTIQUITÉ CLASSIQUE
Publiés par Olivier Reverdin
TOME XVII

ENNIUS

SEPT EXPOSÉS SUIVIS DE DISCUSSIONS

PAR

OTTO SKUTSCH, H. D. JOCELYN, J. H. WASZINK,
E. BADIAN, JÜRGEN UNTERMANN,
PETER WÜLFING-VON MARTITZ, WERNER SUERBAUM

Entretiens préparés et présidés
par Otto Skutsch

VANDŒUVRES-GENÈVE
23-29 AOÛT 1971

CES ENTRETIENS ONT ÉTÉ ORGANISÉS ET CE VOLUME A ÉTÉ PUBLIÉ
AVEC L'AIDE DU FONDS NATIONAL SUISSE DE LA RECHERCHE SCIENTIFIQUE

AVANT-PROPOS

Au cours de ces dernières années, les études sur Ennius ont sensiblement progressé. Le rôle décisif de ce poète, à la charnière entre la littérature grecque, riche d'une longue tradition, et la littérature latine naissante, apparaît de manière toujours plus évidente.

La Fondation Hardt avait consacré ses entretiens de 1962 à Varron; elle a décidé de consacrer ceux de 1971 à Ennius, et elle a chargé le prof. Otto Skutsch de les organiser, avec la collaboration du prof. J.-H. Waszink.

Les savants pressentis ont tous accepté — fussent-ils habitants des Antipodes — à l'exception de M. Sebastiano Timpanaro et de M. Scevola Mariotti. L'absence de ces deux éminents spécialistes italiens d'Ennius a été vivement regrettée.

Il importait de faire tout d'abord le point et de montrer où en étaient parvenues les études sur les œuvres maîtresses du poète. Le prof. Otto Skutsch (Londres) s'est chargé des Annales, *le prof. H. D. Jocelyn (Sydney), des tragédies et le prof. J.-H. Waszink (Leyde) de la* Satura.

On ne peut interpréter et juger valablement une œuvre littéraire qu'à condition de la situer dans son contexte historique et social. Le prof. E. Badian (Harvard) s'est chargé de le faire pour Ennius. Quand on traite d'un auteur qui a contribué à introduire dans une littérature in statu nascendi *des genres et des mètres empruntés à une autre littérature, il est essentiel de soumettre à une analyse critique la langue qu'il a forgée pour y parvenir. C'est à quoi tend l'exposé du prof. Jürgen Untermann (Cologne) sur la grammaire d'Ennius. Epopée en hexamètres dactyliques et tragédie en trimètres iambiques sont des genres littéraires grecs. Ennius, qui est un des premiers à les avoir cultivés à Rome, est donc tributaire de ses devanciers grecs. Au point qu'on peut se demander, avec le prof. Peter Wülfing-von Martitz (Cologne), s'il n'est pas, à certains égards, un poète hellénistique s'exprimant en latin.*

Le sort d'Ennius est semblable à celui d'Archiloque. Sa renommée a été considérable, mais, de ses poèmes, il ne subsiste que des lambeaux. Cette renommée a néanmmoins survécu à la perte presque intégrale de l'œuvre sur laquelle elle était fondée. Elle brille d'un grand éclat chez Pétrarque. Le prof. Werner Suerbaum (Munich) avait préparé, pour les entretiens de Vandœuvres, un mémoire considérable sur Ennius et Pétrarque; faute d'argent, nous avons dû nous résoudre à n'en imprimer qu'un substantiel résumé.

Les sept exposés qui viennent d'être mentionnés et les discussions qui les ont suivis forment la matière du présent ouvrage, qui serait d'une consultation malaisée s'il n'était muni d'index. Ceux qu'on trouvera à la fin du volume ont été établis par M. Bernard Grange, bibliothécaire de la Fondation Hardt, avec l'aide de Mme Martine Vodoz, licenciée ès lettres classiques de l'Université de Genève.

L'organisation de ces XVIIe entretiens et leur publication ont été grandement facilités par un subside du Fonds national Suisse de la recherche scientifique, auquel la Fondation Hardt exprime ici sa reconnaissance.

TABLE DES MATIÈRES

I

OTTO SKUTSCH

Readings and Interpretations in the Annals

READINGS AND INTERPRETATIONS IN THE ANNALS

We need not perhaps reflect at length on the reasons why we are having these *Entretiens sur Ennius*. The title of " Father of Roman Poetry " was not given to Ennius for nothing : it states the facts succinctly but correctly. I am not sure who first applied that title to him. Horace's reference to " Father Ennius ", half reverent, half mocking, does not seem to contain any notion of his being the 'begetter' of Latin Poetry ; and yet who, reading Horace today, can banish that idea from his mind, especially as Ennius himself is not far from claiming paternity ? Nevertheless, as far as a hasty search enables me to judge, it was a scholar of the late sixteenth century, Bonaventura Vulcanius, who first came rather close to calling Ennius the Father of Roman Poetry. In a Greek epigram in the introduction to Merula's commentary on the *Annals* he calls him ἀρχὸς ἀοιδοπόλων, and in the Latin version the corresponding phrase is *vatum pater Ennius*. But whoever may have been the first, he was thinking of Ennius' linguistic achievement, linked indissolubly with his metrical innovation, the introduction of the hexameter. He was certainly not thinking of another aspect of Ennius' art, which to us seems to loom larger and larger : his attitude to Hellenistic poetry, and the conscious stance he took and passed on to later generations of poets. Ennius' linguistic achievement, then, and " Ennius as a Hellenistic Poet " are the topics which Prof. Untermann and Dr. Wülfing have chosen for their contributions. Prof. Badian will deal with historical problems, the nature of which I am not in a position to reveal ; and Prof. Suerbaum will tell us of the influence which Ennius had on later poetry and in particular of the image of Ennius as it was conceived by later centuries down to the Renaissance. I feel almost certain that he will incidentally give us the answer to the question which I raised a minute ago : who was it who first called Ennius the Father of Roman Poetry?

These four contributions and the discussions following them will constitute the more general part of the *Entretiens*. They will be preceded, as it is right and proper in the study of a particular author, by contributions concerned with the actual text of his works. I shall speak of the *Annals*, Prof. Jocelyn of the Tragedies, and Prof. Waszink of the Satires. And if a study of the text is a necessary condition for the assessment of any writer, this is particularly so with a writer who has come down only in fragments. It would be difficult enough to place the fragments in their putative context and thus to build up a picture of the whole if the fragments themselves were clearly understood. But the interpretation of fragments is often uncertain, and the sources which transmit them are frequently either not sufficiently explicit or even actually mistaken. The patient work of scholars over the centuries, beginning with Columna's text and commentary published nearly 400 years ago, and culminating in Vahlen's second edition of 1903, has pieced together a large part of the story. We know, for instance, that the first three books of the *Annals* dealt with the regal period, books IV and V with the early republic, and book VI with the war against King Pyrrhus; that book VII, after an important proem, and (probably) a very brief summary of the First Punic War, began a story of the events of which Ennius himself was an eye witness : the Second Punic War, the description of which came to an end with book IX. Book X, beginning with another proem, was devoted to the war against Philip of Macedon, XI and XII to the activities of Flamininus in Greece, XIII and XIV to the conquest of Antiochus, and XV largely to the achievements of Ennius' patron Fulvius. At this point matters become a little uncertain, and the subject matter of the last triad, XVI to XVIII, which was apparently added by Ennius some time after the completion of I-XV, remains rather obscure. But it is not questions of the arrangement of the subject matter with which I want to deal, nor the old and notorious problems of the proems, which we shall discuss on another occasion. Nor shall I look into the question of how Ennius solved the problem which faced every writer of an historical epic, and especially any Roman epic poet: how was he to use the Homeric backcloth of the Olympic gods in his story? This is the problem which Virgil brilliantly solved by placing his national epic in the mythical past, which Lucan solved by omitting the divine apparatus, which Statius and Valerius avoided by writing purely Greek mythological epics, and which Silius Italicus egregiously failed to solve, with the most ludicrous results. I have made it my task rather to discuss a number of passages, the reading and interpretation of which can in my opinion be advanced. It would seem that even today, nearly seventy years after Vahlen's second edition, some comparatively simple reflexions may achieve some progress. And I have selected passages which can throw a certain amount of light either on Ennius' style and poetic manner or on the method with which such enquiries are to be conducted, or, preferably, on both.

I should like to begin with a very minor linguistic matter, which has perhaps a certain topicality because it was recently mentioned by one of the finest critics of Ennius, whom we have tried in vain, like his friend Scevola Mariotti, to persuade to take part in our deliberations. I am referring, of course, to Sebastiano Timpanaro. In a recent paper [1] he discussed a phenomenon of colloquial language which essentially disappears after Plautus and reappears in late Latin, but is occasionally found as an archaism in the inter-

[1] *Studia Florentina Alexandro Ronconi sexagenario oblata*, Roma 1970, 455 ff., esp. 461.

vening period, especially in the historians. The paper is entitled *Positivus pro comparativo*, and the line of the *Annals* which he adduces as an example is 134 *ferro se caedi quam dictis his toleraret.* He imagines that Ennius took this feature, the omission of *magis* or *potius*, from contemporary language, not observing that it did not suit the epic style. The fragment is, by the source which quotes it as an example of *tolerare* meaning *patienter ferre*, attributed to Book II, and all editors connect it with the story of the surviving Horatius who killed his sister because she wept for her bridegroom, or, in the fertile imagination of Dionysius and of Ennius' commentators, because she insulted him. But it would be most extraordinary, not to say ludicrous, for a man to say that he would rather let himself be killed than so insulted, and immediately to proceed to butcher a woman instead. Moreover, if this were a speech of Horatius, the verb would either have to be in the first person or, as indirect speech, in the infinitive. Timpanaro, a long time ago [1], took the passage to be narrative : " He, Horatius, would more readily have allowed himself " etc. But, unless I am greatly mistaken, that is the style of the *Chanson de Roland*, not of any Greek or Latin epic. Nor is the absurdity of such a statement just before that impatient hero saves his honour by murdering the woman in any way lessened by attributing it to the poet rather than to Horatius. Vahlen correctly saw that the fragment was part of a question, and he suggested : *quis non magis ferro. ...* It is not quite clear to me why Timpanaro rejected this. We all know that Festus, who transmits the fragment, regularly quotes whole lines, ruthlessly cutting off any part of the sentence not contained in that one metrical unit. There simply is no question at all but that the sentence ran : *quis non potius cui uiuida uirtus ferro se caedi quam dictis his toleraret.* I believe that the

[1] *SIFC* 22 (1947), 38.

context must have been an occasion (which we cannot identify) when somebody is by taunts goaded into fighting. But I was not really concerned with the context. My main concern was to show that in looking at fragments we must not be too willing to accept irregularities. The language of Ennius does in fact seem to have been far more normal than the collection of its oddities by modern as well as by ancient grammarians would make it appear.

* * *

A very similar case may continue our story. Festus quotes from book VIII, as an example of *occasus* for *occasio*, line 294 *aut occasus ubi tempusue audere repressit.* This line again has exercised scholars more than just a little. All commentaries note that the infinitive *audere* is here, somewhat boldly perhaps, but not impossibly, used as the object of *repressit*, and our syntacticians follow suit. Here is Wackernagel, *Vorles. über Syntax* 1, 273 : " den Wagemut zurückdrängte ", and Schmalz-Hofmann 577 describes the construction as 'rather bold'. Personally, when I look at the line, I am not so much impressed by the boldness of the syntax as by the fact that the statement made here is absolutely nonsensical. In what conceivable circumstances can 'time and opportunity' be said to *stifle* daring? Don't they usually do the opposite? Let us recall, then, that again our source is Festus, and that Festus quotes whole lines, chopping off parts of the sentence however much they may be required by the sense. So we can, without much ado, supplement: *monuit res aut occasus ubi tempusue audere, repressit*: " when circumstance and time and opportunity called for daring, he repressed it ". An object of *repressit*, such as *cupidos pugnandi animos*, may have preceded, or the general sense of the *ubi* clause was understood to be the object, which is by no means improbable, especially if the next line ran: *et pugnae cupidos hosti dare terga coegit.* What makes me so confident that the phrase cut off by Festus was *monuit res* is the Virgilian line, *Aen.* IX 320 *Euryale, audendum dextra: nunc ipsa uocat res.* We have all learned from Eduard Norden that very often these slightly irregular verse endings in Vergil go back to Ennius; and in fact of the 500 odd hexameters of the *Annals* no less than six end in *res.* And for the use of *res* we may compare *Ann.* 166 *iuuat res*[1], or 430 *quo res sapsa loco sese ostentatque iubetque* " where circumstance itself beckons and bids ", namely " to do and dare "; or Plautus, *Asinaria* 512 *animus hortat, res monet.*

But perhaps Festus was mistaken and *occasus* does not mean " opportunity " here but something like *interitus*? This is indeed how Wackernagel translates: " oder wo der Untergang oder gefahrvolle Umstände den Wagemut zurückdrängte ". There are three considerations, each of them strong enough in itself, to rule out this idea:

1. I shall have to say later that the ancient grammarians were rather stupid; our judgement is incomparably better than theirs, and we must not hesitate to reject their opinion—except where the context which they had before their eyes and which is unknown to us gave them the advantage. And they clearly had the advantage here: Festus or rather his source Verrius Flaccus knew what it was all about, and we do not, and so he must be trusted when he says that *occasus* here means *occasio.*

2. Not only is *occasus* for *mortis periculum* and *tempus* for *tempus aduersum* rather strained, we also know, and everybody who has read Terence's prologues knows, that *tempus atque occasio* is a fixed phrase and bears a positive, not a negative sense. And, lastly,

[1] I would not rule out that in that much-vexed line *monet occasus, iubet res* has to be restored for *tenet occasus, iuuat res.*

3. Our fragment comes from Book VIII. Book VII ended with the battle of Lake Trasumene, and Book VIII began with the gathering of Roman strength, *Marsa manus, Paeligna cohors, Vestina uirum uis*, and continued with the *uictrices morae* of Fabius, the first part of them, later to be followed by the reversal of policy and the battle of Cannae. And what happened during the first part of the *uictrices morae*? We know, of course, that the dictator was criticised and attacked; but read the speech of Minucius in Livy XXII 14, 4-14, accusing the dictator of cowardice, and the speech of M. Metilius XXII 25: *exercitum cupientem pugnare et magistrum equitum clausos prope intra uallum retentos*, and it becomes impossible to deny that this is the ideal context for our *monuit res aut occasus ubi tempusue audere, repressit et pugnae cupidos hosti dare terga coegit.*

It is very pleasant when the slight linguistic correction which one has to make helps to settle the fragment in a definite context. But the essential point which I want to make is that fragments are no happy hunting ground for syntactical peculiarities. It is sometimes said, and with reason, that we must be extremely restrained in correcting fragmentary texts. But with just as much, and perhaps even better reason can it be said that a linguistic irregularity in a fragment can be accepted only with the greatest reserve, and the suspicion that something may have gone wrong, or that the linguistic character of the passage may be affected by the context must be ever present in the mind of those interpreting fragments.

* * *

And the error is not necessarily modern, as it was in the two cases discussed so far. I believe that we have in a number of instances acquiesced too readily in the ancient grammarians' judgement. As I have already pointed out, we have to defer to it where the knowledge of the context assisted their linguistic analysis, but we must set it aside where it did not, and where our own vastly superior linguistic judgement tells us that they may have been, or *must* have been wrong. We have all the context we need for *Annals* 367

omnes mortales uictores, cordibus uiuis
laetantes, uino curatos, somnus repente
in campo passim mollissimus perculit acris.

Here Priscian tells us that *acris* is a masculine nominative singular, taking the place of the classical *acer*, and nobody has ever questioned this (except that I did so myself at Bonn two years ago, and I hope those who were there will forgive me if I bring the matter up again). Now I wonder whether, if the passage had been cited not for *acris* but for some other reason, we would have taken the view that *acris* was masculine singular. With regard to the adjectives ending in *-er* the position of course is that, whereas in the case of the *-ro* adjectives such as *sacer* and *creber* the unsyncopated form has survived only in *sacros* on the Forum cippus, the adjectives formed with *-ri* retained the unsyncopated form much longer, side by side with the syncopated one, and the variant was eventually, by a deliberate decision, utilised to distinguish between the masculine, syncopated, *acer*, and the feminine, unsyncopated, *acris*. This distinction became an absolute rule only with disyllables such as *acris*. Trisyllables such as *illustris*, *salubris*, *terrestris*, and occasionally *equestris*, defy it at all times. As far as *alacris* is concerned it is not quite clear whether it should be classed with the polysyllables, or with the disyllables, since rhythmically it is the equivalent of a trochee. At any rate in the *Athamas* of Ennius we have a masculine nominative singular *alacris*, where this, the old form, is used without any special reason. When Terence later says, *Eun.* 304, *quid tu es tristis quidue es* *alacris* one seems to hear an intended rhyme with *tristis*, and when Virgil *Aen.* 5, 380 has *ergo alacris*, one may suspect that he avoids **er***go alac***er**. As for *acer*, this, the more modern phonetic variant is used even for the feminine by Naevius, *fames acer augescit* and by Ennius himself in *Annals* 424 *post acer hiems it*. So, although the technical writers Celsus and Columella used *acris* masculine singular once each, we should perhaps ascribe that form to Ennius only if we have definite reason to do so. But what reason have we? How did Priscian or his source know that *acris* was nominative here? The context beyond what we have could certainly not have helped him to decide.

So much *a priori*. Now let us look at the text itself. If *acris* is taken as nominative singular, it would have to be used predicative-adverbially to qualify *perculit*, since as an attribute of sleep *acer* is unintelligible. Not even as a translation of a Greek compound such as γλυκύπικρος would it seem to make sense, and we should also have to ask why one part of the compound should be rendered in the superlative and the other in the positive. So *acris* as a singular nominative is difficult: why not take it as accusative plural? This seems to me absolutely required by what precedes. These men are shown in the elation of victory. The conjecture *imis* for *uiuis* is best forgotten: it destroys the alliteration *uictores* ... *cordibus uiuis* ... *uino curatos*, and destroys the sense: the *uiuida uis animi* is vigorously alive in them, they are *acres* or *alacres*. It is then, in that condition, that they are struck by gentle sleep. That is to say we have to do with an oxymoron of the same type as Homer's κιχάνει τοι βραδὺς ὠκύν, 'the slow captures the swift', lame Hephaestus capturing Ares. A similar example is found in the *Philoctetes* of Accius, Philoctetes shooting birds: *occidit tardus celeres, stans uolantes*.

* * *

How misleading in fact the statements of the grammarians can be is amusingly illustrated by *Annals* 149 *postquam lumina sis oculis bonus Ancus reliquit*. R. Frobenius, a man of limited knowledge and intelligence, in his Syntax of Ennius, commenting on this line, followed Vahlen's text without troubling to look at the attestation, and he thus correctly took *sis oculis* to be an ablative (though he classified it wrongly). There can be no doubt at all that it is an ablative, since in *Annals* 532 Ennius quite similarly says *corde relinquite somnum*. But great scholars such as Heinze and Norden *did* look into the attestation, and finding there that Festus speaks of *sis* as a dative they went to great lengths explaining *sis oculis* as a dative of disadvantage: " to the detriment of his eyes King Ancus left the light ". That is the sort of damage which can result from taking these grammarians too seriously. Obviously no context could help Verrius Flaccus to decide whether it was a dative or an ablative, and therefore his opinion is worth nothing. Nor did he really care which it was : he was concerned merely with the attestation of the old pronoun, and was not interested in the syntax at all.

I should like to digress here a little from my present line of argument because two problems arise in connection with this fragment. One, that of placing ; and to that I think I know the answer. The second is an historical one, and to this I should very much like to elicit an answer from Professor Badian. First of all, the place of the fragment. It is attested by Festus as belonging to Book III, and there of course editors print it, but in different positions. In Vahlen, for instance, and in Valmaggi it is the third fragment of that book, in Warmington the fourth. And yet there can be no question but that the much maligned Baehrens was correct in giving it the first place, right at the beginning of the book. That is its natural position. The reign of Ancus was described in Book II. On the other hand, the omens which forecast the future rule of Tarquin were reported by

Ennius in Book III, line 146 and 147-8 in Vahlen. This means that at the beginning of Book III Ennius must have gone back a little in time and have related how under the rule of King Ancus Tarquin immigrated. And how would, how could this narrative have started? " When Ancus was dead" (our line 149) 'the Roman people gave the kingdom to Tarquin' (line 150). And then Ennius began to explain who this Tarquin was, and told of the immigration, the story of Tanaquil, and the eagle portent. This, incidentally, is the order in which Dionysius tells the story, whereas Livy slips it in just before the final note on Ancus.

This accounts for a fact which has not perhaps hitherto been given its due weight. Our line is of course repeated with a slight variation by Lucretius in Book III *lumina sis oculis etiam bonus Ancus reliquit*, where it illustrates the fact that we all must die. But why did Lucretius use the line— unless it was well known, prominent, and almost proverbial? Surely it had all these qualities because it was the first line of a book. And if in Horace King Ancus twice illustrates the fact that all must die, once in company with Numa: *Epist.* I 6, 27 *Numa quo deuenit et Ancus*, and once in the *Odes*, IV 7, 14, in company with Aeneas et Tullus, *nos ubi decidimus, quo pius Aeneas, quo diues Tullus et Ancus*, the reason is not that Ancus had some mysterious connection with the underworld but that his death had been made prominent first by Ennius and then by Lucretius. Let me confirm this by a last observation. Virgil has one book which begins with *postquam*. Which is it? Book III, as in Ennius. Accident, you will say. Perhaps. But let me tell you another fact. Silius Italicus has seventeen books on the Punic War. One of them begins with *postquam*. Which is it? Book III. Just as Silius followed Virgil in this peculiar little detail, so Virgil followed Ennius.

Let me now turn to my other problem, the historical one, although I admit that it has little bearing on Ennius himself.

The question has sometimes been asked why Ancus is called *bonus*, and his concern for the *plebs*, whose common law he is said to have established, has been held to be responsible e.g. by Niebuhr. This may well be so, but in that case it would not be Ennius whose opinion is expressed in that attribute. Ennius may have been an Aufklärer, but we have absolutely no reason to believe that he was a partisan of the *plebs*. His personal friendship with great aristocrats of Rome seems to suggest the opposite. If *bonus* has anything to do with Ancus' pro-plebeian attitudes, Ennius would rather seem to have taken from popular transmission the idea that Ancus was good, without concerning himself with the reasons for that judgement. But of course *bonus* need really mean no more than that Ancus was a just, pious and peaceful ruler, like Numa, whose grandson he is reported to be, and like Servius Tullius, and unlike in some respects at any rate to Romulus, Tullus and the Tarquins.

Bonus need not therefore indicate that Ancus was the patron of the *plebs*, and was certainly not meant by Ennius to do so. We do, however possess certain information proving that Ancus was criticised for currying favour with the people. I am referring, of course, to Virgil's (*Aen.* VI 815) *iactantior Ancus, nunc quoque iam nimium gaudens popularibus auris*. Norden's commentary can make nothing of this, beyond suggesting a confusion with Servius Tullius, although Niebuhr long ago had mentioned the line in connection with his explanation of *bonus*. Here we quite clearly have the aristocratic view of Ancus' attitude to the *plebs*. And how did this tradition of his being the patron of the *plebs* arise? Apart from the transmission that he settled the regions of the Circus valley and the Aventine, definitely plebeian quarters, we may recall the fact that the *gens Marcia* was plebeian and that it was always prominently associated with the *populares*.

But there is another, and perhaps a more interesting explanation. We know that many events in Roman history, if they were not flattering to Roman pride, tended to be eliminated in the transmission, or to be explained away, and in such cases we get only here and there a glimpse of what really happened. The surrender of the city to Porsenna, the fall of the Capitol, the failure of the *deuotio* of Decius Mus at Ausculum are examples of this. Now in the last chapter devoted to Tullus' reign Dionysius of Halicarnassus, III 34, 3, tells us that in the war against Rome the thirty Latin cities appointed two supreme commanders, Spusius Vecilius from Lavinium, and Ancus Poplicius from Cora. These two men are not mentioned anywhere else. It has therefore been suggested that they were invented by Dionysius. Dionysius does invent things, such as the abuse heaped on Horatius by his sister. But this is to adorn a tale. Why should he invent two Latin commanders of whom nobody had ever heard? In the next chapter Tullus is dead and is succeeded by Marcius. We are of course on treacherous ground in the whole story of both Tullus and Ancus. Few of us will believe that Tullus was killed by lightning in his home because he had offended Iuppiter Elicius. I would certainly consider it possible that he was despatched by the Latins and was succeeded by their commander Ancus, whose *gentile*, as given by Dionysius, seems to have given rise to the story that he was a man of the people, seeking *populares auras*. We think of the *Publicii* Malleoli, through whom, according to Ovid, *Fast.* V 289 *rem populus recipit* (they were *aediles plebei* according to Varro, *LL* V 158 and Ovid, but curule aediles according to Fest. 238[B]), and we think of course of Valerius *Poplicola*, whose surname " little poplar " was misunderstood and coloured the picture of his activities. And why should Ancus Poplicius have become Ancus Marcius? One has of course questioned the historicity of King Ancus Marcius because the Marcii are plebeians and do not appear in the *Fasti* before 357. However, the first plebeian *rex sacrorum* was a Marcius, whence that branch of the Marcii proudly called themselves Marcii Reges, and claimed to be descended from a King. But that Marcius *Rex* (*sacrorum*) died in 210 B.C. and it seems hardly credible that Ancus after that date acquired the surname Marcius, unless indeed that surname is an invention of Ennius himself. There are other possibilities : a Publicius and a Marcius are mentioned together as early *uates* by Cicero *De diu.* I 115. There could be confusion here. But it is idle to speculate. The salient facts are these : an Ancus Publicius, otherwise entirely unknown, is mentioned as a leader of the Latins in the wars conducted against them by Tullus immediately before his end. Tullus is succeeded by an Ancus surnamed Marcius, who, though otherwise as pious as his grandfather Numa, was yet in part of the transmission suspected (Dion. III 35, 3) of having killed Tullus. And the *gentile* of Ancus in his earlier role, Publicius, may well have given rise to the story of *iactantior Ancus, ... nimium gaudens popularibus auris.* We must not underestimate the force of etymology in the creation of legend : the same Ancus is said to have fetched laws from the *Aequicoli*, obviously because they *aequom colunt.*

Let me add one more point, and I believe a decisive one. The name Ancus is very rare indeed. King Ancus and Ancus Poplicius are the only known bearers of it [1]. Can we really believe that two separate Anci lived at precisely the same time, one a leading enemy of King Tullus, the other his successor suspected of having murdered him? No, I am convinced that these, the only two Anci known to history, were in fact identical. However, let us now return to Ennius.

* * *

[1] A diminutive *Anculus* must have existed but survives only in the gentile *Ancilius*, found once at Corfinium, once at Tarquinii and once at Praeneste. This distribution alone would be sufficient to discredit Varro's statement (*De praen.*, 4, accepted by Ogilvie on Livy I 32) that the name is Sabine. It is quite likely to be Etruscan ; see W. Schulze, *ZGLE* 165,7 ; Walde-Hofmann, *s.v.*

Sometimes the grammarians working on the text of Ennius deserve some credit for having spotted a problem although they failed to spot the solution. Aulus Gellius, XVIII 5, tells us that he heard an Ennianista read the line which is 232 in Vahlen's edition as *denique ui magna quadrupes equus atque elephanti proiciunt sese*, and that a certain Julianus said this was quite wrong and that the reader should have said *eques* instead of *equus*. Julianus claimed he had consulted an age-old MS of Ennius which Lampadio himself was said to have emended, and found there *eques* and not *equos*. From the concluding words of Gellius it follows that this was an old conundrum of Roman grammarians. And it has remained a conundrum with modern grammarians as well. If the text is correct, it would seem that *eques* is here used in the sense of " horse ". Now we are all nowadays, I think, agreed that when Virgil, *Georg.* III 116, says that the Lapithae *equitem docuere sub armis insultare solo et gressus glomerare superbos* he simply makes the horseman do what in fact is done by the horse. But nevertheless there are those who believe that Ennius used *eques* for " horse ". It seems the straightforward sense of our passage, and there is no denying the fact that in late Latin, in the Vulgate, *uidit currum duorum equitum*, and in Gregory of Tours, *ascenso equite*, *eques* stands for *equus*. But that is a very different matter, for in late Latin *equus* caused phonetic difficulties and tended to be replaced by longer words, such as *caballus*, French *cheval*, and *paraueredus*, German *Pferd*, and apparently also by *equitem*. Note also that in that period there was little phonetic difference between *eques* and *equus*. Now there were obviously no phonetic difficulties in early Latin or in classical Latin; so why should Ennius feel the need to replace *equus*? Bonnet remarks, rightly, that *quadrupes* as an attribute of horse would seem to be a little redundant, and that *eques* should therefore here be the horseman. But we must go a little farther than that. Both as an attribute of *equus* and as an attribute of *eques* "four-footed" is just utterly senseless, and from no poetry known to me in any language can such nonsense be parallelled. Professor Warmington here adopts an interesting idea, which I am unable to trace to its source but which is given in some of our dictionaries. It is that *quadrupes* means "at the gallop". Now, *quadrupedi cursu*, which we find in Apuleius, is perfectly alright, but that is a somewhat different matter. As an attribute of horse *quadrupes* would have to be understood as a back-formation, a hypostasis, of the verb *quadrupedari*, a substitute for its participle *quadrupedans*, which is used as "galloping" both by Virgil and Ennius. But the back-formation would be rather bold and one might also ask why the attribute should attach to *eques* only and not to *elephanti*. I have thought of a different solution: military formations are often referred to in the singular: so *eques* apparently here, and elsewhere, so *miles*, *pedes*, *ueles*, etc. Why then should *quadrupes* be either an attribute or the equivalent of a participle? Why should it not be a noun and mean "the four-footed formations", i.e. τὰ τετράποδα, the cavalry and the elephants? A comma after *quadrupes* puts the whole thing right. *quadrupes* is not attested for the quadrupeds in a military sense, but why should it? It's perfectly possible, and the Romans who did not use elephants had little occasion to employ it. This explanation seems to me far more probable than *quadrupes* in the sense of a participle, especially as the verb is qualified already by *ui magna*. But whichever solution is right, it appears that, when looked at critically, the language of Ennius is far less quaint than it appears at first sight.

* * *

And it is not only word-usage and syntax that loses much of its strangeness on closer inspection. The style, too, is more normal than the state of the text may suggest.

One of the longest fragments of the *Annals* is the one concerned with the familiar friend, lines 234-251 in Vahlen. I have discussed this fragment before now, but want to add a note on it here which nicely, I think, illustrates my point. We have here a detailed description of the friend's character : *ingenium cui nulla malum sententia suadet ut faceret facinus leuis aut mala* : a man who would not be driven by any lighthearted or wicked thought into doing evil : *doctus*, *fidelis*, *suauis homo*, *facundus*, *suo contentus*, *beatus*, *scitus*, *secunda loquens in tempore*, *commodus*, *uerbum paucum*, *multa tenens antiqua*, *sepulta uetustas quae facit* ; knowing many ancient things, which the lapse of time has buried (so, of course. Not : keeping many old-time ways of which a by-gone age long buried is the maker, as the Loeb translator has it). Now this whole piece is in pretty bad shape. I have removed certain difficulties by emendation, and I have simply adopted these corrections here. Others remain, and I do not know how to cope with them : especially the odd transition from *tenens* in one line to *tenentem* in the next one. But there is one which hitherto does not seem to have been noticed, and which I consider not unimportant in its implications. In the piece which I quoted without translating it we had the line 245 *suauis homo facundus suo contentus beatus*. Now is not this really rather peculiar? The whole line is concerned with the sweet nature of the man : agreeable, not in any way jealous, and of a happy disposition. That he is *eloquent* is a statement which does not fit in too well at this point, and though it might be held to be consistent with *secunda loquens in tempore*, it certainly does not consist too well with *uerbum paucum*, because *facundus* always implies a free flow of speech. With these considerations in mind, we realize at once that the word required here is not *facundus*. Quite certainly we must read *iucundus*. Nor is it difficult to see why *iucundus* became *facundus* : *facinus* stood right above it, and the scribe's eye just slipped. Perhaps we can find a little confirmation elsewhere. A. Gellius tells us that Aelius Stilo saw in this piece a self-description of Ennius. The piece was famous and left a good many traces in Latin literature. In Virgil, when the dying Camilla calls a friend to give her a last message, we have verbal echoes, and from there they go to Statius. More importantly, Horace, when he discusses his relationship to Maecenas, can never forget about this passage. And no wonder : Orbilius had seen to it that he knew it by heart, and that he knew what Aelius Stilo had said about it. Now, our piece begins : *quocum bene saepe libenter*. Hor. *Sat.* I 3, 63 says : *qualem me saepe libenter obtulerim tibi Maecenas*. What is remarkable here is not so much the collocation of the two words at the end of the line ; anybody who still composes verse knows that *libenter* more or less has to go to the end of the line, and that *saepe* is liable to settle down next to it. What is remarkable is the application of the phrase to this amicable association, seen in one instance, Ennius, from the point of view of the patron, and in the other, Horace, from the point of view of the client. And connected with this is the fact that *libenter* in both instances has not its normal meaning of " gladly " but the very rare one of " as I (or he) pleased, at will ". So Horace seems to have had the passage of Ennius in mind. A little later in the same satire he says, 93 : *minus hoc iucundus amicus sit mihi*, and in I 5, 44 *nil ego contulerim iucundo sanus amico*. There are a good many passages in Latin literature to show that *iucundus* is just what one does say of a friend. Horace perhaps shows a little more : namely that Ennius did so.

In restoring *iucundus* for *facundus* we have, I think, disposed of a criticism which could have been levelled against Ennius' style : namely that he put his attributes together without any thought other than that of metrical convenience. It is true that there is still no pedantic arrangement : neither is there, for that matter, in the Hellenistic piece about the king's confidant with which I once compared this fragment[1]. But there is certainly no flagrant muddle. In 246 it might be argued that *commodus* was out of place between *scitus*, *secunda loquens in tempore* and *uerbum paucorum*, but actually this arrangement seems rather logical: it is his good sense (*scitus*) which makes him say the right things at the right time, and his adaptability and tact (*commodus*) which makes him say little although he could say much because he knows much.

Further on in the fragment there are serious difficulties: the worst of them that *tenens* in 247 is continued in 248 by *et ... tenentem*. This almost looks as if the poet had chosen the participle of the same verb, *tenere*, and the connection with *et* for the express purpose of drawing attention to the absence of any construction. This I cannot believe, and I am quite certain that there is textual corruption here. However that may be, by restoring *iucundus* we have removed a grave stylistic offence.

* * *

Altogether, I believe, Ennius is much nearer to Greek predecessors and to later Latin poets than might appear from the fragmentary state of the text and the bad transmission of this piece. I would not deny that Ennius often arranges words in ways which are avoided in later poetry: the direct collocation of adjective and noun, and the frequency with which an attribute follows, rather than precedes, its noun. I would not deny that compared to later poetry he can have an archaic stateliness which later poets have given up: as when in the famous scene of the cutting of trees for the cremation of the fallen at Heraclea, 187 ff., three short cola with active verbs, *incedunt*, *caedunt*, *percellunt*, are followed by three short cola with passive verbs, *exciditur*, *frangitur*, *consternitur*, the whole then, after a single return to an active

[1] *Studia Enniana*, 92 ff.

verb, being rounded off by a major colon of long-and-far sounding vowels : *fremitu silvai frondosai.* If one compares Virgil and others in the corresponding scenes, one sees that they aim at variety rather than that archaic stateliness. In this matter we simply have to recognise a different artistic attitude. In the matter of the order of words, it would probably be more correct to say that Ennius marks a stage intermediate between Greek and Latin manner. But what I would deny is that there is lack of artistry, as in the insensate position of *facundus*, or a lack of feeling for what is germane to poetry. Let me give an example of the latter, where editors, guided by their reading of poetry generally, have unhesitatingly corrected a text, until modern ingenuity and modern hyperconservatism began to defend it.

In a fragment possibly describing the region of the Plutonium through which Discordia, having done her work, plunges back into hell, we read, *Ann.* 262 :

longique cupressi
stant sectis foliis et amaro corpore buxum.

Every editor here, following Fulvio Orsini, corrected *sectis* to *rectis*, especially as Ennius elsewhere (490) says *rectosque cupressos.* But then along comes an excellent naturalist, Professor E. H. Warmington, and says : " Why, *sectis* is right. Just look at a cypress and you'll find that cypress leaves appear to be divided up into small parts, being scale-like and imbricated ". And some would even add that the alliteration supports *sectis:* **s***tant* **s***ectis.* Let us take the alliteration first : it proves nothing at all. The function of alliteration in poetry is to heighten the emotional appeal. What emotional appeal is heightened by *stant sectis* " they stand with incisions in their leaves ? " And in any case, if the poet had wanted alliteration here he would have said *celsique cupressi*, not *longique cupressi.* And now to *sectis* itself : Ennius would be quite an extraordinary poet if he were speaking here of those minute incisions in the leaves, so tiny that they are best looked at through a magnifying glass. Surely that is not poetry: that is botany. And what does a poet see in a cypress? We know, from Ovid, *Met.* X 138, where the transformation of Cyparissus into the tree is described. There the poet says of Cyparissus' hair:

et modo quae niuea pendebant fronte capilli

(and the hair that was but now hanging down over his fair brow)

horrida caesaries fieri sumptoque rigore
sidereum gracili spectare cacumine caelum

(grew stiff and rigid and pointed up to heaven).

sumptoque rigore: that is what Ennius means by *rectis foliis.* Let us not cut the father of Latin poetry off from the comity of poets for the sake of preserving an S. He knew as well as Ovid did what was germane to poetry and what was not.

* * *

I should like to attach here an observation which, whether or not my critical decision is correct, shows that Ennius anticipated a stylistic attitude of later poetry: an attitude all the more remarkable in him because it applies to the *Annals* in contradistinction to his scenic poetry.

Donatus, in the *Ars grammatica* IV 394, 6 K. and Pompeius, in his commentary on it, V 291, 25 K., cite as an example of solecism, without naming the author, the line

spoliantur eos et corpora nuda relinquunt.

As Ennius is a likely candidate for the authorship of hexametrical fragments in grammatical tradition, taking into account further that Donatus five lines earlier cites a line, again without naming the author, which we know to belong to Ennius, Columna assigned our fragment to the *Annals*, and editors generally have accepted this. It is line 619 in Vahlen. Quite recently Hubert Cancik, *RhM* 112 (1969), 94, pointed out that we can restore the syllable missing at the beginning from another branch of grammatical transmission : Priscian, II 390, 26 K., apparently following Flavius Caper, testifies that *auctores antiquissimi* used forms such as *careor* for *careo* and *despoliantur* for *despoliant*. It stands to reason that if Flavius uses the third person plural *despoliantur*, he does so because that was the form used in the text to which he refers, and all the chances therefore are that the text was the line which Donatus adduces for *spoliantur*. Now, neither *spolio* nor *despolio* is attested elsewhere to have a deponent variant, and though there are numerous active forms for deponents in Ennius, he has no other deponent form instead of an active form. Both these facts carry comparatively little weight but there is also a very serious objection to the line as it stands. It is well known that most of the forms of the anaphoric pronoun, apart from *is* and *id*, are very rare in poetry. *eos* appears once in the *Georgics*, once in the *Aeneid*, and once in Ovid's ca. 36,000 lines; *eas* appears never in Virgil, and once in Ovid (*Met*. XIV 558, bracketed by Merkel). As to Ennius himself, he uses *is* four times in the *Annals*, and a few times in his other works ; forms such as *ei* (dative), *eum*, *eam*, *ea*, *eos*, *eis* he has fifteen times, but in the plays, of course, not in the *Annals*. You may say that this evidence is not strong enough to show conclusively that Ennius in the *Annals*, in contradistinction to the plays, avoided the oblique forms of *is*. My reply would be that the evidence is indeed conclusive if combined with the fact that, instead of *eum*, *eam*, *eos*, *eas* Ennius uses the highly archaic forms *sum*, *sam*, *sos* and *sas*. It seems quite clear to me that his reason for employing this archaism is his refusal to admit the trite unpoetic forms of the anaphoric pronoun.

What then are we to make of *despoliantur eos*? We could refuse to accept the line as Ennian, although, attested as it now is by both Donatus and Caper, the chances of genuineness are even better than before. Or we can make the bold assumption that the text was corrupt before it was excerpted by our grammarian, say at the end of the republican period. What I would expect Ennius to have written is not *despoliantur eos*, but *despoliant umeros et corpora nuda relinquunt*. The Homeric parallels spring to mind: τεύχε' ἀπ' ὤμων αἴνυσθαι, ἀφαιρεῖσθαι, συλᾶν. It is not easy to see why *umeros* should have become *ureos*, but the possibility certainly exists. Whatever the correct solution here, it is abundantly clear that the peculiar poetic prejudice against the oblique forms of *is* did not arise in the first century B.C.: it was not only foreshadowed but fully developed in the father of Roman poetry.

* * *

In all or almost all the passages we have discussed it was a linguistic feature from which we started, and I do indeed believe that such progress as is still possible will be mainly on these lines. It is true that even in the last few decades occasionally a passage has received a more satisfactory explanation from the comparison of historical narrative concerned with the incidents which the poet must have described; and especially it has been seen that speeches in Livy were strongly influenced by the speeches of historical characters in the *Annals*, speeches which Livy must have learned by heart at school and was never able to forget. Unless, however, I am very much mistaken, the relevant sources have now been so carefully studied that not much progress is to be expected here. But I do not wish to be discouraging, and in order to avoid giving this impression I should like to conclude with one example of how close comparison with Livy can still help to settle both the reading and the precise reference of a fragment. Again I must apologize to those who heard me at Bonn. But I do see some of the detail differently now from the way I saw it then, and so I will venture to repeat the matter.

Festus p. 258[b] cites, without giving the number of the book, a fragment of the *Annals* illustrating the use of *Roma quadrata* :

et quis est erat Romae regnare quadratae

In Vahlen's edition it is line 157. *Quis est erat* is obviously wrong, and Vahlen accepts Hertz's *qui sextus erat* instead. The sixth King of Rome being Servius Tullius, the fragment therefore appears in the third book. More than twenty years ago, however, Timpanaro showed that *qui sextus erat* must be wrong [1]. An infinitive following on *primus* is first found in Silius Italicus, infinitives following other numerals are found nowhere, and since the use, common in the Augustan period, of an infinitive with an ordinary adjective is not found in early Latin at all, *sextus erat* with an infinitive is wholly impossible there. Much better is the version of Salmasius : *et qui se sperat*. It alters only one letter, *p* for *t*, and the construction of *spero* with a present infinitive is quite common in early Latin [2].

Those who follow Salmasius generally put the fragment in the second book and refer it to the deliberations which led to the installation of King Numa. So Lucian Mueller and Valmaggi, and Warmington even maintains that this is the only place possible for it since at a later period Rome was no longer *quadrata*. I do not believe this argument is valid ; for, in the first place, Ennius may not have been as accurate in his antiquarian studies as Professor Warmington ;

[1] *Maia* 3 (1950), 26 ff.

[2] HOFMANN-SZANTYR 357, 4. It is therefore unnecessary to assume that the sentence continued with *posse*.

and secondly, *Roma quadrata* probably does not mean the " square Rome " about the Palatine, but " Rome divided into four parts ", i.e. the four region city of Servius Tullius : *urbe quadrifariam diuisa regionibus*, as Livy I 43, 13 has it. If one refers the fragment to the succession of Romulus, it does not matter greatly whether in the beginning you read *et qui* " and who hopes ? " or *ecqui* (which in the ductus is identical) " does anyone hope ? " But of course *ecqui* could also be an adverb " does he somehow hope ? " This is how Louis Havet took it, and since in that case the subject must be a definite person, much is to be said for Timpanaro's proposal[1] that the subject is one of the three men who during the early republic incurred the suspicion of trying to become king : Spurius Cassius in 485, Spurius Maelius in 439, and M. Manlius Capitolinus in 384. Is it possible to get a little further still, to prove that Timpanaro was right and to determine which of his three candidates is meant ? After what I said about the speeches in Ennius and their influence on Livy, let us look at what Livy says about these three men. Spurius Cassius is dealt with by him very summarily, and the account of Manlius Capitolinus centres on the dramatic gesture with which the accused man turns to the Capitol, the Capitol which he has saved. Matters are different with Spurius Maelius. There in Livy the dictator Cincinnatus delivers a long oration mainly couched in indirect speech, and in its third part, book IV, chapter 15, he says : *nec cum eo tamquam cum ciue agendum fuisse qui natus in libero populo ex qua urbe reges exactos sciret ... in ea Sp. Maelius spem regni conceperit* : " nor had they to treat as a citizen a man who, born in a free state, in a city from which he knew the kings to have been expelled, had yet, he Spurius Maelius, hoped to become king ! " And he continues : *et quis homo ?* Not a member of the great aristocratic families who had

[1] *Maia* 3 (1950), 26 ff.

served the state with distinction, but a grain merchant who could hardly be borne as a senator, let alone as king. *et quis homo?* That is obviously the same as Ennius' *et qui se sperat*, "and, being what kind of a man, does he hope ...?" That is to say we retain the *et qui* as it stands. The matter is so manifest that proof is not really required. But I will point out one detail: why, in Livy, in the midst of indirect speech, do we suddenly have a nominative *et quis homo*, when after all we should expect *et quem hominem*? Ogilvie does not comment. Weissenborn-Mueller say the nominative attaches itself to Spurius Maelius in the preceding sentence—which is of course in the nominative as belonging to a relative clause. That may be a sort of syntactical justification, but the cause is different: the cause is the direct question in Ennius: *et qui se sperat.*

Quite a simple argument, and yet not without interest. Not only can we put the fragment in its historical context and thus into a definite book of the Annals, Book IV; but we can also make a statement about historiography in Rome. Our historians believe, and I think correctly, that the great Cincinnatus had nothing to do with this episode. His ditatorship was, to begin with, connected exclusively with the rescue of Minucius near Mt. Algidus in 458. But the extension of the role of Cincinnatus which has certainly occurred in the annalistic transmission is now shown to be very old and to have been accepted a whole century and a half before Livy. Perhaps you will say: a speech, yes, and also the same speech as in Livy; but how do we know that in Ennius too the speaker was Cincinnatus? Well, perhaps we cannot be absolutely certain. But the chances are that, together with the words, Livy took the person of the speaker from Ennius. Moreover, it is the attitude of Ennius to give great speeches to great men. Münzer once tried to prove that the great speech of Camillus, stopping the Romans from transferring the city to Veji, was an invention of Livy's. No, it belongs to Ennius, and Livy took it over from him, although it clashes with another story which Livy has borrowed from annalistic transmission[1]. Ennius, as a Greek of the Hellenistic period, and as a poet, sees history, as I once tried to put it, as a process shaped by the words and the deeds of great men. If in Livy the speech belongs to the great Cincinnatus, it certainly did so in Ennius.

[1] *Studia Enniana* 12 f.

DISCUSSION

M. Badian : We should perhaps remember, when we look at Horace's *pater Ennius*, that *pater* does not normally mean *genitor* (i.e. begetter). It is a term denoting legal and social status (head of a *familia*), and as such comes to be a title of honour. But no descent is claimed—any more than, when Jupiter is called *pater diuomque hominumque*, it is claimed that he begot them all. It could be, however, that a phrase like *pater Ennius* suggested to a Renaissance scholar (accustomed to the word " father " in a more modern sense) the idea of Ennius as the " father of Roman poetry ".

M. Suerbaum : Der *pater*-Titel für Ennius braucht nicht mehr zu bedeuten, als wenn Aeneas bei Vergil *pater* genannt wird (etwa im Sinne von *uenerabilis*). Ferner ist zu bedenken, dass Ennius als erster wirklicher römischer Dichter gilt (spätestens seit Lucr. I 117 sq.: *Ennius ... qui primus amoeno / detulit ex Helicone perenni fronde coronam*) — eine der Konstanten im Ennius-Bild, über die ich noch sprechen möchte. Wenn er gelegentlich korrekt als *qui primus digne epos Latinum scripsit* oder generalisierend als *Romani carminis primus auctor* bezeichnet wird, entspricht das letzten Endes der Selbsteinschätzung des Ennius, die aus dem Proömium zum VII. *Annalen*-Buch mit der Abwertung der Vorgänger spricht.

M. Jocelyn : Ennius ipse pater may parody a formula of the *Annals*, something like Virgil's *pater Aeneas.* In any case Horace's phrase would simply indicate the present status of Ennius in the family of Roman poets. It has nothing to do with paternity, physical or metaphorical.

Concerning line 294, I am unhappy about the long postponement of *ubi* which results from Mr. Skutsch's supplement as well as about the fact that Ennius' phraseology remains so far from the stock *tempus est* / *datur*—infinitive / gerundive, *occasio est* + infinitive / gerundive, *occasio est et tempus* + infinitive / gerundive (cf. Plautus, *Men.* 552-3, *Pseud.* 958, *Trin.* 998-9). Is it possible that Verrius Flaccus misinterpreted *occasus*? That Ennius was not basing his phraseology on *tempus est et occasio*? Could one interpret *occasus* as " what has just happened " and *tempus* as " general circumstances "? Mr. Skutsch's objections to *occasus* ... *audere repressit* are certainly valid if *occasus* is just a variant of *occasio*.

M. Waszink : I, too, would prefer not to add anything but rather to supply *fuit* : " When there was either an occasion or the moment to show courage, he suppressed it."

M. Skutsch : It seems to me very difficult to assume that an insubstantial and purely formal alternative such as *occasio* and *tempus* should have been introduced by an emphatic *aut*. If, however, to avoid this an addition must be made before *aut*, the chances are that it contained a verb : *monuit res*.

M. Waszink : In my opinion, there is a clear difference between *occasus* (" occasion ", " possibility ") and *tempus* (" urgency ", " necessity ") ; one could paraphrase : " when one could or should be courageous." I do not see any reason to call the use of *aut* in this passage emphatic. But in any case, the comma after *audere* as proposed by Mr. Skutsch seems right.

M. Badian : I am convinced by Professor Waszink's suggestion that *audere* should be taken in an epexegetic sense, governed by *occasus tempusue*, and that (to put it crudely) *fuit* may be understood—i.e. " or when there was an opportunity or time for daring ". This seems much the most straightforward reading of it. However, I do not think that *repressit* can have " opportunity or time " as its object—that does not make sense. We still need a comma after *audere*, with *repressit* referring (just as Professor Skutsch suggested) to the soldiers' eagerness to fight. Hence

I would say that Professor Skutsch's suggested context—a speech attacking Fabius Maximus—still seems to me to be excellent.

If the construction starts with *aut* at the beginning of the line, we agree we need another statement to give the first alternative. This poses no problem. I do not want to invent *pseudo-Enniana*. But one can easily imagine a statement like " When we held a position of advantage " preceding, in some form, the line we have. This reconstruction also answers Professor Jocelyn's justified objection to the excessively postponed *ubi*: it need and should not have anything to do with the preceding line, and in its own clause is only—quite unexceptionally—the second instead of the first word.

* * *

M. Jocelyn: In Mr. Skutsch's interpretation of line 367 it worries me that the victorious soldiers should be described as exulting in their victory (*laetantes*), having their bellies full of wine (*uino curatos*) and then, within the structure of the same sentence, keen in spirit (*acres*). This adjective and its adverb *acriter*, where soldiers are concerned, usually apply to actual fighting (Ennius, *Sc.* 172: *ubi fortuna Hectoris nostram acrem aciem inclinatam dedit*; Livy III 5, 7: *acriter dimicans cecidit*).

M. Untermann: Acer pflegt, wie Herr Jocelyn bemerkt hat, im Zusammenhang mit Kampfszenen die Qualität der Handlung und nicht die der beteiligten Personen zu bezeichnen, und hier bringt *perculit* unmissverständlich das Bild eines Kampfes mit sich. Deshalb sollte man doch versuchen, *acris* nicht auf die *uictores*, die ja soeben gerade nicht *acres*, sondern *laetantes*, *uino curati* sind, sondern auf *somnus* zu beziehen, und es als *adjectivum pro adverbio* zu verstehen : der sanfte Schlaf erschlägt hart, wie ein plötzlich neu hereinbrechender Feind, das siegestrunkene Heer ; das ὀξύμωρον *mollissimus* . . . *acris* ist nicht weniger wirksam, wenn es aus zwei auf das gleiche Substantiv bezogenen Adjektiven besteht.

M. Suerbaum: Eine Auffassung von *acris* als acc. plur. passt besser zur Situation *in campo.* — Eine wirkliche Entscheidung ist nur möglich, wenn man Sinnparallelen zur Auffassung eines *somnus* als *acer* bzw. für die von Mr. Skutsch vertretene Interpretation, dass auch Soldaten, wenn sie einschlafen, noch als *acres* gelten können, vor allem bei Homer nachweisen könnte. (Dort wäre etwa auf *Ilias* XIV 164 f. zu verweisen.)

M. Waszink: What still puzzles me, is that in this interpretation the notions of wine and sleep are separated from each other, whereas it is usual to combine them; I only refer to Vergil *Aen.* II 265: *urbem somno uinoque sepultam.* So I wonder how people who are *uino curati* can be *acres* at the same time.

M. Suerbaum: Beide Verse zusammen (*Ann.* 367/368) sind die Beschreibung einer Hochstimmung. *Acris* dürfte am ehesten als statische Charakterisierung (" die Helden ") zu verstehen sein. (Vgl. etwa die nur scheinbar paradoxe Aussage bei Verg. *Aen.* XI 869 *fugit: acer Atinas.*)

M. Skutsch wishes to add: I overlooked, and Professor Badian points out to me, that Columna took acris *to be acc. plur. — inevitably so since, as shown by his silence, he forget about Priscian's statement.*

* * *

M. *Suerbaum:* Die Argumente dafür, mit dem *postquam*-Vers (*Ann.* 149) das III. *Annalen*-Buch beginnen zu lassen, sind überzeugend. In der Tatsache, dass auch Vergil das III. Buch der *Aeneis* mit einem *postquam* beginnt (und von ihm abhängig Silius das III. Buch der *Punica*) möchte ich eher ein Kuriosum sehen, auch wenn der Auftakt von *Aeneis* III in einer Rückschau raffend erzählt (also, wenn man so will, Ennianisch ist). Der *postquam*-Satz bei Ennius selbst ist keine Rückschau, sondern eine blosse Zeit-Konstatierung des Beginns von Tarquinius' Herrschaft, die kaum anders auszudrücken war.

M. Jocelyn : I agree with Mr. Skutsch that *bonus* here has no political tendency at all. If it did it would be in the opposite direction to radical populism. I should adduce two considerations. Firstly, in the mid first century and doubtless earlier *bonus* was part of the jargon of political debate ; the stout conservative used it of his like-minded fellows. Secondly, the Virgilian Aeneas hardly noticed the existence of the *populus*, much less did he court them, and yet *bonus* was thought an appropriate epithet for him (*Aen.* V 570) as for other equally respectable heroes.

M. Waszink : Es ist auch zu beachten, dass der Anfang von *Aen.* III (*Postquam ... Priamique euertere gentem*) may have been influenced by *Ann.* I 17 : *Cum ueter occubuit Priamus sub Marte Pelasgo* (cf. Vahlen's Praefatio, p. CXLIX).

* * *

M. Badian : Mr. Skutsch's question whether Ancus Poplicius could be identical with Ancus Marcius : I am afraid I cannot comment on Dionysius without careful investigation of what is known of his sources at this point. I certainly agree that he would not invent these names—the question is whether his source might have, and (if so) why. This I cannot answer.

I find difficulty in identifying a Latin leader with one who became a King of Rome, and I cannot understand why memory of this should drop out, when Etruscan and Sabine connections were remembered and stressed ; nor can I understand why he should have changed his *nomen*. Certainly a *nomen* not known for centuries after is no difficulty : compare (e.g.) " Hostilius " ; and many of the *nomina* of the early Republic are of this nature. It is perhaps worth mentioning that Diodorus produces a military tribune " Marcus Ancus " (*sic*), otherwise unknown : an obvious fiction.

The *popularis aura* of Ancus Marcius is hard to explain, but there may be a connection with the aedile M' Marcius, Pliny,

N.H. XVIII 15, who appears to have been the first man to distribute grain to the plebs (at an *as* per *modius*) : if so, he must belong to the mid-fifth century—if he is historical. There was also an early Marcius who passed a law restraining usury. The later Marcii obviously prided themselves on early *populares* in the family.

M. Skutsch : The answer to Mr. Badian's question as to why a Latin successor to the kingship of Rome should have seemed more disgraceful than a Sabine or Etruscan one may well be that the relationship was too close. But in any case we are not concerned merely with a succession here but with the defeat and replacement of a Roman king.

* * *

M. Suerbaum : Wenn *quadrupes* in 232 als Oberbegriff für Kavallerie und Elefanten gebraucht ist, müsste man annehmen, dass beide Einheiten gleichzeitig angegriffen haben. Ist das historisch zu belegen?

M. Skutsch : The relevant section of my commentary shows, following Norden, that the battle was that of the Trebia, in which the rout of the Romans was accomplished by cavalry *and* elephants.

* * *

M. Suerbaum : Zu *iucundus* in 245 möchte ich Folgendes bemerken: Gellius' Paraphrase berücksichtigt auffallender Weise ein *facundus* in 245 nicht und bezieht sich mit *comitate* auf *suauis* und wohl auch auf ein *iucundus*, wie es von Herrn Skutsch konjiziert wird. Das legt nahe, die Textverderbnis als nach-gellianisch anzusprechen. Könnte sich *suo contentus* in 245 auf das Verhältnis zum *patronus* beziehen?

M. Skutsch : suo contentus, in the literal sense the opposite of *auarus*, may easily pass to the more general sense of " content with his lot" ; *beatus* means virtually the same ; cf. Hor. *Epist.* II 1, 139 *agricolæ ... paruo beati.*

* * *

M. Waszink: You think *sectis foliis*, in line 263, too unpoetic ; but are the immediately following words, *amaro corpore buxum*, so much more poetic ?

M. *Skutsch : amaro corpore* would seem to have far more point than the " incised leaves " of the cypress, since the " bitter taste " of the *buxum* would be not purely descriptive but expressive of its nature as the tree of sorrow.

* * *

M. Badian: With regard to 619, I should welcome Mr. Skutsch's great improvement in a very poor line. The decisive question seems to me to be whether the reading we have is indeed likely to go back as far as (say) Verrius Flaccus, not to mention the late Republic : if so, it becomes very difficult to believe that it can be corrupt. Cancik (quoted by Professor Skutsch) showed that Priscian's *despoliantur*, undoubtedly from Caper, would fit well into this line, where Donatus gives *spoliantur*. He suggested a common source (Probus or Pliny), but refuses to discuss, as irrelevant to his purpose, whether Donatus may have found *Ann.* 619 in Caper. For our purpose it *is* important, and it is very likely that Caper was in fact the common source : Priscian attests that he wrote on precisely this problem (" active " for " passive " forms etc.) and refers his reader to him for further information on it. Donatus' text may simply be corrupt, or a slip on the author's part ; or he may himself have had a corrupt text, of Caper or an intermediary.

Caper, who used Probus, is agreed to have lived in the second century A. D. Since Gellius does not know him, I suggest one may assume the latter part of the century. We have no reason to doubt that he collected (or collated) his own material for the work concerned. As Gellius shows, there were texts available, and corrupt texts at that. There are no grounds for assuming that this line, as we have it, goes back to Republican or Augustan times. Hence Mr. Skutsch's suggestion may be accepted.

M. Jocelyn : The verse may sound a little wooden but makes perfectly good sense. I think it is a mistake to impose too much uniformity on Ennius' language. There is a degree of prosodical and morphological oscillation in the *Annals* as in other Republican poems and indeed in Homer's *Iliad.* The oblique forms of *is* are much less common in tragedy than in comedy and epic doubtless reduced their incidence even further but it seems to me unreasonable to suppose a complete ban on them in the *Annals.*

Spoliantur is surely a credible variant of *spoliant.* Admittedly there are no other cases of deponent for active in the *Annals* fragments but the tragic fragments have deponent *contemplatur* (*Sc.* 114) and yet, to judge from Plautus' usage in comedy (on which see P. Langen, *Beiträge zur Kritik und Erklärung des Plautus*, Leipzig, 1880, p. 60), active *contemplo* was normal Latin in the early second century.

Mr. Skutsch's *despoliant umeros* limits the spoilers' activity somewhat. Certainly ἀπ' ὤμων τεύχε' ἐσύλα is one of the *Iliad's* commonest formulae but *et corpora nudant* suggests that Ennius was thinking of more than the corselets worn by the fallen enemy.

M. Wülfing: Für das homerische Vorbild gilt natürlich, dass ὦμοι für den Körper als ganzen steht.

M. Skutsch : I do not quite see the force of Mr. Jocelyn's objection. Since Ennius says they despoil them and leave the bodies naked, why should he not say that they strip the armour from their bodies and leave the bodies naked? Γυμνόν is said by Homer of a body stripped.

II

H. D. JOCELYN

Ennius as a Dramatic Poet

ENNIUS AS A DRAMATIC POET

I. — Introduction

The metre and language of the account which Ennius gave in the first fifteen books of his *Annals* of the establishment and growth of the Roman empire from the arrival of Aeneas in Italy to the return of his patron Fulvius Nobilior in triumph from Aetolia were striking novelties. Ennius was certainly the father of Latin epic poetry. Where other genres are concerned he may not merit this title. A degree of traditionalism seems to have marked the scripts which he wrote for performance at certain regular festivals of the state gods and on special occasions like statesmen's funerals and victory thanksgivings. Some of these scripts were versions of Attic tragedies popular in contemporary Greek theatres, some versions of similarly popular Attic comedies and some dramatisations of events of Roman history. All three types had been performed at the festivals for a number of years when Ennius arrived in Rome. The versions of tragedy and comedy never reproduced exactly the Attic originals. The manner of performance was in many ways different from that of the theatre of Dionysus. How Ennius learnt the craft of writing scripts or whether he ever established sufficient ascendancy over the theatrical environment to make innovations of his own we do not know. The epigrammatist Pompilius knew of no human teacher that Ennius had had and so called him a *discipulus Musarum* [1] but his dramatic fragments are full of the phrases of predecessors [2] and show

[1] See Varro ap. Non. p. 88,5 (= *Menipp.* 356 Buecheler). The reference to Pacuvius shows that Pompilius was not thinking of epic poetry.

[2] Cf. his translation of Euripides, *Med.* 49 οἴκων κτῆμα δεσποίνης ἐμῆς as *erilis fida custos corporis* and Naevius, *Trag.* 21-2 *uos qui regalis corporis custodias/agitatis*. See further below, p. 74.

no rhythms that were not inherited from the same predecessors [1]. The fragments of the plays on Roman historical themes do not differ in verbal or metrical style from those of the versions of Attic tragedies.

The scanty evidence which we possess concerning some thirty scripts allows us to say very little about these scripts as poetic wholes. Fragments are often difficult to disentangle from the text of the authors who quote them and corruption is widespread. The critic of the tragic fragments, which constitute the great majority, has no complete contemporary script to guide him nor even anything written within the direct tradition of Republican tragedy, in the way, for example, that the *De rerum natura* and the *Aeneid* were written by men immersed in the poetry of the *Annals*. He must work with assumptions drawn from Attic tragedy and from the comic scripts of Plautus and Terence, particularly when he wants to do more than interpret the individual words of an ancient quotation or allusion. It is always possible that a false analogy between different dramatic types will lead to a false general assumption and thus ultimately to a false interpretation of a particular fragment. Certainty is unattainable. Minute examination of particular fragments is more likely to demolish old views than to establish solid new ones but seems to me the only way of making progress.

This paper will be concerned with two quotations by Cicero of a version of an Attic tragedy set in the Achaean camp before Troy and with a quotation by Julius Victor of a play organised by Ennius himself around the siege of newly established Rome by an alliance of Sabine communities led by Tatius of Cures. My choice of quotations is not a random one. I wish to avoid repeating things I have said

[1] See further below, pp. 72 ff.

in my book on Ennius' tragic fragments, to correct a number of errors of that book and to open up for discussion an area of Ennius' dramatic writing which borders on epic poetry, the source of his lasting fame. War was a tragic theme which appealed to Roman audiences [1] and often appeared in Ennius' scripts. When he went to Aetolia in 189 as a member of Fulvius' staff he was already a famous poet [2]. His association with Fulvius and love of Homer together seem to have sparked the composition of the *Annals* [3]. Such verses, however, as 139 *heu quam crudeli condebat membra sepulchro*, 195 *non cauponantes bellum sed belligerantes* and 531 *clamor ad caelum uoluendus per aethera uagit* contain locutions quite absent from the *Iliad.* They have many parallels in the scripts surviving from the Athenian stage [4] and this suggests that the translation of tragic ῥήσεις formed some part of Ennius' apprenticeship for relating the major events of Roman history in epic verse.

II. — The passages to be discussed

Cicero, *S. Rosc.* 89-91 (∼ Ennius, *Sc.* 173):

haec tu Eruci tot et tanta si nanctus esses in reo, quam diu diceres. quo te modo iactares. tempus hercule te citius quam oratio deficeret. etenim in singulis rebus eiusmodi materies est ut

[1] Cf. Plautus, *Capt.* 60 ff.; Cicero, *Fam.* VII 1, 2; Horace, *Epist.* II 1, 189 ff.

[2] Cf. Cicero, *Tusc.* I 3.

[3] Cf. on the date of composition of the *Annals* O. Skutsch, *CQ* 42 (1948), 98 f. (= *Stud. Enn.* pp. 38 f.).

[4] With *Ann.* 139 compare Aeschylus, *Theb.* 1020-21 πετηνῶν τόνδ' ὑπ' οἰωνῶν ... | ταφέντ' ἀτίμως. With *Ann.* 195, *ibid.* 545-6 ἐλθὼν δ' ἔοικεν οὐ καπηλεύσειν μάχην, | μακρᾶς κελεύθου δ' οὐ καταισχυνεῖν πόρον. With *Ann.* 531, *ibid.* 348-50 βλαχαὶ δ' αἱματόεσσαι | τῶν ἐπιμαστιδίων | ἀρτιτρεφεῖς βρέμονται.

dies singulos possis consumere. neque ego non possum; non enim tantum mihi derogo, tametsi nihil adrogo, ut te copiosius quam me putem posse dicere. uerum ego forsitan propter multitudinem patronorum in grege adnumerer, te pugna Cannensis accusatorem sat bonum fecit. multos caesos non ad Trasumennum lacum sed ad Seruilium uidimus.

quis ibi non est uulneratus ferro Phrygio?

non necesse est omnes commemorare, Curtios, Marios, denique † *mammeos* †, *quos iam aetas a proeliis auocabat, postremo Priamum ipsum senem Antistium, quem non modo aetas sed etiam leges pugnare prohibebant. iam quos nemo propter ignobilitatem nominat, sescenti sunt, qui inter sicarios et de ueneficiis accusabant; qui omnes, quod ad me attinet, uellem uiuerent. nihil enim mali est canes ibi quam plurimos esse, ubi permulti obseruandi multaque seruanda sunt. uerum, ut fit, multa saepe imprudentibus imperatoribus uis belli ac turba molitur. dum is in aliis rebus erat occupatus, qui summam rerum administrabat, erant interea qui suis uulneribus mederentur, qui tamquam si offusa rei publicae sempiterna nox esset, ita ruebant in tenebris omniaque miscebant; a quibus miror, ne quod iudiciorum esset uestigium, non subsellia quoque esse combusta; nam et accusatores et iudices sustulerunt. hoc commodi est, quod ita uixerunt, ut testes omnes, si cuperent, interficere non possent; nam dum hominum genus erit, qui accuset eos non deerit, dum ciuitas erit, iudicia fient.*

Schol. Gronouianus p. 311, 30 Stangl:

FERRO FRUGIO in Ennio haec fabula inducitur, Achilles (Eberhard: *achillis* cod.) *quo tempore propter Briseidam cum Graecis pugnare noluit; quo etiam tempore Hector classem eorum incendit. in hac pugna Vlixes uulneratus inducitur et fugiens* <*ad*> (add. Graeuius) *Achillen uenit. cum interrogaretur ab Aiace cur fugisset, ille ut celaret dedecus* † *uitium* †: « *quis ibi non est* (*enim* cod.) *uulneratus ferro Frugio?* » *et quo tendit haec fabula?*

scimus Sullam in pueritia turpissimum fuisse, unde Sallustius dixit: « mox tanta flagitia in tali uiro pudet dicere.» Fruges autem dicuntur infames.

Cicero, *Tusc.* II 38-39 (∼ Ennius, *Sc.* 161-172):

cur tantum interest inter nouum et ueterem exercitum, quantum experti sumus? aetas tironum plerumque melior, sed ferre laborem, contemnere uulnus consuetudo docet. quin etiam uidemus ex acie efferri saepe saucios, et quidem rudem illum et inexercitatum quamuis leui ictu ploratus turpissimos edere. at uero ille exercitatus et uetus ob eamque rem fortior medicum modo requirens a quo obligetur

o Patricoles

inquit

ad uos aduueniens auxilium et uestras manus
peto. priusquam oppeto malam pestem mandatam hostili manu
. . .
neque sanguis ullo potis est pacto profluens consistere
. . .
si qui sapientia magis uestra mors deuitari potest.
namque Aesculapi liberorum saucii opplent porticus.
non potest accedi . . .

certe.

Eurypylus hic quidem est. hominem exercitum.

ubi † tantum luctum continuatus † (GKR; *tantum luctus continuatur* ς) *uide quam non flebiliter respondeat, rationem etiam adferat cur aequo animo sibi ferendum sit:*

qui alteri exitium parat,
eum scire oportet sibi paratam pestem, ut participet, parem.
. . .

abducet Patricoles, credo, ut conlocet in cubili, ut uolnus obliget. si quidem homo esset; sed nihil uidi minus. quaerit enim quid actum sit:

eloquere eloquere res Argiuum proelio ut se sustinet.
:: non potest ecfari tantum dictis quantum factis suppetit laboris ...
quiesce igitur et uolnus alliga. etiam si Eurypylus posset non posset Aesopus.
ubi fortuna Hectoris nostram acrem aciem inclinatam ...
et cetera explicat in dolore; sic est enim intemperans militaris in forti uiro gloria. ergo haec ueteranus miles facere poterit, doctus uir sapiensque non poterit? ille uero melius ac non paulo quidem.

C. Iulius Victor, *Ars rhet.* VI 4 (*de locis post rem*), p. 402, 28 Halm (~ Ennius, *Sc.* 370-71):

ab euentu in qualitate ut: « *qualia sunt ea, quae euenerunt aut quae uideantur euentura, tale illud quoque existimetur, ex quo euenerunt*»; *ut* <*in*> (add. Halm) *Sabinis Ennius dixit:*

cum spolia generis detraxeritis ...
...
quam inscriptionem dabitis?

generis Ian : *generi* cod.

III. — Concerning the Achilles

— a —

The Gronovian commentator names Ennius as the author of the three trochaic metra which Cicero quotes at *S. Rosc.* 90. Analysis of the arrangement of quotations at *Orator* 155 shows that Ennius was also the author of the dialogue between Eurypylus and Patroclus quoted at some length at *Tusc.* II 38 [1]. Both quotations are of a play dramatising the

[1] Cf. T. Bergk, *Ind. lectt. Marburg* 1844, VIII ff. (= *Kl. phil. Schr.* I 220 ff.). Delrio and G. Hermann, *De Aeschyli Myrmidonibus Nereidibus Phrygibus Dissertatio*, Leipzig, 1833, p. 8 (= *Opusc.* V 142), had imagined Accius to be the author.

events of the day described by Homer at *Il.* XI 1 to XVIII 239. The play was set in front of the quarters of Achilles in the Achaean camp. Two titles of tragedies with this setting are known, an *Achilles* and a *Hectoris lytra.*

The *Achilles* was a version of a play by the fifth century Attic poet Aristarchus [1]. The only thing which emerges with any certainty from the fragments cited as belonging to it is that it concerned the period of Achilles' refusal to take part in the fighting before Troy and contained an account of a battle involving Ajax [2]. The tone of Nonius' quotation at p. 277, 23 (= *Sc.* 6)

serua ciues, defende hostes cum potes defendere

suggests that danger is immediate, that at the moment of speaking the Achaeans are rather more hard pressed than they were on the night of the embassy of Ulysses, Phoenix and Ajax described in the ninth book of the *Iliad.* The action of the *Achilles* is therefore to be imagined as proceeding during the day which began with the eleventh book of the *Iliad.*

The wording of the last mentioned fragment illustrates prettily one of the difficulties which faced Latin poets adapting Attic scripts and the kind of solution which appealed to Ennius. The authority which Agamemnon had over the contingents from various Achaean communities forming his army was quite different from that exercised by a Roman consul over his officers and troops whether citizens or allies. Achilles' behaviour and even more the reaction of Agamemnon and the other βασιλῆες to it were inconceivable in a Roman camp. Ennius could have used words and phrases

[1] See, in addition to my commentary, pp. 161 ff., *YCS* 21 (1969), 97 ff.

[2] Cf. Festus' quotation at p. 282, 9 Lindsay (= *Sc.* 16) ***prolato aere astitit*** (~ Homer, *Il.* VII 224-5 τὸ πρόσθε στέρνοιο φέρων Τελαμώνιος Αἴας | στῆ ῥα μάλ' Ἕκτορος ἐγγύς et XI 485-6 Αἴας δ' ἐγγύθεν ἦλθε φέρων σάκος ἠύτε πύργον | στῆ δὲ παρέξ.

rendering his dialogue utterly remote from contemporary considerations and more or less faithful to the spirit of the original. Instead he set out to make his audience think of Ulysses, Ajax and the rest as citizens of the same community as Achilles (*ciues*) [1] and to play on the emotions associated with common citizenship. The phrase *serua ciues* [2] would have reminded Roman hearers immediately of one of the deeds of military heroism they most admired and the crown of oak leaves presented *ob ciuis seruatos* [3]. It may even be that the wording and the asyndeton of the two imperative phrases *serua ciues, defende hostes* reflected the way in which this deed was conventionally commemorated. Beside the Ennian fragment should be set Polybius' τοὺς ὑπερασπίσαντας (∼ *defende hostes*) καὶ σώσαντάς τινας τῶν πολιτῶν ἢ συμμάχων (∼ *serua ciues*) [4], the inscription on the Capitoline statue of M. Aemilius Lepidus reconstructible from the legend of a coin of 66 B.C.—AN. XV. PR. H. O. C. S. (= *annorum quindecim progressus hostem occidit, ciuem seruauit*) [5]—and Valerius Maximus III 1, 1 *Aemilius Lepidus puer etiam tum progressus in aciem hostem interemit, ciuem seruauit*, Cassius Dio LIII 16, 4 . . . οἱ ὡς καὶ ἀεὶ τούς τε πολεμίους νικῶντι (∼ *defende hostes*) καὶ τοὺς πολίτας σῴζοντι. At any rate the critic of Ennius' tragic fragments must expect to meet some odd conflations of heroic Greece and second century Rome.

The *Hectoris lytra* enacted the theme of the twenty-fourth book of the *Iliad*, namely Achilles' surrender of Hector's corpse to Priam. The commonly accepted view of the play's

[1] Homer has the word πολίτης only at *Il.* II 806 (talking of the Trojans).

[2] Contrast the Homeric φράζευ ὅπως Δαναοῖσιν ἀλεξήσεις κακὸν ἦμαρ (*Il.* IX 251) and the Aeschylean Ἕλλανα μὴ προδῷς στρατόν (fr. 221, 5 Mette).

[3] This phrase is often found on Augustan coins (*B.M.C. Rom. Emp.* I, 445). Cf. Polybius VI 39, 6-7.

[4] VI 39, 6.

[5] E. A. Sydenham, *Coinage of the Rom. Rep.*, 829.

action [1] has it include the two days on which the Homeric Hector attacked the newly fortified Greek camp, the night during which a new set of armour was manufactured for Achilles, the day on which Achilles drove back the Trojans and slew Hector, the twelve nights and days during which Achilles kept Hector's corpse in his quarters as well as the night on which Achilles surrendered the corpse to Priam. I should now want to argue much more strongly than I did in my commentary against this view.

Aristotle must have deduced his rule demanding that the action of a tragedy should take place within one solar period [2] from what he observed in late fifth and early fourth century scripts. Those scripts which we possess either entire or in large part practically all keep the imagined time of action within twelve hours. The Aeschylean Ἀγαμέμνων and Εὐμενίδες have opening scenes set days before the beginning of the main action but they are early plays, going back to 458 B.C. Sophocles' Τραχίνιαι and Euripides' Ἀνδρομάχη, Ἱκετίδες and Σθενέβοια [3] have journeys performed within the action which in reality would have taken several days but proceed as if such journeys took no more than an hour or two. There is no known example of the kind of play the *Hectoris lytra* has been thought to be.

It is also the case that Attic tragedies had a chorus present in the orchestra during most of the action and that the Latin poets imagined a similar body present on the stage platform for their versions [4]. One of Nonius' quotations (p. 472, 21 [= *Sc.* 186])

[1] Cf. recently A. Grilli, *Studi Enniani*, Brescia, 1965, p. 176 n. 20.

[2] *Poet.* 5, 1449 *b* 12 ff.

[3] On the difficulties of the hypothesis published by H. Rabe, *RhM* 63 (1908), 147 ff., see B. Zühlke, *Philologus* 105 (1961), 1 ff. and 198 ff.

[4] Cf. Cicero, *Fam.* VII 6, 1 (∼ Euripides, *Med.* 214 ff.), [Probus], Virgil, *Ecl.* VI 31 (∼ Euripides, *Med.* 1251 ff.). The Roman theatre had no space

† ser uos et uostrum †
imperium et fidem Myrmidonum uigiles conmiserescite

corrupt though it is [1], reveals without any doubt that the *Hectoris lytra* had a chorus of *uigiles* (νυκτοφύλακες) [2]. Accordingly most of the action of the play must have taken place during one of the watches of the night on which Priam came secretly to Achilles' quarters. From three other Nonian quotations [3] it can be deduced that the watch was the first. Before the *uigiles* arrived on stage there would have been room for no more than a prologue speech describing events prior to the action and one dialogue between actors.

To the prologue speech I should assign the trimeters quoted by Nonius at p. 355, 3 (= *Sc.* 158-9):

Hector ui summa armatos educit foras
castrisque castra ultro iam ferre occupat.

Where their text is concerned, I am ready to abandon my scepticism about Mercier's emendation *ui summa* (*ei summa* codd.) but wish to maintain the hiatus between *castra* and *ultro*. S. Timpanaro has correctly pointed out [4] that *ui summa* need mean no more than "very energetically". Nevertheless, while this phrase might accompany verbs like *expetere* (Plautus, *Cas.* 80) and *niti* (Ennius, *Ann.* 412) appro-

for an orchestra of the Athenian type (see Livy XXXIV 44, 5 and Vitruvius V 6, 2).

[1] S. Timpanaro, *Gnomon* 40 (1968), 669 demolishes some of the arguments adduced in my commentary. I am not convinced, however, that *uostrum imperium* could mean "the *imperium* which you obey (and of which you are in a sense the representatives)".

[2] O. Ribbeck's observation at *Die römische Tragödie im Zeitalter der Republik*, Leipzig, 1875, p. 638 is thus at odds with his reconstruction of the play at pp. 118 ff.

[3] See below, p. 53.

[4] *Gnomon* 40 (1968), 669.

priately enough, it still seems to me out of place with the Ennian *educit.* In such a context Hector surely had to deal with disciplined troops, not stubborn bullocks. *Summa ui* (the adjective normally precedes) is a very common phrase in the military writers Caesar and Livy and *educere* an even more common verb. The collocation *summa ui educere* never occurs. *Summa ui* accompanies verbs and verbal phrases which can be placed in two categories: into one category fall *agere* (Livy XXIV 28, 5), *contendere* (Caesar, *Gall.* III 15, 1; VII 70, 1), *defendere* (Livy X 17, 10; XXVI 6, 6), *hortari* (XXIII 45, 1; XXX 18, 2), *niti* (XLIV 11, 8), *petere* (XXII 6, 2), *tendere* (XXXII 32, 7), *tueri* (XXXII 14, 2), *arma apparare* (IV 1, 5), *bellum parare* (I 56, 13; III 4, 2; XLII 25, 3), *bellum apparare* (III 57, 8); into the other category fall *aggredi* (XXXVI 24, 2; XXXVII 17, 2), *depopulari* (X 27, 5), *expugnare* (IV 35, 10; X 1, 7), *obsidere* (XXV 20, 1), *oppugnare* (VI 9, 10; XXI 7, 1; XXIII 18, 5; XXVII 12, 6; XXVII 28, 13; XXXII 4, 1; XXXII 16, 10; XXXV 25, 2; XXXVIII 5, 10; XL 25, 6; XLI 11, 2; XLII 63, 3); *resistere* (II, 54, 2; II, 56, 4; XXXII 15, 1; XLII 50, 10), *restare* (IV, 58, 4), *ad bellum cooriri* (IV 56, 5), *bellum gerere* (XXXII 21, 19), *eruptionem facere* (*Gall.* VII 73, 1), *proelium conserere* (XXIX 7, 3). In regard to Ennius' *Hector ui summa armatos educit foras*, I should now like to take *ui summa* and *armatos* together, comparing Homer, *Il.* II 65-6 θωρῆξαι ... πανσυδίῃ and Livy I 58, 8 *Tarquinius ... ui armatus* and leaving the exact interpretation open. The text of the next verse, *castrisque castra ultro iam ferre occupat*, has, admittedly, a peculiar look about it. Even such purists as Caesar and Cicero varied the standard military phrase *castra conferre* with the polyptoton *castra castris conferre* [1], but although Vossius' *conferre* normalises both metre and phraseology in Ennius' verse, there are enough cases of the replacement of the compound

[1] See the passages collected by E. Lommatzsch at *TLL* IV 180, 73 ff.

in *con-* by the simple verb in tragedy as well as of hiatus after the fifth element of the trimeter to allow the transmitted text to stand.

Where the substance of the two trimeters is concerned, the prologue speaker seems to me to refer to the beginning of the day upon which Hector was slain, in particular to a movement not described but only hinted at by Homer, *Il.* XX 47-74. There are those who would have him refer to the exit of the Trojans from the city described at *Il.* VIII 55-9 [1] or their exit from their place of bivouac described at *Il.* XI 56-66 [2]. Discussion is difficult because some Attic tragedian stands between Homer and Ennius and because both Attic tragedians [3] and Latin translators tended to write about heroic battles with the military conditions of their own times in mind. Ennius wrote his two trimeters undoubtedly thinking more of contemporary fighting than of the Attic text in front of him. Roman and Carthaginian armies regularly moved from one fortified or fortifiable position to another and when about to join battle manoeuvred for the better fixed position on the terrain. With the Ennian trimeters one might compare Livy XXI 39, 10 *occupauit tamen Scipio Padum traicere et ad Ticinum amnem motis castris, priusquam educeret in aciem, adhortandorum militum causa talem orationem est exorsus* and XXVI 12, 14 *sic ad Cannas, sic ad Trasumennum rem bene gestam coeundo conferundoque cum hoste castra, fortunam temptando.* Homer's Achaeans did not move far from their ships and did not fortify their camp until the tenth year of the war. His Trojans ordinarily kept within the walls of the city [4] and Hector's bivouac on two

[1] Cf. O. Ribbeck, *Die römische Tragödie*, p. 119.

[2] Cf. A. Schöll, *Beiträge zur Kenntnis der tragischen Poesie der Griechen* I, Berlin, 1839, p. 491.

[3] See below, pp. 56 f., 84 f.

[4] Cf. *Il.* V 789; VII 1; VIII 58.

successive nights in the plain between the city and the Achaean ships was an act of unusual boldness; Hector put no fence or ditch around his bivouacking troops [1]. The armies of fifth century Athens and its rivals used as a rule natural rather than artificial fortification for their camping places [2] and, not surprisingly, Euripides' Ῥῆσος represented Hector's bivouac exactly as in the *Iliad* [3]. The prologue of the original Ἕκτορος λύτρα would likewise have begun its description of the day's events in terms more Homeric than those of Ennius'

Hector ui summa armatos educit foras
castrisque castra ultro iam ferre occupat.

Parallel is the way in which Terence altered a Menandrian slave's account of the birth of a child with contemporary Roman customs in mind [4].

To the speech of a messenger describing the battle in which Hector fell I should assign three quotations by Nonius (pp. 504, 30; 510, 32; 518, 3 [= *Sc.* 181, 180, 182-3]):

aes sonit, franguntur hastae, terra sudat sanguine

saeuiter fortuna ferro cernunt de uictoria

ecce autem caligo oborta est, omnem prospectum abstulit.
derepente contulit sese in pedes.

[1] Cf. *Il.* VIII 542; XI 56 ff.; XVIII 297 ff.; XX 1 ff.

[2] Writing in the fourth century Xenophon describes fortifying a camp as a barbarian rather than a Greek practice (*Cyr.* III 3, 26-7). Pyrrhus found the organisation of his Roman enemy's camps quite amazing (see Plutarch, *Pyrrh.* 16, 4) and perhaps introduced it into his own army's practice (hence the peculiar doctrine found at Livy XXXV, 14, 8 and Frontinus, *Strat.* IV 1, 14). Nevertheless, as Polybius VI 42 shows, traditional notions died hard.

[3] Cf. vv. 523-4. For the Achaean wall see vv. 989-90.

[4] Cf. Donatus, *Andr.* 771 *LIBERAE testimonia libera contra seruum. et hoc proprium Terentii est, nam de Romano more hoc dixit.*

A corollary of this is that the author of the original Ἕκτορος λύτρα not only diverged in details from the Homeric narrative [1] but omitted the twelve days which the *Iliad* had elapse between Hector's death and Priam's recovery of his body. For an Attic dramatist to telescope an epic story in this way is entirely credible; for him to extend an action over several days to include everything from the Homeric Hector's first sally from the city at Zeus' behest to the transport back of his corpse is not.

One of Nonius' quotations (p. 469, 25 [= *Sc.* 179])

qui cupiant dare arma Achilli † ut ipse † cunctent

corrupt and obscure though it is, seems to demand an interpretation which cuts across my view of the play's action. This quotation looks as if it should be of a speech made between Patroclus' death and Achilles' acquisition of fresh armour. Such, however, is the strength of the deduction to be made from the quotation of Priam's address to the *uigiles* and from the known structure of Attic tragedy that another interpretation has to be found for *qui cupiant dare arma Achilli † ut ipse † cunctent.* I should suggest tentatively that it comes from a speech reporting conversation or statements made at the time Achilles had no armour to fight in.

A *Hectoris lytra* reconstructed on the supposition that it resembled an Attic drama of the classical period could not accommodate the two untitled fragments with which we are here concerned. The *Achilles* on the other hand could. There is, of course, no absolute certainty attainable in these matters but we shall assume henceforth that it was Aristarchus, a contemporary of Euripides, who reduced the narrative of *Il.* XI 1 to XVIII 239 [2] to the dramatic form we can

[1] With *Sc.* 182-3 contrast Homer, *Il.* XXII 131-7. Mists etc. obscuring vision on the battlefield are common enough elsewhere in the *Iliad.* On *Sc.* 180 see further below, p. 77.

[2] Perhaps even of *Il.* XI 1 to XXII 404. See below, p. 58 f.

glimpse through what Cicero quotes at *S. Rosc.* 90 and *Tusc.* II 38.

— b —

The Gronovian commentator and modern interpreters take the three trochaic metra quoted at *S. Rosc.* 90

quis ibi non est uolneratus ferro Phrygio?[1]

as alluding to deeds perpetrated by Sulla's less worthy followers between the victory at the Colline gate in November 82 and the end of the proscriptions in June 81. The *Sullani* would be identified with the " Phrygians "[2] of Ennius' play. It is odd, however, that in the very next sentence one of the victims of the *Sullani* should be referred to with the metrical phrase *Priamum ipsum senem*[3]. In any case to talk of the *Sullani* first as death-dealing Carthaginians and then as wound-dealing Phrygians makes an unfortunate anti-climax. I would suggest therefore that with *quis ibi non est uolneratus ferro Phrygio?* Cicero refers to prosecutions of certain persons made in the courts near the *lacus Seruilius* during the pre-Sullan era. Those prosecuted would have revenged their metaphorical wounds during the proscriptions. Indeed Cicero says just this four sentences later: *dum is* (i.e. Sulla) *in aliis rebus erat occupatus, qui summam rerum administrabat, erant interea qui suis uolneribus mederentur.*

My hypothesis gives Cicero's oblique and highly literary attack on the effects of the proscriptions much more elegance and point: the victims are imagined at one moment as the

[1] The correct spelling would be *Brugio*; cf. Cicero, *Orat.* 160; Quintilian, *Inst.* I 4, 15.

[2] Unlike Homer the tragedians regularly identified the Phrygians and the Trojans (cf. Euripides, *Rhes.* 75; 585; 727; 814 et al.).

[3] A. Eberhard, *Lectionum Tullianarum Libellus Primus*, Leipzig, 1872, p. 12, has found a number of supporters for his suggestion that the phrase is a tragic quotation.

beleaguered Trojans, the heroic ancestors of the Romans, and at another as the third century Romans who fell at Trasumene and Cannae ; the *Sullani*, on the other hand, are at one moment the Achaean destroyers of Troy and at another the Carthaginian agents of Juno's wrath against the Trojans and their Roman descendents [1]. The verse fragments which appear in Cicero's writings can at times be both quotations of old poems and part of the narrative or argument in hand [2].

The note in the Gronovian commentary describing the scene of Ennius' play from which Cicero's quotation comes is garbled but perhaps not quite as much as some have thought. This scene was based on the narrative of *Il.* XI 396-488 : the whole Achaean army, with the exception of the Myrmidons, is out in the plain and the βασιλῆες are doing deeds of glory in front of the ordinary troops; after suffering a spear wound Ulysses is rescued by Menelaus and Ajax and sent back to camp in his chariot ; Menelaus and Ajax stay in the fight but there is no suggestion of cowardice on Ulysses' part [3]. The tragic dialogue between Ajax and Ulysses in front of the quarters of Achilles to which the commentator refers must have been preceded by a messenger's speech, or some equivalent, narrating a course of battle rather different from Homer's : there has been a general reverse and Ajax, showing an enmity towards Ulysses which arose at a much later stage in the old epic story [4], blames the reverse on Ulysses' failure to stand his ground.

The differences between the tragic dialogue and the Homeric narrative are quite explicable. In dramatising this

1 See Servius, Virgil, *Aen.* I 281 on the end of Juno's wrath in Ennius' *Annals*.

2 Cf. the quotation of the Achilles at *Verr.* II 1, 46.

3 Cf. the way that the other wounded heroes return to camp : *Il.* XI 251 ff. (Agamemnon) ; 369 ff. (Diomedes); 504 ff. (Machaon) ; 581 ff. (Eurypylus).

4 Cf. Homer, *Od.* XI 543 ff. ; Arctinus, *Aeth.* exc. Procl. p. 106 Allen ; schol. Hom. *Od.* XI 547.

narrative Aristarchus had been bound by certain conventions. He could not set a scene on the actual field of battle. He could not, except in very special circumstances [1], shift his action from one scene to another. The 'Ρῆσος of Euripides, based though it was fairly closely on the tenth book of the *Iliad*, related from in front of Hector's quarters in the Trojan camp all the events of the night described in that book and telescoped them within the period of a single watch. There was nothing technically to prevent Aristarchus from making a personage of his 'Αχιλλεύς relate exactly the details of the Homeric fighting or from casting his debates in an Homeric mould. Nevertheless surviving Attic scripts show that Aristarchus' fellow poets neither sought an archaeological accuracy in describing such things as the division of the watches of the night [2] and methods of signalling [3] nor hesitated to represent the epic βασιλῆες as contemporary στρατηγοί [4]. They frequently created scenes of argument informed by a contemporary military ethos [5]. The order of events [6] and the details [7] of epic stories had for them nothing sacrosanct. It is thus not at all surprising to find in Aristarchus' 'Αχιλλεύς a conversion of Ulysses' departure with a wound from the battle field into the rout of a hoplite

[1] The only shifts of scene evidenced in Attic tragedy are in the early Αἰτναῖαι (fr. 26 Mette) and Εὐμενίδες (234; 488) of Aeschylus and Αἴας (815) of Sophocles.

[2] Contrast Euripides, *Rhes.* 5; 527 ff. and Homer, *Il.* X 253 and schol.

[3] Cf. Euripides, *Rhes.* 144; 989 and schol. Eur. *Phoen.* 1377.

[4] Cf. the way in which the Euripidean Eteocles does not set himself at one of the seven gates but exercises a general supervision over all seven (*Phoen.* 1093 ff.; 1163 ff.).

[5] Cf. Euripides, *Heracles* 160 ff.; 190 ff. and particularly Plautus, *Amph.* 238-41 (probably a parody of an Attic messenger's speech at base).

[6] Cf. Euripides, *Rhes.* 501-2 (theft of Palladium).

[7] Contrast Sophocles, *Ai.* 1273 ff. and Homer, *Il.* XVI 112 ff. (firing of Achaean ships); Euripides, *Androm.* 107-8 and Homer, *Il.* XXII 463-5; XXIV 14-17 (dragging of Hector's body).

phalanx and a retrojection in time of the famous enmity between Ajax and Achilles.

With the Attic dialogue lost and less than a verse of the Latin version surviving little can be said about what Ennius himself contributed. Debates about the behaviour of Roman troops and officers in similar circumstances [1] would doubtless have affected his language. Making the piper accompany the utterances of Ajax and Achilles may but need not have been Ennius' idea. A number of arguments set in catalectic trochaic tetrameters are to be found in late fifth century Attic scripts [2].

A later passage of Cicero's speech for Sextus Roscius and the Gronovian commentator's note may have something to tell about another scene of the same play. Describing how Titus Roscius sent Glaucia with news of Sextus Roscius' death to Capito, Cicero calls Glaucia *Automedontem illum, sui sceleris acerbissimi nefariaeque uictoriae nuntium*. This is of a piece with the earlier identification of the villainous *Sullani* with the Achaean sackers of Troy. The commentator writes : AVTOMEDON *Achillis auriga fuit. posteaquam Achilles Hectorem uicit, posuit aurigam suum in curru, ut iret et nuntiaret occisum Hectorem. modo adludit Cicero : Roscium Achillem dicit, Glauciam Automedontem*. This was not Homer's version of the events immediately following Hector's death and it is a reasonable supposition that the commentator, or rather his source [3], had in mind a tragic scene in which Automedon brought back news to the camp of a Myrmidon victory. There could have been no dragging of Hector's corpse behind Achilles' chariot. It looks as if there had not even

[1] For the general Roman attitude to cowardice and indiscipline cf. Polybius VI 24, 9; VI 37, 11-38, 4; Livy VII 13, 4. For the reaction to particular cases cf. Livy XXIII 25, 7; XXV 6, 13 ff.; XXVI 2, 7 ff.

[2] Cf. Euripides, *Heracles* 855 ff., *I.A.* 317 ff., *Phoen.* 588 ff.

[3] Asconius is known to have written a commentary on the speech for Sextus Roscius; see Gellius XV 28, 4-5.

been a single combat of the epic type but rather an engagement between hoplite units in which Hector fell and after which Achilles, like some fifth century στρατηγός, directed a mopping-up operation.

Homer had Ulysses wounded early one morning and Hector killed late in the day following. The conventions of tragedy would have prevented a poet extending his action over such a long period. At the same time they would have allowed him to omit some events of Homer's narrative and to telescope the rest [1] in order to provide a theatrically satisfying plot. It is a possibility worth considering that Cicero had in mind Ennius' version of Aristarchus' Ἀχιλλεύς at *S. Rosc.* 98 as well as 90.

— c —

At *Tusc.* II 38 the dialogue speaker, who is here Cicero himself [2], adduces a tragic Eurypylus as an example of a man who has learnt through habituation to endure pain. He quotes a large number of verses from an episode in which calmly and unweepingly the wounded Eurypylus describes to Patroclus what happened on the field of battle. This scene depended ultimately on the narrative of Homer, *Il.* XI 804-48 [3] and must have belonged to the same play as the one between Ulysses and Ajax from which Cicero quotes at *S. Rosc.* 90.

A chorus would have been required to stand in the orchestra by the script which Aristarchus constructed from Homer's narrative and on the stage-platform by Ennius' version [4]. This circumstance has been neglected by inter-

[1] See above, p. 58.

[2] Cf. *Tusc.* V 32.

[3] Cf. also XV 390 ff.; XVI 27.

[4] See above, p. 49.

preters, who explain the phrases *ad uos*, *uestras manus* and *sapientia* . . . *uestra* in Eurypylus' address to Patroclus as due to the presence of Achilles by Patroclus' side, at the same time failing to say why Eurypylus did not also address by name the Myrmidon leader himself—a grossly discourteous omission by heroic standards. In any case Achilles enjoyed more fame as a medical practitioner than did Patroclus [1]. I suggest therefore that Achilles was quite absent from the stage-platform when Eurypylus arrived and that those whom Eurypylus addressed along with Patroclus were a chorus of attendants (θεράποντες / *caculae*). This hypothesis will also aid interpretation of certain features of Cicero's comments on the exchange between the two heroes.

The relationship between the tragic episode and Cicero's discourse is more complex than has been thought. The episode was obviously a famous one. Aesopus, the leading tragic actor of the first century B.C. Roman stage [2], found the role of Eurypylus a challenge to his powers. Where such episodes were concerned, Cicero often made the speaker in a philosophical dialogue quote selectively, expecting the interlocutor (and ultimately the reader) to supply what had been omitted. At times he even allowed comments to be passed on what had been omitted from the quotation. This is how I should explain the quotation of iambic tetrameters and bits of tetrameters from the address of the Pacuvian Polydorus' ghost to his mother at *Tusc.* I 106 [3] and the following remark about *tam bonos septenarios*. Pacuvius must have made the ghost drop into catalectic trochaic tetrameters (*septenarii*) [4] so as to narrate the story of his murder and it was to these trochaic verses rather than to the introductory

[1] See Homer, *Il.* XI 832 and Pliny, *NH* XXV 42.

[2] See Cicero, *Fam.* VII 1, 2, *Sest.* 120-23, Horace, *Epist.* II 1, 82.

[3] *Trag.* 197-201.

[4] See below, pp. 72 ff., on the metrical structure of such episodes in Roman drama.

iambics that Cicero's remark referred. At *Tusc.* II 38 Cicero assumes his young [1] interlocutor to be similarly familiar with the episode from Ennius' *Achilles*. His manner is very different from that in which in the previous argument about the nature of pain he presented his own versions of speeches by the Sophoclean Hercules and the Aeschylean Prometheus. There he assumed that the young man would find the verses a novelty and tried to explain what he was doing [2].

Five acatalectic iambic tetrameters and the first five elements of a sixth are quoted from Eurypylus' opening address to Patroclus :

o Patricoles ad uos aduenienss auxilium et uestras manus
peto priusquam oppeto malam pestem mandatam hostili manu
neque sanguis ullo potis est pacto profluens consistere
si qui sapientia magis uestra mors deuitari potest
namque Aesculapi liberorum saucii opplent porticus
non potest accedi

Many editors of Cicero's dialogue and of Ennius' tragic fragments treat this as a full, continuous quotation. There are, however, a number of reasons for regarding it as left deliberately lacunose. The adverbial clause *priusquam . . . manu* demands to be preceded or followed by an imperative or a jussive subjunctive or some equivalent phrase [3]. One can hardly press *auxilium et uestras manus peto* into standing for *auxilium et uestras manus date*. Cicero's own phrases, . . . *medicum modo requirens a quo obligetur . . . ut conlocet in cubili, ut uolnus obliget*, strongly suggest that the tragic hero made not

[1] Cf. *Tusc.* II 28.

[2] *Tusc.* II 26.

[3] Cf. Plautus, *Capt.* 831-2: *aperite hasce ambas fores, | priusquam pultando assulatim foribus exitium adfero*; *Curc.* 210: *tene etiam, priusquam hinc abeo, sauium*; *Epid.* 615-16: *quin tu mihi adornes ad fugam uiaticum, | priusquam pereo?* A statement of determination would also be appropriate; cf. Terence, *Andr.* 311 *omnia experiri certumst, priusquam pereo.*

only a general appeal for help but a specific one as well, namely for his wound to be bandaged. The principal statement *neque sanguis ... potis est ... consistere* demands to be preceded by another statement, negative or positive, about Eurypylus' physical condition [1]. The conditional clause *si qui... mors deuitari potest* likewise hangs in the grammatical air [2].

Nobody in this company, I hope, will want to say that Eurypylus' grammar was meant to reflect the state of shock and exhaustion resulting from his wound. It might, however, be reasonably argued that in his tragic scripts Ennius' syntax tended to approach the looseness, redundancy and illogicality of everyday speech more closely than a classical taste would approve and that the utterances given to Eurypylus illustrate this tendency. Two interesting ancient judgments to this effect are to be found in Cicero's *Orator*: at § 36: *Ennio delector, ait quispiam, quod non discedit a communi more uerborum. Pacuuio, inquit alius; omnes apud hunc ornati elaboratique sunt uersus, multo apud alterum neglegentius*; and at § 109: *an ego Homero, Ennio, reliquis poetis et maxime tragicis concederem ut ne omnibus locis eadem contentione uterentur crebroque mutarent, non numquam etiam ad cotidianum genus sermonis accederent : ipse numquam ab illa acerrima contentione discederem?*

The Ennian Eurypylus' discourse contains at least two examples of what might be called colloquial looseness : the

[1] Perhaps about pain (cf. Homer, *Il.* XVI 517-19 : ἕλκος μὲν γὰρ ἔχω τόδε καρτερόν, ἀμφὶ δέ μοι χεὶρ | ὀξείῃς ὀδύνῃσιν ἐλήλαται, οὐδέ μοι αἷμα | τερσῆναι δύναται) or perspiration (cf. Homer, *Il.* XI 811-13 : κατὰ δὲ νότιος ῥέεν ἱδρὼς | ὤμων καὶ κεφαλῆς, ἀπὸ δ' ἕλκεος ἀργαλέοιο | αἷμα μέλαν κελάρυζε).

[2] Cf. Plautus, *Aul.* 390-91 : *aulam maiorem, si pote, ex uicinia | pete ; Bacch.* 870 : *em illoc pacisce, si potes ; Mil.* 1084 : *sinite abeam, si possum, uiua a uobis ; Persa* 30 : *si tu tibi bene esse pote pati, ueni ; Rud.* 1177 : *hunc, si potes, fer intro uidulum* ; Terence, *Phorm.* 197 : *atque id, si potes, uerbo expedi ;* 378-9 : *peto, | si tibi placere potis est, mi ut respondeas ; Hec.* 395-6 : *nunc, si potis est, Pamphile, | maxume uolo doque operam ut clam partus eueniat patrem* ; 635-6 : *ego, Pamphile, esse inter nos, si fieri potest, | adfinitatem hanc sane perpetuam uolo.*

magis of *si qui sapientia magis uestra mors deuitari potest*[1] and the *ut participet* of *eum scire oportet sibi paratam pestem, ut participet, parem.* Most modern editors follow Bentley in altering *paratam* in the latter sentence to *paratum* but produce thereby a use of *participare* and the accusative not evidenced before Gellius XV 2, 7[2]. Timpanaro's explanation[3] of the transmitted text as a contamination of ... *sibi paratam pestem parem*[4] with ... *sibi paratum pestem ut participet parem*[5] runs into the same difficulty. If, however, *participet* be taken as the equivalent of *particeps sit* we have a structure of sentence parallel with Plautus, *Epid.* 606: *exitiabilem ego illi faciam hunc, ut fiat, diem*[6]. Plautus uses *participare* both as a factitive verb ("*aliquem participem facere*")[7] and as an intransitive ("*participem esse*")[8]. A number of first conjugation denominatives have a similar double function in Republican Latin[9]. Ennius' craggy sentence may therefore be allowed to stand.

In writing with such a wide stylistic range as this the critic can find little firm ground. Nevertheless nowhere in the very copious remains of Republican drama is there a sentence at all like one consisting of the first four iambic tetrameters which Cicero quotes at *Tusc.* II 38. Ribbeck

[1] Bergk wrote *magistra* above *magis uestra* in his copy of Ribbeck's first edition of the tragic fragments (*Kl. phil. Schr.* I 682). For Ennius' use of *magis*, cf. the examples collected by Bulhart at *TLL* VIII 58. 78 ff. under the rubric 'res comparata aliis modis indicatur aut certe subauditur'.

[2] Cf. also Apuleius, *Met.* IX 24; *Apol.* 14.

[3] *SIFC* n.s. 21 (1946), 61-2.

[4] Cf. Plautus, *Epid.* 125: *paratae iam sunt scapulis symbolae.*

[5] Cf. Plautus, *Mil* 295: *tibi iam ut pereas paratum est.*

[6] Cf. also Plautus, *Persa* 760: *ego omnis hilaros ludentis laetificantis faciam, ut fiant; Poen.* 453-4: *nec potui tamen | propitiam Venerem facere, uti esset, mihi.*

[7] *Cist.* 165; *Mil.* 232 and 263; *Stich.* 33. Cf. Lucretius III 692.

[8] *Persa* 757; *Truc.* 748.

[9] X. Mignot, *Les Verbes dénominatifs latins*, Paris, 1969, p. 282 lists *celerare, commodare, durare, geminare, maturare, praecipitare* and *superstitare* along with *participare.*

was surely right to propose lacunae before and after *neque sanguis ullo potis est pacto profluens consistere*.

The sentence following the quotations from Eurypylus' address to Patroclus would complete an iambic tetrameter begun with *non potest accedi* :

:: *certe Eurypylus hic quidem est. hominem exercitum.*

Most interpreters follow Bentley in making this an utterance by Patroclus. Pohlenz gives it to Achilles, whom he imagines Eurypylus to be addressing along with Patroclus. There are grave difficulties in both views.

Sentences consisting of *hic quidem est* and a proper name or status indication are indeed common in Roman drama [1]. Such sentences, however, while sometimes preceded by an exclamation of surprise like *atque*, *attat*, *attatae*, *pro di immortales*, *pro supreme Iuppiter* or *sed*, never are by *certe*. Again, they always come from a speaker at the moment he recognises the person named. A dialogue in which persons receive a direct and rather formal address extending to at least six iambic tetrameters and then express a surprised recognition of the person addressing them would be a dramatic monstrosity. At Plautus, *Persa* 788-9, which is superficially similar to the Bentleyan dialogue, the leno's

[1] Cf. Plautus, *Amph.* 660 : *meus uir hic quidem est* ; 1075 : *Amphitryo hic quidem* <*est*> *erus meus; Aul.* 728 : *atque hic quidem Euclio est; Bacch.* 774 : *atque hic quidem, opinor, Chrysalust* ; 1105 : *hic quidem est pater Mnesilochi; Merc.* 365-6 : *attatae,* | *meus pater hic quidem est; Mil.* 361-2 : *pro di immortales,* | *eri concubinast haec quidem* ; 1283 : *nauclerus hic quidem est; Most* 447 : *meus seruos hic quidem est Tranio* ; 1063 : *erus meus hic quidem est; Persa* 14 : *Toxilus hic quidem meus amicust* ; 201 : *Paegnium hic quidem est* ; 309 : *Sagaristio hic quidem est* ; 790 : *Dordalus hic quidem est; Poen.* 1122-3 : *pro supreme Iuppiter,* | *erus meus hic quidem est; Pseud.* 445 : *meus hic est quidem seruos Pseudolus; Stich.* 238 : *Epignomi ancilla haec quidem est Crocotium* ; 458 : *hic quidem Gelasimus est parasitus* ; 464 : *Epignomus hic quidem est* ; 655 : *sed Stichus est hic quidem; Trin.* 1055 : *meus est hic quidem Stasimus seruos; Truc.* 93 : *sed haec quidem eius Astaphium est ancillula*; Terence, *Eun.* 228-9 : *attat, hic quidem est parasitus Gnatho* | *militis.*

o bone uir,
salueto, et tu, bona liberta

is shouted across a distance to persons turned away from him and Toxilus'

Dordalus hic quidem est

is uttered as he sees and recognises the *leno*. An utterance like *Eurypylus hic quidem est* made after Eurypylus' address to Patroclus and his companions could only come from a person standing apart from this group [1] or by a new entrant.

A further point is that *certe* at the head of a statement in dramatic dialogue does not signal novelty but rather takes up a previous utterance in some way. Used alone it confirms the belief of the person who has asked a question, whether this is the speaker himself or another. An instructive contrast is provided by Plautus, *Bacch.* 534-5 : *estne hic hostis quem aspicio meus? | certe is est; Trin.* 1071-2: *estne ipsus an non est? certe is es, | is est profecto*; Terence, *Andr.* 906: *Andrium ego Critonem uideo? certe is est; Ad.* 78 : *sed estne hic ipsus de quo agebam? et certe is est* on the one hand and Plautus, *Amph.* 1072-5 : *quis hic est senex qui ante aedis nostras sic iacet? ... Amphitryo hic quidem <est> erus meus; Aul.* 727-8 : *quinam homo hic ante aedis nostras eiulans conqueritur maerens?| atque hic quidem Euclio est; Bacch.* 773-4: *quis loquitur prope?| atque hic quidem, opinor, Chrysalust* [2] on the other. Followed by *equidem* the adverb counters or corrects the implication of a previous statement; as at Plautus, *Mil.* 430-33 : *persectari hic uolo, | Sceledre, nos nostri an alieni ... :: certe equidem*

[1] During the time between Charmides' question *sed quis hic est qui huc in plateam cursuram incipit?* at *Trin.* 1006 and his recognition of Stasimus at v. 1055 : *meus est hic quidem Stasimus seruos* there is no contact between the two personages.

[2] Cf. Plautus, *Bacch.* 1104-5 ; *Mil.* 361-2 and 1281-3 ; *Persa* 13-14, 200-201 and 308-9 ; *Poen.* 1122-3 ; *Pseud.* 445 ; *Stich.* 237-8 ; *Trin.* 1006-1055 ; Terence, *Eun.* 228.

noster sum; Persa 208-9: *feminam scelestam te astans contra contuor.* | :: *certe equidem puerum peiorem quam te noui neminem* [1]. It would seem therefore to be no accident that the collocation *certe hic quidem* does not occur in dramatic dialogue [2].

Ribbeck gave *certe Eurypylus hic quidem est. hominem exercitum* to Cicero. The same considerations, however, just adduced concerning the usage of *certe* in drama also apply to the usage of Cicero's letters, speeches and dialogues. I suggest therefore that at *Tusc.* II 38 Cicero imagines his interlocutor mentally asking whether the verses just quoted come from the famous scene showing the wounded Eurypylus and represents himself answering with *certe* (" of course ") and following up with a quotation of something said in the course of the scene, namely *Eurypylus hic quidem est. hominem exercitum*, words which would form the end of an iambic trimeter, an iambic tetrameter (acatalectic) or a trochaic tetrameter (catalectic) [3].

Where the speaker of *Eurypylus hic quidem est. hominem exercitum* is concerned, there are three possibilities : (i) Achilles entering the stage unobserved during Eurypylus' address to Patroclus or (ii) Patroclus already on stage and overhearing a monody or monologue uttered by Eurypylus as he enters the stage or (iii) the chorus in similar circumstances. The latter two possibilities would entail that Cicero doubled back

[1] *Certe* sometimes follows *quidem* in a statement (cf. Plautus, *Amph.* 417; *Bacch.* 1177; *Truc.* 963) but the words refer to separate elements of the statement.

[2] *Certe* (Accius, *Trag.* 268) and *quidem* (Ennius ap. Varr. *LL* VII, 93 [= *Sc.* 419]) occur only once each in the remains of tragedy, each word possessing perhaps already a slightly unpoetic tone, and so the absence of collocation is not significant. Both words occur frequently in the remains of comedy on the other hand and these are quite sufficiently extensive to allow firm deductions.

[3] For *certe* in reply to a question cf. Terence, *Haut.* 431 *uenit? :: certe*; for *certe* after the quotation of another person's statement cf. Cicero, *Sest.* 77 '*atque uis in foro uersata est*'. *certe. quando enim maior* ?

to an earlier point in the tragic episode for his quotation [1]. An eavesdropping Myrmidon king seems somewhat implausible and can be ruled out. The degree of sympathy evinced by the exclamation *hominem exercitum* [2] suggests the chorus rather than the unfeeling [3] inquisitor Patroclus.

Something has gone wrong with the text of Cicero's next phrase, *ubi tantum luctum continuatus*. However one corrects it, it must refer to *luctus* on stage. Patroclus is represented as merely inquisitive [4], Eurypylus as an uncomplaining proto-Stoic. I suggest therefore that Cicero had in mind the reaction of the chorus to the sight of Eurypylus stumbling along as the result of his wound rather than treading militarily [5].

Following the exclamation *uide quam non flebiliter respondeat, rationem etiam adferat, cur aequo animo sibi ferendum sit* an undoubted quotation begins:

qui alteri exitium parat
eum scire oportet sibi paratam pestem, ut participet, parem.

This is usually treated as the full reply to an unquoted question from Patroclus. I suggest that Cicero is still concerned with the dialogue between Eurypylus and the chorus, i.e. that Eurypylus answered a question about how he

[1] In comedy the person recognised has usually uttered something. At Plautus, *Most.* 1063 and *Truc.* 93 there has been offstage noise preceding the person's entry.

[2] For the force of *exercitus* here cf. Plautus, *Epid.* 529; *Merc.* 65 and 228; *Persa* 856 et al. For the exclamatory accusative cf. Plautus, *Amph.* fr. VI *ut † laruatus † edepol hominem miserum. medicum quaeritat.*

[3] Cf., however, Homer, *Il.* XI 814-15.

[4] M. Seyffert (Leipzig, 1864) made *heu exercitum ubi tantum luctus continuatur* words uttered by Patroclus.

[5] Cf. the reaction of the chorus in a parallel scene at Euripides, *Phoen.* 1350-1: ἀνάγετ' ἀνάγετε κωκυτόν, ἐπὶ κάρα τε λευκοπήχεις κτύπους χεροῖν.

received his wound, prefixing his answer with the gnome which Cicero quotes.

Cicero's next statement, *abducet Patricoles, credo, ut conlocet in cubili, ut uolnus obliget*, has not been forced by anyone into verse. The alliteration, however, the asyndeton and the anaphora have the flavour of archaic poetry. I suggest, therefore, that Cicero has adapted to his own discourse a hopeful prophecy by the Ennian chorus. The following statement, *si quidem homo esset; sed nihil uidi minus* dismisses the prophecy.

With *quaerit enim quid actum sit* Cicero leaps forward to the dialogue between Eurypylus and Patroclus. The iambic tetrameter.

eloquere, eloquere res Argiuum proelio ut se sustinet

is Patroclus' question. What Cicero quotes of Eurypylus' reply, consisting of a full acatalectic iambic tetrameter and the first three elements of a second

non potest ecfari tantum dictis quantum factis suppetit
laboris

is probably complete in itself. To judge, however, by the structurally parallel dialogue at Terence, *Hec.* 415-23:

:: ain tu tibi hoc incommodum euenisse iter?
:: non hercle uerbis, Parmeno, dici potest
tantum quam re ipsa nauigare incommodumst.
:: itan est? :: o fortunate, nescis quid mali
praeterieris qui numquam es ingressus mare.
nam alias ut mittam miserias, unam hanc uide:
dies triginta aut plus eo in naui fui
quom interea semper mortem exspectabam miser;
ita usque aduorsa tempestate usi sumus.

Eurypylus would have continued his answer after a further enquiry from Patroclus.

The next two sentences, *quiesce igitur et uolnus alliga* and *etiam si Eurypylus posset non posset Aesopus*, are understood by many as addressed by Cicero in his own voice to Patroclus with reference to the dialogue quoted. The point of *igitur* becomes obscure and *ecfari* has to be supplied with *posset*, producing a quite pointless and tasteless insult to the actor Aesopus. Vahlen and Pohlenz take the first sentence as addressed to Eurypylus but in so doing are forced to interpret *alliga* as " allow yourself to be bound up ". The difficulty about *posset* in the second sentence remains. The only way out is to suppose that the two sentences refer to conversation between Eurypylus and Patroclus which Cicero has omitted to quote.

Many critics have tried to treat the first sentence as an actual part of the dialogue between the two heroes but have found themselves obliged to make alterations to the transmitted text: Bentley proposed *PATR. laberis, quiesce. EVR. et uolnus alliga. PATR. tace;* Hermann *EVR. quiesce et uolnus alliga*; Bergk *PATR. tu quiesce igitur et uolnus alligauero.* If it were not for *igitur*, which seems never to be an anapaest in Republican drama, the sentence as transmitted would form the end of an iambic verse. The use of *quiescere* in the sense of *tacere* [1] and perhaps the variation of *uolnus obligare* [2] with *uolnus alligare* give it an unprosaic air. I suggest that Cicero loosely adapted to his own discourse a piece of advice offered to the inquisitive Patroclus by the Ennian chorus. Where the second sentence is concerned, I should supply *quiescere* with *posset* and understand Cicero to be making a joke about stage conventions.

The manner of Cicero's *ubi fortuna Hectoris nostram acrem aciem inclinatam et cetera explicat in dolore* suggests that *ubi*

[1] Cf. Ennius ap. Diomed. *Gramm.* I 387, 30 (= *Sc.* 160).

[2] With *medicum modo requirens a quo obligetur* and *ut uolnus obliget* compare *Nat. deor.* III 57: *primusque uolnus dicitur obligauisse.*

fortuna Hectoris nostram acrem aciem inclinatam begins a fresh utterance rather than carries on from *non potest ecfari*... One would interpret: "he delivers while in pain the speech beginning *ubi fortuna* ..." [1]. This speech was a reply to a specific question about how the survivors of Eurypylus' unit got back to the camp and must have gone to some length. As Eurypylus told the story of the Achaean retreat Patroclus bound his wound.

— d —

The narrative of Homer, *Il.* XI 804-48, on which the episode I have tried to extract from Cicero's argumentative and allusive discourse depends, suffered a number of alterations at the hands of Aristarchus and perhaps also in its turn at those of Ennius. I shall now attempt to elucidate these alterations.

The Homeric Eurypylus limps back into camp with an arrow in his thigh and meets Patroclus in the vicinity of Ulysses' quarters as Patroclus makes his way back across the camp from Nestor's quarters. One of Asclepius' sons, Machaon, lies wounded through the shoulder in Nestor's quarters. The rest of the Achaeans, including Asclepius' other son, Podalirius, are still fighting in the plain. Patroclus puts his arm around Eurypylus' waist, leads him into the latter's own quarters and treats him by removing the missile and sprinkling a pharmaceutical powder upon the site of the wound.

In having the whole action performed or narrated before Achilles' quarters Aristarchus followed the tragic convention of his time [2]. In having one of the heroes, albeit a minor

[1] On whole plays and narrative poems being indicated by their opening words see E. J. KENNEY, *CR* n.s. 20 (1970), 290 and the works there quoted.

[2] See above, p. 57.

one [1], narrate the details of a battle he departed somewhat from convention. Detailed accounts of happenings off stage which affected the interests of those on stage were ordinarily given by a person of low degree [2], a private soldier, herald or personal slave, unnamed as a rule in the tragedian's script [3] and dubbed an ἄγγελος by the ancient editors. Aristarchus could have had Eurypylus' ἡνιοχός or ὑπασπιστής come to Achilles' quarters and ask for Patroclus to come to Eurypylus, reporting by the way the details of the battle. He preferred the unusual but highly dramatic device of making one of the highborn participants, Eurypylus himself, report the battle. I can find only one comparable episode in extant Attic scripts, that in which the Sophoclean Hyllus describes to his mother how Hercules donned the shirt steeped in the blood of Nessus [4]. Hyllus was not physically involved in the events he describes, Lichas having carried Deianira's gift to Hercules, but was much more emotionally concerned than any ordinary ἄγγελος could have been. His narrative gained force in the telling from his own situation. The Aristarchean Eurypylus' narrative of the fighting in which he himself had been wounded would have had an even greater emotional impact.

If I am correct in supposing that Ennius made his chorus utter the identifying *Eurypylus hic quidem est* after a monody

[1] On Eurypylus see Homer, *Il.* II 734-7. *Il.* I 144 ff.; II 404 ff. and XIX 40 ff. make it clear that he was not one of the great βασιλῆες.

[2] Cf. Aeschylus, *Ag.* 503-680; *Pers.* 249-514; *Theb.* 375-652; Sophocles, *Ai.* 719-83; *Ant.* 223-77; Euripides, *Androm.* 1070-1165; *Bacch.* 1024-1152; *El.* 761-858; *Hec.* 484-582; *Hel.* 1512-1618; *Herc.* 909-1015; *Hcld.* 784-866; *Hipp.* 1153-267; *Ion* 1106-228; *I.A.* 414-39; 1532-612; *I.T.* 1284-419; *Med.* 1116-230; *Orest.* 852-956; *Phoen.* 1067-1199; 1335-479; *Rhes.* 728-803, *Suppl.* 634-770.

[3] Talthybius is the exception who proves the rule.

[4] *Trach.* 733-812. The matter is touched on without mention of the Sophoclean scene by E. Fraenkel, *De media et noua comoedia quaestiones selectae*, Diss. Göttingen, 1912, pp. 43 ff.

from the wounded hero then Ennius here altered the original script. Attic tragic scripts as a rule did not have an ἄγγελος arriving after a choral ode identified[1]. Where, however, the ἄγγελος arrived in the midst of conversation between actors or between the chorus and an actor he was identified[2]. The identification always came, except in one special case[3], before the ἄγγελος said anything. A person of high degree making his first appearance, as Eurypylus pretty certainly did in the episode in question, was named either before he reached the centre of the stage or in his own opening speech or in the reply made by the person he addressed. Individual remarks and conversations aside about a newcomer were more the marks of a comic script. Ennius, who had his chorus on the stage platform itself rather than in the area in front of the stage[4] and who, like most, if not all, of his predecessors in the Roman theatre, translated both tragic and comic scripts, seems to have made Eurypylus' entry conform to a local dramatic type.

Ennius almost certainly replaced the metrical pattern of Aristarchus' episode. Extant Attic scripts for the most part have the ἄγγελος arrive uttering iambic trimeters but occasionally, in emotionally tense circumstances, make the piper accompany the newcomer's opening utterance and the utterances of the chorus and the actors already on stage[5]. The narrative, however, always has to be delivered in spoken trimeters[6]. The stichic acatalectic iambic tetrameters with

[1] Cf., however, Aeschylus, *Ag.* 493; *Theb.* 369-74; Euripides, *Erectheus* fr. 65, 11 Austin; *Hipp.* 1151-2.

[2] Cf., however, Euripides, *Androm.* 1070; *I.A.* 415.

[3] Euripides, *Rhes.* 732.

[4] See above, p. 49.

[5] Cf. Euripides, *Herc.* 909 ff.; *Phoen.* 1335 ff.; *Rhes.* 728 ff.

[6] Significant is the way in which at Aeschylus, *Pers.* 176 the Persian queen drops from trochaic tetrameters to iambic trimeters in order to give the chorus the details of her dream.

which the Ennian Eurypylus first addresses Patroclus have no analogues in Attic scripts, tragic or comic, except in an episode of Sophocles' satyr play Ἰχνευταί, where, after the chorus has stated its business to Cyllene and conducted a lengthy conversation with her in trimeters, there is a riddling interchange in tetrameters about the nature of Hermes' lyre [1]. In translating the episode of Aristarchus' Ἀχιλλεύς in question Ennius substituted a traditional metrical pattern of the Roman stage, into whose ultimate origins we need not here go but whose popularity is easily illustrated. A fragment of Ennius' *Hecuba* [2] shows that he turned the entry anapaests of the Euripidean heroine into iambic tetrameters [3]. A noisy newcomer to the door of Achilles' quarters in the *Hectoris lytra* seems to have used similar tetrameters [4]. The speech of this play which describes the battle leading to Hector's death was set in trochaic tetrameters [5]; so too the speech of the *Andromeda* which described the slaying of the sea monster [6]. Comic scripts employed the whole pattern visible in Cicero's quotation of the episode of the *Achilles* with conscious ridicule of the sister genre. Whereas Attic comedians regularly made the bringer of news from off stage speak throughout in trimeters [7], Plautus put many such scenes into musically accompanied verse, lengthening out the news-bringer's opening utterance, filling it full of allusions

[1] 238 ff. Page.

[2] ap. Varr. *LL* VII 6 (= *Sc.* 196).

[3] *Hec.* 59 ff.

[4] ap. Non. pp. 489, 29; 490, 6 (= *Sc.* 156-7). Contrast the noisy entrances at Euripides, *Hcld.* 646; *I.T.* 1307. At *I.A.* 317 and *Rhes.* 11, however, the piper's music sounds.

[5] See above, p. 53.

[6] ap. Non. pp. 20, 18; 183, 18 (= *Sc.* 114 and 118-19).

[7] Cf. Menander, *Aspis* 1 ff.; *Georgos* 31 ff.; *Sicyonios* 169 ff.; *Naucleros* ap. Athen. 474 c (= fr. 286 Körte).

to heroic legend and raising the level of the style to near the tragic. He favoured the acatalectic iambic tetrameter in particular to open with [1] and only rarely concluded with trimeters [2] rather than trochaic tetrameters.

The occurrence of a number of the Ennian Eurypylus' unusual phrases in Plautus' comic scripts, namely *oppeto malam pestem* [3], *hostili manu* [4] and *non potest ecfari tantum dictis quantum factis suppetit laboris* [5], suggests that there existed a large store of traditional scenic vocabulary as well as of metrical patterns upon which the poet could and did draw. It would therefore be idle to come to conclusions about Aristarchus' argumentative and verbal style from the style which Ennius employs in the episode under examination. The extended alliteration and word play of *oppeto . . . opplent, peto . . . priusquam oppeto . . . pestem, potis . . . pacto profluens, paratam pestem . . . participet parem, manus . . . mandatam . . . manu* [6] and the rhyming isocolon of *tantum dictis quantum factis* [7] have a very Roman sound. The metaphor in *res Argiuum . . . se sustinet* was one which Roman statesmen were probably already using in orations about the community's welfare [8]. The substance of *qui alteri exitium parat eum scire*

[1] Cf. *Amph.* 153 ff.; 984 ff. and 1053 ff.; *Bacch.* 925 ff.; *Capt.* 516 ff.; *Merc.* 111 ff.; *Poen.* 817 ff.; *Stich.* 274 ff.

[2] Cf. *Bacch.* 997 ff. (a letter has to be read out).

[3] Cf. Plautus, *Asin.* 21-2 : *ut tibi superstes uxor aetatem siet* | *atque illa uiua uiuos ut pestem oppetas; Capt.* 525-6 : *neque de hac re negotium est* | *quin male occidam oppetamque pestem eri uicem meamque.* The normal phrase was *mortem oppetere* (Ennius ap. Non. pp. 494, 3 ; 507, 19 [= *Sc.* 203]).

[4] Cf. Plautus, *Capt.* 311 : *tam mihi quam illi libertatem hostilis eripuit manus.*

[5] Cf. Plautus, *Pseud.* 108 : *utinam quae dicis dictis facta suppetant.*

[6] An exhaustive analysis of the alliterative patterning in Eurypylus' utterances can be found in A. Grilli, *Studi enniani*, pp. 175 ff.

[7] Cf., however, Aeschylus, *Theb.* 962 ff.; Euripides, *Androm.* 497 ; *Phoen.* 1292.

[8] Cf. Cicero, *Mur.* 3 : *is cui res publica a me iam traditur sustinenda magnis meis laboribus et periculis sustentata.*

oportet sibi paratam pestem, ut participet, parem is thoroughly Greek as one may see from Euripides, *Herc.* 727-8 προσδόκα δὲ δρῶν κακῶς | κακόν τι πράξειν [1]. It was, however, common practice for the Latin translators of tragedy and comedy to insert such gnomes near the beginnings of speeches, especially where, as here, a higher than usual stylistic effect was being sought [2]. The grim irony with which, as in the phrase *malam pestem mandatam hostili manu*, the language of business and commerce is applied to killing looks Ennian, or at least Roman. The receiver of something *mandatum* ordinarily expected no material remuneration for his trouble [3] but neither did he expect any positive harm to result. *Socii ac participes* of an enterprise expected to gain a profit rather than incur a loss from the delivery of something *paratum* [4]. I should not, however, deny the possibility that Aristarchus employed similar metaphors. Both Aeschylus [5] and Euripides [6] affected on occasion to find a paradoxical likeness between the warrior and the businessman.

I turn now from the form of the tragic episode to the substance of what the actors are made to say.

Ribbeck's supplement of the trochees quoted by Cicero

ubi fortuna Hectoris nostram acrem aciem inclinatam <*dedit*>

[1] Cf. Com. inc. 82 *ab alio exspectes alteri quod feceris.* The gnome softened the traditional view expressed at Archilochus, fr. 66 D : ἓν δ' ἐπίσταμαι μέγα, | τὸν κακῶς με δρῶντα δεινοῖς ἀνταμείβεσθαι κακοῖς and Aeschylus, *Theb.* 1049: παθὼν κακῶς κακοῖσιν ἀντημείβετο.

[2] Cf. Ennius ap. Cic. *Nat. deor.* III 65 (= *Sc.* 266-8) and Euripides, *Med.* 364 ff.; Terence, *Andr.* 959-60 and Donatus *ad loc.*

[3] On *res mandatae* see Cicero, *S. Rosc.* 111-113.

[4] For *parare*, 'acquire through commerce', cf. Plautus, *Most.* 67 et al.

[5] Cf. *Theb.* 545-6.

[6] Cf. *Phoen.* 1227-8.

is as probable as such supplements can be [1]. The tragic Eurypylus described a much more serious reverse at this point of time than did Homer; a whole unit of the Achaean army had been forced back, whereas in the *Iliad* Ajax had simply retired from in front of the embattled φάλαγγες [2]. Cicero's discourse makes it clear that Eurypylus got an honourable reception. If this reception is contrasted with the accusations of cowardice hurled at the similarly wounded Ulysses in an earlier scene of the play [3], we may guess that Eurypylus was able to tell of an organised retreat made by the survivors of the Trojan onslaught. The play thus continued to replace the individual combats of the *Iliad* with something like a tactical engagement between fifth century armies. The poet responsible for this alteration of the Homeric narrative was quite certainly Aristarchus.

Rather than *Hector* or *Troiani* the tragic Eurypylus talks of *fortuna Hectoris*. By this phrase Ennius meant either a personal attribute of Hector which conduced to his success or an external success-bringing force which attached itself peculiarly to him. It cannot have the meaning one might expect, namely " Hector's actual success ", without causing an intolerable tautology. In any case only the plural *fortunae* seems to be used in this way in extant dramatic texts [4]. In favour of the first interpretation is a fragment of the *Hectoris lytra* already referred to, *Sc.* 180:

[1] For the use of *dare* with the past participle (absent from the prose of Caesar and Cicero) cf. Plautus, *Cas.* 439; *Cist.* 595; *Mil.* 258 and 1174; *Most.* 298; *Persa* 457; *Pseud.* 881 and 926; Terence, *Andr.* 683; *Haut.* 950; *Eun.* 212; *Phorm.* 974; Virgil, *Aen.* XII 437; Livy VIII 6, 6.

[2] If the Latin corresponds with anything in Homer it is *Il.* XI 544: Ζεὺς δὲ πατὴρ Αἴανθ' ὑψίζυγος ἐν φόβον ὦρσε. Where the phraseology is concerned one might compare *Il.* V 37: Τρῶας δ' ἔκλιναν Δαναοί and VI 5-6: Αἴας δὲ πρῶτος ... Τρώων ῥῆξε φάλαγγα.

[3] See above, p. 56 ff.

[4] Cf. Plautus, *Asin.* 515; 629 et al.

saeuiter fortuna ferro cernunt de uictoria [1]

Here *fortuna* must be an instrumental rather than a circumstantial ablative : luckiness as well as skill in using weapons will decide the outcome of the battle [2]. Where the second interpretation is concerned, it may be noted that the Romans worshipped a number of *Fortunae* with separate spheres of influence, including a *Fortuna populi Romani* whose temple stood on the Quirinal [3]. Ennius may have adapted this latter deity to the more individualistic world of the Achaean and Trojan heroes. The two interpretations suggested do not cancel each other out. In the early second century a number of nouns, e.g. *fides*, *honos*, *mens*, *uenus*, *uirtus*, signalled both personal attributes and external divine forces to which the state paid cult with temples and altars. Certainly the Romans of the Republic valued the luck of the individual commander quite differently from the Greeks of any age, putting it on a level with his courage and tactical skill [4]. There is nothing at all like *fortuna Hectoris nostram acrem aciem inclinatam dedit* in the *Iliad*. Homer usually attributes success in combat to the power of one of the Olympian deities and specifically names the deity on the occasion of the success [5]. In Attic tragic scripts success is occasionally attributed to purely human skill and exertion [6]. Where

[1] Cf. also Livy I 42, 3 : *in eo bello et uirtus et fortuna enituit Tulli*; IX 18, 11 : *quin tu homines cum homine, duces cum duce, fortunam cum fortuna confers ;* XXII 23, 3 : *qui bellum ratione, non fortuna gereret.*

[2] *Fortuna ferro cernere* seems to be a unique phrase. For *ferro decernere* cf. Ennius, *Ann.* 133 ; Virgil, *Aen.* VII 525 ; XI 218 ; XII 282 ; Livy VII 26, 1 ; XXIII 46, 14 ; XXVIII 21, 6 ; XXXIX 15, 14 ; XL 8, 19.

[3] Cf. K. Latte, *Römische Religionsgeschichte*, Munich, 1960, p. 178 and note 3.

[4] Cf. *Antichthon* 3 (1969), 44 f.

[5] Cf. *Il.* XI 318-19 ; XVI 103 ; XVI 844-5 ; XVII 630. At *Il.* VII 288-92 the context makes it clear that by θεός and δαίμων Hector means Ζεύς.

[6] Cf. Euripides, *Hcld.* 841-2 ; *Suppl.* 703-5 and 714-18.

external agencies are admitted the speaker may use Homeric terms [1] but will more often speak of an undefined θεός [2] or δαίμων [3] or θεοί [4] or even ἡ τύχη [5]. Human and non-human agencies are as a rule kept rigidly distinct. The only approximation to the ideas in *fortuna Hectoris nostram acrem aciem inclinatam dedit* that I can find in extant Attic scripts is at Euripides, *Suppl.* 589-93: σοὶ δὲ προστάσσω μένειν Ἄδραστε κἀμοὶ μὴ ἀναμίγνυσθαι τύχας | τὰς σάς. ἐγὼ γὰρ δαίμονος τοὐμοῦ μέτα | στρατηλατήσω κλεινὸς ἐν κλεινῷ δορί [6]. Ennius seems to have regarded contemporary ideas about the factors in military success more than the actual text of Aristarchus' Ἀχιλλεύς.

The tragic Eurypylus had his wound bandaged—quite different treatment from what he received in Homer's narrative [7]. The *Iliad* and the *Odyssey* have two references to bandaging [8], both in descriptions of immediate first aid. Wounds are normally treated with φάρμακα [9] and the function of the military surgeon is described at *Il.* XI 514-15 without any reference to bandages:

ἰητρὸς γὰρ ἀνὴρ πολλῶν ἀντάξιος ἄλλων
ἰούς τ' ἐκτάμνειν ἐπί τ' ἤπια φάρμακα πάσσειν.

[1] Cf. Euripides, *Rhes.* 319-20.

[2] Cf. Euripides, *Rhes.* 64, 583-4, 597-8, *Suppl.* 596-7.

[3] Cf. Euripides, *Rhes.* 995-6.

[4] Cf. Aeschylus, *Theb.* 417-18.

[5] Cf. Sophocles, *Ant.* 328.

[6] Cf. Aeschylus, *Ag.* 1568-70: ἐγὼ δ' οὖν | ἐθέλω δαίμονι τῷ Πλεισθενιδᾶν | ὅρκους θεμένη τάδε μὲν στέργειν. Menander, Fr. 714, 1-3 Körte: ἅπαντι δαίμων ἀνδρὶ συμπαρίσταται | εὐθὺς γενομένῳ, μυσταγωγὸς τοῦ βίου | ἀγαθός.

[7] *Il.* XI 828-32 and 842-8.

[8] *Il.* XIII 598 ff.; *Od.* XIX 456 ff.

[9] Cf. *Il.* IV 189 ff.; V 401 ff.; V 899 ff. See also Virgil, *Aen.* VII 758; XII 391-406. Silius, however, has men bandaged at *Pun.* VI 68-93 (contrast V 344-368).

Nevertheless quite complex bandaging procedures were in use by the time of Aristarchus [1] and vase painters felt able to represent them in heroic scenes [2]. We may suppose that it was Aristarchus who caused Eurypylus to be bandaged. There could have been no arrow protruding from Eurypylus' thigh demanded by the Ennian script. If there had been Cicero would surely have mentioned it. This lack of realism, or avoidance of sensationalism, may also be attributed to Aristarchus.

The address of the tragic Eurypylus to Patroclus refers to the quarters of Machaon and Podalirius as if they were camp hospitals. Now in the *Iliad* the sons of Asclepius are fighting βασιλῆες, like Eurypylus except that they had superior medical skills; professional surgeons are as rare as bandages [3]. Nowhere in the *Iliad* are a number of wounded men treated in the one place [4]. The Homeric Achilles had an αἴθουσα (*porticus*) in his κλισίη [5] and Aristarchus might conceivably have put similarly elaborate structures anywhere in the Achaean camp [6]. If camp hospitals existed in the fifth century he could have turned the quarters of Machaon and Podalirius into hospitals or Machaon and Podalirius themselves into hospital supervisors, if not professional surgeons. It is unlikely, however, that such hospitals did exist in this century. Accounts of Greek armies on campaign in the next century mention ἰατροί often

[1] Cf. Hippocrates, *Medic.* 3 (9, 208), *Ulc.* 1 ff. (6, 400 ff.).

[2] Cf. the late sixth century painting of Achilles tending Patroclus (Beazley, *ARV*[2] I p. 21).

[3] Anonymous ἰητροί are mentioned only at *Il.* XIII 213 and XVI 28.

[4] At *Il.* XI 658-9: οἱ γὰρ ἄριστοι | ἐν νηυσὶν κέαται βεβλημένοι οὐτάμενοί τε. At XI 825-7: οἱ μὲν γὰρ δὴ πάντες, ὅσοι πάρος ἦσαν ἄριστοι, | ἐν νηυσὶν κέαται βεβλημένοι οὐτάμενοί τε | χερσὶν ὕπο Τρώων.

[5] *Il.* XXIV 644.

[6] Αἴθουσα and στόα do not occur in the remains of tragedy; παστάς occurs at Sophocles, *Ant.* 1207 and Euripides, *Or.* 1371.

enough[1] but never camp hospitals[2]. This is no accident for Greek generals as a rule encamped their forces in a naturally protected position and rarely put up artificial defence works[3]. Their camps were notoriously lacking in orderliness[4]. It is significant, I think, that the Hector of Euripides' Ῥῆσος has the wounded Thracian charioteer sent to his palace in Troy for treatment[5], not to any surgeons accompanying the Trojan forces.

Aesculapi liberorum ... porticus is, I suggest, Ennius' transposition into heroic terms of a contemporary Roman camp *ualetudinarium*. The noun *porticus* could denote a temporary verandah made from wood and canvas[6] as well as a permanent colonnade of stone and the working surgeon notoriously needed the light such structures could afford[7]. The fragment of the *Hectoris lytra* quoted by Nonius at p. 355, 3 (= *Sc.* 158-159)

Hector ui summa armatos educit foras
castrisque castra ultro iam ferre occupat

and discussed earlier shows how prone Ennius was to merge the practices of the armies of his own time with what he found described in Attic tragedies.

It will be said with some justice that nothing at all is recorded about medical services in the Roman army in the

[1] Cf. Xenophon, *Lac.* 13, 7; *Anab.* III 4, 30; *Cyr.* I 6, 15; III 2, 12; V 4, 17. See also Hippocrates, *Medic.* 14 (9, 218), Onasander I 13-14.

[2] The implication of Xenophon, *Cyr.* V 4, 17 is that Cyrus did not have anything of the sort in the camps he set up.

[3] See above, p. 53, n. 2.

[4] Cf. Polybius VI 42.

[5] See vv. 872 ff.

[6] Cf. Caesar, *Ciu.* II 2, 3; Columella VII 9, 9; VIII 11, 3; VIII 14, 1; IX *praef.* 2; IX 7, 4; IX 14, 14.

[7] Cf. Hippocrates, *Med.* 2 (9, 206), Galen ad Hippocr. *Off.* 8 (18B, 678).

time of Ennius [1] and argued that the *ualetudinaria* described by 'Hyginus' in his account of the permanent imperial camp [2] and the *optiones ualetudinarii* of imperial inscriptions [3] had no early Republican forerunners. Now, certainly, Polybius does not mention anything like them in his account of second century Roman methods of quartering troops [4]. But neither does he mention armourers or animal attendants or the like. And when, at a later point of his history [5], he describes the Roman method of distributing the spoils of victory he refers to οἱ ἀρρωστοῦντες as a separate category alongside the camp garrison, the reserves and those on special duties. Clearly the wounded were not left to die on the field or to look after themselves. One would indeed expect the care of those likely to be again militarily useful to be organised as diligently as the building of the rampart and the laying out of the camp streets and assembly places, activities which always surprised Greek observers [6]. The links in this argument are tenuous but everything tends towards the conclusion that Ennius put a second century Roman *ualetudinarium* into the Achaean camp before Troy [7].

[1] For speculation see E. H. Byrne, Medicine in the Roman Army, *CJ* 5 (1909-10), 271 ff.; O. Jacob, *AC* 2 (1933), 313 ff.; J. Harmand, *L'Armée et le soldat à Rome de* 107 *à* 50 *avant notre ère*, Paris, 1967, pp. 201-9.

[2] *Munit. castr.* 4, 35. Cf. Vegetius II 10 on the *aegri contubernales*, Macer, *Dig.* XLIX 16, 12, 2 on inspection of the 'ualetudinarii'. For the identification of *ualetudinaria* in remains of imperial *castra* see R. Schultze, *Bonn. Jahrb.* 139 (1934), 54 ff. and I. A. Richmond, *Proc. Brit. Ac.* 41 (1955), 315.

[3] *CIL* VIII 2553; 18047; IX 1617.

[4] VI 27, 1-31, 9.

[5] X 16, 5.

[6] See above, p. 53, n. 2.

[7] However one interprets them, Cicero, *Tusc.* II 39 and the passage of Ennius there quoted provide no evidence for military conditions at the time the *Tusculans* were written. On the other hand it cannot be argued from the fact that some high ranking officers took private physicians on campaign with them at this time (see Brutus ap. Cic., *ad Brut.* I 6, 2; Suetonius, *Aug.* 11;

IV. — Concerning the Sabinae

It is clear from the similarity between the series of questions addressed by the Euripidean Jocasta to her son Polynices come into Thebes to parley

> φέρ', ἢν ἕλῃς γῆν τήνδ' — μὴ τύχοι ποτέ —
> πρὸς θεῶν, τρόπαια πῶς ἀναστήσεις Διί;
> πῶς δ' αὖ κατάρξῃ θυμάτων, ἑλὼν πάτραν,
> καὶ σκῦλα γράψεις πῶς ἐπ' Ἰνάχου ῥοαῖς;
> Θήβας πυρώσας τάσδε Πολυνείκης θεοῖς
> ἀσπίδας ἔθηκε [1];

and the words quoted by the fourth century rhetorician Julius Victor [2] from Ennius' *Sabinae*

> *cum spolia generis detraxeritis, quam inscriptionem dabitis?*

that the Latin poet's knowledge of Attic tragedy affected greatly the way in which he handled stories not previously reduced to dramatic form [3]. The relationship of Roman historical drama to Attic tragedy continued long afterwards to be a close one. The dialogue between the Accian Tarquin and his councillors quoted by Cicero at *Diu.* I 44-5 had as its base that between the Persian queen and the chorus of the Πέρσαι concerning the queen's dream [4].

Plutarch, *Cato min.* 70, 2) that no general provision was made for looking after those wounded in battle.

[1] *Phoen.* 571-6.

[2] P. 402. 30 Halm, writing *de locis post rem.* Victor must be using a fairly ancient source. The second century orator C. Fannius is also cited in this chapter of his work. Cato is quoted at p. 448, 3 and the reading of *comoediae ueteres et togatae et tabernariae et Atellanae fabulae et mimofabulae* recommended at p. 447, 32.

[3] I leave to one side the theory of W. Soltau (*Die Anfänge der römischen Geschichtsschreibung*, Leipzig, 1909, pp. 31 ff.) that Ennius actually invented the story of the Sabine women.

[4] 159-225.

In his reconstruction of the *Sabinae* Ribbeck [1] imagined an episode like that described by Livy [2], Ovid [3] and Plutarch [4], in which Hersilia and others of the Sabine women intervened between the embattled armies of Tatius and Romulus [5]. This flouts all that we know of the conventions of tragedy. The nature of the episode from which Victor's quotation comes must be reconsidered.

It is necessary, however, first to point out that the text of the quotation is even more corrupt than has been imagined and that the connection between it and Euripides, *Phoen.* 571-6, suggested by Vahlen and commonly accepted [6], is far from straightforward.

Ian's *generis* for the transmitted *generi* [7] seems probable enough. It remains, however, impossible to make the words fit any known pattern of Republican dramatic verse [8]. The two clauses, *cum spolia generis detraxeritis* and *quam inscriptionem dabitis* [9], form in themselves unexceptional iambic

1 *Die römische Tragödie*, p. 206. VAHLEN, *RhM* 16 (1861), 580 (= *Ges. phil. Schr.* I 418) was first to suggest that Victor, whose work was first printed in 1823, was quoting from a *fabula praetexta*.

2 I 13, 1-3.

3 *Fast.* III 205-228.

4 *Romul.* 19, 1-5.

5 Ribbeck's reconstruction is followed by F. LEO, *Geschichte der römischen Literatur* I, Berlin 1913, p. 197.

6 Cf. G. WILLIAMS, *Tradition and Originality in Roman Poetry*, Oxford, 1968, p. 254.

7 See the second volume of his Macrobius (Quedlinburg and Leipzig, 1852) p. 527. M. LEUMANN, *TLL* VI ii 1770, 31, s.v. *gener*, thinks that *generi* can stand as a genitive singular. The dative, however, appears regularly with *spolia detrahere* (Varro ap. Fest. p. 189 ; Livy IV 19, 5 ; IV 20, 6 ; XXX 44, 10).

8 T. BERGK, *Philologus* 33 (1874), 294 (= *Kl. Schr.* I 361) argued that Victor paraphrases in prose something from the *Annals*. S. MARIOTTI, *Lezioni su Ennio*, Pesaro, 1951, p. 134 suggested a measurement in Reizian cola but withdrew it in the 1963 reprint of this book.

9 Ian's *dicabitis* is unnecessary. for the type of phrase cf. Ennius' *orationem dare* (*Sc.* 306) and Livy's *impressionem dare* (IV 28, 6).

sequences and in this shape Vahlen leaves them [1]. Ribbeck follows Lucian Mueller in inserting *patres* after *quam*. Warmington marks a lacuna the size of a cretic after *detraxeritis*. I suggest that much more has been omitted, at the very least a reference to where the alleged fathers-in-law will put the *spolia* they take. They might be hung on a battlefield τρόπαιον [2], dedicated in the temple of a deity [3], or nailed up in the principal room of a private house [4]. Only then was there a question of inscribing them [5]. It is significant that Leo has to supplement considerably his paraphrase of the Ennian words : " wenn ihr den Leichen eurer Schwiegersöhne die Rüstungen abzieht *und sie als Tropäon aufstellt*, welche Inschrift wollt ihr darauf setzen, *um euern Sieg zu feiern*? " [6] I leave it to others to guess at the Latin of the missing discourse but warn against the use of Euripides, *Phoen.* 571-6 either in doing this or in mentally interpreting the transmitted Ennian words.

Upon his ἣν ἕλῃς γῆν τήνδ' Euripides hung three sarcastic questions, one about τρόπαια to be set up on the plain before Thebes, one about θύματα of thanksgiving and one about the inscription of armour dedicated in the temples of Argos. Here, as often elsewhere [7], he imported the practices of contemporary Greek states into the heroic world. Homer knew

[1] In his first edition Vahlen wrote *quam <inpie> inscriptionem dabitis* ; at *RhM* 16 (1861), 580 (= *Ges. phil. Schr.* I 418) *quam <nam> inscriptionem dabitis.*

[2] Cf. Sophocles, *Ant.* 142-3 ; Euripides, *Held.* 786-7.

[3] Cf. Homer, *Il.* VII 81-3 ; Aeschylus, *Ag.* 577-9 ; *Theb.* 276-8 ; Livy I 10, 4-7 ; IV 20, 3-11.

[4] Cf. Aeschylus, *Theb.* 478-9 ; Sophocles, *Phil.* 1428-9 ; Polybius VI 39, 10 ; Livy X 7, 9 and XXIII 23, 6.

[5] For a very curious interpretation of Ennius' meaning cf. W. Klug, *TLL* VII i 1849. 80, s.v. *inscriptio.*

[6] *Geschichte*, p. 197. The italics are mine.

[7] See above, pp. 56 ff.

of sacrifices of thanksgiving for victory [1] and the dedication of captured armour to deities [2] but nothing of τρόπαια [3] or of inscriptions [4]. The emotional effect of the first Euripidean question depended on the fact that Eteocles and Polynices came from the one οἶκος and shared one household god, Ζεὺς ἑρκεῖος. It would have been peculiarly impious for one to dedicate the armour of the other to Ζεὺς τροπαῖος. Ennius certainly had Euripides in mind when he wrote the *Sabinae* but the customs of the people in whose language he was writing differed from Athenian customs. The Romans of the early second century had no equivalent of Ζεὺς ἑρκεῖος. Their *Lares* were associated more with the earth than with the upper air. They left nothing on a field of battle except the corpses of the enemy [5]. Their nearest equivalent of Ζεὺς τροπαῖος was *Iuppiter feretrius* but they dedicated captured armour to this god in a temple in Rome itself rather than on a battle field memorial [6]. When we consider how much liberty Ennius permitted himself with the customs and practices described in the Attic plays he actually translated we may be certain that in writing plays like the *Sabinae* he would have ensured that the customs of heroic Italy did not diverge too far from those of the second century [7]. It is most unlikely that the speaker of *cum spolia generis detraxeritis . . . quam inscriptionem dabitis*? referred to τρόπαια.

[1] Cf. *Il.* IV 119-21.

[2] Cf. *Il.* VII 81-3.

[3] Cf. Thucydides II 92, 4-5 ; Gorgias, *Epitaph.* (fr. 6 Diels-Kranz).

[4] Cf. the helmet dedicated by Hiero to Olympian Zeus in 474 (*SIG*[3] 35 B.a.).

[5] The Romans seem to have first set up a trophy on a field of battle in 121 BC (Florus I 37, 6: *cum hic mos inusitatus fuerit nostris*).

[6] Cf. Livy I 10, 4-7 and IV 20, 3-11 ; Plutarch, *Marcell.* 7-8 ; Virgil, *Aen.* VI 855-9 and Servius *ad loc.*

[7] Cf. Terence's excision of Apollodorus' reference to a mourner having his hair cut *ne externis moribus spectatorem Romanum offenderet* (Donatus, Ter. *Phorm.* 91).

Two possibilities are left, one that the *spolia* were to be nailed up in Sabine houses, the second that they were to be dedicated in temples. Consideration of second century Roman practice with regard to *spolia* seems to exclude the first. Whatever the heroes of Homer might have done, ordinary Roman fighting men were not permitted to strip corpses during a battle. Those detailed to do so afterwards did not themselves have the disposal of what they took [1]. The commanding officer distributed items to reward acts of bravery [2] and supervised the burning of what might have been previously vowed to some deity [3]. Those who received an item as decoration would nail it up in a prominent position in the family house [4]. If, however, the commanding officer himself slew the enemy's leader he could dedicate the latter's armour in the temple of *Iuppiter feretrius* [5] and have it suitably inscribed. Ennius, it would seem, had the dedication of *spolia opima* in mind when he wrote *cum spolia generis detraxeritis ... quam inscriptionem dabitis*?

We can now turn to the problem of where in Ennius' *Sabinae* the words which Victor quotes stood. Attic tragedies were always set in front of a temple or a palace or military commander's quarters, never on a field of battle [6]. If, as there is good reason to suppose, Roman historical dramas followed Attic conventions, then Ennius' *Sabinae* must have been set in the Sabine camp. This is precisely whither Dionysius, in his version of the story [7] had Hersilia lead her

[1] Cf. Polybius X 16, 2-9.

[2] Cf. Polybius VI 39, 10.

[3] Cf. Livy I 37, 5 ; VIII 1, 6 ; VIII 10, 13 ; VIII 30, 8 ; X 29, 18 ; XXIII 46, 5 ; XXX 6, 9 ; XLI 12, 6 ; XLV 33, 2.

[4] Cf. (in addition to Polybius VI 39, 10) Livy X 7, 9 and XXIII 23, 6.

[5] See above, p. 85, n. 6.

[6] See above, pp. 56 ff.

[7] *Ant. Rom.* II 45-46.

embassy. One must, however, be careful of the Attic analogy. Comparison of the title *Sabinae* with the like of Ἱκετίδες, Εὐμενίδες, Τραχίνιαι, Βάκχαι and Φοίνισσαι might seem to support the view that Hersilia's companions formed a chorus of the Attic type. Such a chorus, however, would have had to be present from near the beginning of the play right to the end. Hersilia's companions could have formed at most a παραχορήγημα of the type found in the Ἱππόλυτος and the Ἀλέξανδρος [1]. I suggest that Ennius did write a part for a group present through most of the play and that it consisted of Sabine men. These were included in Hersilia's address as the chorus of the *Achilles* were included in Eurypylus' address to Patroclus. *Sabinae* would be a title like the Euripidean Ἡρακλεῖδαι.

There remains the question of who the individual was whom Hersilia addressed. The historians' accounts [2] might lead one to think that it was Tatius, the king of Cures and leader of the Sabine alliance. Yet the tone of what Hersilia says suggests that the man she is primarily addressing is her own father and that the husband she has primarily in mind is her own. On the other hand, her words imply the prospect of a combat between leaders, like the one between Romulus and the king of Caenina or the one between Claudius Marcellus and the Gallic chieftain Virdumar. We are thus brought up against a situation familiar to students of the *Annals*, namely conflict between the poet's version of early Roman history and that of the prose annalists. I suggest that in the *Sabinae* Hersilia was cast as the wife of Romulus, as indeed she was by many of the prose annalists [3], that her

[1] See schol. Eurip. *Hipp.* 58.

[2] Cf. Cn. Gellius ap. Gell. XIII 23, 13 ; Livy I 13, 1-5 ; Ovid, *Fast.* III 205-28 ; Dionysius Hal. *Ant. Rom.* II 45-6 ; Plutarch, *Romul.* 19, 1-5.

[3] Cf. Livy I 11, 2 ; Plutarch, *Romul.* 14, 7. For the story that Romulus assigned her to Hostus Hostilius see Dionysius Hal. *Ant. Rom.* III 1, 2 ; Plutarch, *Romul.* 14, 7 ; Macrobius, *Sat.* I 6, 16.

father Hersilius, whom the annalists ignore, was the principal Sabine leader, a kind of Hector or Turnus, and that Tatius remained in the background, a kind of Priam or Latinus. Ennius would have set his play in front of the quarters of Hersilius and formed the chorus out of *uigiles* like those in the *Hectoris lytra*. This is a tenuous hypothesis, you may say, but one consonant, I think, with the particular evidence provided by Victor's quotation and the general tendencies observable in Attic plays and their Roman adaptations.

DISCUSSION

M. Skutsch: If I may begin with two minor questions they would be : (*a*) You did not mean to suggest that either comedy or Latin play was as assiduously cultivated by Ennius as Greek tragedy ? (*b*) Can it really be said that the situation in Aristarchos is more urgent than in Homer ?

M. Jocelyn : To question (*a*) I should say no. To question (*b*) I should say yes, but not very dogmatically.

* * *

M. Badian : I did not quite understand your interpretation of *Sc.* 179 : in what sort of context would you place it ? It seems to me highly dramatic and rhetorical in form—particularly if you take the *qui* to be an ablative—and difficult to fit into a mere narrative as it stands.

M. Jocelyn : I do not fully understand *Sc.* 179 either as it is transmitted or as Junius emended it. It looks, as I said, at first sight like a remark made by some person between the despoilment of Patroclus' corpse and Achilles' acquisition of a new set of armour. My tentative suggestion was that someone quoted the remark in a conversation held during the night on which Priam ransomed Hector's corpse.

M. Waszink : How are we to translate this verse ? Is *qui* an interrogative or a relative pronoun ? I wonder whether there is not a very sarcastic tone here : " Are there not brave men here who want to give arms to Achilles, in order to be lazy (far from the battle) themselves ? "

M. Jocelyn: I remain unwilling to offer a full interpretation of *Sc.* 179.

M. Skutsch: The greatest difficulty about Mr. Jocelyn's reconstruction of the *Hectoris Lytra* seems to me this : quite apart from line 179 there are several other fragments, 180, 181, 182, which it would perhaps be barely possible to account for in a play as envisaged by Mr. Jocelyn but which taken together with 179 rule out a play strictly to be called *Hectoris Lytra*. Therefore we must either assume that Aristarchos' play included the Trojan attack, the death of Patroclus, the death of Hector and Priam's visits to Achilles—an assumption which seems impossible to me —or we must conclude that a whole trilogy went under a title properly—and perhaps to begin with only—belonging to the third play.

M. Jocelyn: Mr. Skutsch's suggestion is a very interesting one but no exact parallel for such a method of citing tragedies exists even among Greek writers. *Sc.* 180, 181, 182 do not worry me but I must confess that *Sc.* 179 does.

M. Suerbaum: Die Fragmente mit den Kampfschilderungen (*Sc.* 181-184) müssen auf jeden Fall aus einem Botenbericht stammen, der vermutlich vor Priamus erstattet wird und möglicherweise den Tod Hektors behandelt. Der Vers *Sc.* 179 ist aber in einem solchen Botenbericht nicht vorstellbar.

* * *

M. Badian: To turn to the historical interpretation you suggested for the passage from Cicero, *Pro S. Roscio* : I cannot see how you can dissociate the Ennian line Cicero quotes from the " slaughter " at the *lacus Seruilius*, especially since the line contains *ibi*, which seems to refer (*prima facie*) to the same place and occasion ; i.e., if the slaughter at the *lacus Seruilius* refers to the proscriptions, then the line ought to do so as well, embroidering the same theme. If you want it to refer to something totally different, a series of legal actions by the anti-Sullans, preceding and (in part) causing the slaughter at the *lacus Seruilius*—then I can only say that Cicero has expressed himself with unreasonable obscurity and incoherence. That is, unless you have evidence (of which I am not aware at the moment) that the *lacus Seruilius* (referred to by *ibi*) had a proverbial association with prosecution which would suffice to make that meaning clear despite the *prima facie* reference to the proscriptions, with which—even apart from this passage—the *lacus* is particularly associated in our sources.

M. Suerbaum : Das Ennius-Zitat (173) muss in Ciceros Kontext eine bestimmte Pointe haben, nach der *Phryges* (*ferro Brygio*) *Sullani* sind.

M. Badian : I agree that we must look for more than the use of the verse as mere superficial decoration. The scholiast at least did so, and succeeds in giving it some contemporary point. He may well be right, for all we can tell—the allusion would be sufficiently veiled for Cicero to plead innocence if Sulla disliked it. But is there not a far more obvious interpretation of " Phrygian swords "? (I am assuming that I am right in maintaining the traditional interpretation of the line as referring to the proscriptions). An army had just been brought back from Asia Minor to conquer Rome, and this army had in fact executed the slaughter of the proscriptions. The audience can hardly have failed to think of the " Phrygian swords " as Sulla's army. One might add that Mithridates, the enemy of Rome, had become Sulla's ally and furnished him with supplies for the attack on Italy.

M. Jocelyn : I still find the scholiast's explanation beyond belief. Mr. Badian's explanation is much more plausible. Even so, to refer to Sulla's army as a pack of Asiatics at such a juncture of time seems extraordinarily bold.

M. Suerbaum: Es ist schwierig zu sehen, wieso in *Sc.* 173—wie der Scholiast will—eine Entschuldigung des Odysseus liegen soll. Wenn *alle* Griechen verwundet sind, warum flieht nur *er*? *Sc.* 173 würde besser als höhnischer Vorwurf in den Mund des Ajax passen, doch bezeugt der Scholiast ausdrücklich Odysseus als Sprecher.

* * *

M. Waszink: I cannot bring myself to believe that Ribbeck was right in supposing that there are lacunae before 163 *neque* and after *consistere*. The passage contains a closely knit argument: 164 *magis* is motivated by the sentence opened by *namque* (165); and further there is a clear correspondence between 161 *uestras manus* and 164 *sapientia uestra*. These words must remain near each other, and therefore no lacunae need be assumed before or after v. 163. I would rather regard this verse as a parenthesis, which is not surprising in an emotional speech like the present one: after all Eurypylus is in danger of bleeding to death.

M. Skutsch: Lines 161, 162 and 164 fit together very well if we understand, as I think we must, that the *magis* of 164 points forward to *namque* in 165. 163 looks as though it had intruded from somewhere else.

* * *

M. Badian: I am not worried by the fact that *certe* (*Sc.* 166) is not actually attested in this phrase of recognition. With Professor Skutsch, I doubt whether it can be Cicero's. The fact that the phrase is so often introduced by an oath in comedy seems to show that an asseverative particle was called for; and since an oath was out of the question here, the more neutral *certe* seems sufficiently justified. As for the delayed recognition by the chorus (I agree with Professor Jocelyn that this is best assigned to the chorus): could it not be due to the fact that Eurypylus has been very much knocked about in Ennius' version? There is certainly plenty of blood flowing, as both the fragment itself and Cicero's commentary make clear. If dramatic justification is needed, this would amply provide it.

M. Jocelyn: I do not think that such a degree of realism as Mr. Badian's last suggestion implies ever obtained in the classical theatre.

M. Suerbaum: Eine Erklärung des Cicero-Kontextes *etiam si Eurypylus t a c e r e posset, non posset Aesopus* erscheint mir nicht überzeugend ; jedenfalls wäre das ein recht frostiger Witz Ciceros. Er würde dann sagen: Eurypylus fühlt sich ausserstande, das Kampfgeschehen darzustellen (Vs. 170 sq.) — also könnte er schweigen ; der Schauspieler Aesopus aber muss seinen Part unbedingt sprechen. (Von den verschiedenen Erklärungsversuchen dieser Schwierigen Stelle, die ich nachträglich eingesehen habe, hat mir noch am ehesten die von R. Kühner in seinem *Tusc.*-Komm.[4], Jena 1853 vertretene eingeleuchtet: *etiam si Eurypylus haec in dolore explicare posset, non posset idem facere Aesopus* ; Sc. : *ut homo in contemnendo dolore inexercitatus.*)

* * *

M. Badian: You think that at *Sc.* 165 Ennius introduced the idea of a kind of " military hospital " by analogy with Roman conditions. But I do not know of any such institutions in the Roman army during the Republic. A passage in Dionysius (IX 50), obviously based on contemporary conditions, shows soldiers binding up their own wounds—or pretending to do so; and even Caesar mentions no organized medical care for soldiers.

M. Waszink: In this connection I would rather think of an association with healings at the *aedes Aesculapii* built on the island in the Tiber soon after 291 B.C.

* * *

M. Skutsch: As to the fragment of the *Sabine Women*, I believe Mr. Jocelyn overlooks that the situation in the *Sabinae* is different from Euripides' *Phoenissae* 571 ff. Here no town enters into consideration, it is merely a question of the fathers-in-law killing the sons-in-law. I cannot admit that any question such as "what will you do with the spoils?" is missing. In fact, any such question would seem to me to reduce the effectiveness of the sentence, which takes it for granted that the spoils are to be dedicated. The metrical difficulty is minimal: an iamb word is needed to complete two senarii, and L. Mueller's *quam <patres>* not only mends the metre but improves the style by emphasizing *quam*.

M. Badian: I do not think the reference to the *spolia opima* is a necessary, or indeed a very happy, suggestion. This had happened only twice in Roman history; and since it could only happen where a commander killed an enemy commander, the plural seems to make it unlikely that it is in the poet's mind here. Actually, it does not much matter what the Romans usually did with captured armour—certainly Greek *tropaea* are out of the question as early as this. But all that is certainly said here is that the armour will be stripped off and then an inscription will be set up. Now, inscriptions that in various ways celebrate victories were common enough in Rome. If we refuse to believe that Ennius is blindly transferring a Greek custom, we are still not committed to any particular view of what happens to the spoils (dedication, burning, or any combination): all that is assumed is that after victory (and the taking of spoils that marks it) an inscription must be composed to celebrate it.

M. Jocelyn: There may have been a reference to Romulus taking the *spolia opima* from the king of Caenina in the prologue of the *Sabinae*. The Ennian Hersilia, like Eurypylus at *Sc.* 161, addressed a plurality but had one person in mind. Mr. Badian's arguments are weighty ones but I still think that *cum spolia generis detraxeritis* is a particular reference to the stripping of armour from men killed in battle and not a pictorial equivalent of *cum uiceritis*.

M. Waszink : I wonder whether, if one thinks that a word has fallen out, it should not be *soceri* rather than *patres*.

As to the inscription : the habit concerning Greek τροπαῖα is, in my opinion, not entirely out of the question, since we have just heard from Mr. Jocelyn that the *praetexta*, too, was to a high degree influenced by Greek tragedy.

M. Badian : I could accept *soceri*, but I really do not think *patres* will do. First, it is odd for one person to speak to the assembled Sabines and call them " Fathers " ; only one of them is her father. Also—perhaps more important—the word *patres*, as a vocative, is so closely connected with the Senate (as the normal form of address used there, with or without *conscripti*) that I cannot see a poet bluntly using it here in an address to a group of (private) "fathers". I would rather suggest an address to her own father, i.e. *pater*. We have just looked at *Sc.* 161. It will serve as a parallel. *Patricoles* is individually addressed there, and then there is at once a change to the plural (*ad uos*)—as Mr. Jocelyn rightly pointed out at the time, the attendants are included. Similarly here I suggest " *cum spolia generis detraxeritis, o pater* ". (Compare " *O Patricoles* ", l.c., and, of course, the famous and pathetic " *o pater, o patria* " speech).

M. Skutsch : I fail to see why the fact that *patres* in the vocative mostly refers to senators should prevent us from assuming that it could refer to a plurality of fathers, in the rare situation where several girls have to address several fathers. It seems a little unnatural to assume that the senatorial address made it impossible for the girls to say *patres*. What else should they have said?

III

J. H. WASZINK

Problems concerning the Satura of Ennius

PROBLEMS CONCERNING THE SATURA OF ENNIUS

Once I had accepted the invitation to contribute a paper here on the *Saturae* [1] of Ennius, I got an awkward feeling that this subject might be neither important nor extensive enough for an entire lecture, and it is for this reason that I asked for the liberty to add whatever points concerning Ennius' minor works in general might, in my opinion, lead to a fruitful discussion. However, the more I studied the fragments of this work, the more I became convinced that the subject is important and, moreover, still full of problems, so that now I am certain that the time granted to me will have to be used with the greatest efficiency in order to deal at least with the most fundamental problems and to put forward whatever new interpretations I may have to offer.

As to the importance of the present subject, I would like first of all to quote the following assertion from the *Lezioni su Ennio* by Scevola Mariotti, whose absence from our meeting I regret more than I can say : " Le *Saturae* sono la creazione più originale tecnicamente, non solo di Ennio, ma di tutta la letteratura romana " (p. 123) and, a little further on : " Le *Saturae* diventano così l'opera centrale e più tipica,

[1] Before the discussion of the title (p. 105) I quote it in its usual plural form.— It is to be regretted that TERZAGHI, who was one of the great specialists on Lucilius, hardly speaks about Ennius in his book *Per la storia della Satira* (Messina 1944). His main thesis is : " ... rispetto al contenuto, la satira romana non può aspirare a vanto di originalità." I could not get hold of E. BOLISANI, Le Satire di Ennio, *Atti e Mem. della Reale Accad. di Scienze e Lettere in Padova*, 1935. Dr. P. F. Beatrice (Padova) most kindly provided me with a photocopy of Bolisani's rare book *Ennio minore* (Padova, Editrice " Messagero ", 1935), which contains an edition of the fragments of the *Saturae*—to which he also reckoned all the *Varia* with the sole exception of the *Euhemerus*—with an Italian translation and notes on pp. 30-65. When in the sequel I quote Bolisani without adding the title of a publication, it is this work which is meant.

per la loro esperienza stilistica, di Ennio, l'eredità più personale che egli ha lasciato alla tradizione letteraria romana." This statement is the natural outcome of Mariotti's conviction that the most essential feature of Ennius' poetry is the *uarietas* and that, for that reason, " dobbiamo ricercare l''antecedente' (s'intende in un senso ideale, non di necessità cronologico) dell'arte degli *Annali* nelle *Saturae*. "

As to the second point: in studying the history of the interpretation of the fragments of the *Saturae* from Columna, Scaliger and Casaubonus to the present day—and it is at this point that I want to mention with special emphasis the chapter on Ennius' *Saturae* in Professor C. A. van Rooy's important monograph *Studies in Classical Satire and Related Literary Theory* (Leiden 1965)—, I arrived at the conclusion that with regard to this work practically all the essential details have never been established, and in the present state of our knowledge can not be established with certainty, the main reason being, of course, that here we can not, as in the case of the *Annales* and the tragedies, start our investigation from the main rules of a genre already well-known from Greek literature—*satura quidem tota nostra est!* In the first place, we have no certainty about the question whether it was Ennius himself who gave the title *Saturae* or *Satura* to his work. Further, we do not know whether the division into separate books, which we find for the first time in Porphyrio, was made by the poet himself. Next there is a discussion about the question whether minor works as, for instance, the *Epicharmus*, the *Euhemerus*, and the *Sota*, formed part of the whole of the *Saturae* or not. Then there is the question whether Ennius' *Saturae* are directly, or at least somehow, to be connected with a notion which it has become usual to call " the pre-Livian dramatic *satura* ", and this problem is immediately dependent on the more fundamental question whether this term denotes something real or not. A further point of discussion is whether the

Saturae of Ennius had already occasionally a satirical character in the modern sense of the word. And finally there is the question whether Ennius has imitated, or was at least influenced or inspired by, the *Iambi* of Callimachus. From all this it is evident that in this paper a considerable amount of earlier literature will have to be mentioned—it is impossible to discuss problems about which so many controversial things have already been said without at least indicating what has been said. Moreover, any new interpretation which I may have to offer will always have to start from a discussion of what one or more predecessors in the field have said—needless to say that in the course of my study of this subject the number of interpretations which I regarded as new decreased continuously, since I discovered an increasing number of scholars who *ante nos nostra scripserunt!*

Let us now first concentrate our attention on the question of the original title of the work. It has become usual to regard it as self-evident that the title *Saturarum libri IV*, which can be reconstructed from the quotations found in the Roman grammarians, goes back to the poet himself. However, a more accurate investigation shows that in modern literature on Ennius the use of this title derives both its generality and its authority from an entirely apodictic statement by Vahlen in the introduction of his second edition of the fragments, p. ccxiv, which is best quoted in full here: "... quia praeter grandioris poesis opera poemata multa non magni ambitus et varii argumenti variaeque metrorum formae sed quorum hoc commune consilium erat ut suadendo dissuadendo doctrina et exemplis mores regerent facere consuevit, ea in quattuor libros collegit quibus *Saturarum libri* inscripsit nihil significans nisi quod in *satura* voce inesse grammatici docuerunt." [1] No proof is given for any part of this elaborate statement.

[1] In his first edition of the fragments of Ennius, which appeared almost half

The first to doubt the correctness of this assertion was Hendrickson, who was followed by Marx, Deubner, and Pasoli. I also want to mention that Dr. Jocelyn observes that "*The quattuor libri saturarum* mentioned by Porphyrio... and quoted by Nonius, Macrobius and the Danieline Servius must be a late arrangement." [1]

In this context it is first of all necessary once more to consider the evidence. In Roman literature, as far as it has been preserved, the word *satura* as the denomination of either a poem or a collection of poems occurs in a coherent text (not a title) for the first time in Horace. We find it at the beginning of the well-known " consultation " of Trebatius (*Sat.* II 1, 1 s.) : *Sunt quibus in satura uideor nimis acer et ultra | legem tendere opus.* Here *satura* denotes the genre as a whole, as is rightly pointed out in Kiessling-Heinze's commentary ; we may add that the word is used there as a generally known, and therefore certainly as an already traditional term. In the plural, as a designation of definite poems, the word occurs in *Sat.* II 6, 7 : *saturis Musaque pedestri* : here Horace understand by *saturae* the poems which we now call his satires, that is, single poems, not the collection of them.

When from Horace we go back in time, the first author to be taken into account is Varro. About him Friedrich Leo observes (*Gesch. d. röm. Lit.*, 423, n. 1) : " Varro schrieb

a century earlier (1854), Vahlen declared Ennius' *Saturae* to be dependent upon the " dramatic satura " (p. lxxxi); cf. *infra*, pp. 110-111.

[1] HENDRICKSON, *Class. Philol.* 6 (1911), 120 ff. and 334 ff. ; MARX, Römische Volkslieder (*RhM, N. F.*, 78 (1929), 398-426; now also in *Aufsätze zur frühlateinischen Dichtung*, Darmstadt 1969, 45-73), 414 (cf. already the introduction of his edition of Lucilius, I, xiii); L. DEUBNER, Die Saturae des Ennius und die Jamben des Kallimachos (*RhM, N.F.* 96 (1953), 289-292), 289; A. PASOLI, "Satura" drammatica e "satura" letteraria (*Vichiana* 1 (1964), 3-41), 33 ff.; H. D. JOCELYN, *The Tragedies of Ennius* (Cambridge 1967), 13, n. 8. The best " doxography " of this question is given by VAN ROOY, *op. cit.*, 46, n. 8.

saturae und *de compositione saturarum* (er kennt also sicher *satura* schon als Bezeichnung des einzelnen Gedichts ...)." This supposition is indeed the most plausible one; I can not on this point share the scepticism of Pasoli (*op. cit.*, 22) who observes that the four books of *Saturae* mentioned by St. Jerome in his well-known catalogue of Varro's works are mentioned by nobody else, not even by Horace in his Satires, and may, therefore, perhaps be ascribed to Varro Atacinus, whom Horace does mention as a poet of *saturae* (*Sat.* I 10, 46; cf. also H. Dahlmann in his well-known article on Varro, *RE*, Suppl. VI (1935), 1276). Apart from the fact that this hypothesis can not be proved in any way, there is still the work *De compositione saturarum* which, as della Corte supposes (*Varrone, il terzo gran lume romano* [2], Firenze 1970, 250, n. 23), may have been composed "come giustificazione o come apologia dei libri delle 'Menippee' stesse." I am, therefore, inclined to assume that Varro indeed used the word *satura* exactly like Horace, that is, as an indication of the genre as a whole [1] and of a single poem belonging to the genre. I also can not share Pasoli's doubts concerning the use of the word *satura* in connection with Varro's poems and short treatises in prose in the trend of

[1] According to Pasoli, the literary *satura* had nothing to do with the dramatic *satura* which, in his conviction, is a historical entity with an Etruscan name derived from the verb '*śaθr*' which meant *orare* in both senses of the word. For the sake of clearness I quote the summary of his argument (p. 37): "Dunque la filologia ufficiale del II-I secolo a. Chr., quando—secondo la nostra ipotesi—chiamò col nome di *satura*, pensando alla 'pienezza' e alla 'varietà', il genere letterario di Ennio e di Pacuvio prima e di Lucilio poi (escludendo, come sopra dicemmo, Varrone Menippeo), si trovò di fronte il nome di *satura* riferito al melodramma in musica etrusco-latino d'età preletteraria, e credette che il nome della *satura* letteraria e quello della *satura* drammatica non fossero se non due accezioni dello stesso termine; spiegò pertanto il nome di quell'antica forma drammatica dicendo che quei melodrammi si chiamavano *saturae* perchè erano *impletae modis*." Since by this "official philology" he understands "la scuola stiloniano-varroniana", he, too, assumes that Varro also used *satura* as an indication of the literary genre in question.

Menippus [1], though I am not certain that he used the plural in this context.

In the fragments of Lucilius the word *satura* does not occur, a fact which, of course, can not be regarded as conclusive proof for the assertion that he never used it either to designate the whole of his work or single poems. As has been observed by Marx and Pasoli, he uses the terms *ludo ac sermonibus nostris* (1039 M.) and *poemata* as a designation of his poems. Therefore, the possibility exists that he limited himself to the employment of these terms, but there is an equally strong possibility either that both the singular and the plural of *satura* occurred in the lost part of his work or—a possibility which I consider a little more plausible—that he used only the singular to denote the greatly varied collection of his *sermones* (*poemata*), just as is the case in the sentence from Diomedes which I shall quote presently.

Therewith we come to Ennius. The first Roman author to use *satura* in connection with his works is Quintilian who writes (*Instit. orat.* IX 2, 36): *Mortem ac Vitam contendentes in satura tradit Ennius.* Here we can of course not decide whether in the case of Ennius Quintilian understood the term *satura* as indicating the collection as a whole or one single poem forming part of it. Gellius is the first to introduce his quotations from this work by using the plural *saturae* (II 29, 20 and VI 9, 1 *Ennius in saturis*; XVIII 2, 7 *in saturis Quinti Enni*). That, however, this use of the plural in quoting Ennius' work was introduced at a later date may, in my opinion, be regarded as certain on account of the

[1] PASOLI's main argument is (pp. 35-36) that in Cic. *Acad.* I 2, 8, where Varro himself is presented as speaking about this work, the word *satura* is not mentioned: *in illis ueteribus nostris, quae Menippum imitati, non interpretati, quadam hilaritate conspersimus.* But in the conversation which—as usually in Cicero's philosophical works—precedes the treatment of the subject, a paraphrase of a title is more to be expected than an exact quotation of that title, especially when it is the author himself who is speaking.

statement by Diomedes (*GL* Keil I 485, 30 ff.), who is there copying Suetonius (who in his turn may have copied Varro): *olim carmen quod ex uariis poematibus constabat satira uocabatur quale scripserunt Pacuuius et Ennius* [1]. If indeed this sentence goes ultimately back to Varro—a supposition regarded as practically certain by Pasoli, *op. cit.*, 23 and 35—and Varro had real evidence at his disposition, there is little reason for doubt, but the latter premise remains uncertain. As to the division into four books (we can rule out the possibility of the existence of a sixth book, as will be discussed in the sequel), for which Porphyrio is our earliest witness, this may, in my opinion, have been introduced in the period between Gellius and the latter author, that is, in the period of an enhanced interest in archaic Roman literature.

My conclusion must, therefore, be that, though we can not prove anything, there is a possibility seriously to be considered that Ennius used *Satura* in the singular as the title of this work [2].

One further observation. It has frequently been supposed that by means of a title *Saturae* Ennius wanted to render Greek titles *in the plural* which were used in the Hellenistic period, like Ἄτακτα and Σύμμεικτα. If there was such an influence of Greek titles at all, I am much more in favour of the supposition of M. Coffey [3] that Ennius may have imitated the title of the Σωρός of Posidippus.

[1] Cf. also Jocelyn, *op. cit.*, 13, n. 8: "There is no getting round the plain words of Diomedes (Suetonius): *olim ... Ennius.*" Of the *Satura* of Pacuvius nothing is known except this sentence in Diomedes; cf. I. Mariotti, *Introduzione a Pacuvio* (Urbino 1960), 19.

[2] Thus also Krenkel, *loc. cit.* I disagree with van Rooy, *op. cit.*, 46, n. 8, who quotes passages from late authors as Gellius, Nonius and Macrobius in favour of the assumption that Ennius already used the plural *Saturae* as the title of his work.

[3] Cf. the summary of his paper on the Satura of Ennius in: Römische Satire, *Wiss. Zeitschr. der Univ. Rostock* 15 (1966), Gesellschafts- und sprachwiss. Reihe, Heft 4/5, 417.

Next, we have to examine a hypothesis which, in my opinion, has for a long time hampered the study of the present subject. As we all know, Lucian Mueller, followed by Pascal, Bolisani, della Corte, Puelma Piwonka and several other scholars [1], has tried to demonstrate or at least to make plausible that originally *Saturae* was the general title of *all* the minor works of Ennius. As it seems to me, we are by now justified in regarding this supposition as definitely refuted, especially on account of two facts put forward more than sixty years ago by Franz Skutsch [2]. In the first place, it is extremely improbable that the very frequent quotations like *Ennius in Epicharmo*, *Ennius in Euhemero*, *Ennius in Sota* should refer, not to independent works but to parts of a greater work, since this would be entirely against the habits of Roman lexicographers and grammarians. Further, it is equally improbable that a work like the prose adaptations of the Ἱερὸς λόγος of Euhemerus should have belonged to a collection of *Saturae*. Skutsch gives no further comment on this point which he clearly regards as self-evident ; perhaps it is useful to add that Quintilian says explicitly that Varro was the founder (*condidit*) of the kind of *satura* which also contained prose [3].

[1] Lucian MUELLER, *Quintus Ennius* (Petersburg 1884), 107, still expresses himself cautiously : " Dass die Ambracia, die Lehrgedichte Epicharmus, Euhemerus, Protreptica (*sic*) und Hedyphagetica, endlich der Sota und die Epigramme Theile der Satire ausmachten wird nirgends bezeugt, ist aber sehr wahrscheinlich " ; C. PASCAL, Lo Scipio di Ennio, *Athenaeum* 3 (1915), 369-395 ; *id.*, *Riv. di filol.* 47 (1919), 73 ; E. BOLISANI, *Atti del Reale Istituto Veneto*, 1932-1933, and *Ennio minore* (cf. p. 99, n. 1) ; F. DELLA CORTE, Intorno alle Saturae di Ennio, *Atti della Reale Accad. delle Scienze di Torino*, Vol. 71, Tom. II (1936), 198-205 ; M. PUELMA PIWONKA, *Lucilius und Kallimachos* (Frankfurt a.M. 1949), 181-193.

[2] In his article Ennius in *RE* V (1905), 2598.

[3] Gellius II 29, 30 : *Hunc Aesopi apologum Q. Ennius in satiris scite admodum et uenuste uersibus quadratis composuit.* Quintil. *Instit. orat.* X 1, 93 : *alterum illud etiam prius saturae genus, sed non sola carminum uarietate mixtum condidit Terentius Varro.* According to PASOLI, *op. cit.*, 20 and 24, *condidit* does not

I further want to eliminate right here what I regard as a second serious mistake, *viz.*, the supposition that Ennius' *Scipio* was identical with the third book of his *Saturae*. This hypothesis was first formulated by L. Lersch: De Ennii Scipione, *RhM* 5 (1837), 416, on account of the similarity of two fragments, *viz.*, one quoted by Nonius Marcellus, p. 66, 27: *Ennius satyrarum lib. III: testes sunt | Lati campi quos gerit Africa terra politos* and one which occurs in Cic. *De Oratore* III 42, 167: *Testes sunt Campi magni.* The identification was adopted in his first edition by Vahlen, who in his introduction, p. lxxxiv, is strongly critical of Lersch's argumentation without, however, adding any argument himself; he rejected it in his second edition, p. ccxvi. Lucian Mueller also accepted the identification and made an attempt to blend the two fragments into one [1]. However, we know that Ennius was by no means averse from repeating himself: I only mention the use made of the motive of the revelation in a dream in both the proem of the first book of the *Annales* and the *Epicharmus* (cf. p. 136, n. 1). There is, therefore, no reason to regard the *Scipio* as a part of the *Satura*. And therewith we may inversely regard the *Satura* as an independent work existing by the side of the other minor works of Ennius.

It is now with the greatest possible circumspection that I want to consider the much-discussed question whether Ennius' *Satura* can have been influenced in any way by what it has become usual to call " the dramatic *satura* ".

denote the *inventor* but the " perfezionatore " of the genre; cf. also BOLISANI, 13-15.

[1] In his edition (p. 75) he combines these two verses into one fragment (*Sat., Lib.* III / *Scipio*, fr. VII): *testes sunt campi magni ... | lati campi, quos gerit Africa terra politos.* In the critical apparatus he adds: " *add. in priore versu ut puta:* virtuti' meai." In his book *Quintus Ennius*, 108-109, he put these words into the text; in this he is followed by Bolisani.

In the famous discussion concerning the authenticity or the degree of authenticity of Livy's description of the evolution of Roman drama I take the side of those who are convinced that in general the facts mentioned by Livy—that is, by Varro—belong to historic reality but that the connection made between them is due to Varro's reconstructive (or merely constructive) tendencies : the performances by the Etruscan dancers in 364 B.C., the *Fescennina licentia* with its exchange of *uersus alterni* as well as the activity of Andronicus consisting in *argumento fabulam serere* belong to reality, and for that reason I am inclined also to believe in the reality of the *impletas modis saturas* mentioned there. As I have expounded elsewhere [1], I find a strong support for this supposition in the fact that still in 115 B.C., there existed performances by "a Latin singer and a Latin flute-player" (*Latinus cantor et tibicen*), who were clearly regarded as truly vernacular artists, since they were excepted from the expulsion of *histriones* which took place in that year. However, we should under no condition assume the existence of more than is mentioned in Livy's report. It is worth while to quote the relevant sentence here again : after mentioning the professional *histriones* Livy says : *qui non, sicut ante, Fescennino uersu similem incompositum temere ac rudem alternis iaciebant, sed impletas modis saturas descripto iam ad tibicinem cantu motuque peragebant.* I entirely agree with the interpretation of this sentence by Dr. Jocelyn in the introduction to his edition of the fragments of Ennius' tragedies, p. 13 : "The word—*viz.*, *satura*—must have denoted at one time some sort of stage performance. It can hardly be a mere invention on the model of Aristotle's τὸ σατιρικόν. All, however, that Livy's story at VII 2, 4 ff. implies is that the

[1] In my paper Tradition and Personal Achievement in Early Latin Literature (*Mnemosyne* IV 13 (1960), 16-33), 20 ; a further elaboration in my 'Fachbericht' Zum Anfangsstadium der römischen Literatur, *Aufgang und Niedergang der römischen Welt*, *Festschr. Joseph Vogt*, I (Berlin 1972).

histriones presented on a *scaena* at public festivals arrangements of words in a variety of metrical patterns accompanied by pipe music and called *saturae*. There is no suggestion that these *saturae* involved consistent acts of impersonation." To the last words he adds the wise observation: "Talk of 'dramatic' *satura* is confused and misleading."

It is this very point which we must keep in mind continuously when we try to imagine—there can be no question of a real investigation—how an influence of such performances on various poems in Ennius' *satura* could be possible at all. Such an influence, which was already assumed by Vahlen in his first edition (p. lxxxi) was postulated with great emphasis by Otto Weinreich [1], who assumed that the dramatic element—we may as well say: the dialogue—was particularly important in the *satura*. The possibility of such an influence is discussed with much greater reserve by Mariotti in his important paper Titoli di opere enniane, *Maia* 5 (1952), 271-276, in which his chief aim is to point out that, as Ennius in his *Annales* conferred an entirely new meaning upon a long-existing Latin term, he did—I would rather say: he may have done—exactly the same thing in the case of the *Satura*. I must, however, strongly disagree with a suggestion by Timpanaro to which Mariotti assents (*op. cit.*, 272, n. 2), *viz.*, that we may find a parallel for the dramatic *satura* as a whole of loosely connected "little scenes" in the second part, *viz.*, the part which comes after the parabasis, of the comedies of Aristophanes. In fact we should keep the *satura* apart from any truly *dramatic* performance, that is, a performance involving impersonation, a distinction already made in the chapter of Livy: for there it is said explicitly that a real drama was first introduced at Rome by Andronicus—the words *argumento fabulam serere*

[1] *Römische Satiren... eingeleitet und übertragen von* OTTO WEINREICH (Zürich 1949), xviii-xix.

are quite clear in this respect, for they show that the real essence of a drama is found in the plot which is immediately connected with the *diverbium*. It is, in my opinion, evident that in this chapter the *satura* is presented by Varro as the prototype of the *canticum* of Latin comedy—the very element which failed in the νέα.

It is for the same reason that I can not possibly believe that the fragment which Festus p. 257 M. quotes from a *Satura* of Naevius, *viz.*, *Quianam Saturnium populum pepulisti?* can stem from a dramatic satura, as was first assumed by Hendrickson, *Amer. Journ. Philol.* 15 (1894), 19 s., and then by Lejay (edition of the *Satires* of Horace, xcvii f.) and, with particular gusto, by Weinreich, *op. cit.* Mariotti (*Maia* 5 (1952), 272, n. 1) thinks of a *fabula togata*, Marx (*op. cit.*, p. 416) of a political pamphlet. I must confess that, like Eduard Fraenkel (*RE*, Suppl. V, 640), I am entirely at a loss about this fragment [1]. But to return to the *satura* of Ennius : If we find traces of a dialogue in the fragments of this work we should not, with Weinreich, regard these as an element deriving from the old *saturae*: we must either trace them back to popular tradition, the *Fescennina licentia*—let us not overlook Livy's statement that in the *saturae* the *histriones* no longer *uersum alternis iaciebant*—or assume (and this is in my opinion quite plausible) that Ennius' *Satura* shows already an influence of full-fledged comedies, and most probably already of Roman comedies. I can thus completely agree with the negative attitude of Vahlen in his

[1] Pasoli's view that a dramatic satura did exist at Rome but that it had no connection at all with the dramatic *satura* (cf. p. 103, n. 1) is shared by VAN ROOY, 23 ff.—The *Satura* of Pomponius must have been a fabula Atellana, since Pomponius is not known to have written anything which belonged to a different genre. FRASSINETTI in his edition of the *Fab. Atell.* (Rome 1967), 108, thinks in this context of " un tentativo di riesumazione della *satura* preliviana, con musica e danza e senza *Oscae personae* ". I could not get hold of C. MARTIN, *Etude sur la satura dans la littérature latine archaïque des origines à Pacuvius*, thèse, Univ. libre, Bruxelles, 1942.

second edition (p. ccxiv) and of Deubner (*op. cit.*, 290) towards those scholars who postulated a thorough influence of a dramatic *satura* on Ennius' collection of various poems.

On account of the preceding considerations I arrive at the conclusion that the only thing which the *Satura* of Ennius can have owed to a preliterary (not : a dramatic) *satura* was a tendency to strive after *uarietas* in the choice of both the metres and the subjects (in order to prevent misunderstandings, I add that it is only the variety of the subjects, not their proper characteristics, which, in my opinion, should be connected with such an influence). However, it may be more correct to say that the preliterary *satura* only strengthened in Ennius an older, more general, and typically Roman tendency to create *uarietas*, a tendency of which this *satura* was only one more manifestation. In fact, such a tendency is equally present in the technique, probably invented by Naevius, of blending together the plots of two Greek dramas (cf. on this question H. Drexler, *Plautin. Akzentstudien*, 369, and his paper Der Anfang der römischen Literatur, in *Das neue Bild der Antike* (Leipzig 1942), II, 74 f.). It must also lie at the root of Plautus' continuous creation of new and fantastic words, and of *numeri innumeri* in the *cantica* of his plays (cf. on this point my *Fachbericht* mentioned in n. 1, p. 108).

We now come to the much-discussed question whether the *Satura* of Ennius contained satirical elements in the sense in which this adjective is used nowadays. I can be brief on this subject, because it has already been treated with as much exactness as sagacity by van Rooy in his chapter on Ennius ; I feel justified in limiting myself here to quoting the main sentence of his argument. Against the statement of Friedrich Leo (*op. cit.*, 206), " die Gedichte hatten kein 'satirisches Element' ", which he rightly qualifies as merely apodictic, van Rooy observes (*op. cit.*, 32-33) : "... the relevant fragments of his work manifest a clearly satirical tendency in so far as he hits out or mocks at harmful elements in contemporary Roman society " ; he is equally right in pointing out a little further on that the satirical element is manifest here " only as one *out of many* "[1]. However, a second point should be added here, *viz.*, that Ennius does not seem to have attacked definite individuals, a thing which Lucilius must have done from the very beginning of his career, for the early satire from the twenty-sixth book which contains his 'program' can only have been caused by complaints about such attacks. In this he continues, and in my opinion imitates, though in a different genre, Naevius' endeavour to introduce the habit of ὀνομαστὶ κωμῳδεῖν at Rome. This is a habit of which, as far as our knowledge goes, no trace can be found in the work of Ennius[2].

If I am not mistaken, it is these personal attacks in the *Saturae* of Lucilius together with his gradual giving up of polymetry in favour of the dactylic hexameter which makes us too much inclined to overlook the *primary* importance of the element of *uarietas* in Lucilius—after all quite a number of his *Saturae* are not " satirical " at all—and, in connection with that fact, a priori to underestimate the still quite important similarities between the *Saturae* of Ennius and

[1] We must certainly reject the exaggerated ideas on this subject of E. M. PEASE in his paper The Satirical Element in Ennius, *Transactions of the Amer. Philol. Assoc.* 27 (1896), xlviii-l. I limit myself to quoting the essential sentence of the paper : " Nothing could be more natural then (*viz.*, after Andronicus had introduced the Attic New Comedy at Rome) than that Ennius should remodel the old satirical medley into the literary *Satura* ", *etc.* Also DEUBNER in his paper *Die Saturae des Ennius und die Jamben des Kallimachos*, 290-291, overstresses in my opinion the importance of the satirical elements in Ennius' *Saturae*. The same holds good for Altheim's judgement of the Crested Lark, for which cf. *infra*, p. 125.

[2] One may wonder whether Ennius' famous allusion to Naevius by means of the purposely vague plural *alii* in *scripsere alii rem* (*Ann.* 213) is not a silent criticism or correction of the very man to whom he alludes. On the possible influence of Naevius on Lucilius' aggressivity cf. my paper Tradition and Achievement (cf. n. 1, p. 108), 32.

Lucilius. I need hardly say that I disagree entirely with Puelma Piwonka, who made a sharp distinction between the *Saturae* of Lucilius, which he regarded as highly dependent on the *Iambi* of Callimachus, and the, in his opinion, more moralizing *Saturae* of Ennius and Varro (*op. cit.*, 192). It is these similarities which are rightly emphasized by, for instance, Vahlen, Marx and Mariotti [1]. Now among these similarities we must mention in the first place the habit of both poets to speak in these poems about their personal lives and about their poetry. I think it appropriate to discuss this subject in the first place.

Lucilius had chosen both the character and the social function of his poetry as the subject for the " programmatic " poem which had been included in, and which probably opened, the earliest book of his *Saturae* which was written in *versus quadrati* and which in the final edition of his poems became the twenty-sixth book. This poem contained a discussion between the poet and an adversary, or a critical friend. From the fragments so much at least is clear that Lucilius underlined the fact that in his poetry he could only be just himself: I remind you of the well-known verses (622 and 623 Marx) *ego si qui sum et quo folliculo nunc sum indutus non queo* and *ita ut quisque nostrum e bulga est matris in lucem editus.* Now Mariotti ('Titoli', 274, n. 4) has already connected another verse from this poem, *ego ubi quem ex praecordiis ecfero uersum* (590 M.), with the famous lines quoted by Nonius from the third book of Ennius' *Saturae* (vss. 6-7 V.).

Enni poeta salue, qui mortalibus
Versus propinas flammeos medullitus.

[1] Cf. the excellent paraphrase of the main thesis of Puelma Piwonka's book and the acute criticisms by H. Herter in his review in *Deutsche Literaturzeitung* 71 (1950), 490-496.—The passages to which I allude in the text are: Vahlen [2], *Praefatio*, ccxv; Marx, ed. of Lucilius, xiv; Mariotti, Titoli di opere enniane, 274, n. 4.

I would like to discuss this fragment for a moment in spite of the fact that Professor Suerbaum has already said the most essential things about them in his book *Untersuchungen zur Selbstdarstellung römischer Dichter*, p. 262 with note 744, a passage to which I want emphatically to refer you.

Mariotti underlines the importance of the similarity of the expressions *ex praecordiis* and *medullitus* : evidently in his opinion the adverb *medullitus* is to be connected with the verb *propinas*. The same interpretation is given by Weinreich, *op. cit.*, 4, in his German translation : " Heil, Dichter Ennius, dir, der du den Sterblichen | Kredenzest Verse, feurige, aus tiefster Brust ! " We may add the paraphrase by Friedrich Leo, *Gesch. d. röm. Lit.*, 206 : "der sich so anreden liess, brachte seine Gedichte ans Licht weil sie in seiner Seele wohnten. " After long considerations I have arrived at the conclusion that this interpretation is the most plausible one [1] —we may indeed say that both poets declared to have put their heart into their poetry.

I agree with Mariotti—I may also add a similar statement by Leo, *op. cit.*, 161 [2]—that in the two present verses Ennius also refers to his own poetry. There remains, of course, the important difference that Ennius thus in his *Satura* refers to a different genre, *viz.*, to his epic poetry, whereas Lucilius speaks in a *satura* about his *Saturae* in general.

The first question now is, who is addressing Ennius here. However, before I begin to discuss this point, I want to put forward that—as must already be evident from what I said at the beginning of this paper—I recant my earlier adherence [3]

[1] There is an alternative, *viz.*, that *medullitus* refers—or at least *also* refers—to *flammeos* ; but at the moment this is not of primary importance.

[2] " In den Satiren liess er sich anrufen mit dem Wort : ' Heil, Dichter Ennius, der du den Sterblichen flammende Verse zutrinkst aus innerster Brust ! ' " Thus also KRENKEL, ed. of Lucilius, 14 : " Du kredenzt den Sterblichen deine Verse, die stets voll flammenden Feuers, aus tiefster Brust."

[3] The Proem of the *Annales* of Ennius, *Mnemosyne* III 3 (1950), 236.

(an adherence which had no further importance there for my argument) to Pascal's assertion that the two verses under discussion belonged to the *Scipio* (Pascal just borrowed this view from Lucian Mueller who, as we mentioned already, regarded this poem as identical with the third book of the *Saturae*) [1].

Now several scholars, of whom I mention here Till, Knoche and Bieler [2], assume that Ennius is here presented as addressing himself, whereas others, among whom Weinreich is to be mentioned in the first place [3], suppose that the verses belong to the description of a symposion, where the poet is addressed by his host or one of his fellow-guests. Not knowing that here again I had a predecessor, *viz.*, Lucian Mueller, as I was admonished by Professor Suerbaum[4] —who, I am glad to say, agrees with my interpretation,— I have defended in my first paper on the proem of the *Annales* the supposition that Ennius was addressed here by the Muses. Since my argument is rather different from that of Mueller, I ask for your permission to quote a few lines from that paper (p. 237) : "... if I am not mistaken, the verses under discussion are much too solemn for the atmosphere of a symposion (*mortalibus* = fellow-guests?) : it seems considerably more probable that they allude to the central fact of Ennius' inner life, *viz.*, to his access to real poetry or, to use his own language, to his initiation at the *fontes Musarum*

[1] Cf. *supra*, p. 107, with n. 1.

[2] R. Till, Die Anerkennung literarischen Schaffens in Rom, *Neue Jahrb. für Antike und deutsche Bildung* 3 (1940), 162; U. Knoche, *Die römische Satire*[2] (Göttingen 1957), 18; L. Bieler, *Geschichte der römischen Lit.*, I[2] (Sammlung Göschen, Berlin 1965), 49.

[3] *Epigramm und Pantomimus* (Sitzungsber. Heidelberger Akad. d. Wiss., Phil. hist. kl., Jahrg. 1944-1948, 1. Abh.), 147; *Id., Röm. Satiren*, 7.

[4] L. Mueller, *Quintus Ennius*, 110; adopted by Maxim. Richter, *Priscorum poetarum et scriptorum de se et aliis iudicia* (*Comm. Philol. Jenenses* XI 2, Leipzig 1914), 26 (both quoted by Suerbaum, *loc. cit.*).

from which he 'drank his gift to mankind'." I do not want now to enter into a discussion on the *fontes Musarum* but I want to make a few further observations which, as it seems to me, have some importance in the present context [1].

The first point to be inquired into is the meaning of *propinare* in the present context. In his *Studi sugli scrittori latini* (Torino 1900), 46, Carlo Pascal has already drawn attention to the verses of a Hellenistic poet, *viz.*, Dionysius Chalcus, which are quoted by Athenaeus, XV 669 E: δέχου τήνδε προπινομένην | τὴν ἀπ' ἐμοῦ ποίησιν and, two lines further on, ἀοιδὰς ἀντιπρόπιθι. Since this Dionysius was a poet of skolia, it may be regarded as practically certain that these verses served as an introduction to a poem sung at a symposion. Pascal takes it for granted that Ennius knew the epigram of Dionysius from the first hand (*uel uertisse uel imitatione expressisse*).

Now here we may indeed find an excellent specimen of Ennius' method in making use of his examples in Hellenistic poetry—perhaps we had better say: in working up the suggestions which Hellenistic poetry had to offer him. The important thing is that, if indeed it is the Muses or one special Muse, probably Calliope, who was presented as speaking these lines, Ennius has brought this image into an entirely different atmosphere, *viz.*, that of the *genus sublime*, though, on the other hand, he has left intact the main element of the original idea. The Hellenistic poet offers a poem to a fellow-guest as if it were a cup of wine, or rather wine in a cup of which he has drunk a small part himself before offering it to his fellow-guest. This typical grecism (a Greek verb incorporated into the Latin first conjugation) has not

[1] I want to observe here in passing that I entirely fail to see, why, as is postulated by A. Marastoni, Studio critico su Ennio minore (*Aevum* 35 (1961), 1-27), 6, the two verses under discussion should be thought to betray once more (together with the proem of *Annales* I and the *Epicharmus*) an influence of the doctrine of Pythagoras.

been introduced by Ennius into the Latin language: we find it, almost certainly before Ennius began the composition of his *Satura*, three times in Plautus, *viz.*, in the *Stichus* (probably composed in 200 B.C.), 468: *propino tibi salutem plenis faucibus*, in the *Pseudolus* (191 B.C.), 1282: *manu candida cantharum dulciferum propinat amicissima amico*, and in the *Curculio* (date uncertain), 359: *propino magnum poclum: illa ebibit.* In the dictionary of Lewis and Short it is assumed that in the verses under discussion *propinare* has a metaphorical meaning, for it is placed there under the heading: "C. In general, to give, deliver, furnish to one". If I am not mistaken, it is this interpretation of the verb which lies at the root of Friedrich Leo's paraphrase which I have just quoted ('brachte ... ans Licht'). However, the purport of the passage is lost, if we do not assume that the verb is used here with its original meaning: it is said that Ennius offers to mortal beings, to mankind, a drink of fiery verses, after first having such a drink himself.

If this interpretation is correct, the next question is what exactly we are to understand by this fiery drink. If I am not mistaken, two ideas have been blended together here, *viz.*, that of the drinking of wine and that of a draught from the sources of the Muses.

About the association with the drinking of wine there can, in my opinion, not be any doubt. The strongest argument is, of course, the very use of the verb *propinare.* In the second place, the adjective *flammeus* evokes an association with the idea of the *calor vini*, for which an endless number of passages can be quoted. I only refer here to two passages from Horace, *viz.*, *Epod.* 11, 14: *calentis ... feruidiore mero* and to the famous words from the Ode to the *pia testa* (III 21, 11-12): *narratur et prisci Catonis | saepe mero incaluisse uirtus*; I may also remind you of the well-known sentence from Euripides' *Alcestis* (758-759): ἕως ἐθέρμην' αὐτὸν ἀμφιβᾶσα φλόξ | οἴνου.

We may perhaps add the consideration—it would be too much to call it an argument—that for the composition of his verses Ennius used to seek his inspiration in wine, as we are told in the famous line from Horace, *Epist.* I 19, 7-8 : *Ennius ipse pater numquam nisi potus ad arma | prosiluit dicenda.* It is to this fact that he alludes in the line which Hug, followed by Vahlen, has first attributed to the *Satura : numquam poetor nisi* (*nisi si* Vahlen) *podager*, and in his first edition the latter scholar regarded this line as belonging to the same poem as the two verses under discussion. However, this would lead to the conclusion that the poem in question was written in a mocking tone, which does not tally with the loftiness of the two verses. I want to observe in passing that, since the line from Horace clearly echoes the verse of Ennius, I regard it as certain that we should not follow Vahlen in reading *nisi si* instead of the simple *nisi* which we find, also after *numquam*, in the later poet (equally unnecessary is Lucian Mueller's addition of *sim*).

Now I venture to suppose, in the first place on account of the choice of the solemn word *poeta*, that in these verses there was also a solemn element, *viz.*, an association with the sources of the Muses which certainly must have been mentioned in the proem of the seventh [1], and almost certainly in the proem of the first book of the *Annales*. This association is practically obvious if indeed these verses were presented as spoken by the Muses (or, more probably, by Calliope). But however this may be, the really important thing is that in this poem, as is evident from the second line of the fragment, Ennius spoke about what I have called " the central fact of his inner life ", *viz.*, his composition of

[1] Pasquali's observation is mentioned by Timpanaro, *Studi ital. di filol. class.* 1948, 22, n. 2. The fact that the priority belonged to Pasquali was noticed by Mariotti, *Lezioni su Ennio*, 144 ; however, Suerbaum, *op. cit.*, 278, n. 787, has found that there is a much earlier predecessor, *viz.* Pascoli (*Epos* I [2], Livorno 1911, 34).

a really great epic poem in the metre of Homer. It is this emphasizing of the value of his achievement which shows Ennius' pride, and, if I am not mistaken, also the not unusual concomitant of pride, *viz.*, his uncertainty: indeed the present verses are the second description of the value of his epic poetry after the ὕψος of the proem of the first book of the *Annales*, for the proem of the seventh book of this poem had been both a retort to criticisms and a renewed vindication of his importance as an epic poet. Therewith Ennius created one of the main features of the literary *satura*: Mariotti (cf. pp. 113 f.) was certainly right in pointing out a similarity between the 'programmatic' satire of Lucilius and the fragment under discussion. A similar reaction to the acceptance by the Roman public of a *new* form of poetry, *viz.*, his *Odes*, is found in Horace's first letter concerning Roman literature (*Epist.* I 19); it is a curious coincidence that it is this very poem in which Horace speaks about Ennius' *prosilire ad arma dicenda*.

Thus, though Ennius may have found the first suggestion for the composition of the present verses in a Hellenistic poet, who connected the idea of προπίνειν with that of ποίησις, we may yet say—as was already emphasized by Friedrich Leo [1]—that the verses bear the stamp of his personality and that, moreover, they find their natural explication in his situation as a poet. It is for this reason that I have not yet raised the much discussed question whether we are to suppose a direct influence of the book of *Iambi* of Callimachus on the composition of his *Satura*.

Let us begin by stating that the existence of such an influence is by no means impossible or even improbable.

[1] *Gesch. d. röm. Lit.*, 206, n. 1: "Dass der Ausdruck *poesin propinare* auch griechisch vorkommt..., nimmt ihm nichts von seiner Unmittelbarkeit und persönlichen Prägung."

Of the remaining minor works of Ennius four show a direct influence of Hellenistic literature, *viz.*, the *Euhemerus*, the *Sota*, the *Hedyphagetica* and the *Epigrams*. A second interesting point to be mentioned here, be it in passing, is that three of the authors translated or imitated are natives of Sicily, *viz.*, Epicharmus of Syracuse, Euhemerus of Messene and Archestratus of Gela. This fact should undoubtedly be connected with another fact, *viz.*, that it is by no means accidental that the first performances of regular dramas at Rome took place one year after the end of the first Punic war, which was a *bellum Siculum* in the first place; it is in Sicily that great numbers of Romans must have become acquainted with Greek tragedy and comedy [1]. Further, an influence of the narration of the dream at the beginning of Callimachus' *Aitia* on the proem of the first book of Ennius' *Annales* remains probable—let us be cautious and say, *pace* Erich Reitzenstein and Marconi [2], that it is probable rather than improbable. I can find no serious objection against the careful formulation by Mariotti [3]: " Comunque si pensi dell'inizio degli Annali, non sembra facile negare la vicinanza della produzione minore di Ennio allo spirito callimacheo, e a me continua a parer probabile che la stessa concezione delle Saturae enniane sia ispirata di Giambi di

[1] Cf. the famous third chapter (Die Anfänge, pp. 47 ff.) of LEO's *Geschichte der römischen Literatur*.

[2] The supposition that the dream narrated in the proem of the *Aitia* has brought Ennius upon the idea of introducing a dream into the proem of the *Annales* is accepted by MARIOTTI, *Lezioni su Ennio*, 60; O. SKUTSCH, *The Annales of Quintus Ennius* (London 1953), 10; PUELMA PIWONKA, *op. cit.*, 187; W. H. CLAUSEN, Callimachus and Latin Poetry, *Greek, Roman and Byzantine Studies* 5 (1964), 181-194. It is contested by E. REITZENSTEIN in *Festschrift für Richard Reitzenstein* (Leipzig-Berlin 1931), 63 ff.; R. PFEIFFER, ed. of Callimachus, I (Oxford 1949), 4; G. MARCONI, Il proemio degli *Annales* di Ennio, *Riv. di Cult. Class. e Medioev.* 3 (1961), 244-245.

[3] In his review of K. ZIEGLER, *Das hellenistische Epos* [2] (Leipzig 1966), in *Gnomon* 43 (1971), 150.

Callimaco... Questo naturalmente non vuol dire che Ennio fosse un callimacheo osservante."

Before giving a brief survey of the development of this hypothesis and of the various arguments which have been advanced, I would like to make a preliminary observation. Already the interpretation of the two verses to which I have perhaps devoted too much time, and, to a much higher degree, the examination of the fragments of the *Annales* show with perfect clearness that, whenever Ennius is imitating earlier poets or at least following suggestions offered by their work, there is never question of slavish imitation in the modern sense of the word—he has always put the stamp of his personality on anything he wrote. The most striking example, at least in my opinion, is his use of the motive of a dream which, if he did borrow it from the proem of Callimachus' *Aitia*—as I am convinced he did—received an entirely different function in the proem of the *Annales*. We should, therefore, be very much on guard against any tendency to exaggerate the importance, or rather the intensity, of an influence of Callimachus on his *Satura*.

A few words then about the history, and hence about the gradual development, of this hypothesis. It was expressed for the first time by Wilhelm Kroll in his revision (with Franz Skutsch) of the sixth edition of Teuffel's *Geschichte der römischen Literatur* (Leipzig-Berlin 1916), 193; he gave a further elaboration of his thought in his well-known paper Hellenistisch-römische Gedichtbücher (*Neue Jahrbücher* 37 (1916), 93-106), 95. As it seems, his hypothesis did not become known to Gallavotti, who in his edition of the fragments of the *Iambi*, which appeared in 1946[1], put the

[1] Callimaco, *Il libro dei Giambi a cura di* CARLO GALLAVOTTI (Naples 1946), 11. I want to quote in this context the following excellent remark by A. LESKY in his *Geschichte der griechischen Literatur*[2], 766, on the *Iambi* of Callimachus: "In seiner Buntheit war das Buch eine rechte *satura lanx*, wie die Römer die Opferschüssel voll verschiedener Gaben nannten. Es ist verständlich, dass

following question : " Ci è forse dato di scorgere qui più che altrove la vera origine della satura latina ? " The most thorough elaboration of this hypothesis is given in a short but important paper by Ludwig Deubner, Die Saturae des Ennius und die Iamben des Kallimachus, *RhM, N.F.* 96 (1953), 289-292. Deubner assumes a strong dependency of Ennius on Callimachus ; among other things he assumes " dass Ennius zu seinen *Saturae* durch die Iamben des Kallimachos angeregt wurde ". As the two main arguments for this hypothesis he mentions the fact that each volume of poems was written in a variety of metres and, further, the circumstance—or rather his personal opinion—that in both a satiric element must have been quite prominent. After him, Ulrich Knoche in *Die römische Satire* [2], 17-18, gave a more reserved version of this supposition. Finally, van Rooy in his monograph on the satura, 35-37, successfully reduced Deubner's somewhat exaggerated statements to an acceptable presentation of the case, which I can not describe here in detail but which will be mentioned in the discussion of the most important fragments ; at the moment I limit myself to quoting an essential part of van Rooy's conclusion (*op. cit.*, 37) : " Let us not doubt that Ennius had read the *Iambi* of Callimachus and had been inspired by their varied content. No doubt the *Iambi* were also a main source of his interest in iambic poetry as a genre, and led him to the reading of Archilochus and other exponents of this genre. Undoubtedly he also found himself more attracted to the comparative mildness of Callimachus than to the scathing and abusive temperament of Archilochus."

man gerade von den *Iamboi* des Kallimachos die Linie zur frühen römischen Satire gezogen hat. Solche Betrachtung verträgt sich durchaus mit der Anerkennung dessen, was an der Leistung der lateinischen Dichtung eigenständig ist, und bedeutet nur eine Einschränkung, nicht aber eine Widerlegung von Quintilians Wort : *satura quidem tota nostra est* (X 1, 93)."

It is in this context that the interpretation of a passage from the tenth satire of the first book of Horace becomes important. Horace discusses here the fact that, if Lucilius lived in the Augustan period, he would certainly see that the verses which he had written were quite clumsy and asked for correction, even if it is true that they were more polished than those of older Roman poets (vss. 65-67): *fuerit limatior idem | quam rudis et Graecis intacti carminis auctor | quamque poetarum seniorum turba*. A great number of scholars from Ianus Dousa down to the present day (I limit myself to mentioning Vahlen, Knoche, Büchner and van Rooy [1]) are convinced that by the *rudis et Graecis intacti carminis auctor* Horace must mean Ennius. Büchner even considers the possibility that the adjective *rudis* may contain an allusion to Ennius' birth-place without realizing, as it seems to me, that almost four centuries ago no less a scholar than Isaac Casaubonus took an even further step by regarding *Rudius* instead of *rudis et* as the original reading (he forgot that Ennius called himself a *Rudinus*, *Ann.* 377). If this interpretation were certainly correct, we would have to state the surprising fact that Horace had not noticed any influence of Greek literature on the *Satura* of a poet who was so deeply under the spell of that same literature. However, this interpretation is not certain at all and not even plausible; it is, in fact, considerably less probable than that defended by Nipperdey, Lucian Mueller, Leo, Heinze, Eduard Fraenkel and Rudd, *viz.*, that *auctor* only indicates, to say it in Nipperdey's words, *eum, qui condiderit... carmen aliquod rude, et in quo nulla Graecae artis vestigia insint*, which,

[1] The "doxography" of this question is given by RUDD, *Phoenix* 14 (1960), 36 ff., to which should be added the further literature mentioned by BÜCHNER, *Gnomon* 22 (1950), 243-244. See also VAN ROOY, *op. cit.*, 45, n. 6; KRENKEL, ed. of Lucilius, 13; J. CHRISTES, *Der frühe Lucilius. Rekonstruktion und Interpretation des XXVI. Buches sowie von Teilen des XXX. Buches* (Heidelberg 1971), 200.

as he rightly observes, amounts to the same thing as saying : *non dico rudem esse Lucilium, et Graeca arte Graecisque litteris destitutum.* So we are not forced to assume that Horace regarded Ennius' *Satura* as a *Graecis intactum carmen.*

I now turn to the elements in Ennius' *Satura* which, in my opinion, can somehow be traced back, be it only to a certain degree, to the *Iambi* of Callimachus. In the first place I want to mention—of course—the treatment of questions concerning literature—we may also say : the emphasis laid on the importance of both poetry and poets. Let us not forget for a moment that words like *Enni poeta salue* were in more than one respect something entirely new for Rome. They refer, of course, to the proem of the *Annales*, and may be called the outcome of it; but firstly the proem owes almost certainly its most vital element to Callimachus and, moreover, the idea of speaking about a *poeta* in a special poem does come from Greece, and it is Callimachus who in his poetry discussed literary questions all the time.

In the second place I regard it as probable that the idea to insert fables—which as such belong to a much simpler level of culture than Alexandrian poetry was!—in a volume of variegated poems was suggested to Ennius by Callimachus. Further I am, like van Rooy (*op. cit.*, 36), very sceptical about the possibility that the famous contest between Life and Death should owe anything to this poet, but, on the other hand, I wonder whether the fragment concerning mustard and onions (vss. 12-13) is not somehow to be connected with the traditions of iambic poetry. Finally, the origin of the moralizing character of a number of the fragments will require further investigation. Let us now consider these various points.

Though the material is much too scanty to admit of any further conclusion, I yet venture to conjecture that in the domain of literature Ennius has only spoken about his own endeavours and achievements and, therewith, about his own situation as a *poeta*—the polemics against Naevius were almost certainly confined to their common ground, that is, to epic poetry (*i.e.*, the *Annales*). It may be—but we do not have any certainty about this—that these effusions were a starting-point for telling a number of either proud or amusing things about himself, and Ulrich Knoche (*op. cit.*, 18) may be right in supposing that the *Satura* is the source of the rather numerous anecdotes about Ennius' peculiarities.

Let us return to the second point : as I said already, we may regard it as fairly probable that the *Iambi* of Callimachus at least influenced Ennius in his decision to include fables in his *Satura*, though, apart from the observations made a moment ago, we must certainly remain alive to the fact that an influence of the very famous αἶνοι of Archilochos is not out of the question ; cf. pp. 108 and 130, n. 1. The second *Iambus* of Callimachus, which contains a fable, is written in choliambic trimeters ; on this account, two points at least have to be considered. In the first place, I am inclined to assume that in Callimachus this fable had a rather strongly satirical character ; in the second place, I want to point out that no fragment of the *Satura* is known which has this metre ; but this may be due to mere accident. In Ennius' *Satura* there must have been at least three fables (to which Buecheler endeavoured to add a fourth by his transposition of the fable of *Cura* which we find in Hyginus, *Fab.* 220, into *uersus quadrati* in *RhM* 41 (1886), 5-6), *viz.*, the famous one of the Crested Lark, of which Gellius gives a paraphrase in prose, and two others of each of which only one line has been preserved. The first of these is quoted by Varro (*LL* VII 35), of course without indication of its provenance, and runs as follows (vs. 65) : *Subulo quondam marinas propter astabat plagas.* The attribution of this verse to a fable is certain on account of the fact that it fits in completely with the fable told by King Cyrus in Herodotus I 141. The circumstance that the same story is told by this author is particularly important in this context, because Callimachus was greatly interested in Herodotus ; in the fragments of his *Iambi* two passages certainly show his influence [1] ; I shall return to this point in the sequel. Further, I would like to add the observation that the line contains the word *quondam* which often occurs in the first line of a fable as, for instance, Phaedrus I 6, 3 : *Vxorem quondam Sol cum uellet ducere* ; *id.* I 24, 2 : *In prato quondam rana conspexit bouem* ; I 28, 3, *etc.* Then there is the next verse in Vahlen's collection (66), which is probably also a *uersus quadratus* [2]*: Propter stagna ubi lanigerum genus piscibus pascit...*; perhaps we should add *mare* or *lacus*, for Paulus ex Festo says that the poet is speaking here about a *palus.* I agree with Krenkel (*op. cit.*, 15) that this verse may have been the first, or at least one of the first lines of a fable.

With regard to these three fragments of fables I want to make the following observations. In the first place it should be noted that two of them certainly, and the third probably, were written in the ancient Roman *uersus quadratus* and that —as far as my knowledge goes—there are no traces of any Greek fable written in trochaic tetrameters ; it is, in my opinion, quite probable that it is Ennius who first used this metre for this genre. In the second place, I want to point out that there is nothing particularly satirical and caustic in

[1] The ninth *Iambus* (on the Ἑρμῆς ἐντεταμένος) is certainly influenced by Herod. II 51, cf. PFEIFFER, *ad loc.*, and C. M. DAWSON, The Iambi of Callimachus, (*Yale Class. Stud.* 11 (1950), 1-168), 94.—In *Iamb.* 12, 58 the mentioning of the enormous Indian ants certainly comes from Herod. III 102, cf. PFEIFFER, *ad loc.*, and DAWSON, *op. cit.*, 113, n. 58. An entirely different interpretation is given by BOLISANI, 43, who reads *quidem* instead of *quondam* and, following PASCOLI, thinks that an *omen* is described which presented itself to Scipio, and which was similar to the *omen* which Caesar received on crossing the Rubicon (Suet. *Caes.* 32).

[2] I can not subscribe to the—entirely apodictic—statement by A. GRILLI, *Studi enniani* (Brescia *s.a.*), 116, that this verse should be a dactylic hexameter.

these fragments of Ennius' fables, though this has been asserted from several sides [1]; so no conclusions concerning the sources which made Ennius write these fables can be drawn from the tone in which they are written. Finally, we should not lose sight of the fact that Lucilius, too, narrated a fable, *viz.*, the well-known one about the lion and the fox (vss. 980-981 Marx). This once more brings his *Saturae* nearer to the *Satura* of Ennius and provides us with one more argument against Puelma Piwonka's thesis of a fundamental difference between the *Saturae* of the two poets.

I think it is the right place here to add a few words concerning a verse about the localization of which I am completely at a loss, *viz.*, the famous hexameter *Simia quam similis turpissima bestia nobis*! Knoche (*op. cit.*, 20), regards it as entirely uncertain that this verse, which is quoted by Cicero (*De nat. deor.* I 35, 97) as a verse of Ennius without any further indication, should have been part of the *Satura*. Against this view I would like to observe that a part of this line is quoted by Serenus in his *Liber medicinalis*, 819 : *siue homo seu similis turpissima bestia nobis | uulnera dente dedit*, and that it is this very author—who, as it seems, possessed a certain knowledge of older Roman literature—who elsewhere [2] alludes to a verse which almost certainly formed part of the *Satura*, *viz.*, *numquam poetor nisi podager*. The possibility that this verse was part of a fable is not excluded, though I must confess that I can not easily imagine a context in which it may have occurred. I only want to mention the sup-

[1] For instance by ALTHEIM, *Gesch. d. lat. Sprache* (Frankfurt a.M. 1951), 359 : " In der von Gellius nacherzählten Fabel der Haubenlerche ist das Verhalten derer gegeisselt, die meinen, sich auf Verwandte und Freunde statt auf eigene Kraft verlassen zu dürfen."

[2] On Ennius' podagra he writes (vss. 706-707): *Ennius ipse pater, dum pocula siccat iniqua, hoc uitio tales fertur meruisse dolores.* It is evident that Serenus knows both the verse of Ennius and that of Horace, which has the same beginning. On Serenus' rather remarkable quotations from old Latin literature cf. SCHANZ-HOSIUS, III, 28.

position of Puelma Piwonka (*op. cit.*, 189) who assumes for this verse an influence of the Cynic-Stoic diatribe, as also for vs. 63 : *Meum non est, ac si me canis momorderit* (quite improbable is the connection of this verse with Scipio by Lucian Mueller and Bolisani, who thought that the *Scipio* was identical with the third book of the *Saturae*).

We now come to a fragment which has been left unexplained by Vahlen, Lucian Mueller and Warmington and which may perhaps prove to be of particular interest. I mean the only fragment from book IV (vss. 12-13), which is quoted by Macrobius in order to provide an example of *tristis* with the meaning " bitter ", *viz.*, *neque ille triste quaeritat sinapi neque cepe maestum.* Krenkel (ed. of Lucilius I, 14) gives the fragment under the title " Der Triefäugige " (" The Blear-eyed Man ", *lippus*). I wonder whether a different hypothesis is not to be preferred, *viz.*, that mustard and onions are rejected here as a particularly disagreeable or even disgusting kind of food. In this context one might consider the possibility that before *ille* something like *quisquis sapit* should be supplied. This leads us to various observations. In the first place we should note that this same qualification of onions is mentioned by the two authors of *saturae* after Ennius, *viz.*, Lucilius (194 M.) : *flebile cepe simul lacrimosaeque ordine tallae* (*talla* is the peel of the onion)—from the description of a *rustica cena*, according to Charisius —and Varro, *Sat. Men.* 250 : *flebile esitet caepe*, and from this we may infer that it has come to belong to the traditional material of the Roman *satura*. We can, however, take a further step, for the same subject is touched upon in two verses from Naevius' comedy *Apella* (which almost certainly means " The Jew " [1]). We find there a formal execration

[1] *Apella* with Alpha privans=*sine pelle*, *i.e. sine praeputio* ; cf. Ribbeck's note in *Com. Lat. Fragm.*, *ad loc.*, and V. Pisani, Apella, *Paideia* 8 (1953), 8. Whereas in Egypt onions were regarded as holy plants which it was not allowed to eat (Plin., *NH* II 16 and 101 ; Juven. 15, 9 ; cf. *TLL* III 847,

of the man who introduced onions as a nourishment: *Ut illum di perdant qui primus holitor caepam protulit*, and in a iambic senarius we find once more mentioned the discomfort caused by onions: *cui saepe edundod oculus alter profluit*. We have here a specimen of that typical execration of an inventor, which also occurs in a famous fragment of Plautus, in which the inventor of *horologia* is cursed by a hungry parasite. This is a theme which occurs already in Euripides and Aristophanes, and further in Middle and New Comedy; we can refer to Eubulus and Menander [1].

There is, however, also another poem in which a quite similar vegetable is cursed in a somewhat different form, which may be regarded as a variation of the first one, *viz.*, the third *Epode* of Horace, where it is said that garlic should only be eaten by a man who has killed his father. In this connection it is worth while to observe that Nonius mentions in one breath all the three vegetables under discussion: *acria, ... ut est sinapi caepe alium*. No Greek model of this poem is mentioned by Kiessling-Heinze *ad loc.* and by Eduard Fraenkel in his discussion of it (*Horace*, 68-69). However, I like to quote the latter's excellent characterization of this poem as containing "a good deal of mocking pathos and quasi-Archilochean indignation delivered with feigned grandiloquence".

7-13), they are mentioned as the food of the Jews during their stay in Egypt in *Numeri* 11, 5 (cf. *TLL ibid.*, ll. 28-35). Cf. the verse in the well-known 'Alphabet' of WILHELM BUSCH: "Die Zwiebel ist der Juden Speise."

[1] Cf. for this subject LEO, *Plautin. Forsch.*², 154, and K. THRAEDE, Art. Erfinder II (geistesgeschichtlich), in *Reallexikon für Antike und Christentum* V (1962), 1225-1226.—As entirely improbable I regard the interpretation of this fragment by WEINREICH who says (*op. cit.*, 4-5) that the mustard and the onion are mentioned here as the characterization of a frugal meal—he entirely overlooks the fact that the present passage is quoted by Nonius because *tristis* there means *amarus*, a notion which has nothing to do with frugality, and the further passages which he quotes are not relevant in any respect.

We thus see ourselves faced with two possibilities; our material is, of course, much too scanty to admit of any decision. There is a possibility that Ennius found a subject like this described in a volume of *Iambi*, either by Callimachus or by Archilochus. For the sake of completeness I want to observe, firstly that convincing proofs of an influence of these poems of Callimachus on the *Epodes* of Horace have not become known to me [1], secondly that at all events Lucilius mentions the name of Archilochus, whom he seems to have followed in one of his *Saturae* [2]; therefore I do not want to exclude the possibility of a direct influence of Archilochus on Ennius. But there is also a second possibility which, in my opinion, deserves more serious consideration than it has received till now, *viz.*, that in his *Satura* Ennius worked up suggestions offered, not by the entirely enigmatic " dramatic *satura* ", but by existing drama, which in this case amounts to an influence of the then already flourishing Roman comedy. After all the author of the comedies *Cupuncula* and *Pancratiastes*—literally tenth-rate according to the canon of Volcacius Sedigitus—may well have realized that in this field at least he had no reason to look down upon the poet whose epic poem he so thoroughly despised.

It is this latter point about which I want to add a few observations before summing up the result of my investigations. I must begin here by eliminating at once what

[1] No convincing examples of an influence of the *Iambi* on the *Epodes* are mentioned by PASQUALI in his famous book *Orazio lirico* in which he stresses throughout (and occasionally overstresses) the influence of Hellenistic poetry on Horace's *Odes* and *Epodes*.

[2] Lucil. 698 M. (732 Krenkel): *metuo ut fieri possit: ergo <anti> quo ab Archiloco excido*. IANUS DOUSA already connected this line with the famous fragment of Archilochus (74 D.): Χρημάτων ἄελπτον οὐδέν, *etc*. PUELMA PIWONKA, *op. cit*., 50, conjectures: *ego <hoc anti> quo*, on which KRENKEL *ad loc*. observes: " Da Lucilius dem Archilochus offenbar über einen längeren Abschnitt gefolgt war, hat die Konjektur..., in diesem einen Punkt weiche ich von A. ab, von PUELMA PIWONKA viel für sich." Cf. also the note by E. BOLISANI, *Lucilio e i suoi frammenti* (Padova 1932), 268.

might at first sight seem to provide by far the strongest argument in favour of my hypothesis, *viz.*, the graphic description in six verses of a parasite which Vahlen, though with great hesitation, has included in his edition as a fragment of the sixth book of the *Saturae* (vss. 14-19). This fragment is mentioned by Donatus in his commentary on Terence, *Phormio* 339-342, as the model imitated in these verses. The indication of the passage is entirely corrupt in the manuscripts of Donatus: the words *sed ex sexta satyrarum Ennii* are a very audacious conjecture by Stephanus. The most important manuscript reads *sed de cen*..., for which Leo (*Gesch. d. röm. Lit.*, 206, n. 2) conjectured " vielleicht Caecilius " which is considerably more plausible, since the verses in question are strikingly good and therewith far above the level of Ennius in the domain of comedy.

Yet there remain a number of cases in which an influence of definite comedies, or rather of the general activity in this field in Ennius' time, must be regarded as possible and even probable. Van Rooy has already observed (*op. cit.*, 49, n. 56): " There are, of course, interesting similarities of style between the Ennian *Saturae* and Roman Comedy "; he also points out the fact that Caecilius Statius was at one time a friend of Ennius. I wonder whether we may not quote in this context the second fragment of the second book (vs. 5) which, as it seems to me, describes a general turmoil of highly active or nervous people: *restitant occurrunt obstant ostringillant obagitant*. (Bolisani, 33, refers it to " la vita tumultuosa del foro "). Deubner (*op. cit.*, 290) quotes this verse as an example of " iambisches Ethos " which may amount to the same thing, and a similar view seems to be held by Puelma Piwonka (*op. cit.*, 186, n. 3), whereas Weinreich (*op. cit.*, 5) thinks that it may belong to the description of a battle.

In the second place there are the four well-known verses containing a lengthy pun, by means of endless repetition, on *frustrari*, *frustra* and *frustra esse* (*fr. inc.* iii, vss. 59-62). These have already been connected by Dr. Jocelyn with the equally lengthy word-play on *otium* and *negotium* in the chorus of Ennius' *Iphigenia* (fr. xcix Joc.) and, moreover, with some similar passages in Plautus (*Amph.* 33-36 ; *Capt.* 255-256 ; *Pseud.* 704-705). We may add *Bacch.* 548 where we find the same words as in Ennius : *atque i se cum frustrant, frustrari alios stolidi existimant.* This striking similarity with a passage from Plautus is, in my opinion, particularly important, since I have the impression that Ennius was acquainted with Plautus' plays—after all by no means a surprising fact, or rather what was to be expected—and has borrowed at least several expressions from this great master of the Latin language. In this connection I do not want to mention the verb *propinare* (cf. *supra*, pp. 117 f.), which may be a Grecism belonging to colloquial Latin like *graecari* and *obsonare*, but I wonder whether Ennius did not borrow from Plautus the adverb *medullitus* which occurs twice in the latter's comedies (*Most.* 243 ; *Truc.*—from 189 B.C.—439).

A puzzling case is the fragment in hexameters quoted by Varro *LL* VII 71 : *decem coclites quas montibus summis* | *Ripaeis fodere.* This fragment, which Hug attributed to the *Satura*, must be connected, as was first seen by Otfried Mueller, with the statement in Herodotus III 116 (cf. *ibid.* IV 27) that in the North of Europe much gold is found which the one-eyed Arimaspoi get hold of by stealing it from the griffions ; it is, therefore, quite possible that to *quas* we should with Lachmann supply *massas.* It is interesting to see that, in support of this conjecture, Lachmann refers to a passage from Plautus, *viz.*, *Mil. glor.* 1065 : *nam massas habet : Aetna mons non aeque altust.* Warmington translates : " ten nuggets which the One-eyed have mined on the Ripaean mountain-tops " with the explication : " The fr. suggests a mocking allusion to ostentatious wealth." Although we may reckon with a certain influence of Herodotus on early Roman historiography [1], which makes it probable that his work was known at Rome during the life-time of Ennius, I wonder whether we should not take into account the possibility of an influence of Callimachus. I have already (pp. 120 f.) discussed the fact that this poet and scholar was particularly interested in Herodotus, as was demonstrated by Ernst Howald in an important paper [2]. Since the verse seems to betray a mocking tone, as was suggested by Warmington, we come once more to think of the *Iambi* of Callimachus.

The *certamen* between Life and Death (*Inc.* 1), which is unfortunately only mentioned by Quintilian (IX 2, 36), certainly has its place in an old tradition of Greek comedy but in this case it is not Roman comedy of which I am thinking. It is in fact by no means impossible that Ennius was influenced by the particularly famous ἀγών between Earth and Sea in a comedy of Epicharmus, since it is certain that he was acquainted with what in the Hellenistic period was regarded as 'Epicharmean literature'. In the summary of the lecture given by Mr. Coffey at the symposion on the *Satura* at Rostock (cf. n. 3, p. 105) I find the judicious remark that the staging of discussions between personified abstract notions was in the Greek tradition chiefly connected with Epicharmus. Quite interesting is the fact that Novius wrote a *fabula Atellana* with the same title. Van Rooy, *op. cit.*, 36, has rejected Deubner's attempt to find a model for this poem of Ennius in the contest between laurel and olive-tree in Callimachus' first *Iambus* [3]; I agree with van Rooy's

[1] W. Soltau, *Die Anfänge der römischen Geschichtsschreibung* (Leipzig 1904), 267; cf. also H. Ball, *Die Bekanntschaft römischer Schriftsteller mit Herodotus* (Progr. Berlin 1890).

[2] In his paper Ionische Geschichtsschreibung (*Hermes* 58 (1923), 113-146), 133-139. W. Schmid, *Gesch. der griech Lit.*, I (München 1934), 666, n. 4 adds the observation that both authors are greatly interested in aetiologies.

[3] Cf. M. Coffey, *op. cit.* (see n. 3, p. 105). The last discussion of the influence of 'Epicharmean' literature on Ennius is given by A. Marastoni, Enniana

emphasis on the different character of the highly literary poem of Callimachus but I regard it as probable that this poet, too, influenced Ennius' decision to devote a poem to an ἀγών.

A last problem to be treated here—I repeat that in this paper any attempt at completeness is out of the question—concerns the problem whether Ennius' *Satura* contained poems possessing a certain amount of ὕψος. This question pertains particularly to the first fragment of the second and the third fragment of the third book. The first fragment (vss. 3-4) runs as follows: *contemplor | inde loci liquidas pilatasque aetheris oras*. Here we find two expressions which belong to the *genus sublime*, *viz.*, *inde loci* and *aetheris oras*. The first expression occurs twice in the fragments of the *Annales* (vss. 22 and 530), whereas the combination *aetheris orae* is found five times in Lucretius, and *aetheriae orae* three times [1]; this makes it practically certain that this locution, too, was borrowed by Ennius from his epic poem. Thus it is quite credible that the present fragment is from a poem which possessed a certain ὕψος. The explication of *pilatas* given by the Servius Danielinus, *viz.*, *firmas et stabiles* ... *quasi pilis fultas* is, in my opinion, not correct in so far as the *quasi* should disappear: the verse is evidently to be connected with passages like *Odyssey* I 53, where the columns " which

minora quaedam ex opusculis decerpta, *Miscellanea critica*, II (Leipzig, Teubner, 1965), 219-227. — In his edition of the fragments of the *Fabulae Atellanae* (*Poetarum Latinorum Reliquiae: Aetas rei publicae*, VI 1, Rome 1967), 111, P. Frassinetti proposes the following supposition: " si incentrava probabilmente su un contrasto nello stile della vetusta commediola epicarmea." Cf. also Vahlen [2], ccxiii, who observes at the end: ... *certe ei suam partem* παραινέσεως vel νουθετήσεως, *ut par est in satura, non defuisse non ambiguum est.* Leo, *op. cit.*, 206, is uncertain: " Wir haben leider die Wahl, ob wir uns das Gedicht des Ennius mehr in die Nähe von Novius' ' Tod und Leben ' oder von Kallimachos' ' Lorbeer und Ölbaum ' denken wollen." Cf. also A. Dieterich, *Pulcinella*, 78, und R. Hirzel, *Der Dialog* I (Leipzig 1895), 423.

[1] *Aetheris orae:* II 1000; III 835; IV 215; V 143,683.—*Aetheriae orae:* IV 411; V 85; VI 61.

keep heaven and earth apart" are mentioned. Puelma Piwonka, *op. cit.*, 183, n. 1, quite erroneously refers to Sophocles *Aias* 108, where Sophocles speaks about pillars supporting the roof of a house. On the other hand, Puelma may well be right in supposing that Ennius is here describing one more dream (besides those narrated in the proem of the first book of the *Annales* and in the *Epicharmus*), this time combined with a contemplation, a θεωρία, of the universe. One feels inclined to put the question whether the first line of the first book of Lucilius, *aetheris et terrae genitabile quaerere tempus*, is a quotation from a poem belonging to a *satura* which the younger poet regarded as not suited to the genre —in this context it may be of importance that the first line of the first satire of Persius, *o curas hominum, o quantum est in rebus inane!* is perhaps also a quotation. At all events Lucilius may, as Marx observes, have coined the adjective *genitabilis* after the example of Ennius' *genitalis* (*Ann.* 115). Lucian Mueller thought of a reference by Lucilius to Ennius' *Epicharmus* and *Euhemerus* but in my opinion the interpretation given by Marx is more probable, *viz.*, that here a friend of the poet is speaking who advises him to compose, rather than a *Satura*, a *carmen physicum*, for which then an example could be found in one of the poems forming part of Ennius' *Satura*. When, after all, it is probable that the fragment *Enni poeta salue* is, to a certain degree, the repetition of a scene from the proem of the *Annales*, the poet may have included in his *Satura* a similar repetition of the verses *de rerum natura* [1] in that same proem.

[1] I use this opportunity to point out once more that this revelation of the *rerum natura* by Homer in this context (Lucr. I 126) should not be imagined as a lengthy discussion on this subject but that almost certainly it contained only as much as was necessary in order to understand the doctrine of the transmigration of souls. It had in fact the same function as the revelation (vs. 723 *ordine singula pandit; expandere* in Lucr., *loc. cit.*) by Anchises of the same subject in *Aen.* VI 724-751. Cf. on this subject what I have written in *Mnemosyne* IV 3 (1950), 221-222. It is for this reason that in the well-

I am quite uncertain about the localization of the fragment from the third book *testes sunt* | *Lati campi quos gerit Africa terra politos* (vss. 10-11), which is so surprisingly similar to the fragment from the *Scipio* : *testes sunt* | *Campi magni*. There is, of course, a fairly great possibility that Ennius repeated himself once more [1] and that, after or before writing the *Scipio*, he included a *laudatio* of Scipio maior in his *Satura*, as is supposed by Mariotti [2]. Weinreich (*op. cit.*, 5) seems to think of a reminiscence of personal experiences of the poet ; however, we have no record that the second Punic war ever brought Ennius to Africa.

As to the verses 2, 8 and 63, Friedrich Leo (*op. cit.*, 207) supposes that they stem from a moralizing context (" einen moralischen Zusammenhang "). It is indeed quite plausible that Ennius' *Satura* contained more moralizing poems—or poems with a moral—than the three fables of which we know. Probably the proverbial expression found in the hexameter (v. 70) *Quaerunt in scirpo soliti quod dicere nodum* should be added to this group. Some scholars speak, though rather vaguely, about the possibility that Ennius should have experienced the influence of the famous *Diatribes* of Menippus. As regards chronology, this is quite possible but I am still not much inclined to regard this as probable, since the qualification of Varro's *Satura* or *Saturae* by means of the adjective *Menippeus* looks like the announcement of a novelty. Further, I can not, in the absence of any further

known sentence of Fronto *magister Enni Homerus et somnium* the importance of the word *magister* should not be overstressed.

[1] To the examples quoted above (p. 107) more can be added ; a particular striking instance is the similarity of *Sc.* 185 *Constitit credo Scamander, arbores uento uacant* and *Varia* 12 (from the *Scipio*) : *Constitere amnes perennes, arbores uento uacant.*

[2] *Lezioni su Ennio*, 125 ; *Titoli di opere enniane*, 274, n. 4 (here he refers to the fact that the eleventh book of Lucilius (394 ff. M.) may have contained a similar *laudatio* of Scipio Minor).

proof, follow Deubner when he asserts (*op. cit.*, 290) that the verses which he regards as moralizing, *viz.*, vss. 1, 2, 5, 8-9 and 59-62, show a " iambisches Ethos " and are therefore —he does not say this explicitly but it is evident from the context that we should infer this—primarily due to the influence of the *Iambi* of Callimachus.

Illuc unde abii redeo. I entirely agree with Mariotti that the most essential feature of the *Satura* of Ennius was a continuous striving after *uarietas*, which may be regarded as typical of ancient Roman culture. This *uarietas* showed itself in the wide range of *uaria poemata* which together constituted this *Satura* and which show both the influence of Greek Hellenistic literature, which Ennius had studied and imitated with so much zeal, and of the still quite young Roman literature, of which the comedies of Plautus should perhaps be mentioned in the first place. The question whether Ennius' Roman models also included the remnants —preserved in whatever form—of a preliterary *satura* will probably never be solved.

DISCUSSION

M. Skutsch: The first point I wish to make is really a query only: does Mr. Waszink hold with Mariotti that the *Annals* are, if not in a chronological sense, yet in some sense a *Satura?*

M. Waszink: Ich glaube nicht, dass diese Formulierung die Meinung von Mariotti richtig wiedergibt: Mariotti will m.E. nur sagen, dass man die *Satura* sozusagen als eine Vorarbeit oder —um mit ihm jeden Gedanken an Priorität auszuschliessen— als eine Bearbeitung auf einem mehr bescheidenen Niveau der verschiedenen Fazetten seiner Dichtung in den *Annales* zu betrachten hat.

M. Wülfing: Ist der Eindruck ganz falsch, dass Ennius' hochbewusster, zuweilen spielerischer Umgang mit der Sprache auch witzig wirken konnte, selbst an einigen *Annalen*stellen, dass mindestens Ennius so etwas nicht ganz streng vermied?

Ich denke an das onomatopoetische *taratantara* (*Ann.* II 140), an das Unwort *gau* (ich bin mir bewusst, dass Ennius auch homerische Sonderformen mag haben nachbilden wollen; bei *do*, vielleicht auch bei *cael* naheliegend) oder an die 'tmesis' *Massilitanas* (*Ann.* 610) und *cere - comminuit - brum* (*Ann.* 609). Übermut des Könners?—Da kann dann manches zwischen *Saturae* und den anderen Gattungen hin- und hergewirkt haben.

M. Suerbaum: Aus der mehrfach bezeugten Anführung *Ennius satyrarum libro* ... würde auch ich nicht schliessen, dass der originale Titel *Saturarum libri quattuor* gelautet hat. Ennius ist nämlich ein Vertreter des *Satura*-Typs, den Diomedes als *carmen quod ex uariis poematibus constabat* charakterisiert. In diesem Sinne ist also *Satura* ein Synonym zu *liber*, das ja auch eine Zusammenfassung von x *uaria poemata* ist. *Saturarum liber* wäre also eine

Tautologie. Ich neige deshalb zu der Annahme, dass der originale Titel der Ennianischen Sammlung *Satura* (oder aber, falls Ennius diese seine vermischten Gedichte nicht in einer einzigen Rolle, sondern in Einzelpublikationen veröffentlicht haben sollte, evtl. auch *Satura prima*, *Satura secunda* usw.) gelautet haben wird.

M. Skutsch : Is it not legitimate to infer from *De compositione saturarum* that a plurality of compositions are meant? Would the author not have used the singular if the genre as such had been in mind?

M. Waszink : I reckon with a possibility that Varro was thinking of the *Satura* of respectively Ennius, Lucilius, himself, etc., at all events of a plurality of authors.

M. Suerbaum : Die These, der Ennianische *Scipio* sei eine *satura*, beruht nicht einfach auf der hypothetischen Zusammengehörigkeit oder gar Identität des Fragmentes aus dem III. Buch der *Satiren*, *Sat.* 10 sq. *testes sunt | Lati campi quos gerit Africa terra politos* mit dem wahrscheinlich aus dem *Scipio* stammenden Fragment *Var.* 8 : *Testes sunt Campi Magni*, sondern in erster Linie auf dem Tatbestand, dass der *Scipio* nachweislich aus Partien verschiedenen Versmasses (mindestens Septenaren und Hexametern) bestand. Damit können wenigstens wir ihn als *satura* jenes älteren Typs bezeichnen, die Diomedes als *carmen quod ex variis poematibus constabat* definiert. Ob der *Scipio* dagegen in der Antike zu den sog. *libri saturarum* des Ennius gezählt (und mit Buch III identifiziert) wurde, ist eine andere, davon zu trennende Frage. Vgl. dazu meine *Untersuchungen zur Selbstdarstellung älterer röm. Dichter*, Hildesheim 1968, S. 239 f. mit Anm. 701.

M. Jocelyn : One should not build too much on a single quotation occurring in a context like Macrobius, *Sat.* VI 4, 6. Items in blocks of quotations by grammarians tended to become confused.

M. Badian: I should point out that, while I quite agree on the grammarians, the assignment of a hexameter (*Var.* 14) to the *Scipio* comes from Macrobius, who cannot be lightly dismissed. Polymetry therefore seems securely attested.

M. Skutsch: I have long held the view (although I cannot here set it out in detail) that in the notorious Livy chapter and in the (partly contradictory) statements on the banqueting songs in Cato and Varro we have the *disiecta membra* of a peripatetic theory on the beginnings of literature adapted to the circumstances of Rome. I do not see any connection between any earlier dramatic satire and the work of Livius Andronicus.

M. Suerbaum: Mir scheint aus dem vieltraktierten Livius-Kapitel VII 2 hervorzugehen, dass—zu verstehen ist immer: nach der Darstellung des Livius—bereits auf der sog. *satura*-Stufe der Entwicklung ein Dialog vorhanden war und nicht erst durch Livius Andronicus (auf der *fabula*-Stufe) eingeführt wurde: sogar schon die Fescenninen-Stufe ist dialogisch (*alternis iaciebant*). Die sog. dramatischen *saturae* scheinen einzelne Sketche ohne zusammenhängende Handlung gewesen zu sein. Neu auf der *fabula*-Stufe ist nicht die Rollendarstellung (die kann es durchaus in den *saturae* gegeben haben), sondern die zusammenhängende Handlung: bei *Liuius ... ab saturis ausus est primus argumento fabulam serere* ist nicht nur das *argumento*, sondern auch das *serere* bedeutungsvoll.

M. Waszink: I do not see any reason to change my opinion in these matters: there remains the possibility of performances without improvisation, as Mr. Jocelyn has observed. And the source of Livy, almost certainly Varro, may have regarded those performances, which he clearly contrasts with the *plots* of a full-fledged comedy (*argumento fabulam serere*), as the *exempla* of that part of Latin comedy which is not the dialogue (*diuerbium*, on which the plot is based), *viz.* the *cantica*.

M. Badian : I am already on record as totally disbelieving the " tradition " on *Tafellieder*, which I suspect Cato made up (see my chapter on The Early Historians in *The Latin Historians*, ed. T. A. Dorey). Did Ennius know that story? We are not told in which book of the *Origines* Cato mentioned it, but it might well be the first. This seems to have been written early, perhaps some time in the 180s : he is said by Plutarch to have written it for the education of his eldest son. If so, Ennius may well have read it in Cato before he wrote this passage.

M. Jocelyn : I do not believe that *Sat.* 6-7 was meant as the utterance of a Muse or that it had any direct connection with the *Annales* proem. The principal metaphor, as Mr. Suerbaum reminds us, came from the area of the symposium. Archilochus, Aeschylus and Cratinus had established a tradition of poetic bibulousness and to this tradition Ennius clearly attached himself somewhere in his writings (*numquam nisi potus ad arma prosiluit dicenda* etc.). If, however, Ennius described himself drinking anything in the *Annales* proem, it was water, not wine. Again the verses of the *Annales* came from the Muses (*insece Musa manu Romanorum induperator quod quisque in bello gessit cum rege Philippo*) not from the poet's spinal marrow. Ennius *Sat.* 6-7, like Lucilius fr. 590, surely refers to satirical poetry, concerned as this was with contemporary life, the poet's own personal experience etc.

M. Waszink : As I have expounded in my first paper on the proem of *Annales* I (*Mnemosyne* 1950), I am convinced that in 217 *Nos ausi reserare* we should supply *fontes* (cf. my paper, p. 116, n. 1). Combining this with *Musarum scopulos* (215), I regard it as certain that in the proem of *Ann.* VII *Musarum fontes* were mentioned. This again must be combined with Propertius III 3, 6, *Unde pater sitiens Ennius ante bibit*, where *unde* refers to Hippocrene mentioned in III 3, 1. It is said by many scholars (not by all) that we should explain this as a mere metaphor. I only want to say now that the *onus* of proof does not rest upon those who defend the literal interpretation, *viz.* that Propertius alludes to a scene actually described by Ennius. Finally, I see a confirmation of this supposition in the well-known line of Lucilius (1008 M.): *quantum haurire animus Musarum e fontibus gestit*, which may, in my view, certainly be regarded as a parody of the proem of the *Annales*.

M. Skutsch: Would Professor Waszink say that there is a direct connection between *Enni poeta salue* and the proems of the *Annals*?

M. Waszink: Yes, I would say so. I am convinced that the fragment refers to the *fontes Musarum* which, as I expounded, were certainly mentioned in the prologue of *Ann.* VII, and almost certainly in the prologue of *Ann.* I.

M. Skutsch: I would still hold that the object of *reserare* in *Annals* VII is not *fontes* but *fores*. It is remarkable that in Plato's *Phaedrus*, 245 a, where the ποιητικαὶ θύραι of the Muses are mentioned, the context is exactly the same as here: the relationship between τέχνη and inspiration (see *Stud. Enn.* 125).

M. Suerbaum: In *Ann.* 217 *nos ausi reserare* möchte ich noch immer (vgl. meine *Untersuchungen*, S. 278 ff.) *fontes* ergänzen: einmal weil Ennius eher als an Platos *Phaedr.* 245 a (mit der Tor-Metaphorik) an die im Hellenismus, zumal bei Kallimachos, so stark ausgeprägte Symbolik des Wassertrinkens angeknüpft haben wird, zum andern weil Vergil in einer im Ethos und offenbar im Wortlaut von Ennius abhängigen Stelle *Georg.* II 175 *sanctos ausus recludere fontis* gebraucht. Auf Vergil fusst Stat. *Silu.* II 2, 38 sq. *reseret ... fontes* und auch Columella X 435 *ueteres ausus recludere fontes*.

M. Jocelyn: The fact that drinking water of inspiration is a commonplace of classical Latin poetry proves nothing about *Ann.* 217. It was also a common place of Greek poetry (as early as Pindar, *Ol.* VI 84-7, *Isth.* VI 74-5). I find Columna's supplement *fores* more convincing than Pascoli's *fontes*. Admittedly this involves a philosophical rather than a poetical common place but there are many traces of philosophical doctrine in the *Annales*, apart from the account *de rerum natura* in the first book (cf. *Ann.* 163, 211, 218-9, 518, 521-2, 542-3).

M. Skutsch : I should have thought that *nec quisquam* in *Ann.* 218 can only be meant to be illustrative : " just as nobody can dream of philosophy before he has studied it." If the sentence referred to Ennius himself we should have to write *coepi* with H. Fränkel or to insert *prius quam sam «hic» discere coepit.*

M. Badian : I think it is genuinely possible to take lines 218-19 in the two opposite ways that have at times been suggested : one, that Ennius worked hard at philosophy before he had his vision ; the other, that he was the first man to have a vision of philosophy before he had studied it. Cicero only tells us (probably from Ennius) that, through familiarity with Homer's works, he came to have his vision of Homer. But Homer is not philosophy (which is clearly his Pythagorean revelation). So it is still possible that Ennius said that, through knowledge of Homer, he had his dream of Homer, and then his revelation of philosophy before he had actually studied that subject. This is by no means *better* than the alternative interpretation. I merely want to insist that it should be left open, and that we should not claim to be certain where we cannot be.

M. Suerbaum : Das Vorkommen von Fabeln in Ennius' *satura* sollte man nicht einseitig auf literarische Einflüsse, etwa auf das Vorbild von Kallimachos' Iamboi (in denen offenbar nur vereinzelt Fabeln vorkommen), zurückführen. Gerade wenn die nächste Parallele zu einer der Ennianischen Fabeln (*Sat.* 65) bei Herodot (I 141) vorliegt und es einzelne Fabeln vor Ennius z.B. auch schon bei Hesiod gegeben hat, ist nicht einzusehen, warum generell Kallimachos' Iamboi Ennius in diesem Punkt beeinflusst haben sollen. Ich möchte vielmehr in der Fabel — nach der Definition von Jolles — eine «einfache Form», ein unliterarisches, volkstümliches Erbe sehen, auf das immer wieder von einzelnen Literaten zurückgegriffen werden konnte. Als erster der Fabel als selbständiger Gattung den Rang wirklicher Poesie verliehen zu haben, kann sich Phaedrus rühmen, weil er als erster eine Reihe von Gedichtbüchern geschrieben hat, die nur aus Fabeln bestanden. Das gelegentliche Vorkommen von Fabeln in der römischen Satire wird dadurch nicht berührt. Es scheint von Ennius inauguriert zu sein ; jedenfalls bieten auch die späteren römischen Satiriker, z.B. Horaz, Fabeln. Doch ist zu bedenken, dass hier neben Ennius (oder gar durch Ennius ?) die popularphilosophische Diatribe eingewirkt haben wird (vgl. dazu G. A. Gerhard, *Phoinix von Kolophon*, Leipzig 1909, 246 f. ; M. Puelma Piwonka, *Lucilius und Kallimachos*, Frankfurt a.M. 1949, 184 f. 356).

M. Waszink : Ich habe aber *nur* gesagt, dass Ennius durch die Lektüre der Iamben des Kallimachos *mit*angeregt sein kann, um Fabeln unter die *uaria poemata*, die seine *satura* ausmachten, aufzunehmen. Es ist sehr wohl möglich, dass Ennius in diese *satura* auch mehr Volkstümliches aufgenommen hat, aber es ist doch evident, dass er in fast allen seinen Gedichten griechische Dichtung als sein, wenn auch mehr oder weniger nahes, Vorbild betrachtet hat.

M. Suerbaum : Es ist unleugbar, dass autobiographische Elemente in der Ennianischen *satura* eine grosse Rolle spielten und nach ihm bei Lucilius in einem Masse, dass Horaz *Sat.* II 1, 30 ff. von ihm sagen konnte : *ille uelut fidis arcana sodalibus olim* | *credebat libris . . .*, | *quo fit ut omnis* | *uotiua pateat ueluti descripta tabella* | *uita senis.* Dabei drängt sich mir die allgemeine Frage auf, warum wir geneigt sind, den autobiographischen Angaben in satirischer Dichtung (z.B. auch bei Horaz) zu vertrauen, den scheinbar autobiographischen Elementen z.B. in der Lyrik oder Elegie dagegen nicht. Offensichtlich hängt diese Einstellung (die allerdings nicht immer herrschte, wenn man z.B. an die Rekonstruktionen eines « Liebesromans » Catulls denkt) mit dem verschiedenen literarischen Genus zusammen. Anscheinend ist die (traditionslose?) *satura* nicht so stark der « Gefahr » ausgesetzt gewesen, traditionelle Motive zu übernehmen und als quasi-individuelle Erlebnisse zu stilisieren. Die *satura* scheint von Anfang an unverfälschter gewesen zu sein, sie scheint unstilisierter, direkter, wenn man so will, prosaischer zu sprechen.

M. Badian: Mr. Suerbaum has made an important point. I should add that we have the ancients' own assessments of their genres and of the credibility of each to guide us. Horace plainly tells us that Lucilius' autobiographical passages should be (on the whole) accepted. Elsewhere we are told no less clearly that a poet's account of his amatory experiences should *not* be believed. Of course, we must always be watchful and critical. But until we have evidence to the contrary, we may surely be (and we normally are) guided by the ancients' own assessment of their conventions.

M. Wülfing: Die Glaubwürdigkeit autobiographischer Angaben hält immer so lange, bis wir mit der topischen Wiederkehr konfrontiert werden. Diese Entdeckung ist tatsächlich in der hochformalisierten Elegie und Lyrik häufiger gemacht worden als in den Ich-Aussagen der *satura*. Das *sermoni propiora* hat eben auch seine Bedeutung für den Inhalt.

M. Suerbaum: Die Erklärung von Hor. *Sat.* I 10, 66 *rudis et Graecis intacti carminis auctor* im Sinne von *si quis Graecis intactum carmen scripsit* befriedigt nicht recht, weil es zum Stil der Polemik gehört, konkrete, nicht fingierte Gegner anzugreifen. (Wer hat denn überhaupt ein solches *Graecis intactum carmen* verfasst, wenn die *poetarum seniorum turba* ausgeschlossen ist?) Man möchte erwarten, dass mit jenem *rudis et Graecis intacti carminis auctor* ein bestimmter Autor gemeint ist und Lucilius anschliessend dann *überhaupt* über die *poetarum seniorum turba* gestellt wird (mit dem üblichen Übergang von der individualisierenden zur generalisierenden Aussage). Nach der Argumentation des Horaz braucht es nicht unbedingt ein Satiriker zu sein, dem Lucilius an *lima* überlegen ist; denn Lucilius hatte nach Vs. 53-55 Accius und Ennius (und zwar Ennius offenbar — und in Wirklichkeit — als Epiker), also Nicht-Satiriker, getadelt (zur Entsprechung von Vs. 53 ff. / Vs. 64 ff. vgl. meine *Untersuchungen*, S. 340). Jenes *Graecis intactum carmen* ist darum nicht notwendigerweise auf die *Satura* zu beziehen, zumal Horaz diese ja zu Beginn von *Sat.* I 4 ausdrücklich an griechische Vorläufer, die alte attische Komödie, anknüpft.

Der *Graecis intacti carminis auctor* braucht nicht der Begründer einer Dichtungs g a t t u n g zu sein, an der sich die Griechen überhaupt nicht versucht haben (eine solche Gattung könnte, jedenfalls nach der späteren Theorie, nur die *satura tota nostra* sein); es könnte vielleicht auch der Verfasser einer Einzeldichtung gemeint sein, die von griechischem Einfluss unberührt ist; also evtl. auch Naevius als Verfasser des *Bellum Poenicum*.

Nachträglich sehe ich, dass sich eine Beziehung des *Graecis intactum carmen* auf die *satura* halten lässt, ohne dass Horaz dabei mit seiner eigenen Betonung griechischen Einflusses auf die *satura* zu Beginn von *Sat.* I 4 in Konflikt gerät, wenn Horaz sagen wollte, dass die *satura* erst seit Lucilius unter griechischem Einfluss gestanden hat, dass die *ältere* Form der *satura* dagegen noch ein *Graecis intactum carmen* war. Dann wäre der *rudis auctor* von Vs. 66 doch Ennius, und zwar *auctor* nicht nur im Sinne von *scriptor*, sondern auch von εὑρετής.

M. Badian: We are informed—I could not say how reliably—that Naevius wrote satires. If so, Horace may well refer to this; though I agree with Professor Suerbaum that his wording does not wholly exclude a reference to other kinds of verse (i.e. verse of any kind in Saturnian metre). It seems to me more likely that the author here referred to is one who has not been previously named; and the judgment seems too absurdly inappropriate to Ennius to be applicable to him. On the other hand, it clearly echoes the spirit of Ennius' own judgment on Naevius, and Horace may be following this and even be alluding to it. I cannot easily accept the suggestion that the *auctor* is intended to be imaginary and understood with an " indefinite article " : for this, Latin normally uses a *si quis* construction. I suspect this suggestion is based on a modern-language type of thinking really irrelevant to Latin.

M. Skutsch : I must confess that as long as we have no more than a title *satura* for Naevius, citing a piece as unconnected with anything which we know about later Satire as *quianam Saturnium populum pepulisti*, it seems to me illegitimate to suspect Naevius in Horace's *auctor*.

M. Wülfing : Es mag schwierig sein, *auctor* im Sinne von « irgend ein Verfasser » zu verstehen — diese Probleme sind ja längst von Nipperdey und Eduard Fraenkel, *Horace* 131, A. 3, behandelt worden — aber unvergleichlich schwieriger dürfte es doch sein, an der Stelle « Ennius » zu verstehen. Warum ist sein Name vermieden, obwohl er im Vs. 54 genannt war (etwa *weil* er dort genannt war ?). Wie soll ihn das Publikum in der Beschreibung *rudis et Graecis intacti carminis auctor* erkannt haben ? Alle Beweislast liegt bei denen, die Ennius in diesem *auctor* sehen wollen.

Naevius kommt auch nur dann in Frage, wenn Unberührtheit vom Griechischen gängige Charakteristik für ihn war. Oder, wenn man den früher immer betonten « Urheber »- (*auctor*) Begriff auf seine *satura* (?) anwenden zu können glaubt.

M. Waszink : I can only say that in the remarks by Messrs Suerbaum, Badian and Skutsch I cannot find an argument for giving up Nipperdey's and Fraenkel's interpretation of the passage under discussion.

IV

E. BADIAN

Ennius and his Friends

ENNIUS AND HIS FRIENDS

A discussion on Ennius is not really a promising place for a historian *qua* historian. First of all, unlike the study of (say) Vergil or Ovid in more recent times, the study of Ennius has never attracted the narrow and esoteric kind of literary specialist : from Colonna and Merula to scholars like Jocelyn, Suerbaum and Skutsch, those working in this field have invariably approached the subject in the only way in which it can properly be approached—from the broadest possible base of general Classical scholarship, as true *Philologen* (*dicti studiosi*). Hence it would be absurd for a professed historian to pontificate on relevant historical matters before colleagues who are as well informed about them as he is himself. The historian must himself become—as the best ancient historian always is, but even more profoundly so—*dicti studiosus*, making what contribution he can from (as it were) the inside, though inevitably against the background of his special training and interests.

Moreover, there is a singular scarcity of facts for the historian to work on. The ancient historian is never blessed with a superabundance of good evidence, but in this case Clio has been singularly ungenerous. For the historical background of Ennius' life Livy is our principal source ; and Livy, like most of his annalistic predecessors, was more interested in the striking incident—battle, sedition, stirring oratory—than in the working of the political system of the age, with its constitutional conventions and its shifting and kaleidoscopic personal and family manoeuvring for power and position [1]. Nor was it his aim—and by his day it could

[1] The most ambitious attempt to trace that working is H. H. SCULLARD, *Roman Politics 220-150 B. C.* (1951)—based on F. MÜNZER's classic *Röm. Adelsparteien und Adelsfamilien* (1920). Scholars have been found to deny the nature of the working of the system, largely because Livy does not report it ! See, e.g.,

perhaps no longer have been perfectly achieved even if it had been—to separate truth from myth, character from image. As for the life of a mere poet : no one cared enough about it to record any facts, and the scholars of the late Republic already had no solid ground under their feet except for what could be gleaned from the works themselves [1]. For us, of course, the task is made infinitely harder by the tantalisingly fragmentary nature of those works. I shall therefore devote much of my time to trying to separate fact from fiction, in the full knowledge that the goal is beyond proper attainment : let it be stated at the outset, since it would be tedious to repeat it in each instance, that much of what I am going to say—like much of what the rest of us here have been saying—must rest on what subjectively seems the most reasonable interpretation of scattered tatters of evidence : pieces that others will think it more reasonable to combine in a different way. Even so, I hope that some points of interest, both positive and negative, may emerge and perhaps gain some acceptance ; though such has been the amount of care devoted to this field of study that I shall say little that has not been said in some form before ; indeed, those better versed in the long history of the scholarship of the subject may well find that it *all* has been. However,

C. Meier, *Res Publica Amissa* (1966), 187 : " Scullard, Syme und die Ihren haben nun diese These [of the manoeuvring of aristocratic politics] niemals aus den Quellen begründet, in denen von solchen Faktionen keine Silbe steht."

[1] W. Suerbaum, *Untersuchungen zur Selbstdarstellung älterer römischer Dichter* (1968), provides the most thorough and scholarly investigation of what we can thus glean, both directly and at second hand. He incidentally discusses all the points concerning Ennius' life (and nearly all those concerning Ennius' work) noted in my paper. My indebtedness to his careful collection of all relevant facts and to his sober judgments will appear (to the initiate) on every page and must here be gratefully recorded. I shall not in each case give particular references to his discussion, since his excellent index makes it readily accessible, and I need merely state, with due emphasis, that it should always be consulted ; as should his bibliography, which has often dispensed me from the need for extensive research and listing.

as one thing leads to another, we may find incidental gleanings by the wayside, which I shall feel quite free to pick as I come to them, even at the cost of a detour; and if the resulting product may perhaps be called a *satura*, the subject of our enquiry would not be one to have objected.

The solid facts that we know about the life of Quintus Ennius are very few, and the main ones are all too quickly listed: his date of birth, since he seems to have mentioned it in whatever book of the *Annals* it was that he wrote when he was sixty-seven [1]; also his *patria* (presumably, although not necessarily, his actual place of birth) of Rudiae and his Messapic descent, which he again chose to record and others chose to preserve for us [2]; and we may add his gout, whether

[1] See Vahlen, pp. cxcvi and 67 (with references to his earlier discussion); Suerbaum, pp. 115 f. (bibliography p. 117[381]), 133 f., 145. As is known, Gellius XVII 21, 43 quotes Varro as giving Ennius' date of birth and reporting that he himself stated this (it seems) in Book XII of the *Annals*, where he gave his age as his 67th year. It will appear below (pp. 176 f.) that book numbers transmitted by Gellius must not be lightly changed—but also that I agree with those who think a change in this instance essential. (Suerbaum too, I think, would make this the only such figure in Gellius that he admits must be changed.) Since Gellius (who certainly had access to a text) did not choose to check the statement in Ennius, his information here is at second hand and may have been corrupt when it reached him. It should be noted that he does not *pretend* to have checked—a point to be borne in mind, in his favour, where he quotes Ennius directly.

[2] *Ann.* 376 (Servius *in Aen.* VII 691), 377 (*nos sumus Romani, qui fuimus ante Rudini*) with Book XII, fr. IV. Suerbaum (p. 325, App. 29) collects the various attempts that have been made to assign a home in the *Annals* to line 377. No one has ever proved that it (or, for that matter, 376) belongs anywhere in that work. The statement about his age (and the famous simile of the retired horse, 374-5) presumably stood at what he conceived of as the end of his work (Book XV, as Suerbaum has made plausible). It is the only purely personal statement securely assigned to the *Annals* (the literary controversy of the *prooemia* seems of a different nature, and irrelevant), and is both understandable and acceptable in its presumed place. For line 377 no such poetically proper place can be found; while there is no objection whatever to placing it in the *Satires*. It follows (*i.a.*) that the line is irrelevant to the date of composition of the *Annals*.

or not he died of it [1]. We know that he accompanied M. Fulvius Nobilior, the consul of 189, to Aetolia and celebrated his achievements there, to Cato's disgust [2]; and there are no doubt one or two minor points one might add. But we soon enter the realm of legend and error, e.g.—as we shall see—with the story that he received the Roman citizenship as a reward from M. Fulvius' younger son [3]; and even the date of his death, attested by Varro, cannot be regarded as absolutely certain, as Münzer pointed out long ago [4].

But it is not mere dearth of fact that is conspicuous—it is the growth of distortion and legend, only too often accepted to this day. We all know how Cicero's cautious statement, in the context of a case, that Ennius' statue was *said* to be in the tomb of the Scipios was soon inflated, only a generation later, into positive assertion—and it may well be that Cicero himself already knew it as such and rejected it [5]; a little later still, we hear [6] that the great Scipio had

[1] Attested in *Satires*, line 64, from which his death of the disease was most probably deduced (Hieronym. *Chron.*, *s.a.* 1849: *articulari morbo*; Seren. Samm. 706 f. (using Horace too); Jerome's information on Ennius is a weird mixture of fact and various layers of fiction).

[2] Evidence in VAHLEN, pp. XIII-XV. Vahlen's stricture on Cicero's statement that Ennius *in Aetolia militauerat* ("*Cicero parum accurate scribit*") is strangely misconceived: Ennius was technically *miles* under his commander M. Nobilior, though he might have been described as *contubernalis*. Cicero does not mean to imply that he did any fighting.

[3] Cic. *Brut.* 79. See below pp. 183 f.

[4] MÜNZER, *Hermes* 40 (1905), 66 (accepted LEO, *Gesch.* I 156[1]) pointed out that Cicero's statement that he died at the age of seventy may be based, ultimately, on the mere fact that his *Thyestes* (which Cicero dates in the year of his death, at the *ludi Apollinares*) was the last play of which there was a *didascalia* date. Jerome (*l.c.*) says *septuagenario maior* and may be following a more accurate tradition, which recognised the nature of the evidence.

[5] Cic. *Arch.* 22: *in sepulcro Scipionum* putatur *is esse constitutus ex marmore*; Ovid, *a.a.* III 409 f.; SUERBAUM, pp. 210-3, with earlier literature.

[6] Val. Max. VIII 14, 1, and later sources collected VAHLEN, p. xix (with the just comment: *Apparet non tenuiter crevuisse fiduciam rei narratae*).

himself given the order for this (presumably before his own death, hence many years before the poet's) because Ennius had celebrated him in the poem *Scipio*. That story, in the present company, is hardly worth refuting [1]. But it is important in showing us, with welcome clarity, the way in which such legends grow and gain acceptance. We must apply the lesson elsewhere.

Cicero, in his *Cato de senectute* [2], presents Ennius as a *familiaris* of the elder Cato, in a context in which he tries hard to stress Cato's cultural interests (in his usual way of seeing his heroes, in the dialogues, through spectacles coloured by the rosy glow of his own ideal *humanitas*): Cato is made to cite poetry every few sections! Cato, in the same context, mentions and dates his own quaestorship and goes on to give high personal praise to Ennius. Yet there is no word of Cato's having brought Ennius to Rome. In the *prooemium* to the *Tusculan Disputations* [3], Cicero gives a list of Roman poets and of cultured Roman aristocrats (Cato is included as *studiosus*); he mentions Fulvius' taking Ennius with him to Aetolia and Cato's consequent attack on Fulvius—yet once more there is no mention of Cato's having brought Ennius to Rome himself. In the *Brutus* [4] Cicero cites Ennius for the consuls of 204 and mentions—quite irrelevantly, and uniquely in the dialogue, as far as contexts of this sort are concerned—the fact that Cato was quaestor in that year. Ennius is emphatically introduced as the source

[1] The facts, ever since Vahlen, have been generally recognised. But fiction still finds determined defenders, e.g. G. Hafner, *Das Bildnis des Q. Ennius* (1968) 42 f.

[2] Cic. *Cato* 10 (quaestorship and consular date; reference to Q. Fabius : *de quo praeclare familiaris noster Ennius*).

[3] Cic. *Tusc. disp.* I 3 f.

[4] Cic. *Brut.* 57-60. Note 60 : *at hic Cethegus consul cum P. Tuditano fuit bello Punico secundo, quaestorque his consulibus M. Cato ... et id ipsum* [perhaps merely Cethegus' oratorical skill ; but it could refer to the whole complex of facts] *nisi unius esset Enni testimonio cognitum, ...*

of information on the consuls ; but again there is no mention of Cato's bringing him to Rome in that very year. One argument from silence might be impugned : perhaps Cicero merely did not bother to tell the obvious story. But *three* such cases, each in a context where positive mention was very much to the point, add up to a strong argument. We may safely assert that Cato's reported action in bringing Ennius to Rome from Sardinia, which we in fact first find in Nepos [1], was either not yet known to Cicero, or deliberately rejected. It is, in fact, parallel to the tale of Ennius' statue, except that here, where he is not straining evidence to the limit in court, Cicero does not even mention the suspect story as a rumour ; it is most likely that he ignored it. It follows, we may add, that Ennius himself did not mention it in his poems, which Cicero knew well [2].

Of course, the story might still be based on good tradition ; but the onus of proving that it is surely belongs to those who would defend it. Particularly since it is not at all obvious what Cato, who was Scipio's quaestor in Sicily and Africa, was doing in Sardinia on his way back. Where the point has been discussed, it has usually been held that he must have been driven off course by storms (and then, it is implied, found Ennius in Sardinia, waiting—if one may put it that way—for a kind passer-by to give him a lift to Rome). I find it difficult to believe this, especially since the difference in course (reckoning from the Gulf of Tunis to the Gulf of Cagliari) is more than 90 degrees and the distance nearly 200 miles [3].

[1] Nep. *Cato* 1, 4 ; hence (ultimately) Hieronym. *Chron. s.a.* 1777.

[2] SUERBAUM, p. 142, recognises mention of the incident by Ennius as doubtful. But he regards the story itself as *gesichert* (p. 308) and tries to connect it with the " vision at Portus Lunae " : Cato is supposed to have put Ennius ashore there. On this see below, p. 193, n. 3.

[3] VAHLEN (p. x) notes several difficulties in the story (*non uno nomine obscura est*), but regards it as quite certain (*certum est*), on the strength of Nepos'

On the other hand, it is well known that Cato's quaestorship attracted other legends, to the point where the facts and even the date became obscured. Different sources put it in 205 (especially Plutarch) and 204 (especially Cicero), and with the date 205 goes the story that Cato left his province and went to Rome, to take part in the attack on his commander Scipio launched in that year in the Senate [1]. It is now generally held that 204 is the true date and 205 due to the legend of the attack on Scipio; I concur with this judgment for the reasons usually given, to which I would add another point: Cicero, both in the *Cato* and in the *Brutus* passages that we have looked at, mentions the date in an Ennian context—in the *Brutus*, as we saw, putting it in quite irrelevantly with that of the consuls. I would suggest that the date of the quaestorship was in fact mentioned by Ennius under the consular date 204.

The facts of Cato's quaestorship were soon deformed by legend. In the case of the supposed connection with Ennius we can see legend developing. We have seen that in Nepos Cato brought Ennius back with him from Sardinia as quaestor. Now, Cato did in fact go to Sardinia, not (however) as quaestor, but as praetor in 198; and the *De uiris illustribus* (47, 1), which does not have the Nepos story about the quaestorship, instead tells us that Ennius taught Cato Greek during Cato's Sardinian praetorship! [2] Just like the

word (*mera fide Nepotis*). LEO (*Gesch.* I 155 [2]) thinks Cato went to Sardinia on business. *What* business?

[1] MÜNZER, *Hermes* 40 (1905), 68 f. first thoroughly discussed the whole matter and came to the conclusion that 205 (and the attack on Scipio) was true, with the Ciceronian version deriving from a deliberate apologia by Atticus for what was, by Roman standards, a shocking violation of *pietas*. See BROUGHTON, *MRR* I 310 [4] for brief and sound discussion.

[2] The author (as Professor Suerbaum points out to me) does not make it clear whether Cato is supposed to have taken Ennius with him or found him there. In any case, the story is irreconcilable with the one in Nepos. The facts appear to be that Ennius returned from Sardinia in 204 (when Cato

tale of the statue of Ennius in the tomb of the Scipios, the story of Cato's connection with Ennius can be seen growing under our eyes, from a rumour unknown to (or unrecognised by) Cicero, to an accidental and brief connection in Nepos, then to a close and essential one in the later source. Although this accretion does not in itself disprove the truth of the story in its original version, it suffices (I think) to do so when added to the serious and all but conclusive considerations already advanced, which make it unlikely enough in any case.

It might be suggested that Nepos drew on Varro's *De poetis* and should therefore be believed. If this source could be established, it would certainly inspire more (though not absolute) confidence. But we must recall that Nepos is here writing on Cato and not on Ennius : indeed, the short *Life* that we have is a summary based on a major work on Cato [1] and undoubtedly comes from the sources Nepos there used. I.e., the story is based on what we might call a Cato source and not an Ennius source. It should be noted that Nepos, like Plutarch, has what we must (with most scholars) regard as the wrong date for Cato's quaestorship : he shares 205 with Plutarch, where (we recall) it is part of an elaborate fiction involving Cato in the attack on Scipio made in that year. In fact, an enigmatic remark seems to show that Nepos knew that story, though—at least in the short *Life*—he did not choose to tell it [2]. Hence

was quaestor elsewhere), while Cato only got to Sardinia in 198 (as praetor) : those wishing to report a meeting of the two in Sardinia had to accommodate one of these facts to the other. WARMINGTON (*Rem. of Old Latin* I, p. xviii) combines the accounts into one glorious stew, without noticing the contradiction.

[1] As Nepos himself tells us (*Cato, ad fin.*). That work was undertaken at Atticus' request.

[2] *cum quo* [*i. e.* Scipio] *non pro sortis necessitudine uixit*—he applies the remark to the whole of their later lives, but its insertion here suggests that their quarrel in 205 (as in Plutarch) was known to Nepos and recounted in the full *Life*.

Nepos had an annalistic source contaminated with legend. This does not help to confer respectability on the Ennius part of the story—the less so if I am right in my conjecture that Ennius himself gave 204 as the date of Cato's quaestorship.

Now, why should anyone make up such a legend? We must certainly ask this question; indeed Leo considers that the report bears "the stamp of authenticity" [1], since he could think of no reason why anyone should make it up at a time when neither Cato nor Ennius had yet attained special fame. Yet, given the undoubted fact that some annalists were totally unscrupulous in tendentious invention, there is no special reason for surprise that one of them—possibly the same one who made up the attack on Scipio, or else a successor expanding his work—should hit on this story. It makes a pleasant and obvious foil to the story of Cato's later attack on Fulvius for taking the poet with him to his province, if Cato himself had brought the same man from a province to Rome. This, in fact, was seen by Ennius' first editor, who used the report in precisely this way [2]. It is perhaps the most obvious explanation for the blatant fiction, especially since we first find it in close connection with the tendentious misdating of the quaestorship.

But there might be a more elaborate background, which we can only suggest with due caution. It is known that the early history of Latin poetry was a much debated subject in the late Republic, with the facts neither clear nor always the principal consideration [3]. Livius Andronicus is last

[1] LEO, *Gesch.* I, 155 [2]. That useful mark, often appealed to by scholars, is (alas) usually discernible only to the author's inner eye. Leo did not consider the possibility that the legend (like that of Cato's attack on Scipio, which he knows) was made up later, when the men concerned were famous.

[2] COLONNA, p. XI. We must again ask why Cicero, in a similar context, should have overlooked this obvious point.

[3] See SUERBAUM, p. 2 [2] and App. 1 (pp. 297-9), for recent discussion.

firmly attested in 207, as the author of an expiatory hymn or hymns addressed to Jupiter and Juno [1]. The honour of founding his *collegium* was granted to him after his sacred endeavours had borne fruit, hence a little later [2]. This is the last we hear of him, and he must by then have been over seventy [3]. By 200 he was certainly dead [4]. If the date of his death was ever known, it has not reached us. But it is unlikely that it was : as in the case of other early poets, he was probably assumed to have died soon after his last public appearance, hence around 206. The case of Naevius is more complicated [5]. He is last heard of in 204, the year in which some of the ancients put his death. Varro objected, but had (it seems) no actual date to suggest, except that he thought 204 too early. It has often been suggested that the reason for Varro's objection, despite his ignorance of a precise alternative, was that he found the notice of Naevius' death in Utica and accepted it (as one no doubt should) ; and this implies that Naevius cannot have died before 202, while that city was enemy territory [6], perhaps not before 201,

[1] Livy XXVII 37 (esp. 7 f., 13 f.).

[2] Presumably after the battle of the Metaurus and the triumph of his patron M. Livius (see *MRR* I, 294). This, incidentally, will be the time when (according to Ennius, *Ann.* 291) Juno at last came over to the Roman side—a poet's success in bringing this about would give a later poet a splendid theme.

[3] LEO, *Gesch.* I, 58.

[4] A poet unknown to us (P. Licinius Tegula) performed a sacred task that would have been his, had he been alive (Livy XXXI 12, 10).

[5] It has recently been discussed by H. D. JOCELYN, *Antichthon* 3 (1969), 32-47. Cf. also SUERBAUM, pp. 299 f. (especially on the *ueteres commentarii*). Hence I can be brief.

[6] It was still being unsuccessfully besieged by Scipio in 203 (Livy XXX 8-10), and it cannot have admitted any Roman or ally of Rome until after the battle of Zama in 202, unless he was a traitor or deserter (which we do not hear about Naevius). It is not clear from Livy (XXX 36) whether Scipio occupied it at that stage ; in any case, the final truce followed almost at once. The argument from Utica is cautiously accepted by SUERBAUM (p. 300—with a less plausible alternative) and JOCELYN (p. 42).

when peace with Carthage was formally made. This indeed seems to me the only probable explanation of Varro's reported view [1]. But the date given by the *ueteres commentarii* quoted by Cicero—whatever they were—must also have had a reason, presumably the obvious and usual one that no more work of his was on record after that date. Hence it is, in the light of Varro's objection, his exile that should be put in 204, or perhaps 205, if the *commentarii* allowed a year after his last known work. Either date would be historically plausible in the light of the career of Naevius' chief noble enemy, Q. Metellus [2]. It might in any case be tempting for a scholar fashioning the history of these early poets in the light of more rationalisation than knowledge to make Cato conveniently bring in another poet, just when Livius had died and Naevius, the poet hostile to

[1] H. DAHLMANN, *Studien zu Varro, ‹De poetis›* (1962), 56 f., believes Varro thought of a date much later than 201 for Naevius' death, since (he claims) Cicero (*Brut.* 60) gives Plautus' date of death as twenty years later and regards this as the reason for Varro's view on Naevius' death. I fear that this interpretation is based on a misunderstanding of *nam*. Cicero says that Varro *uitamque Naeui producit longius. nam Plautus*... [184 B.C.] *mortuus est*. The *nam* has nothing to do with giving the reason for the previous statement, but is used 'elliptically'. See LEWIS and SHORT, *s.v. nam*, B 3 and 4.

[2] Thus F. MARX, *Ber d. kgl. sächs. Ges. d. Wiss.* 63 (1911), 72 f. (choosing 204). JOCELYN, *Antichthon* 3, p. 42, believes that the story of Naevius' exile should be wholly rejected, as its author "misjudges badly the social conditions of third-century Rome and the status of Naevius. The latter was no Marius or Cicero driven into exile by the legal machinations of opponents of higher birth". The point had already been made (unknown to Jocelyn) by LEO (p. 78 [5]): "wie wenn es sich um die Verbannung eines Staatsmanns handelte". Though later ideas may have influenced the verbal formulation, this in no way invalidates the story of the exile. Being (probably) a *ciuis sine suffragio* (JOCELYN, p. 34), Naevius could be expelled without much formality, by mere edict. In 205 his enemy Q. Metellus was dictator and could easily have banished him. Since in that capacity Metellus held the elections, 204 saw friends of his in high office, e.g. the urban praetor M. Marcius Ralla (see SCULLARD, *Rom. Pol.* 77), who would readily have done him this favour. Marx (l.c.) believes he was a lower-class citizen and subject to trial by the *tresuiri capitales*. Even this would be easy to manage. The story of the exile cannot be so cavalierly dismissed.

the Metelli and (in legend at least) to Scipio, had disappeared from the scene, whether by death or by exile. Point would be added by the fact that the poet introduced by Cato turned into a flatterer of Scipio and was later attacked by Cato himself. All this, however, though tempting, must remain speculation, and the obvious and straightforward explanation suggested above is sufficient.

Strictly speaking, we therefore perhaps cannot tell whether Ennius was ever in Sardinia or when he came to Rome. But here I would agree with Professor Suerbaum [1] that Silius will not have spun his own story about Ennius' military service in Sardinia out of whole cloth. When, in *Pun.* XII 390 f., he makes the poet serve as a Roman centurion, he merely exposes his own astonishing ignorance and failure to do the most elementary research on his subject [2]. But why Sardinia, if not because there was a tradition ultimately based on Ennius himself—whether or not Silius had read him—to the effect that Ennius had served there, presumably as an auxiliary? Similarly, why Sardinia as the place from which Cato brought him, unless there was such a reference? As for the date, we have already seen reason to believe that the poet emphasised the year 204, with a eulogy of the consul M. Cethegus—long since dead, as the wording of lines 306 f. shows—and a mention of the quaestorship of M. Cato, to whom, as we know from *pro Archia* 22, Ennius gave special praise (no doubt as an example of *Romana uirtus*). If we want a factual basis for the story that Cato brought him to Rome (which would be pleasant, though not absolutely essential), it could most

[1] Suerbaum, p. 46[146]; p. 138[440] (where, for 'Prätor' (l. 5), read "Quästor").

[2] In this he has been followed by some modern scholars, e.g. Warmington, *Rem. of Old Latin* I, p. xviii, at least adding, "according to Silius"; and now Krenkel, *Lucilius* (1970) I 13, without warning or doubt. Jocelyn (*The Tragedies of Ennius* (1967) 43) calls him "a soldier of fortune". In fact he can only have been a conscript (perhaps an officer) in an auxiliary unit from his area.

easily be found if we assume that Ennius mentioned his coming to Rome in the year in which Cato was quaestor. On all counts, therefore, we may (if we wish—there is nothing compelling in it) still believe that the information about Ennius' service (not as a centurion !) in Sardinia and the date of his arrival in Rome does go back to the poet himself: it is only the Cato story that must be discarded.

That, after his arrival, Ennius was a teacher [1] we may well believe : it was an obvious way of making a respectable living. There is no sign, for a long time, of attachment to one particular patron, and we shall see that Ennius did know several eminent Romans of the younger generation ; though, of course, we need not conceive of him as a *grammaticus* running an actual school. Jerome adds that he lived on the Aventine, with only one maid to wait on him and in fact in poverty. The story of the one maid has often been doubted : it may be built on nothing more substantial than the Scipio Nasica anecdote told by Cicero, which we shall soon have to discuss. The " poverty ", similarly, may come from Cicero's *Cato*, where Ennius is praised for having borne old age and *paupertas* like a man. It is in any case no more than a conventional *locus* in the biography of a poet. Both the " poverty " and the residence on the Aventine have recently been traced by Professor Skutsch to Porcius Licinus —about whom we know very little indeed, except that he was of noble family and that, in this particular account, he was making a highly polemical point regarding the ingratitude of rich patrons [2]. At least as far as Ennius' residence

[1] Suet. *Gramm.* I 2.

[2] O. Skutsch, *Studia Enniana* (1968), 27 [2]. On Porcius Licinus (*RE*, *s.v.* Porcius, no. 48) much ignorant nonsense has been written. He was identified by Büttner with a slave freed by C. Gracchus' widow and called Licinius (see *RE*, *s.v.* Licinius, no. 5). A L. Porcius Licinus was *cos.* 184, and the poet must belong to the same family, since a freedman could not adopt the family *cognomen*. A L. Porcius Licinus, in or soon after 118 (M. H. Crawford,

is concerned, however, I think the statement can perhaps be confirmed and slightly greater precision attained.

Professor Otto Skutsch has recently argued for positing a hitherto unknown gate in the Servian Wall, the Porta Tutilina [1]; and he places Ennius' residence there. I am not entirely convinced; but I think that his discovery has opened the door to renewed investigation, and that his basic points are sound, even though I would arrange them to show a slightly different pattern.

First, it seems to me that, in the present state of our topographical knowledge, we cannot see any need for another gate on the Aventine. Gates naturally lead from major thoroughfares inside the city to major roads outside, just as their modern equivalents—traffic roundabouts or interchanges—do. In the area with which we are concerned [2], the Porta Capena is much the most important gate, leading from the Circus Maximus to the Viae Appia and Latina and serving the main city street that runs between Palatine and the Caelian; the Porta Naevia, of the location of which we can be only approximately certain [3], connects that same street with the Via Ardeatina; while the Portae Rauduscula and Lavernalis drain the two main streets on the Aventine (as well as the street conventionally called 'della Piscina Publica') into the Via Ostiensis, one of Rome's

Roman Republican Coin Hoards, Table xi), minted some of the famous 'Narbo' *serrati* (SYDENHAM, *CRR*, no. 520). He may well be the poet.

[1] SKUTSCH, *BICS* 17 (1970), 121 f., for the first time properly analysing Varro, *LL* V 163.

[2] I.e. the Caelian and the Aventine: the Porta Capena lies in the depression between them. See A. P. FRUTAZ (ed.), *Le Piante di Roma* II, tav. 118 (Lugli-Gismondi, 1949). H. KIEPERT, *Atlas Antiquus*, Tab. IX, though now in need of correction elsewhere, still seems to give a good idea of what is known of the topography of "Servian" Rome in this area. A. MERLIN, *L'Aventin dans l'Antiquité* (1906), 119 f., discusses the gates mentioned by Varro.

[3] For discussion see MERLIN, *l.c.*, and cf. PLATNER-ASHBY, *Top. Dict.*, *s.v.* Porta Naevia.

major trade and traffic arteries. Between the Portae Capena and Naevia, where the new " Tutilina " must be postulated, no roads are known (nor indeed topographically particularly likely, in view of a ridge in the terrain), nor—as far as we know—would there be any city streets to drain off apart from those already amply served. The distance between the Capena and the probable site of the Naevia is only about 600 metres : perhaps five to ten minutes' walk. This, of course, is not decisive, since our information on " Servian " Rome is so poor ; but it strongly suggests that no gate was needed here, and none should be assumed, especially if other explanations are possible.

At the same time, we know where—much later, at least—the goddess Tutilina was : according to Tertullian she was in the Circus Maximus, and the *loca Tutilinae* mentioned in connection with Ennius ought to be in that neighbourhood. Now, the Porta Capena, as we have seen, leads straight out of the Circus Maximus, in the dip between the Caelian and the Aventine. Surely that cannot be coincidence. Skutsch made the important discovery that Varro's reference to Tutilina here is inexplicable unless she had given her name to a gate in the Wall. This should be accepted and seems irrefutable. The obvious answer, in the light of all these facts, is that Varro, interested in antiquities as he always was, here mentioned an archaic name for the Porta Capena itself (which would be precisely in its right place here). We owe the discovery to Professor Skutsch's alertness.

As for the *loca Tutilinae*, we obviously cannot put them in any precise place ; indeed, the word " loca " suggests that Tutilina may have featured in various scattered places over a certain area : a statue in the Circus, a gate a little east of it ; perhaps even an altar on the Aventine side of the gate. It is instructive to compare those other ancient goddesses, the Camenae, attested in various places along the

Caelian[1]; there is, in fact, a noticeable overlap in their respective territories. Tutilina may be another archaic deity, gradually—like the Camenae—displaced in historical times. In any case, nothing follows with any certainty about Ennius' habitation: unless we emend the first fragmentary word in our Varronian snippet from *-ligionem* to *regionem* (which, in a fragment of this nature, one has no justification for doing), Porcius may well here have spoken, as indeed Vahlen thought, of a cult specially honoured by Ennius. We shall see that this would tie in with the Camenae once more. However, if, on the strength of this, we want to posit that Ennius, when he first came to Rome, took up residence on the eastern slope of the Aventine, this cannot strictly be refuted.

We must remember that, when Ennius came to Rome, the Aventine was still the stepchild of the city—even though it had had one street ever since 240. There were as yet no drains, no public water, no secular public buildings[2]. It was only between 200 and about 140 that proper urban development took place. In 193 the *porticus Aemilia* was built by the aediles L. Paullus and M. Lepidus; in 192 another portico was added; 184, under the censors M. Cato and L. Flaccus, saw the first drainage; and there was more work done under the censors of 179 and 174. The state and appearance of the Aventine towards the end of the third century can be gathered from the fact that, at the time of Hannibal's half-hearted attack on Rome in 211, a unit of 1200 Numidian cavalry deserters was stationed there[3]—unfortunately it is not clear precisely where; but the amount of vacant space needed for this purpose was clearly consider-

[1] See Platner-Ashby, *s.v.* Camenae. On Tutilina, see Skutsch (*l.c.*) and Wissowa, *RKR*², p. 202 (taking an excessively narrow view of her *loca*).

[2] On all this see Merlin, *op. cit.*, pp. 246 f.

[3] Livy XXVI 10, 5 f. (the details are not very clear).

able. It was therefore not a thickly populated part at the time of Ennius' arrival, and we must wonder why he settled just there.

The usual explanation [1], that it will have been because of the nearness of the guild centre of the poets in the temple of Minerva on the Aventine, is probably near the truth; though perhaps it does not dig deeply enough. The temple, at any rate, stood on the eastern part of the main (northern) peak of the Aventine. Where Ennius lived—at least later in life, if we believe that he lived near Tutilina country earlier on—can in fact be gathered with fair certainty. Cicero reports—and the report reads as if it were based on a statement by Ennius himself—that he was a neighbour (*uicinus*) of Ser. Sulpicius Galba [2]. Now, we know where some of the estates—perhaps the main urban properties—of that family were: on the western slope of the Aventine, down to the Tiber and what is now Monte Testaccio. That is where we later find the *horrea Sulpicia* (or *horrea Galbae*), perhaps built by the consul of 108, who appears to be the Galba whose tomb was in that area [3]. If Ennius was the *uicinus* of these estates, he must have lived on the western slope of the Aventine, overlooking the Tiber—perhaps near the present S. Anselmo (a very pleasant location). There he would be only about 500 m from the temple of Minerva along the "*uicus Armilustri*". It was clearly not a bad area, though, if he lived there from the start, it would at first be without public amenities. But people have at all times been prepared to sacrifice public amenities for a pleasant location. The area was certainly far from overcrowded and the *uicinitas*

[1] See Vahlen, p. xi.

[2] Cic. *Ac.* II 51. Vahlen (*l.c.*) admits bafflement as to any topographical implications.

[3] See Platner-Ashby, *s.v.* Horrea Galbae; the inscription: *ILLRP* 339. (Possibly the homonymous *cos.* 144.)

of the Galbae guarantees respectability: despite Porcius' emphasis on his *paupertas*, it would be a mistake to imagine him as living in the slums. At the same time, it was, of course, not one of the really fashionable quarters: the "Good Companion" passage, which we shall soon discuss in detail, shows that Ennius knew his station and was not likely to make the kind of social blunder characteristic, in their different ways, of a Cicero and a Trimalchio. The old connection of the Aventine with the Plebs and early Plebeian movements may be relevant, in a roundabout way. Not that we may see Ennius, hobnobbing with aristocrats and celebrating the aristocratic qualities in his poems, as a class-conscious champion of an oppressed Plebs! No, the real connection is probably to be found in the fact that the Aventine will have been the residence of the upper stratum of Plebeians: the merchants and prosperous artisans, who wanted to be near the Tiber and for whom the temple of Minerva provided a guild centre. These were not the proletarians of the Subura and the centre of the city, which must even at that period (and especially during the crisis of the Hannibalic War) have been overcrowded and unhealthy. These were the men who had provided leadership for the early Plebeian movements—or rather, those of them who had not (or not yet) joined the new aristocracy. It was there that Ennius would be precisely among men of his own station: we must remember that the poets, as artisans, also had their guild centre at the temple of Minerva. That temple thus has its relevance to Ennius' choice of a residence, though the relevance is a little more complicated than a first glance might reveal.

In due course, Ennius, of course, acquired several aristocratic connections and even friends. Some are better attested than others. Thus, as we have seen, Scipio and Cato are dubious, both enveloped by myth. Not, of course, that Ennius did not know and celebrate them. In the case of Scipio that is guaranteed by the poem he wrote about him, in the case of Cato by Cicero's emphatic words in the *Pro Archia* [1]. It is a pity that the lavish praise for Cato has not yet been attested in our fragments. Perhaps, indeed, an attempt can be made to do so. Cicero's context suggests chiefly military achievements; and we know that Ennius was in fact most interested in those. Cato's most distinguished success was his pacification of Spain in his consulship, after a major revolt caused by the Roman decision to annex the provinces occupied in the Hannibalic War [2]; and the first part of that war—a prolonged and difficult campaign, leading to what was perhaps the decisive victory—centred on Emporiae, where a friendly Greek settlement provided a base for action against a hostile Spanish settlement, which became a centre for resistance in the area [3]. Perhaps it is in this context that we should place the mysterious line that appears in Vahlen as the last of the *Annals* (628): *apud emporium in campo hostium pro moene.* Once we write the second word as a proper name [4], its precise applicability to Cato's campaign stands out, and the difficulty of making sense of it in its traditional form vanishes. Of course, if it is to make a hexameter and find its place in the *Annals* (where, from the subject-matter, it belongs), we shall have to emend—not unusual in our text of Festus. One might suggest, purely *exempli gratia* (for we can never hope to

[1] VAHLEN, pp. 212-4; Cic. *Arch.* 22.

[2] See *MRR* I 339; *RE, s.v.* Porcius, coll. 112-5 (Emporiae 113-4); cf. my *Foreign Clientelae* (1958) 120 f.

[3] Livy XXXIV 11-14 has a detailed account.

[4] The Latin form *Emporiae* is generally considered to be due to the dual nature of the city (Greek and Spanish); see *RE, s.v.* But the place is not mentioned in any surviving Latin author before Livy. Whatever the Latin form 150 years before Livy, Ennius was in any case quite likely to transliterate the Greek, which is always Ἐμπόριον. (I should like to thank Professor Suerbaum for obtaining, and the editors of *TLL* for giving, information from the *TLL* files.)

reach the true original wording of any thoroughly corrupt fragmentary line !) : *in campo apud Emporium pro moene* | *hostium*. Cato's *hiberna* were three miles from the hostile Spanish city, and after a major battle fought there the city surrendered [1].

However this may be, there is no evidence for a close personal attachment of Ennius to either Scipio or Cato, although both were imagined by later fiction. Two other aristocratic friends are better attested as such : the *uicinus* Ser. Galba, whom we have already met ; and Nasica (not otherwise specified), who appears in an anecdote related by C. Caesar in the *De oratore* (II 276), which brings in the one maid, later perhaps to become a symbol of poverty. Both these stories merit acceptance. In the case of Galba there appears to be a direct reference to a statement by Ennius ; while the Nasica story is to some extent guaranteed by Cicero's using it as he does : he had plenty of examples of wit and had no need for dubiously authentic ones, and we all know the immense care he devoted to authenticity in the setting of his dialogues. Of course, his judgment may have been at fault ; but it is safe to assume that he found the story in a source that he thought he could trust (perhaps even once more Ennius himself, telling a joke at his own expense in the *Satires*).

[1] O. MUELLER thought the line a Saturnian (almost anything can be !), BAEHRENS (*cit.* Vahlen) vindicated it for Ennius, to whom our source (Festus) assigns it. STRZELECKI did not admit it to his edition of Naevius. As far as we can judge, the quotation (as here reconstructed) makes quite acceptable Ennian verse. (For this type of spondaic ending, cf. lines 204, 304, 624.) Elision in a word of the type *hostium* is rare: line 11 (*animam et*) is not parallel. We could, however, assume that the *i* became consonantal—a phenomenon known in Latin poetry down to Vergil (see M. LEUMANN, *Lat. Laut- und Formenlehre* (1963), 110). In Ennius, those who would retain the MS reading in 251 (*compellat Servilius sic*)—as Professor Skutsch would do—should have no objection to this. The assumption of a quotation overrunning a line is admittedly a difficulty in Festus, though it would be easy enough (e.g.) in Nonius. But the reference in subject-matter seems to me clear, and the exact form of the line is irrecoverable.

However: who were the two men? In each case a father and a son are possible: Galba may be a little-known praetor of 187 or his very eminent son, the consul of 144, known for unusual distinction in oratory and genocide [1]; Nasica may be the consul of 191 or his son, consul in 162. In each case, the older man has generally been preferred by modern scholars [2]—probably mistakenly, I submit. Let us first stress that in each case either man is possible. For the older pair this need hardly be established. As for the younger, Ser. Galba was probably born in 191, P. Nasica *c.* 205 [3]. The younger Nasica, therefore, could have associated with Ennius for quite a long time; Galba, while a young man when Ennius died, could certainly have been taught by him. The real point for preferring the younger man is different in each case, and much stronger in that of Nasica. In the case of Galba, Cicero mentions his name merely as Ser. Galba, without any explanation. Now, to Cicero, Ser. Galba (in the context of that period) was always and inevitably the great orator: it is doubtful whether he even knew of the obscure father. There can thus be no doubt that Cicero intended a reference to that man. However, Cicero may, of course, have been wrong, especially if he had no more to go on than the name in Ennius. Even so, there is no positive reason to disbelieve him, especially in the light of the second case. For in that story, the actual content makes the reference to the younger man certain. It is strange that the distinguished scholars who know the "Good Companion" passage so

[1] *MRR* I 456 f.; *RE, s.v.* Sulpicius, no. 58.

[2] See, e.g., LEO, p. 160; F. SKUTSCH, *RE, s.v.* Ennius, col. 2591 (Galba only —following Cichorius); MARIOTTI, *Kl. Pauly* II, 270 f.

[3] Galba presumably got his praetorship (151) *suo anno*, though his consulship was delayed by his appalling record in Spain. Nasica was aedile in 169, but his praetorship was delayed a year until 165 (presumably by his active part in the Macedonian War), and his consulship duly followed in 162. A date of birth in 206 or 205 may be assumed.

well have more often discussed its textual and literary intricacies than recognised its social significance : in the light of that passage, which was at least *supposed* to be a self-portrait, it is inconceivable that Ennius could have associated with a distinguished consular, a Patrician of almost his own age, on a footing of such easy familiarity bordering on rudeness. This was possible only in the case of a much younger man, where the moral authority of an older man and a teacher would make up for the vast difference in social status : the friendship of Polybius and the younger Scipio Africanus, of course, provides the chief example. It is clearly in terms such as these (though this relationship was perhaps not as priggishly philosophical, as the anecdote shows) that we must conceive of Ennius' relations with a Scipio Nasica—and, I suggest, also with a Sulpicius Galba : Cicero's instinct was surely right, whatever the nature of his actual evidence. Ennius knew his station, and took as much pride in knowing it as in his actual aristocratic connections.

This brings us to another great family connected with Ennius, the Servilii. They are an interesting lot, especially at this period. Rising from what one may call inconspicuous nobility to hold—through two brothers and a cousin—the chief power in Rome towards the end of the Hannibalic War, they then fade out—though probably both the power and its fading are exaggerated in our sources [1]. That this is so in the latter case can be demonstrated : one of the brothers, C. Geminus, is both a pontifex and a *decemuir s.f.*—a very unusual cumulation of sacred offices at the highest level.

[1] Two brothers, C. and M. Geminus, and a remote cousin, Cn. Caepio, held high office in 203, Caepio and C. Geminus as consuls and M. Geminus as *magister equitum* to the dictator P. Galba appointed during that year. The dictator held the elections and M. Geminus was elected one of the consuls for 202. That year again saw a dictator, appointed by the consul M. Geminus—he named his brother C. Geminus. Throughout the year, one of these brothers was in Rome and the other had an army in Etruria. See SCULLARD, pp. 78 ff., and *RE*, *s.v.* Servilius, nos. 44, 60, 78 (also for what follows).

He became chief pontiff in 183 and, in the 180s (he died in 180), must have been a man of particular distinction and *auctoritas*. That he is rarely mentioned by Livy merely underlines what we have already had to note : that historian's lack of knowledge of, or interest in, the real working of the Roman 'Establishment'. The other brother, M. Geminus, lived much longer—indeed, he was still alive in 167, when Livy's narrative fades out for us, so that we do not know when he died. He—not unexpectedly—was an augur, complementing his brother's offices. His historic moment (for Livy, at least) came in 167, when, in a dramatic speech, he threw the full weight of his *auctoritas* as an elder statesman and distinguished soldier behind L. Aemilius Paullus and succeeded in fending off opposition to Paullus' triumph [1]. It is against the background of the record of this family that we must see the 'Good Companion' piece (*Ann.* 234-51), to which we can now at last turn our attention.

Precisely what the *historia Servilii Gemini* was, no one has ever discovered. The word itself, especially in Gellius, means no more than "story" [2]. Was it merely a piece of lengthy description, or a major excursus summarising a great man's life at a decisive moment? It is unfortunate that we know far too little about Ennius' technique to be able to answer this question. Its length, at any rate, must have been considerable : the portrait of the companion, which is all we have, alone takes up eighteen lines. Before it, there must have been a speech by Servilius, presumably after a battle (see below) ; then an address to the companion, with some kind of conversation ; then a period of rest and a new battle scene. This is the bare minimum, even without any additional summary of Servilius' life. Although speeches

[1] Livy XLV 36-39. It would be pleasant to think that Ennius lived to hear that great speech in 167. Alas, we do not know (see above, p. 154, n. 4).

[2] See *TLL*, *s.v. historia*, col. 2839.

in Ennius need not have been long, and battle scenes seem to be mainly a collection of striking incidents, 100 lines seems the very least we must allow for the *historia*. It reinforces the judgment of many good scholars, that the *Annales* were far from being annalistic in any proper sense. We must imagine them as a series of episodes and comments rather than as any kind of 'history'. With all his great gifts, Ennius seems to have been no master of composition and structural planning [1].

We must now approach the thorny problem of the identity of the Geminus who is the hero of the passage. Opinions have varied widely [2]. The one that may be said to hold the field now is that of Cichorius, as expressed in Norden's book. It is worth noting, as a matter of interest, that when he first treated the question [3], Cichorius casually and without argument assumed that the numeral in Gellius was mistaken and thought that M. Geminus (*cos.* 202) was intended. But by 1915, when he came to write a long commentary (pp. 135-42) in Norden's book, he fully committed himself to the younger Publius and the battle of Cannae, as had been claimed by Hug. This, of course, also implied a change in the numeral in Gellius, and he explained it as

[1] LEO, p. 171. TH. BERGK, Kritische Studien zu Ennius, *Jahrbücher* 7 (1861), 322, put it very well: "Bedeutende Begebenheiten wurden teils ganz übergangen, teils mit summarischer Kürze abgetan, während der Dichter dann wieder geringfügigen Ereignissen die ausführlichste Darstellung widmete." He applies this mainly to the later books. But it is obviously true (e.g.) of the First Punic War, if we combine the poet's own statement with the facts of the fragments (see O. SKUTSCH, *Studia Enniana* 34-36, 128 [3]).

[2] Some representative examples: VAHLEN was sure it referred to Publius (*cos.* 252 and 248), and LEO, *i.a.*, accepted this; HUG rejected it and thought it must refer to that man's son Gnaeus (*cos.* 217), who died heroically at Cannae (this involved changing the book number VII in Gell. XII 4, 1 to VIII—*audacius fortasse*, as Hug admitted); HEURGON, in his edition of the *Annals* (1958), does not decide between VII, VIII and IX, with a different identification in each case (p. 81).

[3] CICHORIUS, *Unt. Luc.* (1908) 277, on Lucil. 221 M.

probably due not to an error in the manuscript, but to one by the author himself, who had got the passage from Varro, and had added a mistaken book number from a faulty memory.

This view, which may fairly be said to be the commonly held one, seems to me unlikely; and since the matter is important, it must be discussed. (Of course, as I have stressed before, no one can lay any claim to certainty or to arguments that are really decisive.) First, I do not think *inter pugnas* can mean 'between the individual engagements of a single battle'—or that, as others have claimed, it can mean *inter pugnandum* [1]. In fact, it seems to me that it ought to mean what at first sight it does mean, namely, *inter pugnas*: between two battles. A battle has just been fought, and another is expected; the scene would be set either in the evening, after the end of the first, or the following morning, just before its resumption as the second. No one needs to be told that such a situation—a battle divided into two parts, i.e. two battles, by nightfall—is common enough throughout antiquity. I do not see why the phrase should be taken in anything other than its natural sense; and this entirely excludes the battle of Cannae. Secondly, I think it appears from the phrase *summis rebus regundis* (237) that the man is more likely to be consul at the time; though,

[1] Professor Skutsch tells me that he also rejects Cichorius's explanation of the phrase as referring to incidents of the same battle, but defends the meaning *inter pugnandum*. Among the parallels he kindly let me see (phrases like *inter arma*, *inter proelia*), some are indecisive, possible only in the plural (*inter arma*); the others (type *inter proelia*) seem to me, when checked in the context, to mean at most " in the midst of *battles* " (etc.)—never " in the midst of fighting " (etc.) where only a single specific occasion is meant. Hence I do not find this meaning—essential for the Cannae interpretation—established. Skutsch's point on the stylistic contrast between the fighting mentioned at the end and the dining at the beginning of the passage (*Studia Enniana* 101 [17]) is, of course, valid; but it does not help in deciding which occasion(s) of fighting is/are meant: this must still be disengaged from the phrase *inter pugnas* itself.

of course, a reference to a consulship in the previous year is not actually excluded. Finally, and most important: I do not think we have any right to change the book number in our text except for the gravest of reasons.

As far as I have been able to check, in the case of surviving works (such as Cicero, Lucretius, Vergil), Gellius' record for accuracy on Republican and Augustan Latin authors is absolutely perfect [1]. Where this is so (and Gellius shares the distinction with Macrobius), and the instances on which one can check amount to many dozens and not merely an isolated few, there is, as a point of method, no legitimate reason for a change unless there is either serious division in the manuscripts or a totally compelling reason of interpretation.

I admit the temptation of making changes, where they seem convenient. I myself should very much like to put the Fabius Cunctator fragment in Book XVII: the change from XII to XVII [2] is easy, and the context there is admirable and obvious—the address of L. Paullus to restive soldiers in Liguria [3]. On the other hand, in Book XII no one has ever found a plausible context, except for Vahlen, whose elaborate theory making it plausible was chiefly invented *ad hoc* and is now generally and rightly rejected. Yet, having said all this, I must admit that I regard Macrobius'

[1] NORDEN (p. 66), trying to discredit Gellius' accuracy, found (in Books I-X !) only one error. (Contrast this with a mass of errors in the very first book of Nonius.) In I 2, 6 he cites Book I instead of Book II of Arrian's digest of Epictetus. But this was *contemporary* literature, much more readily cited carelessly than the "Classics". In I 22, 8 Gellius cites as from Book II of Cicero's *De republica* a passage that modern editors put in Book III (III 32). But this is simply another instance where an illicit change has been made: our text of that work is far too incomplete to justify the arrogant claim that Gellius must be wrong and we know better.

[2] Macr. VI 1, 23. A Salzburg MS cited by VAHLEN (p. 66) gives VII. But it is not cited by Willis, hence presumably not good evidence.

[3] See CICHORIUS, *Unt. Luc.*, 275.

record for numerical accuracy as so perfect that the change is not justified, except perhaps with an expression of doubt (*audacius fortasse*), and in the apparatus. In fact, I would say that the rules of evidence here apply: the judge and even the jury may feel sure they know that the man is guilty, but they have no right to say so unless he is convicted by evidence that removes all reasonable doubt. Their intuition is simply not enough.

But this merely by way of illustration. Cichorius's suggestion that the fragment may come from Varro, quoted without book number, and with a mistaken one supplied by Gellius, seems to me quite inadequate. Gellius does take things over on trust—he certainly did the report that Ennius gave his age as 67 in whatever book it was. In that case, he neither checked nor (in fact) quoted. This among other facts probably justifies a change from the transmitted XII in that instance [1]. But the man who caught Caesellius out in a defective quotation [2] was not likely to add, without checking, a mistaken book number from an imperfect memory—or at least, this ought not to be suggested unless the reasons for a change in this instance were far more overwhelming than they in fact are. It seems to me that, with the difficulties that still becloud identification with the battle of Cannae, there is anything but the kind of evidence going beyond all reasonable doubt which we need for justifying a change. A mere feeling that perhaps the balance of probability is in favour of Cannae—a feeling which I myself do not share—would be nowhere near enough, from the point of view of method, to justify a change such as would be necessary [3].

[1] Gell. XVII 21, 43. See SUERBAUM, pp. 115 f. (bibliography pp. 117 [381]); 133 f.; 143 f. As far as I can see, it is the only book number in Gellius that S. is prepared to change. Cf. his splendid statement of principle p. 150 [469].

[2] Gellius VI 2, 3 (*Ann.* 381-3).

[3] This, of course, is a principle that applies more widely, covering not only

This is perhaps the place to illustrate what harm can be done to our understanding of our author by illicit and irresponsible conjecture of this kind. Macrobius quotes two well-know lines on the indestructibility of Troy from Book X of the *Annals* [1]:

> *quae neque Dardaniis campis potuere perire,*
> *nec cum capta capi nec cum combusta cremari.*

Vahlen reports the readings as *in undecimo*, and so they appear in the majority of MSS in Eyssenhardt's old edition of Macrobius. Willis reads X in two of three main manuscripts (the third, as often, omits the figure), with no basis whatever for XI [2]. I cannot help wondering whether the idea first came from editors of Ennius who, like Vahlen, wanted to connect the lines with an imaginary great speech by Titus Flamininus to the Greeks at Corinth—a context for which no historical evidence exists and which Ennius is most unlikely to have made up, since the speech actually delivered was very famous. Nor would the physical indestructibility of Troy itself seem very relevant to that situation.

In fact, once we accept the transmitted book number X, a conjectural placing of the fragment becomes easy, and it secures a place in Ennius' work for a well-known incident. In 197, the people of Lampsacus decided to appeal to Rome, especially for help against Antiochus the Great, who was then subduing Asia Minor. In this they based themselves both on an old συγγένεια with the Romans, as living in the Troad, and on the help of Rome's old ally Massalia. The

the book written in Ennius' 67th year, but the uncomfortable Histrians in Book XV (Macr. VI 3, 3). But as we saw and shall see, these two cases provide instances where change appears legitimate. (Cf. p. 177, n. 1 and Appendix, pp. 198 f.)

[1] Macr. VI 1, 60 (lines 358-9).

[2] On the figure XI Willis notes: "*vulg., nescio unde.*"

text of a well-known document attests the embassy of Hegesias of Lampsacus [1]. The first Roman whom the envoys met was Lucius Flamininus (the brother of Titus), whose answer to them clearly accepts the plea of συγγένεια and reassures them at length. It seems to me obviously in this context—probably from a flattering speech by the envoys of Lampsacus, perhaps from a propagandist speech by Lucius Flamininus or another Roman—that this fragment should be placed. Ennius used the incident—as indeed the Romans had done—as an occasion both for proclaiming the Trojan descent of Rome, which was of the greatest long-term cultural significance for Rome as it entered the Hellenistic world, and at the same time for stressing the existence of Roman " relatives " surviving in the Troad itself—which was, at the time of our document, of great immediate political advantage and which the Romans henceforth eagerly insisted on when it suited them [2]. The return to the proper manuscript reading in our source thus secures for Ennius a mention of a well-known and not uninteresting incident concerning the political events of the exciting years of the Second Macedonian War.

[1] *SIG*³ 591. Note especially lines 17 f., 21 f. On that famous inscription see E. Bickermann, *Philologus* 487 (1932), 277-99.

[2] Roman συγγένεια with Troy and its descendants became politically important in the First Punic War, where Segesta and Rome found the myth mutually profitable (see my *For. Client.* 37⁷; 44³). A letter to King Seleucus in Greek, interceding on behalf of Ilium, was quoted by the Emperor Claudius (Suet. *Claud.* 25, 3). The date would be the reign of Seleucus II or III (between 246 and 223) and the letter was probably a later forgery (M. Holleaux, *Rome, la Grèce*... (1921), 45-60; but see *For. Client.* 44³). If so, it fits into the tradition that invented (as is generally agreed) the *adscriptio* of Ilium in the Peace of Phoenice (see *For. Client.* 59). In fact, Rome had not, by then, as yet decided to stake a claim in the East. The opportunity presented by Lampsacus seems to have been the first (Holleaux, *l.c.*), and was eagerly seized. By the time of the war with Antiochus, the connection with Ilium was stressed on every possible occasion (Livy XXXVII 9, 7; 37, 1 f.; XXXVIII 39, 10). Ennius had stressed a turning-point in Roman policy.

We must now return to our story in Gellius, about the unknown exploit of our Geminus. I think we ought to accept that he was the consul of 252 and 248. After all, that P. Servilius was re-elected (with his colleague C. Cotta) after four years in a major crisis in the First Punic War: it was just after the disaster of P. Claudius, who had offended the gods by ignoring the sacred chickens [1]. These, let us add, were the first consuls to be re-elected as a pair since 272, in another year of crisis, and the *last* pair in the history of the Roman Republic to achieve this distinction. That we do not know in what way they deserved this surely shows our lamentable ignorance of the period, rather than anything about the men themselves. Admittedly, the panegyrist can pick out for lavish and detailed praise what is not of really major significance in history; and we may admit that the exploits of Servilius and Cotta cannot have been of really major significance in the longer term, if they escaped the attention of Polybius. But the fact that the Romans bestowed this signal honour on Servilius and his colleague at a time of major crisis shows us that we do not know enough of the period of history concerned (any more than we do of the structure of the *Annals*) to make a change in our manuscript reading here, arrogantly transferring the whole incident to a person whom it will (to say the least) not very easily fit.

It may be added that the very fact that the exploits of the consuls of 252 had not been properly recorded by Fabius Pictor, the authoritative historian of that War, as is proved by Polybius, may have led his grandsons to ask our poet to accord him special treatment. After all, we have good reason to think that Ennius, in treating the War, concentrated precisely on what had not been properly done before. It does show, however, that Ennius stood close to the family of the Servilii, to oblige them in that way; the more so since

[1] See *MRR* I, 212, 214, 215 for the sources.

the fact that he took the opportunity of putting in a sketch of his own character—idealized and, as Professor Skutsch has pointed out, modelled on a known Hellenistic *genre*—and disarmingly proclaimed his own view of his social status confirms it. We have the word of Lucius Aelius Stilo for it, and I am glad to see that nowadays he is generally believed.

We know little about Stilo, except that he overcame the handicap of obviously low birth, through pure literary and scholarly merit. His name shows his origin : L. Aelius the Writer (Stilo), son of the Town-crier (Praeconinus), he was the son of a *praeco* from Lanuvium—by no means a member of the municipal aristocracy of that town, several of whom we know from coins and in other ways. It is, I suggest, quite likely that he was of freedman birth. Cicero tells of a Q. Mutto, *homo sordidissimus*, who was prosecuted by a L. Aelius, *libertinus homo litteratus ac facetus*. Cichorius thought this man might be a freedman of the erudite scholar [1]. It is possible. But another possibility exists : he might be Stilo's father ! A *praeco* was very low in the social scale—next to an undertaker and close to a pimp—and might well be a freedman. But wit was his stock in trade, and he might have a kind of clown's licence. Compare the Campanian Q. Granius [2]. L. Stilo's rise to equestrian status was perhaps an even greater achievement than appears on the surface.

[1] The Mutto of Cic. *Scaur*. 23 may be identical with the man in Lucilius 1031 M, as urged by Cichorius (*Unt. Luc.*, 206 f.).

[2] *RE*, *s.v.* Granius, no. 8. Though there is no evidence of freedman birth for this man, a metrical tombstone of an A. Granius M. l. Stabilio Praeco survives (*ILS* 1932; *RE*, *l.c.*, no. 10). Bücheler tried (wrongly) to identify him with Q. Granius (see *RE*, *l.c.*), but it is obvious that there was a relationship. Caesar's municipal law excluded *praecones* from municipal senates (Cic. *Ad fam*. VI 18, 1). See the *tabula Heracleensis* (*FIRA* 13), lines 94, 104 (and cf. 108-25 for other exclusions).

If he came from a client family of the aristocratic Aelii, he certainly had access to excellent information on the subject concerning us. A P. Aelius Paetus was *magister equitum* to the dictator C. Servilius in 202, and was made consul for 201 under his presidency. The Aelii Paeti have been called a family of " particular eminence " in the decade 203-194, specially distinguished as jurists [1]. Of course, other families of aristocratic Aelii were also eminent. Stilo, in fact, moved in the highest circles, and must in any case have been able to gather much authentic information on Ennius. A statement he apparently made without hesitation or qualification should certainly be accepted. Moreover, support comes from the fact that the 'good companion' of Servilius apparently had no name. Of course, it is technically possible (as Professor Skutsch says) that the name was mentioned in the actual speech that follows our quoted fragment. But I think it unlikely : for would not Stilo (or Varro, or Gellius) have then more naturally said that 'under the name of' So-and-So Ennius painted a portrait of himself ? In fact Stilo put it quite anonymously. He merely said that the passage as quoted was a self-portrait of Ennius. This looks like a pointer to real anonymity in the passage, and this means that the person thus introduced was probably fictitious, and his introduction can only be explained as a cloak for the idealized self-portrait.

It should perhaps be mentioned that one or two younger Servilii Gemini are known to have lived at this time, though their precise relationship to the eminent pair of brothers is unknown. It can safely be assumed, however, that they also stood in some sort of relationship with Ennius, as young Galba and others did [2]. We have seen that the scholar,

[1] T. A. Dorey, *Klio* 39 (1961), 192.

[2] A C. Servilius C.f. issued coins, probably in 58 B. C. (M. H. Crawford, *Rom. Rep. Coin Hoards*, Table xiii), with Flora and the legend FLORAL

whether foreigner or merely of low citizen birth, must remain on a footing of inferiority and clientship with his own generation of aristocrats, but can become a personal friend of a younger generation whom he trains and advises.

And so to M. Fulvius Nobilior, Ennius' chief and most important patron. Clearly, Ennius was an established poet and teacher when he was asked to accompany Fulvius to Aetolia. As a reward for his poetic services to this man, we are told by Cicero (*Brutus* 80), Ennius was given the Roman citizenship by his son Quintus in 184. The son is quite explicity identified by Cicero, as the consul of 153 and as interested in literature—though this is perhaps a mere deduction from his supposed service to Ennius. Now, this identification, as it stands, is totally unacceptable. In fact, we almost certainly know the career both of young Quintus and of his elder brother Marcus, and it emerges that Quintus must be six years younger than his brother. Their aedileships and praetorships as well as their consulships seem to be separated by exactly that interval [1]. This means that he

PRIMVS on the obverse (*CRR* 890). Since this cannot refer to the first institution. of the games (by two Publicii about 240: see *MRR* I, 219, 220 [3]), it is usually taken as referring to their conversion into an annual event in 173—presumably (in view of the moneyer) by a Servilius as aedile. A M. Servilius (the *praenomen* makes him a Geminus, son of one of the famous brothers) was military tribune under L. Aemilius Paullus in Liguria in 181 (*MRR* I 385—add in Index). He may, but need not, be the unkown aedile. The Ligurian campaign—by what may, but need not, be coincidence—was singled out for attention by Ennius in Book XVII (see Cichorius, *Unt. Luc.* 277). There are multiple interrelationships here, which can only be glimpsed. The Floralia, instituted at the behest of the Sibylline Books, were certainly fashioned after Greek models. In due course they developed into licentious performances (see Val. Max. II 10, 8 ; Sen. *Ep.* 97, 8), of which Ennius would perhaps not have approved. But we do not know how or when this came about.

[1] See *MRR* I, 437 (Aediles) and 445 (Consuls) for Marcus, *ibid.* 445 (Aediles) and 452 (Consuls) for Quintus. Though there is some doubt about the aedile of 160 in isolation (*MRR* I, 445 [1]), the picture fits together—and also fits the *epulo* of 180 (see text)—so well that doubt seems unreasonable.

would indeed, as the date of his consulship suggests, be born around 196; and this would make him twelve years old in 184, when he is supposed to have given the citizenship to Ennius![1] But there is more. A Q. Fulvius M.f. was made an *epulo* in 180 while still a boy (*praetextatus*)—an extraordinary event on which Livy (and presumably his source) comments[2]. Clearly, to attain that office, he cannot have been *much* below coming of age. That means that we may put the date of birth of that young priest precisely around 196, which makes him almost certainly the son of M. Nobilior, the consul of 189 and Ennius' patron. Cicero was simply mistaken. He was not well informed on details of family relationships long before his own time; compare his ignorance of the early career even of P. Sempronius Tuditanus, consul as recently as 129, on whom Atticus had to put him right[3]. An error about the early career of a much less distinguished consul of a generation earlier need not surprise us. Modern scholars have found the proliferation of Fulvii at this precise period enough of a puzzle, and there is good evidence to show us that the ancients also did[4]. Even Atticus may have slipped up in this case.

If, as seems quite certain, the man who gave Ennius his citizenship in 184 was not Quintus, the son of the consul

[1] The identification is doubted in Weissenborn-Müller on Livy XXXIX 44, 10; XL 42, 7; but there is confusion with Q. Flaccus, aedile 184.

[2] Livy XL 42, 7. The age for assuming the *toga uirilis* varied, but 17 was common and was the official minimum age for military service.

[3] See my discussion of this in *Homm. M. Renard* (1969), 54-65.

[4] Livy XL 41, 8 produces a *frater* of Q. Fulvius Flaccus (*cos.* 180) who is called M. Fulvius Nobilior—a notorious crux (see *MRR* I, 391 [3]). The Terentian *didascaliae* for the *Andria* and the *Hecyra* fail to give the *cognomina* of two Fulvii—almost the only such cases. (Of course, no *cognomen* could stand on an official record at that time and for many years after.) There were no fewer than five Fulvii about at the time (see *RE*, nos. 57, 60, 61, 93, possibly 44, and stemma coll. 231-2) who might have been on such a commission, though to us not all are equally plausible.

of 189, it becomes quite uncertain who he in fact was : most probably the annalistic tradition was simply mistaken in his *cognomen*, or Livy misunderstood what he found in his source. M. Nobilior (*tr. pl.* 171, *cos.* 159, therefore born about 202) could be *tresuir* for founding a colony at the age of eighteen in 184 ; in fact, Livy or his source may even have meant this [1]. But Livy's wording may suggest that he did not know which *cognomen* belonged to which man ; and originally, of course, no *cognomen* would appear in the contemporary record. So it may be that Cicero's statement is based on no more than misinterpretation of an annalistic notice just like the one that we have in Livy. On the other hand, it may well be that we simply have another instance of legend concerning Ennius, in this case spinning a *cognomen* out of the poet's known association with M. Nobilior. There may well be nothing in it at all. However, though uncertainty must remain, it is unfortunately certain that Cicero's statement must be rejected. It may serve as a demonstration, together with the contemporary story of Cato and Ennius, of how little was really known by the first century B.C., even where much was asserted.

M. Fulvius Nobilior leads to another man, not so often named in this connection : A. Manlius Vulso, *cos.* 178, the younger brother of Cn. Manlius Vulso, *cos.* 189 (the colleague of M. Fulvius Nobilior and the man sent to supersede the Scipios in Asia and make the treaty with Antiochus). Gnaeus had been elected in a peculiar way [2] : at first Nobilior alone secured the necessary majority ; then Nobilior held a new election, at which Vulso was made his colleague—clearly not without his cooperation. Now, this man's brother Aulus, obviously closely connected with Ennius' patron M. Nobilior, was the consul of 178 who fought the war in

[1] Livy's text reads " M. et Q. Fulvii, Flaccus et Nobilior ".

[2] Livy XXXVII 47, 6 f.

Histria that made Ennius take up his pen again and write Book XVI of the *Annals*. Pliny, of course, says he did so to celebrate the achievements of the two brothers 'Caecilii' Teucri, and we must assume that this is what Ennius himself stated. The names and identities of these two young men provide a well-known crux which must be separately discussed, since we have now come to them; but that is best left to an Appendix. What I want to say here is that perhaps Ennius did not tell the whole truth in his own Preface, for personal and political reasons. It is difficult to believe that he resumed writing a work that he thought he had completed, simply in order to celebrate the (to us) impenetrable achievements of two young men whose identity is not certain and who (and this *is* certain) are not heard of again. We have seen that the consul involved in the war in Histria was a brother of a special friend of Ennius' patron M. Nobilior—and we must now note that this consul Aulus got into serious trouble over that war, which he had started without proper authority and which he very nearly lost. Livy shows how he was attacked by two tribunes and finally handed over his troops to his successor, the consul of 177, only after serious insubordination [1]. In view of Ennius' personal connections, it is clear which side he would be on. I think this gives a much more serious and satisfactory reason for his continuing the *Annals*: the desire to exculpate and assist A. Manlius Vulso, no doubt at the request of his friend M. Fulvius Nobilior. As it happens, Nobilior held the supreme dignity of the censorship in that very year, and it is known that Ennius congratulated him and his colleague M. Lepidus on their public reconciliation in that office. Ennius was clearly still on very close terms with his patron. If all this is correct, it naturally reinforces the reasons often advanced for thinking that Book XVI must have been topical, i.e.

[1] Livy XLI 7, 4 f.; 10 f.

started in 178 or 177, and not many years later—which has an obvious bearing on Ennius' statement of his own age as being sixty-seven, supposedly in Book XII [1]. But this needs no further development here.

It is to this war, incidentally, and to the exploits of the two brothers, that I would assign *Ann.* 367-9, unhesitatingly changing XII to XVII in Priscian (twice) and ascribing the error, as so often, to that author himself and not to a copyist. The striking story is told at length in Book XLI of Livy, and there is no parallel for it, with its elaboration, in the rest of his extant work. In the circumstances, the reference seems almost certain [2].

This is far from exhausting the importance of M. Fulvius Nobilior's connection with Ennius. For we must now say a few final words on the Temple of Hercules of the Muses, which was the most important result of this connection. I am not alone in thinking it very probable—though I cannot prove it, any more than others who have thought so could —that the discovery of this divine decad helped to inspire Ennius to transfer the Muses to Rome in song, as his patron had transferred them physically. Nothing, indeed, forces us to assume that the *Annals* were started before 187—in fact, Vahlen quite independently of this came to prefer a

[1] See p. 177, n. 1 and p. 178, n. 3. It should be obvious that, if there is anything in the suggestion here advanced (which seems to offer the only satisfactory reason for Ennius' resumption of his epic that I have seen), it deals the death-blow to any attempt to retain Book XII for the statement. That XVI-XVIII were known to Verrius in a separate publication was shown by O. Skutsch, *Stud. Enn.*, 20, with notes 3 and 4. Nobilior and Lepidus: *MRR* I 392; Ennius, *Ann.* XVII, fr. X. (But the book number is merely Vahlen's guess.)

[2] See Livy XLI 2-4: the Roman camp is lost, but recaptured after the enemy soldiers fall into a drunken sleep. Colonna (pp. 111 f.) at once saw that this was the reference; though he did not yet know enough about the probable structure of the work to worry about the book number. He also (rightly) explains the fragment as referring to criminal negligence in those concerned. But his comment seems to have been lost from view by recent scholars.

later date. The *Scipio* would be quite enough to give M. Nobilior an assurance of glory, if he persuaded Ennius to celebrate him. Nor is there any sign that Ennius had had any converse with the Muses before [1]. Whether or not he visited Delphi while he was in Greece is not very important; though he had plenty of time to do so and it would be strange if he missed his chance. In any case we know that the divine decad was discovered in Ambracia. The discovery must have seemed nothing short of an omen to M. Nobilior and his poet. The Muses, of course, were the patron goddesses (*i.a.*) of Greek poetry, and poetry had been much in the general's mind when he took Ennius with him. But Hercules was the god of victory and of success, the god to whom men dedicated a tithe after achieving their aims [2]. Under the name of Hercules Victor (or Invictus), he had long had a round temple in the Forum Boarium near the Ara Maxima, where he received sacrifice. Thus victory and song were happily combined, and it was no wonder that the divine decad was transferred to Rome and given a special habitation in the Campus [3].

The details of this complex are not in all respects clear, but the outline of its shape is known from the Severan Marble Plan of Rome. It is clear that Hercules must have stood in one of the round buildings marked within the enclosure: this shows a connection with the old home of Hercules Victor. How the Muses were arranged, we cannot tell; though, as it happens, we know precisely what they

[1] There is no reference to them in any fragment from his other works (as against 5 in the *Annals*). As O. Skutsch has pointed out (*Stud. Enn.*, 18), the word is not found in Latin before Ennius. We shall see that the Muses still needed to be explained to a Roman audience.

[2] See Wissowa, *RKR*², 277 f.

[3] For the temple (of "Hercules of the Muses", not "Hercules *and* the Muses", as might be thought possible but for the evidence of the coin *CRR* 810), see the outline on the Severan Marble Plan of Rome (best in E. Nash, *Pictorial*

(as well as Hercules) all looked like [1]. It might be a little hazardous, but one ought to conjecture that there was one in each of the eight niches that we see in the inner enclosure, with the ninth at the back of that enclosure, where the picture on the plan is unfortunately not clear. In any case, it was on the walls of the enclosure that M. Nobilior must have put up his annotated copy of the *Fasti*, the product of much learning and research, fittingly under the protection of the Muses. In fact, it has recently been rightly pointed out that the whole structure was a *Mouseion*. Later it was known as the centre of the *collegium poetarum*, which met there (it seems) for recitations. It was there, too, that Accius dedicated his over-lifesize statue. Clearly, this function of the structure was no accident—it must have been the immediate purpose of the founder. His *Mouseion* could not but become the centre of the poets' guild. Of that guild, we know very little. We have references to occasional meetings and poetic competitions, but not before the late Republic. It was there, one may conjecture, that the critic Tarpa officiated [2].

Dictionary of Ancient Rome I (1961), 471). The best reconstruction, which (on the whole) I follow, is by B. Tamm, *Opuscula Romana* III (1961), 157 (see also H. Cancik, *MDAIR* 76 (1969), 323 f., not adding much). She collects the evidence on the name of the temple and on the *collegium poetarum*. On Hercules Victor (or Invictus) see Platner-Ashby, *s.v.* Hercules Victor.

[1] See Sydenham *CRR*, pp. 134-6 (with Plate 23). Hercules is shown playing the lyre (no. 810). Since Ambracia had been Pyrrhus' capital, the notice (Pliny, *NH* XXXVII 5) that Pyrrhus had a gem that (supposedly in its natural markings!) showed Apollo, playing the lyre, with the nine Muses, needs reappraising : it must be suggested that somewhere along the line of (apparently not scrupulously truthful) tradition the more usual Apollo was substituted for the most uncommon Heracles as *Musagetes*. This links the divine decad with Pyrrhus and, to the poet who recorded the Pyrrhic War in such splendid verse, would add further point to his vision of the Muses as the patron deities of his epic. Ennius' admiration for Pyrrhus, usually (and in part rightly) put down to his native environment in Magna Graecia, may at least in part stem from what he saw (and no doubt heard) at Ambracia.

[2] For the guild and its meetings, see Tamm, *op. cit.*, 166 f. On Tarpa, see *RE*, *s.v.* Maecius, no. 24. For the *Fasti*, clearly a lengthy work

It was undoubtedly a major (though still limited) step in the progress of poetry in Rome. Later, around 100, we find the Patrician senator C. Julius Caesar Strabo attending meetings of the guild—and Accius refusing to get up when he came in ! [1] The incident shows that Caesar was not properly a member of the guild, on the same footing as Accius. But both he and other dilettanti nobles and senators —men like Porcius Licinus or Q. Catulus—will have been *patroni* of the college : all *collegia* had eminent patrons of this sort, as masses of inscriptions show. It was no doubt in that capacity that they attended : hence an obligation to get up when they came in. An inscription recently published and discussed shows a professional civil servant of freedman status as president of the guild of poets about the end of the Republic or early in the age of Augustus : apparently the actors were no longer in it, and this change—eliminating men of very low status—may well go back to the rise in prestige of the guild, consequent on the move from the temple of Minerva, which they shared with other tradesmen, to the protection of the Muses. However, the inscription also reveals the continuing low social status of the actual members of the *collegium* : we must conclude that no senator could be an ordinary member of it [2]. Let me add, without

of scholarship (perhaps underrated in our tradition), see the intriguing speculations of P. Boyancé, *RPh* 29 (1955) 172 f., linking these *Fasti* with the so-called books of Numa and with Pythagorean 'astral mysticism'. Though this is all highly speculative, I accept the contention that these *Fasti* contained an extensive calendar commentary ; but I regard them as an inscription, since the idea of a book as an *anathema* (Boyancé, p. 174) is rather far-fetched. The date of the building of the temple (which is not mentioned by Livy) remains a mystery. See also E. G. Sihler, *AJP* 26 (1905), 1 f., especially 19 f.

[1] Valerius Maximus III 7, 11 (note *numquam*—not merely one meeting).

[2] E. J. Jory, *BICS* XV (1968), 125 f. The man is a Cornelius P. l. Surus, *nomenclator*, *praeco ab aerario ex III decuriis*, *accensus cos. et cens.* (whatever this last phrase means : *accensus* was not a regular professional status, but a personal appointment, and the phrase is added at the end of the inscription ; probably

any evidence (I admit), that I believe that M. Fulvius Nobilior was chosen the first patron of the reconstituted college. It would be a fitting, and indeed an inevitable, gesture.

One further aspect of this deserves investigation. We know that, when Greek literature was first translated into Latin, the Camenae took the place of the Greek Muses and became the patron goddesses of letters :

uirum mihi, Camena, insece uersutum.

Ennius, as is known, put his epic clearly under the protection of the Olympian Muses. It is almost invariably asserted (sometimes in quite extreme tones) that he would have nothing to do with the older goddesses : he was the first who had scaled (?) the rocks of the Muses. One can even go on to deny that the corrupt and (admittedly) anonymous line from Varro that appears in Vahlen as *Ann.* 2 is Ennian [1], though this is uncommon nowadays. However, it is well known, and must not be forgotten, that when Ennius' patron built his temple of Hercules of the Muses, Numa's old *aedicula* of the Camenae, which had had no proper home since it was struck by lightning some time after 205, was deposited there, and the temple is in fact

Surus served as *accensus* to one man—his patron?—as consul and censor). He is *mag. scr. poetar.*, thus giving us the fact that the guild preserved its ancient name (see Festus 446 L f.), but had lost the actors. I would suggest that this may have been part of the social upgrading connected with the move to the temple of the Muses : actors were generally regarded as particularly disreputable. The date of the inscription is late Republican or early Augustan.

[1] I read *Ann.* 2 *Musas quas memorant nosce(s?) nos esse Camenas*. Ennian authorship denied by Leo, p. 184[5]. O. Skutsch, rightly stressing the connection between Fulvius' building of the temple and Ennius' invocation of the Muses (*Stud. Enn.*, 18 f.), seems here to imply no antipathy to the Camenae (cf. also 3 f.), though stressing the ways in which their associations differed from those of the Muses. Yet *ibid.*, 21 he speaks (without discussion) of Ennius' " contempt for the Camenae ". See further p. 192, n. 2.

sometimes referred to as *aedes Camenarum* [1]. It is to be gathered that the *aedicula* was quite prominently displayed within the new complex. It is clearly one of the two round structures featured in the plan—the other, as we have seen, must be the home of Hercules. In any case, the Camenae were not deities to be lightly dismissed or offended. They were connected with the most sacred mysteries of Roman religion : the *ancilia*, and the spring where the Vestal Virgins drew their holy water [2]. We have also observed that they may well be connected with our old friend, the goddess Tutilina. In fact, we have seen that the area of the Porta Capena, in the middle of the country of the Camenae, must at one time have been called after Tutilina. The *aedicula* of the Camenae had been just outside that gate when it was struck by lightning, and had found a refuge in the temple of Honos and Virtus simply because it was the nearest available temple, only a few yards away. Tutilina, however, was of deep religious significance to Ennius among others.

The Camenae have perhaps been undeservedly neglected or played down by students of Ennius, who then have difficulty in accounting for the second line of the *Annals*, not to mention the special attention to the Camenae attested in the case of Ennius' patron M. Fulvius Nobilior. The action of M. Nobilior guarantees the Ennian authorship of

[1] Tamm, *op. cit.*, gives the evidence (see also Sihler's old, but useful, study *AJP* 26 (1905), 1 f.).

[2] See (conveniently) *RE*, *s.v.* Camenae, col. 1427. The importance of the Camenae is duly appreciated by J. H. Waszink, *C. et M.* 16 (1957). 139 f. ; cf. *Mnemosyne* IV 3 (1950) 228 f. Suerbaum, pp. 347 f., in a careful discussion of *Ann.* 2, rightly rejects Waszink's apparent translation of the line. I do not see, however, how Suerbaum arrives at the conclusion (p. 349) that—on the reading recommended by Skutsch and (except for the precise form of the verb) to be regarded as certain—it cannot be the Muses who are speaking : it must be the Camenae. It is clearly the Muses, explaining that they *are* the Camenae. This suffices to show that Ennius can have felt no contempt for the Camenae—quite the contrary.

the line and explains it. Ennius never meant to attack or belittle the Camenae, only to elevate them to higher standing by giving them their Greek name, with all the overtones that that name had acquired. Professor Skutsch rightly saw [1] that the line is taken from a personal (dream) appearance by the Camenae to Ennius. *Where* this was placed is anyone's guess. Those who believe (as I do, with perhaps the majority of scholars) [2] that Ennius met the Muses near the beginning of Book I will certainly wish to put it just there, with Vahlen. The Muses introduce themselves to Ennius (and his audience), explaining who they are—we recall that the word had not been used in Latin before, though students of Greek no doubt knew them. They explain that they are identical with those familiar and very sacred Roman figures, the Camenae. No doubt they reveal some further mysteries, perhaps explaining their connection with Olympus, with Helicon and/or Parnassus, the " rocks of the Muses " [3]. In other words, I except they said something like this : " We,

[1] O. SKUTSCH, *Stud. Enn.*, 18 f., on *Ann.* 2.

[2] Certainly including Suerbaum and Waszink (for the latter's most recent opinion, see *Maia* 16 (1964), 327 f.).

[3] I cannot pretend to certainty on whether Ennius, in his dream, 'visited' any or all of these mountains : at least, Persius' allusion in *Sat.* VI does not enable us to decide this. Nor can we be at all confident about the structure of the prologue as a whole. I should add that I have ignored the 'vision at Portus Lunae' (a myth based on *Ann.* 16), after SKUTSCH's demonstration (*Stud. Enn.*, 25 f., following Housman) that the line probably does not come from the *Annals*. The fact that there is a lemma mark between *cor iubet hoc Enni* and the scholion on *postquam destertuit* (Pers. *Sat.* VI 10) vitiates most of the older arguments ; and SUERBAUM's reference (see pp. 51 f.) to the scholion on VI 1 (which does assert the provenance of the line from the *Annals*) is rightly rejected by SKUTSCH (*op. cit.*, 29 [12]) with the argument that this scholion is late and based on nothing but interpretation of the text. As Professor W. Clausen has confirmed to me, the lemma marks can be trusted and go back to the oldest and best tradition; against them, the text of a scholion giving nothing that goes beyond a deduction—in fact mistaken—from the text cannot stand. *Portus Lunae* was probably mentioned in the *Satires*, in a jocular and mock-heroic way.

whom the Greeks call Muses, are really the Camenae, whom you have known all along and revered as most sacred in Rome. In Rome, we have looked after poetry of late. But if you want to be a genuine poet, you must now come with us to scale our mountain haunts in Greece." Precisely how this ties in with his vision of Homer, no one can tell; but if one may guess, I suspect that they may have introduced Ennius to his vision of Homer after taking him with them. In any case, Ennius went with them, and with the physical transfer the use of the Latin name becomes inappropriate.

Nobilior's action in transferring Numa's sacred and mysterious *aedicula* of the Camenae to the new complex of his *Mouseion* is not a contradiction of Ennius' attitude. We should not conceive (as many do) of the poet as suddenly having to fall in with his patron by publishing a recantation —or, according to Leo and others, not even going that far, but maintaining a stubborn silence and contempt for the goddesses whom his patron was conspicuously honouring. And the whole story becomes absurd if, as most scholars at the same time rightly believe, Ennius only began the composition of the *Annals* after his return from Greece, at the very time when his patron was commissioning the new temple! In any case, Ennius may well have specially honoured the Camenae himself, if our notions on Tutilina are at all on the right track.

The poet's attitude and achievement must be seen as parallel and complementary to that of his patron, not as diametrically opposed. Both of them, without destroying the essential continuity with Rome's past—the last thing either of them would want to do—integrated that past into the less provincial past of Greece. The poet who celebrated Roman *uirtus* and victory, and the commander who, besides winning a war for Rome, put up Roman *Fasti* in his temple of the Muses, would be the last persons to renounce the past of Numa and the Vestal Virgins and the sacred *ancilia*. The Muses start by explaining that they really are the Camenae —just another name for them. They do not supersede them, or oppose them, since they are the same. But in the end the Camenae must be absorbed into the Muses, just as their *aedicula* had to be absorbed into the temple structure of M. Fulvius Nobilior. Rome must make its individual contribution within the cultural framework of Greece. That was what philhellenism in Rome was really about, for those to whom it meant anything at all. And here we may fittingly take our leave of Q. Ennius and his patron.

APPENDIX: *CAELI PUGNAE*

Pliny, *NH* VII 101 says that Ennius added Book XVI to his epic in order to celebrate the exploits of T. Caecilius Teucer and his brother. This is generally, and rightly, understood to mean that Ennius had originally stopped at the end of Book XV and later took up his pen again, going on to add (in fact) three more books. What interests us is the identity and exploits of the men who caused him to do so.

Macrobius (VI 3, 3) mentions *pugnam Caeli tribuni* and quotes lines 401-8 for this battle. Since the lines describe a brave stand by a Roman against Histrians, it is natural to connect the battle with the Histrian War related in Livy, Book XLI. There, indeed, we find two tribunes called (according to our text) T. and C. Aelii prominent in the fighting (XLI 1, 7; 4, 3); although the particular exploit recorded by Ennius is not mentioned and another tribune (as was noted long ago) plays a more prominent part than the Aelii. Are any or all of these to be identified? The attempt has often been made, for two or all three, and there are difficulties, pointed out and stressed in a careful review of the evidence by Suerbaum (pp. 146-51). I accept many of his strictures against poor arguments, though I think he is at times hypercritical. (Thus, the fact that Livy does not explicitly call his Aelii brothers seems no argument at all against identification with the brothers attested by Pliny.) The case for identification has not recently been popular, no doubt in view of Vahlen's firm rejection. Although not all the difficulties can be removed, it seems to deserve reviving, basically along lines long ago sketched (though perhaps not forcefully enough) by L. Havet, *Bibl. de l'Ecole des Hautes Etudes* 35 (1878), 34 f.—dismissed by Vahlen, *Ges. phil. Schriften*

II 252 f.) : there is probably only one name involved, and that name is Caelius. Macrobius, as so often, has it right.

There is certainly no valid excuse for those scholars who, identifying the incidents referred to in Livy and in Macrobius, have emended Macrobius according to Livy and produced "*pugnam C. Aeli*"—an error committed by Merula and unfortunately still found in Willis's edition of Macrobius, without discussion. Our version of Livy XLI, especially for the first nine chapters, inspires no confidence. It rests on an apograph by Grynaeus from the Vindobonensis, which does not survive for these chapters. (See Giarratano's edition for a convenient summary of the facts.) Now, the Vindobonensis is full of spelling errors, especially in names, and illustration is only too easy. Wrong *praenomina* are common (e.g. XLI 14, 11 ; 15, 6 ; 17, 1 ; etc.); the abbreviation "Q." is expanded to "*que*" and added to the preceding word (XLI 14, 4 ; XLII 4, 4). Sometimes gibberish results, e.g. (XLI 28, 5) "*Ci. Furius Grassus pars*" for M. Furius Crassipes. *Nomina* are frequently distorted, e.g. "Aemilium" for "Aelium" (XLII 9, 8). Most interesting for our purpose, wrong word division (sometimes with consequential errors in "adjustment") is frequent. I quote some striking examples : XLII 22, 7 *rogationem M. Arcia* for *rogatione Marcia* ; 27, 8 *Sedicitius* for *Sex. Digitius* ; and even better 26, 7 *C. P. Laetorius* for *C. Plaetorius.* (Such inventions as *Tullium Quintium Flamininum* (XLV 44, 3) sufficiently show the scribe's standard of competence.)

In the light of these examples (and they are a small random selection) it should be clear that this text should never have been taken as a basis for emending the relatively good one of Macrobius. It might be urged that the reason for doing so is that the names concerned occur twice : hence less likelihood of repeated error. But here Havet rightly pointed out (p. 36[3]) that the uniformity may have been introduced by Grynaeus. It is a well-known fact that Grynaeus and other scholars of his age emended the texts they copied as they saw fit, without giving any indication of the changes they were making. Madvig (*Emend. Liv.*[2] (1877), 592) put it very clearly: "nec tamen, quod illius aetatis mos minus postulabat, quid in codice repertum, quid a se profectum esset, indicaret"; and, on the first chapters of XLI (p. 601): "ita Grynaei fide nituntur ut, quid ille in codicis scriptura mutarit, nesciatur". That consistency (in correctness or error) need not be postulated for the scribe of Vindobonensis is obvious. Thus a man who in XLII 28, 5 is called L. Iunius Annalis appears *ibid.* 31, 9 as C. Iulius Annalis—both, incidentally, mistaken!—even though the fact that the same man is referred to is clear to anyone who is aware of what the text actually means. If one of the two references to T. and C. Caelii referred to them as Aelii and the other did not (whether it got the name right or introduced a different error), Grynaeus would inevitably eliminate the discrepancy.

There is, therefore, no need to emend Macrobius, and emendation must, in fact, go the other way. As for Pliny, this leaves the easy change from "Caecilius" to "Caelius" in his text. As it happens, this very confusion can be demonstrated in Pliny's text in the vicinity of our passage. In VII 165 M. Caelius Rufus, Cicero's client, is given the *nomen* Caecilius (and thus again XXVII 4); while a medical writer about whom we know nothing else appears once as Caelius Bion (XXVIII 200) and once as Caecilius (XXIX 85). And the very passage concerning the Caecilii (?) Teucri shows textual confusion over the *praenomen* of Ennius.

As to the incident itself, it was pointed out long ago by L. Mueller and confirmed by Cichorius (*Unt. Luc.* 187 f.) that Lucilius 1079 M (*Caeli pugnas*) uses an Ennian reminiscence to describe another Histrian War—that of C. Sempronius Tuditanus (*cos.* 129). This must surely be accepted, and it shows the fame gained by the description. (Lucilius' plural is obviously generic—cf. the singular in Macrobius.)

It is true that Macrobius' text does not quote the passage from Book XVI: the MSS divide evenly between XII and XV.

This, however, does show confusion and illegibility at an early stage, and there is no objection to emending that figure—and not accepting either version precisely as it stands. The change to XVI can be supported by obvious palaeographic arguments. It has been urged (most recently by Suerbaum) that Histrians appear elsewhere in Book XV, in connection with a siege (see fr. IV, from Macrobius, with no textual confusion). But it was shown long ago that the siege is probably that of Ambracia—the centrepiece of that book, as far as we can see, and the original triumphant conclusion of the whole epic. (For the evidence on the Histrians, see Vahlen, p. CXCIX, referring to Florus I 26, 1, where Histrian support for the Aetolians is explicitly reported.) One could (like Vahlen) put the *Caeli pugna* in the same context and dissociate it from the Histrian War of Book XVI. This, however, is made less than plausible by Cichorius's demonstration of Lucilius' use of the phrase for a Histrian War ; and since Livy offers us the " Aelii " who can so easily become Caelii, it seems to me the least difficult interpretation of the evidence to link the whole episode with the great Histrian War in Book XVI and Pliny's comment on it (no doubt from Ennius' own *prooemium*). That the reason Ennius gave for resuming his task may not be the whole truth is argued in the text above, pp. 185-7.

DISCUSSION

M. Suerbaum: Die Nepos-Notiz in der *Vita Catonis* 1, 4 scheint mir doch etwas mehr Vertrauen zu verdienen. Zu bedenken ist, dass diese Biographie nur eine Abkürzung einer ausführlicheren *Vita Catonis* ist, auf die Nepos am Schluss (3, 5) verweist. Die uns vorliegende Fassung will den Historiker Cato würdigen. Nun erscheint aber jene Ennius-Nachricht, die doch die literarischen Interessen Catos unterstützen könnte, eben nicht in dem « literarischen » Teil der *Vita* (cap. 3), sondern in dem allgemein-chronologischen Teil (cap. 1/2). Zudem ist der von Nepos berichtete Sachverhalt *praetor prouinciam obtinuit Sardiniam, ex qua quaestor superiore tempore ex Africa decedens Q. Ennium poetam deduxerat* chronologisch so kompliziert, dass man ihn kaum für eine Erfindung halten möchte ; denn dann würde man eher die einfache Lösung erwarten, die Ps. Aur. Vict., *De uir. ill.* 47 — offensichtlich Nepos missverstehend, ihn jedenfalls chronologisch vereinfachend — bietet. Dort nämlich steht sinngemäss : *praetor prouinciam obtinuit Sardiniam, ex qua Ennium poetam, qui eum ibi instituerat, deduxit.* — Wenn Mr. Badian mit seiner These recht haben sollte, die Erfindung dieser Verbindung Cato/Ennius durch einen Annalisten habe eine anticatonische Tendenz, weil man Catos Kritik an Fulvius durch den Hinweis auf Catos (angebliche) eigene parallele Praxis entwerten wollte, so ist immerhin zu konstatieren, dass Nepos daraus einen strahlenden Ruhmestitel Catos gemacht, die Tendenz also ins Gegenteil verkehrt hat : ... *quod non minoris aestimamus quam quemlibet amplissimum Sardiniensem triumphum.*

M. Jocelyn: I do not think that the absence of a reference to the story of Ennius' arrival in Rome from Sardinia at *De sen.* 10 indicates either ignorance or disbelief on Cicero's part. Cicero was writing an imaginative dialogue for an audience (or readership if you like) which knew the stories circulating about Ennius and other early poets and did not need to be reminded of the details. He represented Cato (perhaps falsely, but no matter) as a cultivated Roman gentleman, not as some pedant anxious to give an exhaustive account of his own learning.

At *Tusc.* I 3 Cicero is talking about the ill repute of poets in early Rome. The fact (if it is a fact) that Cato brought the man Ennius to Rome with him fifteen years or so before has no relevance. There was no reason at all why it should have been mentioned.

The next great orator after Cethegus was Cato. It is not therefore surprising that at *Brut.* 60 Cicero should remark the fact that Cato was quaestor in the year Cethegus was consul. Such synchronisms were common in ancient literary histories. Ennius would hardly have referred to a quaestorship in the *Annals*.

M. Badian: The *Brutus* passage is (as I said) marginal: one could argue as Mr. Jocelyn has done, that Cato's quaestorship is mentioned in 60 because he is the next great orator to be treated (61 f.). One could also argue that, in view of that immediate treatment to follow, reference to the quaestorship was unnecessary—and note that in the whole of the *Brutus* no other quaestorship is mentioned for such a purpose. At *Tusc.* I, 3 ff. Cicero mentions Cato's attack on Fulvius " for taking poets to his province " and takes care to explain that, *ut scimus*, the poet concerned was Ennius. It is at least odd that he fails to add that (equally *ut scimus*, on Professor Jocelyn's view) Cato had actually " taken the poet from a province to Rome "; the more so as in 5 he proceeds to describe Cato as *studiosum*. In *Cato de sen.* 10 Cato is an old man reminiscing about his youth, and (as I said) quoting his *familiaris* Ennius. He also mentions his quaestorship. I cannot see why he should refrain from saying that (*ut scitis*, if you like) he had brought the poet to Rome in that office. One such omission might be ignored, or explained away. Three seem to me decisive. As for Mr. Suerbaum's question, I think it far more likely that Cicero knew the story and ignored it as gossip, perhaps because he had found it in a bad source.

M. Jocelyn : I do not think that Ennius would have singled out for special prominence even the deeds of Cato's consulship. The *Annals*, it is commonly agreed, were written under the patronage of Fulvius Nobilior.

M. Badian : Cicero in the *Pro Archia* says so and we have no reason to deny it : Cicero and his educated audience knew their Ennius. As I have often said elsewhere : one must not think of Roman social and political life in terms of " parties " and " party " loyalties. Ennius legitimately could, and did, keep out of these *inimicitiae*.

M. Jocelyn : I do not deny that Ennius described Cato's military achievements. Cicero, *Arch.* 22, however, merely lists Cato among other successful generals eulogized in the *Annals*.

M. Skutsch : I wonder whether Professor Badian could explain why Porcius Licinus should know of Ennius' earlier habitat. Would it not be more natural to assume that he knew where he lived later when he had risen in the world?

M. Badian : Yes ; though if there were two locations, I do not see why he should not know of both ; and if he did, he might choose (for his polemical point) to stress the first and (necessarily) less comfortable one. However: I am by no means committed to the view that Ennius did move house, or that he ever lived near the *loca Tutilinae*.

M. Jocelyn : Is it likely that an immigrant with a sophisticated Greek education paid attention to an obscure local deity like the *dea Tutilina*?

M. Badian : If the text says so, it is a fact we have to accept. I admit it is uncertain, but unless we emend it, this does seem to be what it says. Since we know practically nothing about *Tutilina*, except that she was a very old goddess, we cannot even try to guess whether or why Ennius should or should not feel specially interested in her.

M. Skutsch : The multiple transposition of *Ann.* 628, to produce so improbable an hexameter as— ⏑⏑ —*in campo apud emporium pro moene hostium* seems to me unconvincing, although I fully see that the context suggested by Prof. Badian is excellent.

This was followed by a general discussion of this line, and Prof. Badian repeated that his reconstruction was given only exempli gratia.

As to the identification of Galba, I have the feeling that if Cicero had meant the younger Galba he would have said *cum Galba adulescentulo*, provided he knew that it was the younger Galba.

M. Jocelyn : The story of Ennius and Nasica seems to me too neat to be literally true. It is perhaps a floating anecdote which attached itself to Ennius and Nasica. The fact that Cicero reports it is no warranty. In the philosophical dialogues Cicero often used stories which men of education and good manners were given to relating. The truth or falsehood of such stories did not concern him.

M. Badian : On Galba, it seems to me pretty certain (from the form of Cicero's quotation) that Ennius told the story ; also, since Cicero always does mean the great orator by this form of reference, I think he did in this case. I doubt whether he sufficiently checked the chronology to realize that Galba would be *adulescens*. I repeat that, if Cicero thought so, it does not follow that it was true. But I think my point from social conventions supports it (though less so than in the case of Nasica), and there is nothing improbable in Ennius' taking a walk with a young pupil. As for Nasica, I can only say that we know Cicero takes great care over the historical background and does not retail mere gossip (e.g. the Cato story). Also, I cannot imagine why a man like P. Scipio Nasica, of all people, and not one of the great men of the age, should be chosen as the hero of this story, if it were really no more than a floating anecdote.

M. Suerbaum : Ist das anmassende Verhalten des Ennius gegenüber Scipio Nasica in Ciceros Zeit naheliegend? Doch offenbar nicht. Deshalb möchte man erwarten, dass die Anekdote keine Erfindung der ciceronischen Zeit ist, sondern einen historischen Kern hat.

M. Waszink : What must the words *haece locutus* in *Ann.* 234 refer to?

M. Badian : I should think the consul has been addressing his *consilium* and now withdraws to talk to his friend.

M. Skutsch : It seems to me that the phrase *inter pugnas* is fully explained by the deliberate contrast of the second line of the fragment. *Epulae* and *bellum* are used as contrasting spheres of life both by Ennius himself, *Sc.* 314 : *scibam me in mortiferum bellum, non in epulas mittere*, and by Petron. V 22 : *dent epulas et bella.*

M. Suerbaum : Bei der Interpretation von *Ann.* 234-251 sollte man den Gegensatz zwischen dem vorhergehenden Handeln des Servilius (*haece locutus* weist auf eine Ansprache) und dem jetzigen Geschehen, der Aussprache mit einem « guten Gefährten », stärker berücksichtigen. Die Beschreibung des « guten Gefährten » ist zwar allgemein gehalten ; sie hat aber an dieser Stelle nur einen Sinn, wenn ihre Aussagen auch für die jetzige Situation *inter pugnas* passen. Nach diesem methodischen Grundsatz muss Servilius *zuvor* in einer Weise beansprucht worden sein, die eine Parallele zu einem harten Verhandlungstag im Senat bilden kann, d.h. — wenn man *locutus* und *inter pugnas* berücksichtigt — Servilius muss eine Ansprache im Kriegsrat oder (weniger wahrscheinlich) vor den Soldaten gehalten haben. J e t z t aber wendet sich Servilius seinem Vertrauten zu. Wenn die Beschreibung des sonstigen entspannenden Verkehrs mit ihm einen Sinn haben soll, muss sie auch für die jetzige Szene gelten, von der wir nur den Auftakt (234 *uocat*, 251 *hunc inter pugnas Seruilius sic conpellat*) kennen. Das Milieu des sonst gepflegten Umganges ist offensichtlich der Abend, *otium*. Deshalb scheint mir die jetzt anhebende Szene in der Tat am besten für den Abend eines Kampftages zu passen, an dem der Feldherr sich im Gespräch mit seinem Vertrauten entspannt oder auch — was ebenfalls nicht ausgeschlossen ist, wenn man *cui res audacter magnas ... eloqueretur* bedenkt, — offen über den Ernst der augenblicklichen Lage *inter pugnas* (zwischen zwei Kampftagen) ausspricht. Die sich abzeichnende Szene braucht — entsprechend der Schilderung des typischen Verhaltens — mehr Zeit, als ein *inter pugnas* im Sinne von « während einer Kampfpause an einem Schlachttag » einräumen würde.

M. Waszink: Ich kann der Meinung von Herrn Suerbaum nicht beipflichten : der Gebrauch des Verbums *conpellat* lässt mich vermuten, dass es sich in der jetzt gegebenen Situation um eine recht kurze Mitteilung oder auch um eine Bitte handelt.

M. Skutsch: The prominence given by Silius Italicus to Servilius and his glorious death at Cannae (X 222 ff. *Seruilius optima belli, post Paullum belli pars optima, corruit ictu barbarico magnamque cadens leto addidit uno inuidiam Cannis*; cf. VIII 665 ; IX 272 ; XVII 308) makes it in my judgement impossible to imagine that the Servilius mentioned by Gellius should not be the Servilius thus celebrated.

M. Badian: Silius uses material not in Livy and probably read some of the late annalists — perhaps more often than we can prove, since Livy used them himself. The legend of Cn. Servilius' exploits at Cannae is not in Livy, but is in Appian's *Hannibalic War*, hence was in some late annalist. There is no reason to think that Silius is here based on Ennius.

Let me finally repeat that it is not enough to show that Cannae and Cn. Servilius will fit (though even this, I think, is still very much open to question). Those who want to change a book number in a practically perfect source have to show that the change is not only possible, but necessary and indeed inevitable. I do not see that anyone has come anywhere near showing this.

M. Jocelyn : I am not persuaded that Aelius Stilo might have drawn from an oral tradition of the Servilii the idea that in describing the general's companion at *Ann.* 234-51 Ennius gave a portrait of himself. It was an old scholarly game to find in poetic texts concealed references to the poet and his contemporaries (cf. *Schol.* ad Eur. *Orest.* 772 ; 903). The rules of this game were very elastic.

M. Suerbaum : Mit Mr. Jocelyn glaube ich, dass die Bezeichnung der Charakteristik des « guten Gefährten », *Ann.* 234-51, als indirektes Selbstporträt des Ennius eine philologische Interpretation ist, für die Aelius Stilo nicht aus einer hypothetischen Familientradition der Servilier zu schöpfen brauchte. Dass Ennius einem Mitglied der Familie der Servilier erklärt haben sollte, er habe sich in dem « guten Gefährten » selber abbilden und damit den Serviliern ein Kompliment machen wollen, ist eine eigenartige Vorstellung. Dass er ein indirektes Selbstporträt geben wollte, ist möglich, bei dem Umfang der historisch an sich bedeutungslosen Szene sogar wahrscheinlich. Wichtig ist, dass jedenfalls Aelius Stilo von dem Charakter und der sozialen Stellung des Ennius eine Vorstellung hatte, wie er sie in *Ann.* 234-51 konkret dargestellt fand.

M. Badian : One naturally cannot prove, against those who choose not to believe it, that Aelius Stilo had genuine information. I was merely concerned to show one way in which genuine information might have reached him. I cannot agree with Professor Suerbaum's suggestion that it is somehow absurd to think of Ennius' and his patron's discussing his poetry and of this as giving rise to some genuine oral tradition about it. This has happened in the case of many other poets, ancient and modern.

M. Untermann : Bezüglich der Frage, wie Ennius zu seinem Vornamen *Quintus* gekommen sei, möchte ich darauf hinweisen, dass es einigermassen sicher ist, dass der messapische Vorname *dazimas* « decimus » bedeutet. Man darf also annehmen, dass die Messapier, ebenso wie die Römer und Osko-Umbrer, Ordinalzahlen als Namen kannten. Ennius' einheimischer Vorname könnte somit lateinisch *Quintus* entsprochen haben ; leider können wir keinen der erhaltenen messapischen Namen mit Sicherheit mit dem Zahlwort « fünf » verbinden ; man vergleiche allenfalls *penkeos* (Gen. sg.), das mit idg. *penq*^{u}*e* (gr. πέντε) zusammengebracht werden könnte. Er kann also seinen einheimischen Namen durch dessen lateinische Entsprechung ersetzt haben, sobald er in näheren Kontakt mit Römern kam.

M. Suerbaum : Spekulationen, die die verschiedenen Nachrichten über die Aelii, Caelii oder Caecilii auf ein einziges Brüderpaar beziehen, habe ich in meinen *Untersuchungen* (S. 148 ff.) besprochen und abgelehnt. Wenn nur im XVI. Buch der *Annalen* vom Istrier-Krieg und den Heldentaten der Brüder Caelii die Rede war, wie sind dann die beiden Istrier-Erwähnungen im XV. Buch (*Ann.* XV fr. IV und 408) zu erklären?

M. Badian : It was suggested long ago that, since at *Sat.* VI 3, 1 the main manuscripts of Macrobius are evenly divided between XII and XV (three each), the original had obviously become illegible in detail, and emendation to XVI is justified if there is good reason for it. (This accounts for *Ann.* XV 401 sqq.). As for XV fr. IV, Vahlen showed that the siege is probably that of Ambracia, with the Histrians there as mercenaries (compare Florus I 26, 1).

M. Waszink : One remark with regard to this " reconciliation " of *Musae* and *Camenae* : I regard it as certain that Ennius only wants to show or to underline the *identity* of these groups of goddesses. More than once in the *Annals* he mentions a Greek word together with its Latin translation (148 *uentus aer*; 218 *sophia-sapientia*). Let us not forget in this context how extremely important Ennius thought his knowledge of more than one language, which for him was much less self-evident than it is for us; it is in this light that we should see his statement about his *tria corda.*

M. Jocelyn: Like Mr. Badian I find quite incredible the common notion that Ennius displayed in the *Annals* a degree of contempt for the *Camenae*, goddesses who figured prominently in the legend of Numa, the founder of the pontifical college. An idea strikes me which I shall probably dismiss on further reflection, namely that the *dea Tutilina* was one of the *Camenae*. There were legends in which the *Camenae* were individualized, e.g. that of Egeria.

V

JÜRGEN UNTERMANN

Entwürfe zu einer Enniusgrammatik

ENTWÜRFE ZU EINER ENNIUSGRAMMATIK

Grammatik sei hier verstanden als ein Modell, mit dem wir das Gefüge von Elementen und Regeln abzubilden versuchen, das die Äusserungen eines Sprechers gestaltet und verständlich macht. Wir setzen voraus, dass dieses Gefüge systematisch geordnet ist, fordern also auch für die Grammatik eine systematische Ordnung, in der jede Äusserung des Sprechers ihren Platz finden muss. Bei nicht mehr lebenden Sprechern ist die Zahl der Äusserungen begrenzt, sie stellen ein « Corpus » dar, aus dem wir die Grammatik als « Corpus-Grammatik » zu konstruieren haben. In unserem Fall sind es alle Äusserungen, die durch antike Zeugen und durch die moderne Philologie dem römischen Dichter Quintus Ennius zugeschrieben werden.

Eine Grammatik kann zwei Schwerpunkte haben: 1) synchronisch-deskriptiv, — die Beschreibung des belegten Materials und der daraus zu gewinnenden Grammatik, 2) diachronisch-evolutiv, — Beschreibung der gleichen Gegebenheiten als etwas, was zu dem Zweck, in dessen Dienst wir es vorfinden, verändert worden ist.

Wir können also folgende Fragen stellen:

1) Wie spricht (schreibt) Ennius? Wie macht er sich seinen Hörern (Lesern) verständlich? Was vermag er ihnen mitzuteilen?

2) Wie verändert er die ihm verfügbare Sprache, um seine Mitteilungen zu gestalten? In welchem Grade konnte er eine Sprache gebrauchen, die seinen Hörern (Lesern) neu war?

Wir fragen damit nach der Sprache des Ennius und zugleich nach der Leistung, die Ennius vollbracht hat, als er die sprachliche Form seiner Werke schuf. Alles, was auf diese Fragen antwortet oder hoffen lässt, sie einer Antwort näher zu bringen, hat Anspruch darauf, in eine Enniusgrammatik einzugehen [1].

Zunächst einige allgemeine Bemerkungen zur Methode (die im übrigen nicht nur für eine Enniusgrammatik gelten, sondern ebensogut auf andere Autoren angewendet werden könnten) : man wird als Erstes die Texte betrachten, die uns unter Ennius' Namen erhalten sind. Sie s i n d schon Leistung des Dichters, in dem Sinne, in dem jede noch so triviale Äusserung die persönliche Leistung eines Sprechers ist. Daran ändert auch der Umstand nichts, dass dann die Sprache des Ennius weithin übereinstimmt mit dem, was man « Latein des 3./2. Jahrhunderts », « Altlateinische Dichtersprache » oder ähnlich nennen kann. Nur so, also nur wenn wir die Frage nach der Originalität im üblichen Sinne zunächst zurückstellen, erhalten wir eine homogene Basis, die unserer Grammatik einen klaren Status gibt.

Hier sei gleich angemerkt, dass ich mich trotz vieler Bedenken entschlossen habe, bis auf weiteres die Sprache der *Annales*, der Tragödien und der kleinen Opera als e i n Corpus zu betrachten. Das geschiecht einerseits im Vertrauen darauf, dass sich hinter dem Namen Ennius e i n e grosse, wenn auch gewiss vielschichtige Sprecherpersönlichkeit verbirgt, dass man also die epische und die tragische Sprachkunst des Autors als Facetten e i n e r Sprachfähigkeit zu betrachten hat. Andererseits hat es den rein praktischen Grund, dass die knapp tausend Sätze, die unter Ennius' Namen erhalten sind, ohnehin schon eine recht schmale

[1] Mein Versuch ist also anspruchsvoller, aber auch grösseren Gefahren ausgesetzt, als es die Bemühungen um eine Darstellung der Sprache des Ennius waren, die R. Frobenius in seiner *Syntax des Ennius* (Diss. Tübingen 1910) und N. Catone in seiner *Grammatica Enniana* (Firenze 1964) unternommen haben : die genaue Bestandsaufnahme in diesen beiden Büchern bleibt selbstverständlich immer eine unentbehrliche Voraussetzung für alle sprachlichen Arbeiten über Ennius.

Grundlage darstellen ; jede weitere Aufsplitterung des Materials würde die daraus gewonnenen Modelle wirklichkeitsfremder und subjektiver machen.

Zweitens — und das ist eine ganz neue Fragestellung — ist das aufzuspüren, was Ennius aus der Sprache seiner Zeit gemacht hat, um die Verse zu bauen, die wir von ihm besitzen. Die Bekannte in dieser Rechnung sind Ennius' Verse, die grosse Unbekannte ist die Sprache seiner Zeit. Allgemeine Regeln, nach denen man vorgehen könnte, sind bei der Zufälligkeit und Vielfalt der Situationen kaum zu erhoffen. Man wird sich vielmehr bemühen, geeignete Einzelerscheinungen aufzugreifen und von ihnen aus angemessene Kriterien zu entwickeln. Im Folgenden sollen solche Einzelerscheinungen und skizzenhafte Erörterungen über ihre Deutung vorgelegt werden ; sie stellen gleichsam eine lose Folge von Paragraphen einer noch zu schreibenden Enniusgrammatik dar. Meine Andeutungen werden nur Fragen stellen, Probleme zeigen und kaum eines davon lösen können. Aber wenn eine Aufgabe, wie sie hier gestellt ist, überhaupt durchführbar ist, wenn man versuchen darf, eine Enniusgrammatik zu entwerfen, dann müssen schon die ersten Schritte auf dem Weg zu ihr von der Kritik der Spezialisten begleitet werden.

L a u t p r o b l e m e . Eine Beschreibung der Laute, die in der Sprache des Ennius verwendet sind, wird man nicht vom Enniustext aus in Angriff nehmen. Wir dürfen annehmen, dass für Ennius der lateinische Lautbestand seiner Zeit und dessen Reglen galten, und diese Gegebenheiten sind weitaus zuverlässiger aus lateinischen Inschriften und antiquarischen Zeugnissen [1] zu ermitteln : es gibt längst eine

[1] In einer Enniusgrammatik sollte allerdings sorgfältig gesammelt und bewertet werden, welche lautlichen und orthographischen Mitteilungen über das vorklassische Latein die antiken Grammatiker an Ennius und anderen tragischen und epischen Dichtern seiner Zeit exemplifizieren.

gewisse communis opinio — fixiert in den Handbüchern der historischen lateinischen Grammatik — wie der Lautbestand um 200 v. Chr. ausgesehen haben könnte.

Hier war Ennius sicher nicht « originell », und nach einem messapischen *accent* wird man in seinem Schriften vergeblich suchen. Das einzige, was hier zu nennen wäre, ist die Überlieferung (Festus 374 L.), er habe *graeco more* die Doppelschreibung von Konsonanten in die lateinische Orthographie eingeführt, — interessant immerhin im Zusammenhang mit Klangfiguren wie

era errans (*Sc.* 253),
sum summam seruare decet rem (*Ann.* 98),

und besonders,

feroque | *ornatur ferro* (*Ann.* 183 f.),

die graphisch allzu unklar bleiben, wenn man nicht gedehnte Konsonanten durch Doppelschreibung erkennbar macht.

Unsere eigentliche Frage an den Text lautet somit nicht : welchen Lautbestand lässt er erkennen ? sondern : wie verhält sich der überlieferte Text zu dem, was wir auf Grund der Inschriften über das damalige Latein wissen ? Kaum mehr als statistische Aufmerksamkeit sollte man rein orthographischen Fragen widmen : ob *deico* oder *dico*, *uorto* oder *uerto*, *oquolto* oder *occulto* zu schreiben ist, bleibt dem Temperament des Editors überlassen [1], — volle Zeittreue wird man kaum erreichen, solange auch von den Inschriften her noch kein absolut geschlossenes Bild gewonnen ist.

Nicht ganz ohne Belang sind Lautfragen dort, wo es um Alliterationen oder andere Klangfiguren geht ; so ist in *Ann.* 306 *olle* statt *ille* neben *olim* (damals * *ollim* ?) gestützt, das auch später nicht durch * *illim* ersetzt wird ; *ae* alliteriert

[1] Eine sehr angemessene Stellung bezieht Timpanaro, vgl. besonders *SIFC.* 22 (1947), 41 f.

viel häufiger mit *a* als mit *e* [1], eine Aussprache [*ai*] oder [*ae*] gegenüber einer bereits monophthongisierten Aussprache [*ē*] wahrscheinlich macht; die Schreibung *erumna quod mentem eruat* (*Inc.* 49), die Charisius für Ennius bezeugt, wird damit zum Produkt einer etymologischen Spielerei entwertet.

Wo die Inschriften des 3. Jhdt. noch *du* vor Vokal schreiben, hat der Enniustext *b*-, — ausser *Ann.* 559, wo *duellis* dreisilbig gemessen wird, und *Sc.* 396 in *perduellibus*, einem Wort, dessen archaische Schreibung nie aufgegeben wurde. Es ist nicht auszuschliessen, dass Ennius' Zeit noch, wie das *Senatus Consultum de Bacchanalibus*, *du* schrieb und (nicht positionsbildendes) [*dw*-] sprach. Parallel dazu [*sw*], das vor *o* (auch vor *o* aus *e*) zu *s* wird, und im Reflexivpronomen früh zu Doppelformen führt; geschrieben *su* dort, wo es auch im klassischen Latein geschrieben wird (*suauis*, *suadet*); nur *s* erscheint in *sonus*, *soror*, *socrus* usw. und in *sis*, der einsilbigen Variante von *suis* (*Ann.* 149, mit dem eindeutigen Zeugnis des Festus zu dieser Stelle), und *sas* (*Ann.* 101), dessen Deutung als *suas* freilich umstritten ist [2]; ob einsilbiges *suos* (*Ann.* 221) [3], die graphische Modernisierung eines ennianischen *sos*, oder Relikt der Orthographie jener Zeit ist, ist nicht zu entscheiden. Es ist nicht unwahrscheinlich, dass sich *sw*- im Anlaut des Reflexivpronomens dort länger gehalten hat, wo eine Verwechslung mit dem Demonstrativum *so*- möglich war, dass also *se*, *sibi*, *si* (osk. *svai*) früher fest werden konnten, als *sos*, *sis* aus *suos*, *sueis*.

[1] Sicher z.B. *extra aedis exanimata eliminas*, *Sc.* 256 (vgl. weiteres bei Jocelyn, *ad loc.*, S. 378); dagegen beweist das Wortspiel *Ann.* 187 *incedunt* ... *caedunt* eher, dass *e* und *ae* verschieden gesprochen worden sind (trotz *cedre* = *caedere* *CIL* I² 376).

[2] Festus 432,20 f.L.: *sas Verrius putat significare eas, teste Ennio qui dicat: « Virgines ... sas », cum suas magis uideatur significare.*

[3] Der Text (bei Festus) ist entstellt; zu den Verbesserungsversuchen vgl. Valmaggi *ad. loc.* (frgm. nr. 125).

A r c h a i s c h e F l e x i o n s e n d u n g e n. Vom *-d* des Ablativs fehlt bei Ennius jede Spur, selbst nach *re* kann Synaloephe stattfinden (*Sc.* 3). Ennius steht also, im Gegensatz zu den Verfassern des *SC. de Bacchanalibus* und im Gegensatz zu Naevius und seinem *Troiad* (*Bell. Pun.* 5, 2 Strz.), auf der Seite der Modernen in einer Entwicklung, die einen wichtigen Schritt von der vorklassischen zur klassischen lateinischen Grammatik darstellt.

Demgegenüber gibt es vorklassische Nominalendungen, die bei Ennius fest verankert sind: am wichtigsten *-ai* im Gen. sg. der *a*-Stämme, der dadurch vom Dativ mit einsilbigem *-ae* deutlich unterschieden werden kann, z.B.

Lunai portum, est operae, cognoscite, ciues (*Ann.* 16).

Zu Stellen, wo *-ai* eindeutig überliefert ist (z.B. *Ann.* 33) kommen andere, an denen es wiederhergestellt werden muss (*Ann.* 119 u.a.), und so stellt sich im Rahmen einer Enniusgrammatik die Frage, ob überhaupt und unter welchen Bedingungen daneben andere Formen, einsilbiges *-ae* und *-as*, in gleicher Funktion anzunehmen sind. Dass in der damaligen Umgangssprache *-ae* die Norm war, wird man aus Plautus' Sprachgebrauch schliessen, und es ist vielleicht kein Zufall, dass in Ennius' Tragödien nur ein Fall von *-ai* nachweisbar ist (258), dem ein völlig sicherer Beleg für einsilbiges *-ae* (85) gegenübersteht:

ex opibus summis opis egens, Hector, tuae.

Andere Formen auf *-ae*, die man als Genitive auffassen könnte, lassen gleich gut oder besser die Deutung als Dativ oder Lokativ zu: so *o lux Troiae* (*Sc.* 72), wenn man *Sc.* 46 vergleicht,

eum esse exitium Troiae pestem Pergamo,

ebenso *Ann.* 112.

qualem te patriae custodem di genuerunt

und wohl auch *Sc.* 120

liberum quaesendum causa familiae matrem tuae,

wo *familia* dem *sibi* in *Sc.* 129,

uxorem liberorum sibi quaesendum gratia

entspricht.

Es bleiben einige Fälle, in denen man entweder einsilbiges *-ae* anerkennen, oder schon recht gewagte Auswege suchen muss:

contempsit fontes quibus exerugit aquae uis (*Ann.* 379),

kann an einen Vers, der auf *aquai* endete, angelehnt sein, und vom Dichter für den vorliegenden Zweck unter Heranziehung der modernen Genitivform umgestaltet sein. In *Sc.* 252

régis Péliae, pér dolum

könnte Ennius die metrische Struktur der Genitivform griechisch Πελίου vorschweben, die zur Aufnahme der modernen Genitivformen geführt haben könnte. Dass Ennius sie verwendet, ist aus dem oben zitierten Vers *Sc.* 85 ohnehin ersichtlich.

Was Ennius bewog, *-ai* beizubehalten, ist schwer zu sagen. Archaisches Pathos sucht er sonst nicht gerade in den Flexionsendungen (zu einer Ausnahme gleich weiter unten) und die spondeische Schwere dieser Form ist der Eleganz des Hexameters alles andere als zuträglich; eben deshalb ist es auch kaum glaubhaft, dass Ennius aus irgendwelchen metrischen Gründen am Versende *-ai* vorgezogen habe.

Merkwürdig ist schliesslich, dass einmal eine dritte Genitivendung der *a*-Deklination bezeugt ist, *-as* in

dux ipse uias (*Ann.* 441).

Die für das gleiche Buch (XVII) bezeugte Erwähnung einer Grotte

tum caua sub monte late specus intus patebat
(*Ann.* 440)

verführt dazu, an so etwas wie eine νέκυια und damit an das VI. Buch der *Aeneis* zu denken : ist 441 das Fragment eines Gebets, etwa *esto tu dux ipse uias*? Einem solchen Enniusvers könnte dann Vergil, *Aen.* VI 94, nachgebildet sein,

este duces, o, si qua uia est,

gerichtet an die Tauben, die Aeneas zum goldenen Zweig geleiten werden. *Vias* wäre dann als ein « sakraler » Archaismus motiviert. Unklar bleibt freilich, welchen Platz eine solche Episode in den Berichten des XVII. Buches eingenommen hat.

Normierung der Flexion. Zunächst eine methodische Bemerkung : nicht nur aus den Autoren, auch aus den Inschriften lässt sich für das Jahrhundert vor der klassischen Epoche des Latein eine rasch voranschreitende Normierung beobachten [1], die zu dem klassischen System geführt hat, das als optimales Instrument sprachlichen Ausdrucks jahrhundertelang im Gebrauch der Gebildeten bleiben sollte. Eine der treibenden Kräfte für diese Tendenz war wohl der griechische Einfluss, der seit dem Ende des dritten Jahrhunderts in Rom Boden gewann, — die Konfrontation mit der hochstandardisierten attischen Grammatik und mit deren Lehrern und Theoretikern, die Begriffe wie Paradigma, Analogie, Regel, in die lateinische Sprache hineingetragen haben. Es liegt nahe, zu vermuten, dass der griechisch

[1] Neben dem Standardwerk zu diesem Vorgang, J. Marouzeau, *Quelques aspects de la formation du latin littéraire* (Paris 1949) jetzt eine vorzügliche kurze Zusammenfassung : G. Neumann, Sprachnormung im klassischen Latein, *Jahrbuch des Inst. für deutsche Sprache* 1966/67, 88-97.

gebildete Ennius einigen Anteil an diesem Prozess hatte; leider fehlen direkte Nachrichten darüber, abgesehen von jener winzigen Notiz über die Einführung der Doppelschreibung, und so bleibt es unsere Arbeit, in seiner Hinterlassenschaft nach Spuren einer systematisierenden Sprachgestaltung zu suchen.

Welche Kriterien stehen uns zur Verfügung? Ennius' Sprache kommt uns ja eigentlich schon recht normal vor, gemessen einerseits an Livius Andronicus, Naevius und deren Schwerfälligkeit, andererseits an Vergils aufs Höchste geschliffenen Formen. Es war wohl Ennius selbst, der einen sicheren Blick für die sich abzeichnenden Bestrebungen nach einer ausgewogeneren lateinischen Grammatik hatte und ihnen durch seine Werke bleibende Geltung verschaffte. Man darf vielleicht sagen: nicht Ennius ist erstaunlich nah an den von Vergil repräsentierten Normen, sondern Vergil und seine Zeitgenossen hatten erstaunlich wenig hinzuzufügen, um die von Ennius geformte Sprache zu letzter Ausgeglichenheit weiterzuentwickeln. Aber eben dieser Umstand machte es schwer, das bewusste Wirken des Ennius von dem abzuheben, was damals in der lateinischen Welt allgemein im Kommen war. Eine Möglichkeit, sein Wirken zu beobachten, bietet sich wohl kaum dort, wo seine Sprache schon klassische Norm erreicht hat, sondern viel eher an den Stellen, an denen seine Bemühungen ohne Erfolg geblieben, d.h. von der Sprachgemeinschaft und den literarischen Nachfolgern nicht akzeptiert worden sind.

Für Beispiele zurück zu den Flexionsendungen. Bis in die klassische Zeit hinein lassen sich in der lateinischen Sprache Tendenzen beobachten, die sogenannte 3. Deklination auszubauen und zu ordnen: eine dieser Tendenzen strebt eine Vermehrung und Vereinheitlichung der sogenannten «Mischklasse» an, am konsequentesten durchgeführt in den Adjektiven vom Typ *facilis*, *-e*. Aus diesem Bereich finden sich bei Ennius «hochmoderne» Formen, die in der späteren Literatur nicht mehr zugelassen waren. Einige lassen sich unter der Überschrift « Vermehrung der Parisyllaba » zusammenfassen :

NSg. *Laurentis* statt *Laurens* (*Ann.* 34) [1],
cuiatis statt *cuias* (*Ann.* 281),
trabes statt *trabs* (*Ann.* 616, *Sc.* 247),
Iouis neben *Iuppiter* (*Ann.* 63, 258 u.a.),
lacte statt *lac* (*Ann.* 352),
sale statt *sal* (*Ann.* 385, ohne metr. Zwang) ;

und drei Fälle, in denen statt einer synkopierten Nominativform die unsynkopierte wieder eingeführt wird :

mentis statt *mens* (*Var.* 51, 53),
acris (mask.) neben *acer* (*Ann.* 369 [2] und 424),
plebes statt *plebs* (*Sc.* 228) ;

das Gleiche durch Verkürzung der obliquen Kasusformen :

hebem statt *hebetem* (*Ann.* 426),
lapi statt *lapidi* (*Ann.* 398),
praecipe statt *praecipite* (*Ann.* 399),

hier vielleicht in Anlehnung an die Struktur von *praepes* (vgl. Versschluss *praecipe casu* mit *praepete ferro*, *Ann.* 407), indem *cip-* auf *capere* wie *pet-* auf *petere* und nicht auf *caput* bezogen wird ; in 398 hätte statt *ferroque lapique* auch *ferro lapidique* stehen können ; vielleicht hatte Ennius ein Nominativpaar *ferrumque lapisque* vor Augen, aufgrund dessen er die neue Form wagte.

Andere Neubildungen fügen sich in jene Tendenz, die zu klass. lat. *honor* statt *honos*, *arbor* statt * *arbus* geführt hat:

[1] Die Beispielserien bei Priscian 133 f., 337 f. zeigen, dass dieser Beleg als einer unter vielen für eine und dieselbe Tendenz galt.

[2] Von Priscian ausdrücklich als NSg. masc. zitiert ; vgl. aber die Diskussion zum Vortrag von O. Skutsch, oben, S. 32 f.

ueter zum Genitiv *ueteris* (*Ann.* 17),
itiner neben *iter* zu *itineris* (*Sc.* 336),
Hectōrem statt *Hectŏrem* (*Sc.* 82, 101 u.a.),
homonem (*Ann.* 138) neben *hominem* [1].

In der Verbalflexion findet sich als « missglückte » Modernisierung vor allem die Ausbildung der *i* -Konjugation zu einer autonomen vokalischen Klasse, genau parallel den *a* - und *e* - Stämmen, ablesbar an den Futurformen auf *-bo*, an *i* statt *ie* in den *b*-Tempora und in der Verwischung der Grenze zwischen *i*- und *io*-Flexion :

audibo (*Sc.* 315)
expedibo (*Sc.* 148),
stabilibat (*Ann.* 43),
scibam (*Sc.* 314 u.a.),
parire (*Ann.* 10), neben *parere* (*Sc.* 35, 263) [2].

Fraglich ist, ob das bei Varro überlieferte *pinsibant* (*Sc.* 411) zu halten ist [3], und wenn ja, ob es der gleichen Tendenz seine Entstehung verdankt.

A u s b a u p a r a d i g m a t i s c h e r K a t e g o r i e n. Unter etwas anderen Bedingungen steht die Auseinandersetzung des Ennius und seiner Zeitgenossen mit der Frage, welche Endungen und Suffixe als paradigmatisch, d.h. als frei verwendbar, dem Hörer frei zumutbar empfunden werden können. Dass hier bis zur klassischen Zeit starke Einschränkungen durchgeführt wurden, ist vielfältig zu

[1] *homonem* muss nicht, wegen osk. *humuns*, älter sein ; durch germanische Verwandte und durch das sicher schon vor Ennius festgewordene *nemo*, *neminis* ist die ablautende Flexion als ursprünglicher erwiesen. Im Osk. und Lat. kann jeweils selbständig die Analogie zu dem nicht-ablautenden *-n*-Stämmen gewirkt haben.

[2] Vgl. noch *paribis* Pomp. 19 (Ribb.) und *parire* Plaut. *Vid.* 116.

[3] Ernout-Meillet, s.v. und Sommer, *Handbuch der lat. Laut- und Formenlehre*, 523, vermuten Verschreibung aus *pinsebant*.

beobachten — so verschwinden z.B. die berühmten *s*-Modi (*faxo, ausim*) aus der Sprache, so wird die Verwendung des « deiktischen *-c* » beim Pronomen strenger geregelt. Dass bei Ennius solche vorklassischen Formen noch allenthalben begegnen, ist weder verwunderlich noch signifikant. Beachtung verdienen aber alle Anzeichen dafür, dass er eine Endung oder ein Suffix, das später nicht mehr paradigmatisch verfügbar ist, mit einem fest umrissenen Inhalt zu Neuschöpfungen verwendet.

So vielleicht bei den Adverbialendungen, von denen die klassische Zeit nur noch drei zulässt — *-e* bei Adjektiven der 1./2. Deklination, *-er* bei den Stämmen auf *-t* und *-ter* bei allen übrigen. Wie bei allen vorklassischen Autoren hat zunächst in der Sprache des Ennius diese Distribution noch keine Geltung, insbesondere gibt es allenthalben *-ter*-Adverbien zu *o*/*-a* -Adjektiven, — man sollte vielleicht festhalten, welche Fälle bei Ennius tatsächlich begegnen : einmal *prognariter* in

> *ut pro Romano populo prognariter armis*
> *certando prudens animam de corpore mitto*
> (*Ann.* 209 ff.),

in einem Adjektiv mit Partizipialbedeutung, synonym mit dem folgenden *prudens* und vielleicht nicht ohne Einfluss des Adverbs *prudenter* gebildet ; zum andern in den Formen

> *duriter* (*Sc.* 306),
> *saeuiter* (*Sc.* 180, 307),
> *tam toruiter* (*Ann.* 76),
> *tam proteruiter* (*Sc.* 374),

von denen das erste häufiger, die beiden folgenden selten in der altlat. Kunstsprache wiederkehren, und das letzte nur hier belegt ist. Alle vier Adjektiva gehören in den Sinnbereich « böse, grausam, aggressiv », zwei sind durch *tam* gesteigert. Hat Ennius die ursprünglich komparativische (genauer: oppositive) Funktion des Suffixes noch gekannt? Man denke an das berühmte *praeter propter Sc.* 241, das die Paare der voraufgehenden Zeilen *otium - negotium*, *domi - militiae*, *huc - illuc* wiederspiegelt und wohl zu übersetzen ist durch « bald weiter weg, bald näher ». Hat Ennius mit den oben genannten Adjektivadverbien Bedeutungen wie « allzu hart », « härter als angemessen » geben wollen?

Das Adverbialsuffix *-tus* hat seinen Ursprung wohl in der Endung eines dem Ablativ nahestehenden lokalen Herkunftskasus. Man sieht im allgemeinen *intus* « von innen » als den Ausgangspunkt seiner Verbreitung im Lateinischen an. Von hier aus seien inhaltsverwandte Ableitungen von Substantiven wie *penitus*, *funditus* (*Ann.* 128, 620), *medullitus* (*Sat.* 7), *radicitus* usw. geschaffen worden. Es scheint mir aber nicht ganz ausgeschlossen, dass im 3. Jahrhundert die Funktion von *-tus* als einer Art Kasusendung geläufiger war, als es ausschliesslich aufgrund von *intus* möglich gewesen wäre. Ennius wagt jedenfalls mehrere situationsgebundene Ableitungen von substantivisch (kollektiv) gebrauchten Adjektiven,

> *diuinitus* « von göttlicher Seite her » (*Ann.* 11),
> *humanitus* « aus (meiner) menschlichen Art heraus » (*Ann.* 125),
> *publicitus* « aus öffentlichen Mitteln » (*Ann.* 183);

letzteres kehrt öfters wieder, u.a. bei Pomponius (27 Rib.) in ganz ähnlichen Zusammenhang, und weitere Beispiele, wie *germanitus*, *sollemnitus*, finden sich anderswo in der vorklassischen Kunstsprache.

Das Suffix *-tim* ist bei Ennius und seinen Zeitgenossen noch frei verfügbares deverbatives Adverbialsuffix; in klassischer Zeit war es sicher nicht mehr paradigmatisch.

> *qui rem cum Achiuis gesserunt statim* (*Sc.* 17),

wo *statim* « stehenderweise, auf der Stelle bleibend» (nicht

« sofort ») bedeutet ; einen volleren Zusammenhang bietet Plautus, *Amph.* 238 f.,

sed fugam in se tamen nemo conuortitur
nec recedit loco quin statim rem gerat.

Dazu *tractim Annph.* 435, « im Vorbeistreifen », nicht — wie später — « gedehnt », also noch enger an das nomen actionis * *tractis* = *tractio* angelehnt als an das *-to*-Partizip. Daneben findet sich dann auch schon bei Ennius eine Bildung wie *fortunatim*, *Ann.* 108, die nur auf ein Pseudo-Partizip *fortunatus* bezogen werden kann. In Gestalt von *guttatim*, *Sc.* 206, « Tropfen um Tropfen » zu einem nicht existierenden * *guttare* « tropfen » *uisceratim*, *Sc.* 119, « Stück um Stück (des Fleisches) », neben dem es nur ein Verbum *euiscerare* gibt, sind bei Ennius die zahlreichen Gelegenheitsbildungen — meistens Pseudodeverbativa — des vorklassischen Latein vertreten, die durch *-tim* ein die Haupthandlung begleitendes duratives oder iteratives Geschehen zum Ausdruck bringen. Ganz unklar ist *propritim*, das bei Lukrez, II 975, belegt ist und *Ann.* 95 von einigen wiederhergestellt wird.

Auf die grosse Häufigkeit, also wohl paradigmatische Verfügbarkeit der sogenannten Iterativa auf *-(i)-ta-* im vorklassischen Latein ist oft hingewiesen worden, wenn man auch bisher die semantischen und syntaktischen Bedingungen noch nicht präzise genug erfasst hat, unter denen der Sprecher die « iterativen » Formen wählt. Man wird mit mehr Gegebenheiten für « verbale Pluralität » [1] rechnen dürfen, als man es getan hat, und man muss diese Gegebenheiten in einer Grammatik sorgfältig differenzieren : z.B. wiederholte Handlung, weil mehrere Urheber agieren,

[1] Dieser Terminus und die gründliche Behandlung des Phänomens anhand des Lateinischen und des Hethitischen bei W. DRESSLER, Studien zur verbalen Pluralität, *SBer. Österr. Ak. d. Wiss.*, *Phil.-hist. Klasse* 259, 1. (Wien 1968).

multi alii aduentant (*Sc.* 49),
qui ... homines ... aeuum agitabant (*Ann.* 307),

« die vielen, die ihre Lebenszeit (jeder seine Lebenszeit) verbrachten ».

Wiederholte Handlung eines Urhebers, entsprechend der Natur der Handlung :

flammam halitantes (*Sc.* 184),

« bei jedem Atemzug eine Flamme hervorstossend »,

Bacchico insultans modo (*Sc.* 127),

« Tanzsprünge nach bacchischer Weise ausführend »,

capitibus nutantis pinos (*Ann.* 490).

Von Atlas heisst es

qui caelum uersat (*Ann.* 29),

« der ständig den Himmel dreht » ; dagegen wird eine einzelne Umdrehung des Himmelsgewölbes beschrieben durch

uertitur interea caelum (*Ann.* 211).

Oder, weil eine Handlung speziell in dem gegebenen Kontext aus vielen Einzelhandlungen besteht :

Hectorem curru quadriiugo raptarier (*Sc.* 101),
tractatus per aequora campi (*Ann.* 137),
pars ludicre saxa
iactant, inter se licitantur (*Ann.* 73 f.) ;

wohl auch *abnutas*, *Sc.* 352, « durch wiederholte Gesten (die die vorangehenden Worte 349-351 begleiten) ablehnen », dagegen einfach konstatierend *certare abnueo* (*Ann.* 279). Oder, weil die Möglichkeit, eine Handlung immer wieder auszuführen, zur Charakterisierung gehört :

qui sui quaestus causa fictas suscitant sententias (*Sc.* 394),
omnes mortales sese laudarier optant (*Ann.* 560).

Vergleichbar damit

adsectari se omnes cupiunt (*Inc.* 8),

wo die « Pluralität » nicht am Verbum für « begehren », sondern am Objekt des Begehrens, *adsectari*, ausgedrückt ist.

Erst wenn man den Komplex « iterativ » in die Einzelfunktionen zerlegt hat, aus denen er sich zusammensetzt, wird man sagen können, ob und, wenn ja, in welchem Umfang Ennius die *-ta*-Iterativa als paradigmatische Kategorie gekannt und verwendet hat : je präziser sich eine Funktion ermitteln lässt, desto wahrscheinlicher ist sie einer paradigmatisch verfügbaren Formkategorie zuzuordnen.

Hingewiesen sei noch auf die auffallend umfangreiche Gruppe der intransitiv-ingressiven Verben auf *-esco-* mit ihren zuweilen fast passivischen Konstruktionen :

horrescit telis exercitus (*Ann.* 393),

« das Heer wird gesträubt (wird so wie ein Fell mit gesträubten Haaren) durch die Waffen » ;

sanguen exalbescat metu (*Sc.* 26),

« das Blut wird weiss durch Furcht » ;

uites laetificae pampinis pubescere (*Sc.* 152) [1],

« die Weinstöcke werden durch die ausschlagenden Ranken zum Blühen bereit » (wie junge Menschen mit dem Spriessen des Haars mannbar werden), parallel dazu mit passivischer Form im gleichen Zusammenhang

herbis prata conuestirier (*Sc.* 155).

[1] Vgl. aber Jocelyn, 285, der die Verse 151-155 V. nicht für ennianisch hält.

Lexikon und Syntax. Bisher war von den formalen Mitteln der Sprache, den Lauteinheiten und den paradigmatisch geordneten Morphemen die Rede, einem Instrumentarium, das Ennius gewiss nur in ganz beschränktem Umfang verändert und verbessert hat. Interessanter ist es, weiter zu fragen, wie Ennius Wörter (Lexikon) und Satzbau (Syntax) verwendete, um das zu sagen, was er sagen wollte.

Der Aufbau des Lexikon und Ennius' Verhältnis dazu, ist wohl dadurch am besten zu fassen, dass man zunächst herausstellt, was Ennius mit Sicherheit vorgefunden hat, was vor ihm in der lateinischen Sprache üblich war, und von ihm ohne nennenswerte Abweichung vom Üblichen verwendet wurde.

Leicht zu fassen sind technische Begriffe, die Ennius sicher nicht erfunden hat, etwa *caeli templa*, *laeua auis*, *augustum augurium* aus der Auguralpraxis, *foedus ferire*, *bellum indicere*, *forum degrumare* aus der staatsrechtlichen Sphäre, *auster*, *aquilo*, *clauum tenere* aus der Seemannssprache. Schwerer ist es festzustellen, was der alltäglichen Umgangssprache ohne jede Verschiebung entnommen worden ist. Hier kann der Vergleich mit den Inschriften, vor allem aber mit Plautus weiterhelfen, der sicher in höherem Grade als alle anderen Autoren der damaligen Zeit den *sermo quotidianus* in seine Werke hineingenommen hat.

Gewiss wäre aber Ennius' Dichtkunst nicht das, was sie ist, hätte der Dichter sich mit dem vorgegebenen Repertoire an Wörtern und semantischen Möglichkeiten zufriedengegeben. Er hat neue Wörter in die lateinische Sprache eingeführt [1] — gewiss nicht immer nur auf eigene Faust, sondern auch in Kontakt mit den anderen Gebildeten seiner Zeit und insbesondere mit anderen epischen und tragischen

[1] Hor. *Ars poet.* 56 f. *cum lingua Catonis et Enni sermonem patrium ditauerit et noua rerum nomina protulerit*, — auch hier (vgl. S. 213, Anm. 1) gehört zur Enniusgrammatik eine Sammlung aller Wörter, die ihm die antiken Grammatiker und Philologen zugeschriben haben.

Dichtern, — und er hat existierende Wörten mit neuen Inhalten aufzuladen versucht.

Hier ist zuerst die Aufnahme neuer Wörter von aussen, nämlich aus dem Griechischen, zu nennen, die der *poeta doctus* zuweilen ganz ausdrücklich und lehrhaft kommentiert :

> *Musas quas memorant nosce nos esse Camenas* (*Ann.* 2),
> *uento quem perhibent Graium genus aera lingua* (*Ann.* 148),
> *sophiam sapientia quae perhibetur* (*Ann.* 218).

Meist aber tauchen sie einfach als Fremdwörter auf — manches davon ist bei Plautus geläufig, also vielleicht bereits Bestandteil der Umgangssprache, wie *pausam facere*, *machaera*, manches bei Plautus nur um einer besonderen Wirkung willen verwendet, z.B. *tyrannus* (*Ann.* 109, Plt. *Cu.* 208, *Ps.* 703) ; anderes fehlt bei Plautus, z.B. *lychnus*, bei Ennius in der kommentierenden Genitivverbindung *lychnorum lumina* (*Ann.* 323).

Die auch aus der Gegenwart bekannte Erscheinung, dass Fremdwörter in der empfangenden Sprache eine höheren Glanz haben als sie ihn in der gebenden gehabt haben, zeigt sich in der Verwendung von gr. βραδύς « langsam, schwerfällig, träge » in lateinischem Kontext

> *primus senex bradys in regimen bellique peritus* (*fatur* o.ä) (*Ann.* 423),

wo offenbar ein Senator gemeint ist, dessen so eingeleiteter Rede sicher ein Teil der bei Vahlen anschliessend angeordneten Verse mit ihrem gnomisch-moralisierenden Inhalt zuzuweisen ist. *bradys* hat hier nicht den negativen Sinn, den es im Griechischen hat, sondern bedeutet so etwas wie « gewichtig, verantwortungsbewusst » [1]. Das Wort kehrt

[1] Die genaue lateinische Entsprechung dürfte *grauis* sein : vgl. A. Weische, *Studien zur politischen Sprache der römischen Republik* (Münster 1966) 38-52, der diese Qualitätsbezeichnung noch einmal genau untersucht hat.

sonst nirgendwo in der lateinischen Literatur wieder : wahrscheinlich darf seine Verwendung und seine (sozusagen unkorrekte) Überhöhung Ennius persönlich angelastet werden.

Unmittelbar neben den Fremdwörtern sind die Lehnübersetzungen zu nennen wie

dicti studiosus (*Ann.* 216),

zu denen auch Anlehnungen an epische Formeln gehören wie

dia dearum (*Ann.* 22),

etwas lateinischer

sancta dearum (*Ann.* 64) ;

und derartige Anlehnungen leiten über zu der Frage des epischen Vokabulars überhaupt, das Ennius als *alter Homerus* in die lateinische Kunstsprache hineingebracht haben muss.

Ein Ansatzpunkt zu seiner Erfassung scheint mir das Epitheton zu sein, wie er es in den beiden zuletzt genannten Beispielen unmittelbar übernehmen konnte. Es muss dem Dichter bewusst gewesen sein, dass es in der griechischen Poesie eine gewohnheitsmässige zusätzliche Eigenschaftsangabe zu bestimmten Wörtern, die unabhängig war von der jeweiligen Situation des Kontexts, gegeben hat.

Wie gut Ennius das gewusst hat, sieht man daran, dass er bei der Imitation eines griechischen Verses Epitheta einführen kann, die weder im Vorbild gegeben sind, noch den Sinn des Satzes verändern :

Assaraco natus Capys optimus isque pium ex se
Anchisen generat (*Ann.* 30 f.),
'Ασσάρακος δε Κάπυν, ὁ δ' ἄρ' 'Αγχίσην τέκε παῖδα
(*Il.* XX 239).

Vorbilder hierfür wird es innerhalb des Lateinischen kaum in der Kultsprache und noch weniger in der Sprache des Staatswesens gegeben haben ; der einzige Bereich, in dem wir sie erwarten können, ist die Alltagssprache : man denke an heute übliche Wendungen, wie : « mein lieber Mann », « junger Freund », « gute Frau », in denen einige wenige Adjektive in bald euphemistischer, bald ironisch-hyperbolischer Verwendung die Funktion solcher Epitheta ausüben. So scheint es verständlich, dass Ennius in dem Augenblick, in dem er für seine Kunstsprache Epitheta brauchte, zunächst einmal auf einfache Adjektiva zurückgriff : *magnus*, *bonus*, *pulcher*, *ingens*, *summus*, *optimus*, *altus*, sind auffallend häufig mit sehr verschiedenen Substantiven verbunden ; und auch als stärker qualifizierende Epitheta dienen durchweg noch Adjektiva der alltäglichsten Schicht wie *saevus*, *crudelis*, *acer* und andere.

Es ist jedenfalls bemerkenswert, dass vollere Formen daneben verhältnismässig selten sind, etwa zwei Epitheta zu einem Substantiv, wie

somno leni placidoque (*Ann.* 5),
per caerula laetaque prata (*Ann.* 516).

Mit jener Art von Epitheta, die im griechischen Epos eine beherrschende Rolle spielt, dem komponierten Adjektiv, stellt zwar Ennius mancherlei Experimente an, aber es ist später, dem griechischen Vorbild zum Trotz, nie zu grosser Blüte gelangt ; bei Ennius etwa

terrai frugiferai (*Ann.* 489),
Iouis altitonantis (*Ann.* 541),
mortiferum bellum (*Sc.* 314),
uites laetificae (*Sc.* 152),
in altisono caeli clipeo (*Sc.* 215 f.),

und, als Streiflicht auf die Möglichkeiten formaler Variation, über die Ennius verfügte,

nauibus uelivolis (*Ann.* 388),
naues ueliuolas (*Sc.* 79),
ueliuolantibus nauibus (*Sc.* 67 f.),
oratores doctiloqui (*Ann.* 582 f.),
additur orator Cornelius
suauiloquenti ore (*Ann.* 303 f.),

Eine andere Erscheinung, in der sich Ennius' gestaltende Kraft äussert, möchte ich vorsichtig die Verdichtung des semantischen Repertoires nennen. Ich gehe dabei von der Annahme aus, dass ein sogenannter « primitiver », noch nicht für die gehobene Literatur erschlossener Wortschatz verhältnismässig weitmaschig ist, und dem Dichter die Aufgabe und zugleich die Möglichkeit bietet, immer mehr freie Räume in diesem weitmaschigen Netz auszufüllen und damit das semantische Instrumentar immer mehr zu vervollkommen.

Natürlich ergeben sich Möglichkeiten der semantischen Verfeinerung schon aus der Anwendung morphologischer Gegebenheiten, und so wäre hier manches von dem bisher Besprochenen noch einmal anzuführen : z.B. die Adverbien auf *-tus* und *-ter*, oder die Verbalstammbildung, wie sie anlässlich der Verben auf *-ta-* und *-sko-* behandelt wurde. Eine viel grössere, wenn auch schwerer zu fassende Rolle dürfte aber der Ausbau des Wortschatzes selbst gespielt haben. Ein Zugang dazu scheint mir die Untersuchung von Synonympaaren zu sein wie sie Ennius und andere frühe Dichter gern und oft sehr originell verwenden.

Aus der Rechts- und Sakralsprache waren den Römern suppletive Synonym- und Oppositivreihen geläufig, mit denen die lückenlose Erfassung eines Bedeutungsfeldes gesichert werden sollte :

sei deo sei deiuae (*CIL* I² 801),
neque exuehito neque exferto (*CIL* I² 366),

neue coniourase neue comuouise neue conspondise neue conpromesise (*CIL* I² 581),

und auch Ennius wendet solche 'Suppletiva' reichlich an, z.B.

arce et urbe orba sum (*Sc.* 88),
omnia arcet, terram mare caelum (*Ann.* 542),
dictum factumque (*Ann.* 314).

Aber über diesen Ansatzpunkt hinaus geht es wohl, wenn zu dem Alltagswort *pater* das Synonym *genitor* hinzugefügt wird (*Ann.* 113), zu *avis* die Umschreibung *genus altiuolantum* (*Ann.* 80 f.). Die Belege, die in diesem Kapitel zu registrieren sind, reichen von Umschreibungen durch ganze Sätze,

it eques — et plausu caua concutit ungula terram (*Ann.* 439),
audibo — atque auris tibi contra utendas dabo (*Sc.* 315),

über Paraphrasen

qui tum uiuebant homines — atque aeuum agitabant (*Ann.* 307),

in umgekehrter Reihenfolge, d.h. die Paraphrase zuerst

accipe daque fidem — foedusque feri bene firmum (*Ann.* 32),

bis zur Wiederholung einzelner Wörter durch bildhaftere oder in irgend einem anderen Sinne gewähltere Synonyma

exitium Troiae pestem Pergamo (*Sc.* 46),
imperium simul et sola regni (*Ann.* 150),

und, in umgekehrter Reihenfolge,

expedibo atque eloquar (*Sc.* 148),
profiteri et proloqui (*Sc.* 337).

Eine dreigliedrige Reihe findet sich in

Marsa manus Paeligna cohors Vestina uirum vis (*Ann.* 276),

wo erst ein untechnischer Alltagsausdruck, dann der militärische Terminus und dann eine poetische Umschreibung eine und dieselbe Sache bezeichnen.

Manche Unklarheit wird sich freilich daraus ergeben, dass wir über den Status vieler Wörter im damaligen Latein ganz ungenügend unterrichtet sind. So etwa

uiduae et uastae uirgines (*Sc.* 233) :

uidua ist ein paarmal als Adjektiv zu *virgo* anzutreffen [1], *uasta* nur hier : konnte *uastus* damals allgemein im Sinne von « allein » auf Personen bezogen werden ? Oder hat Ennius gewagt, ein nur auf Räumlichkeiten und Landschaften anwendbares Wort auf Menschen zu übertragen ? Servius' Notiz zu dieser Stelle *sane uasto pro desolato ueteres ponebant* gibt gerade auf diese Frage keine Antwort, und das Synonympaar in Catos Lustrationsgebet, *De agr.* 141, *uiduertatem uastitudinem* zeigt wohl, das die synonyme Verwendung als solche nicht Ennius' Erfindung war, lässt aber nicht erkennen, ob die Anwendung auf Menschen — *uirgines* — ungewöhnlich oder allgemein üblich war.

Ein ähnliches Problem zeigt sich in

contra carinantes uerba atque obscena profatus (*Ann.* 563).

Zunächst zur Lesung : *carinare* wird durch *obtrectare* oder *probra obicere* paraphrasiert, war also ungefähr bedeutungsgleich mit *obscena profari* ; dann ist es unwahrscheinlich, dass nach *atque* ein anderes Subjekt gemeint ist als vorher. Man

[1] Vgl. Jocelyn *ad. loc.* (S. 341 f.).

muss also entweder vorher einen Singular herstellen [1] oder nachher einen Plural; letzteres ist zweifellos einfacher — *profati* statt *profatus* und passt besser zu dem Bild einander schmähender Gegner, das durch *contra* nahegelegt wird. Man wird übrigens an *Ann.* 135 erinnert, einen bei Festus fragmentarisch überlieferten Vers, in dem aber Vahlens Ergänzung dem Sinne nach die überzeugenste ist [2]. Kann man 563 darauf folgen lassen? Das ergäbe

haec inter se totum (egere diem tuditan)tes
contra carinantes uerba atque obscena profat(i).

In 563 wird man auf jeden Fall mit einem Paar synonymer Ausdrucksweisen rechnen dürfen — damit zurück zu unserem Hauptthema: wir kennen das Verbum *carinare* nur aus Ennius [3]. Führte er es als ein ungewöhnliches Wort, sei es als einen Archaismus, sei es als ein Dialektwort, in seine Dichtung ein? Fügte er *obscena profat(i)* gleichsam glossierend hinzu? Oder war *carinare* damals geläufig, so dass die zweite Vershälfte keine andere Rolle spielt als *aeuum agitabant* neben *uiuebant* oder *genus altiuolantum* neben *aues* in den oben zitierten Beispielen?

Deutlicher als in diesen nur vage nachzuzeichnenden Verfahren sehen wir den Dichter Ennius dort am Werk, wo er sich wiederum als *poeta doctus* erweisen kann, — beim Spiel mit etymologischen Figuren, in die zweifellos eine Menge Reflexion über die lateinische Sprache eingeflossen

[1] Denkbar wäre etwa *contra carinans das(dat) uerba atque* ... oder *contra carinans is*... mit *is* als Pronomen nach einem Subjektswechsel: « dieser dagegen... ».

[2] Andere Versuche bei VALMAGGI *ad. loc.* (frgm. nr. 120); *tuditantes* ist durch den Kontext bei Festus gesichert.

[3] Hier und *Ann.* 564, dort freilich in der zweiten Silbe kurz gemessen; die antiken Etymologien geben aber so einhellig die Herleitung aus *carina*, dass die Langmessung zumindest als Produkt dieser Lehrmeinung für möglich gehalten werden muss.

ist. So etwa, wenn er mit verspielter Penetranz alle verfügbaren Ableitungen eines Grundworts in einen Vers presst:

qui cupida mente cupiens cupienter cupit (*Sc.* 298),

oder, etwas weniger gewollt,

qui uincit non est uictor nisi uictus fatetur (*Ann.* 493).

Darüber hinaus an vielen Stellen, an denen er etymologische Figuren einzuflechten versteht, die seinen Lesern keine zusätzliche Information über den berichteten Sachverhalt geben sondern nur innersprachliche Zusammenhänge vor Augen führen wollen. Das sind oft ganz vordergründige Verbindungen:

uoce uocabam (*Ann.* 50),
curantes magna cum cura (*Ann.* 77),
hastati spargunt hastas (*Ann.* 284),
statuam statui (*Ann.* 567),
iudicauit inclitum iudicium (*Sc.* 70),
nominatur nomine (*Sc.* 249),

und viele weitere Beispiele dieser Art; das sind aber auch Wendungen, in denen der Dichter über das unmittelbar Evidente hinausgeht, wie

quidue ferat fors (*Ann.* 197),

hinter dem man den Satz einer gelehrten Abhandlung — etwa *fors dicta a ferendo* — zu wittern meint; ähnlich

stipendia pendunt (*Ann.* 265),
ut faceret facinus (*Ann.* 244),
ex ore orationem dedit (*Sc.* 306),
peruince . . . peruicacia (*Sc.* 379),
acrem aciem (*Sc.* 172),

und anderes mehr. Nur einmal wird — im Zusammenhang mit Eigennamen — direkt eine etymologische Deutung gegeben

quae nunc nominatur nomine
Argo quia Argiui in ea delecti uiri
uecti petebant pellem inauratam arietis (*Sc.* 249 ff.).

S y n t a x. Unter dieser Überschrift sollte innerhalb einer Grammatik sichtbar gemacht werden, mit welchen Mitteln und nach welchen Regeln die fertigen Sätze einer Sprache geschaffen werden, — die Summe aller Wechselwirkungen zwischen Semantik und Morphematik. Das ist ein sehr hochgestecktes Ziel, und man wird in einer Enniusgrammatik zunächst die kürzeren Syntagmen für sich untersuchen dürfen, um dann zu grösseren Einheiten und schliesslich zu Sätzen und Texten vorzudringen.

So muss hier ein Kapitel über das Kompositum als ein relativ einfaches Syntagma geschrieben werden. Hierbei decken z.B. die Verbalkomposita einen Bereich, der tief in das Lexikons hineinreicht und damit interessante Probleme der Trennung (bzw. Verflechtung) von Semantik und Syntax mit sich bringt.

Die Komposition ist zweifellos ein Mittel feiner semantischer Differenzierung, wenn z.B. *noscere* in

nosce nos esse Camenas (*Ann.* 2),

« merke, wir sind die Camenen », variiert wird mit dem Kompositum

Lunai portum, est operae, cognoscite, cives (*Ann.* 16),

« nehmt es zur Kenntnis » ; oder, wenn Ennius den gradlinig und schwer gebauten Satz mit dem Simplex *quatit*,

summo sonitu quatit ungula terram (*Ann.* 277),

umbaut zu einem sehr viel kunstvolleren, der stattdessen *concutit* erfordert :

plausu caua concutit ungula terram (*Ann.* 439).

In beiden Fällen ergibt die Verwendung des Präverbs *con-* eine glattere, weniger altmodische Information über den gleichen Sachverhalt bei gleicher syntaktischer Struktur.

Aber unter anderen Bedingungen kann das gleiche Präverb über das Verbum hinaus in den Satz hineinragen und durch dessen Gesamtinhalt motiviert sein.

undique conueniunt uelut imber tela tribuno (*Ann.* 401) :

undique und *con-* vermitteln die gleiche Information, aber der Dativ des Betroffenen, *tribuno*, fände in einem Simplex *ueniunt* allein keinen hinreichenden Rückhalt ; ebenso unentbehrlich für den Satz ist *con-* in

o magna templa caelitum commixta stellis splendidis (*Sc.* 196),

wo keine « Vermischung » gemeint ist, wie in

ceu lacte et purpura mixta (*Ann.* 352),

sondern zweifellos dasselbe, was in den Annalen mehrfach durch *aptus* « versehen mit, behaftet von » wiedergegeben wird, z.B.

caelum prospexit stellis fulgentibus aptum (*Ann.* 159).

Oder, wieder etwas anderes, in

pacem inter sese conciliant conferunt concordiam (*Sc.* 343) ;

conferre kann nicht durch *ferre* ersetzt werden, ohne dass die Kraft der gesamten Aussage gefährdet wird.

Hier stellt sich weiter die Frage, wie Ennius die Wahl zwischen Adverb, Praeverb und Präposition trifft ; in

aestatem autumnus sequitur, post acer hiemps it (*Ann.* 424)

sucht er zweifellos nach einem Synonym zu *sequitur* und findet es in der Verbindung des Adverbs *post* mit dem Verbum *ire*. Ähnlich scheint *ante* an der unsicher überlieferten Stelle

ante tenentes (*Ann.* 227)

zu stehen ; es wird von Ruderern gesagt, die auf den Befehl zum ersten Ruderschlag warten. Hieran schliessen sich zwei Möglichkeiten an, beide bei Ennius belegt, *ante* als Praeverb,

plebes in hoc regni ante stat (*Sc.* 228)

statt *plebes ante regem stat* und *ante* als Praeposition

non enim rumores ponebat ante salutem (*Ann.* 371)

statt *rumores saluti anteponebat.*

Die Präzisierung der Ortsbeziehung wird beim Nomen wiederholt, sobald das Adverb, das sie ausdrücken konnte, als Praeverb mit dem Verbum verschmolzen ist, d.h. als lexikalischer Funktionsträger beim Verb und nicht mehr als syntaktischer Funktionsträger in Satz aufgefasst wird : man vergleiche

quos ubi rex epulo spexit de cotibus celsis (*Ann.* 421),

wo an *de* sowohl die Mitteilung, dass der König herabblickt, als auch die Angabe des Orts, von dem aus er es tut, gebunden ist ; dagegen werden lexikalische Präzisierung des Verbs und Ortsangabe getrennt ausgedrückt in

ibi tum derepente ex alto in altum despexit mare (*Sc.* 310).

Oder, am Beispiel von *ex-* verfolgt : zunächst finden sich Simplicia, wo auch Komposita stehen könnten,

quam tibi ex ore orationem duriter dictis dedit (*Sc.* 306),
tunc timido manat ex omni corpore sudor (*Ann.* 418),
spiritus ex anima calida spumas agit albas (*Ann.* 518) ;

daneben Beispiele, in denen dem Praeverb jeweils das Nomen,

dem dieses Praeverb als Praeposition zuzuordnen wäre, voraufgeht :

> *nam numquam era errans mea domo efferet pedem* (*Sc.* 253),
> *at ego, omnipotens, te exposco* (*Sc.* 177),
> *contempsit fontes quibus exerugit aquae uis* (*Ann.* 379) ;

das Substantiv ebenfalls ohne Praeposition, aber anders gestellt :

> *exterrita somno* (*Ann.* 36).

Schliesslich die letzte Stufe : Wiederholung der Ortsangabe beim Substantiv

> *ibi ex oraclo uoce diuina edidit* (*Sc.* 43),
> *quam mox emittat pictis e faucibus currus* (*Ann.* 86).

An den Verbalkomposita lässt sich ein Prozess in der Sprache des Ennius wiederfinden, der nicht nur in der gehobenen Literatur stattgefunden hat : viele Belege aus Plautus würden dies bestätigen, im klassischen Latein ist die angedeutete Entwicklung in allen Schichten durchgedrungen, und die romanischen Sprachen zeigen, wie vollkommen letzten Endes Praeverbien aus syntaktischen Elementen zu semantischen Morphemen geworden sind.

Anderes in der Syntax des Ennius trägt deutlicher kunstsprachliche Züge, — so etwa das Bemühen, syntaktische und semantische Abhängigkeit in ein Spannungsverhältnis zueinander zu bringen. Es lohnt sich beispielsweise, die Verwendung adnominaler Genitivkonstruktionen daraufhin zu betrachten, ob das abhängige (im Genitiv stehende) oder das regierende Nomen den grösseren Informationswert im gesamten Satz besitzt.

Informationsärmer ist das regierende Wort sicher dann, wenn *genus* als Träger für spezifische Bezeichnungen auftritt :

uento quem perhibent Graium genus aera lingua (*Ann.* 148),

wo gegenüber der einfacheren Aussage,

quem Graeci uocant aerem, qui uentus est (*Var.* 54 f.) [1],

das Subjekt durch ein semantisch überflüssiges *genus* syntaktisch zerlegt wird, in diesem Fall zudem noch unter Beibehaltung der Pluralform des Verbums. Als Träger eines Epithetons finden wir *genus* an zwei Stellen :

seruat genus alte uolantum (*Ann.* 81),

Variation von *auem seruat* im vorrausgehenden Vers, und

lanigerum genus (*Sat.* 66),

dem man, mit semantisch etwas enger determinierten Regens,

balantum pecudes (*Ann.* 186) [2]

zur Seite stellen kann.

In anderen Fällen ist durch das Regens eine Eigenschaft desjenigen Begriffs ausgedrückt, der im Genitivattribut dazu genannt wird :

per teneras caliginis auras (*Ann.* 21),

fast ersetzbar durch *per teneram caliginem,* — *auras* ist nahezu synonym mit *caligo* und mehr Träger des Adjektivs *teneras* als Übermittler einer Information.

ad caeli caerula templa (*Ann.* 49, *ähnlich* 65 f.)

[1] Noch näher : *Grai perhibent aethera*, Pacuv. 90 (Ribb.) ; vgl. auch Valmaggi, *ad. loc.* (frgm. nr. 81).

[2] Die beiden kenning für « Schaf », *laniger* und *balans*, liefern gute Beispiele für eine solche Variationsfreudigkeit : bei Ennius noch *hostiis balantibus*, *Sc.* 39 ; *pecus balans*, Iuv. XIII 233 ; *lanigeros greges*, Verg. *Georg.* III 287 ; *balantum gregem*, *ibid.* I 272 ; *pecus lanigerum* Accius 20 (Rib.).

lässt sich vereinfachen zu *ad caelum caerulum* ; dass der Himmel von den Auguren in *templa* eingeteilt wird, spielt an keiner der beiden Stellen eine Rolle ; *templa* ist also nichts weiter als Umschreibung für *caelum* selbst.

Romani scalis ; summa nituntur opum vi (*Ann.* 161) :

wie der Beginn des Verses zeigt, geht es um die Erstürmung einer Stadtmauer ; *opes* « Mittel » ist somit am besten als Sammelbezeichnung für die Belagerungsapparatur zu verstehen ; *summa opum vi* weicht also nur wenig von einer syntaktisch einfacher gestalteten Aussage *summis opibus* oder *opibus ualidissimis* ab. Noch knapper, aber trotzdem zu einer Genitivverbindung syntaktisch vertieft, sind Aussagen wie

in infera noctis (*Ann.* 89)

statt *in noctem inferam*, « in die weiter unten liegende Nacht »,

per aequora campi (*Ann.* 137)

statt *per campum aequum* oder *planum*. Oder auch :

fructus uerborum aures aucupant (*Sc.* 281)
irarum effunde quadrigas (*Ann.* 513).

Hier werden Eigenschaften — der Wert der Worte und die Gewalt des Zorns — in Metaphern von hoher Bildhaftigkeit dargestellt und, wie in den vorhergenannten Fällen, umgekehrt zum semantischen Abhängigkeitsverhältnis in den Satz eingefügt : sie sind die syntaktischen Träger der Begriffe, zu deren Illustration sie dienen.

Viele weitere Versuche einer solchen weit von der Alltagssprache wegführenden Verflechtung von Satzbau und Inhalt lassen sich in der Verwendung von Verbalabstrakten auffinden : beispielsweise wiederum in Genitivverbindungen, bei denen die für den Kontext wichtige Gegebenheit als Genitivattribut hinter einem sie begleitenden Geschehen zurücktritt :

ager oppletus imbrium fremitu (*Sc.* 384),

wo kaum das Geräusch, wohl aber der Regen die relevante Mitteilung darstellt.

draconis saeui sopiui impetum (*Sc.* 274) :

nicht der Angriff, sondern der Drache wird eingeschläfert ; das Verbalnomen, das syntaktisch als Regens von *draconis* erscheint, malt nur das Bild des Drachens genauer aus : *saeuum draconem*, *impetum facientem*. Konkurrierend mit anderen Ausdrucksweisen :

quo ... auxilio exili aut fuga freta sim (*Sc.* 87),

wo *fuga* und *auxilio* einander syntaktisch, *fuga* und *exili* einander semantisch gleichgestellt sind ; *auxilio*, der Form nach zwar kein Verbalnomen im strengen Sinne, bezeichnet wieder das Geschehen, das mit *exilium* verbunden ist : *quod mihi auxilium ferat*. Zwei verschiedene Konstruktionen mit Verbalnomina kommen zusammen in

concurrunt ueluti uenti, cum spiritus austri
imbricitor aquiloque suo cum flamine contra ... certant
(*Ann.* 443 ff.).

Informationskern (a) sind die Namen der Winde : *auster*, *imbricitor*, *aquilo* und der Umstand, dass diese gegeneinander wetteifern ; aus diesem Kern ableitbar und deshalb weniger belangvoll ist die Mitteilung (b), dass sie dies durch ihr Blasen, *spiritus*, *flamen*, tun. Dieser Inhaltskomplex *auster*, *imbricitor aquiloque contra flando certant* wird dadurch seiner trivialen Sachlichkeit entrückt, dass erst (b) Subjekt und Regens von (a), dann (a) Subjekt und Regens eines praepositionellen Attributs mit dem Inhalt (b) sind, wobei die enge Zuordnung, die im ersten Teil durch das Genitivsyntagma gesichert ist, im zweiten Teil ausdrücklich durch *suo* widergespiegelt wird.

In dem soeben genannten Beispiel ist die auf den ersten Blick adverbiale Gruppe *suo cum flamine* durch den Kontext deutlich als adnominal erwiesen (auf das Verbum *certant* bezogen wäre sie inkompatibel mit dem ersten der drei Subjekte, *spiritus*). Anderswo sind gleichartige Gruppen verwendet, um dem vom Verbum bezeichneten Geschehen mehr Relief zu geben : so in dem oft imitierten

leni fluit agmine flumen (*Ann.* 173),

wo zunächst *ein* Vorgang in Nomen und Verbum als Subjekt und Praedikat, *fluit flumen*, zerdehnt wird, dann noch ein fast synonymes adverbiales Nomen, *agmine*, hinzugefügt wird, das seinerseits das Adjektiv *lenis* als den Träger der einzigen zusätzlichen Information in den Satz einführt.

omne sonabat
arbustum fremitu siluai frondosai (*Ann.* 190 f.) :

die nominale Folge *fremitu siluai frondosai* ist syntaktisch dem verbalen Syntagma *omne sonabat arbustum* als adverbiale Bestimmung untergeordnet, semantisch als fast synonyme Spiegelung zur Seite gestellt. Ähnlich, aber einfacher :

plausu caua concutit ungula terram (*Ann.* 439).

plausus « Stampfen » und *concutere* « stossen, erschüttern » sind fast inhaltsgleich ; syntaktisch einander untergeordnet spielen die beiden Wörter semantisch die Rolle von suppletiven Synonyma, wie *pugnant proeliant*, *Sc.* 5, *differt dissupat*, *Sc.* 118, und viele andere.

Ein recht kunstvolles Gebäude finden wir in

tinnit hastilibus umbo
aerato sonitu galeae (*scil. tinniunt* - *Ann.* 402 f.) ;

Das semantisch schon verhältnismässig eng begrenzte Verbum *tinnire* « klirren (metallisch) klingen» steht zunächst allein als Praedikat zu *umbo*, und wird dann, durch *aerato sonitu* weiter eingeengt, auf *galeae* ausgedehnt. *sonitu* bringt keine neue Information — es ist weiter gespannt als *tinnere* —, sondern dient nur als Träger von *aeratus* ; und dieses nimmt, in kühner Anwendung als Adjektiv zu einem Wort mit der Bedeutung « Klang », eine Eigenschaft des Subjekts, *galeae*, in das Bild hinein.

Die verfügbare Zeit verbietet es, mehr als einige wenige solcher Hinweise zu geben, die — immer wieder unter anderen Bedingungen — Ennius' kunstsprachliche Technik und deren Verhältnis zu den Möglichkeiten des damaligen Latein sichtbar machen. Als Facit wäre nun eine zusammenfassende Würdigung dessen am Platze, wie weit es denn Ennius in seinem Bemühen um eine lateinische Literatursprache gebracht hat. Statt einer solchen Würdigung, die bei dem gegenwärtigen Stand meiner Einsichten doch nur in hohlen Worten bestehen könnte, will ich zum Abschluss zwei Sätze anführen, in denen mir das, was in dem bisher Gesagten als Ennius' Leistung sich abzuzeichnen begann, besonders vollkommen zur Verwirklichung gelangt zu sein scheint.

> *clamor ad caelum uoluendus per aethera uagit*
> (*Ann.* 531) :

das kongruierende Grundgerüst *clamor* ... *uoluendus* ... *uagit* schliesst den Satz zusammen, symmetrisch unterbrochen durch zwei praepositionale Syntagmen. Diese beiden nennen zuerst das Ziel, *ad caelum*, dann den zu diesem Ziel sich erstreckenden Raum *per aethera*. Die Bewegung auf das Ziel hin wird getragen durch das Futurpartizipium *uoluendus* « das sich wälzen wird ». Was diese Bewegung durch den Raum trägt — unabhängig davon, ob das Ziel erreicht wird oder nicht — erfahren wir aus dem Hauptverb, *uagit* « brüllt ». Dieses ist seinerseits semantisch aus dem Subjekt *clamor* « Gebrüll » abgespalten, Subjekt und Praedikat beherrschen eine Szene, die vor den Augen des Zuschauers sich ins Unermessliche, *ad caelum per aethera*, auszuweiten im Begriff ist.

Das Verbum, das diese Bewegung eines akustischen Geschehens zum Ausdruck bringt, *uoluendus*, ergänzt zudem das Gemälde durch eine optische Vision : *uoluendus* erzwingt die Vorstellung von der Staubwolke, die sich über dem Schlachtfeld auftürmt und ahnen lässt, was, von ihr verhüllt, auf der Erde geschieht.

missaque per pectus dum transit striderat hasta (*Ann.* 364) :

wie das Plusquamperfekt erkennen lässt, vervollständigt dieser Vers den voraufgegangenen Bericht vom Fall eines Kriegers. Trotz der auf den ersten Blick fast primitiv wirkenden Reihung sind die Satzglieder kunstvoll gebündelt : durch *missaque* ist Ursprung und Bewegung des Geschehens an den Anfang gestellt, die semantische Indifferenz von *missa* wird sogleich durch *per pectus* eingeengt und aktualisiert ; dieses wieder ist zugleich als Ortsangabe verflochten mit *dum transit*, das seinerseits sofort weiterführt zu *striderat*, dem es als Zeit- und Umstandsbezeichnung untergeordnet ist. *striderat* hat für die Beschreibung des grausamen Geschehens einen minimalen Wert als Information, aber grosse Bedeutung für die Stimmung, die der Dichter erzeugen will. Das nun endlich folgende, für die Information und für den Satzbau unentbehrliche Subjekt *hasta* lässt die Spannung verebben. Einer lückenlosen syntaktischen Verkettung entspricht ein Spannungsbogen von ungewöhnlicher Anschaulichkeit.

Annalistisches Aufzählen ist in derartigen Versen ersetzt durch geschlossene, in sich bewegte Bilder ; episches Voranschreiten ist umgewandelt in Szenen von zwingender Eindringlichkeit, die fast das grosse Geschehen der Geschichte vergessen lassen und doch das, was geschieht, besser als alle Ereignisberichte dem Hörer nahezubringen vermögen. Hier ist, wenn auch erst nur in wenigen Versen, Vergils Meisterschaft syntaktischer und semantischer Architektur erreicht.

DISCUSSION

Remarque : les circonstances n'ont pas permis à M. Untermann de présenter oralement l'ensemble de son exposé. La discussion ne porte donc que sur une partie de celui-ci.

M. Badian : Do you think the Ennius who wanted to write *erumna* for *aerumna* because it came from *eruo* was the poet or the later Ennius who is reported by Suetonius as having perhaps written grammatical works and a work on augural science? If our Ennius, where did he speak about this?

M. Untermann : Die etymologische Motivierung der Schreibung *e-* statt *ae-* scheint mir auf jeden Fall spät zu sein. Mir kommt es nur darauf an, zu sagen, dass die Schreibung *e-* dem Dichter Ennius zugewiesen werden kann, da wir gleichzeitig auch schon in Inschriften *e* statt *ae* finden.

M. Waszink : In my opinion, Ennius may really have produced this etymology himself, and may have done so in his *Satura* (cf. the hidden etymology in the famous verse *Simia quam similis*, *Sat.* 69). Lucilius also discussed several semantic and etymological questions in his *Saturae*. And when Accius chose the form of poetry for his works on language and literature, it is *this* tradition which he may have wanted to continue.

M. Badian : We should add *Ann.* 308 to your short list of first declension genitives in *-ae* : *Suadaeque medulla* certainly cannot be changed to *-ai* and I do not really believe in the *-as* alternative (which you will no doubt discuss).

M. Untermann : Auch ich weiss keine gute Lesung von *Ann.* 308 und habe deshalb die Stelle nicht in meine Statistik einbezogen. Ich gebe gern zu, dass nicht viel Aussicht besteht, hier *-ai* herzustellen.

M. Skutsch : I am greatly impressed with Prof. Untermann's interpretation of *dux ipse uias* as belonging to a " sacred " context, comparable to Virgil's *este duces, o, si qua uia est.* This really seems to solve a great difficulty. A νέκυια, however, in the seventies of the second century seems somewhat improbable.

M. Suerbaum : Die *-ai*-Formen müssen für die archaische Dichtung und speziell Ennius charakteristisch gewesen sein ; das zeigt Martial XI 90, 5. — Eine grundsätzliche Frage : Ist es gerechtfertigt, in einer deskriptiven Behandlung des Stoffes bei der Besprechung des Problems, ob neben *-ai* noch andere Genetivendungen « anzunehmen » sind, sinngemäss zu sagen « ich möchte dies und das lieber nicht akzeptieren ? » Das scheint doch eine normative Aussage zu sein.

M. Untermann : Man versteht mich falsch, wenn man « systematisierend » mit « normativ » gleichsetzt (letzteres im Sinne der Schulgrammatik verstanden) : selbstverständlich akzeptiere ich jede Form im Enniuscorpus, aber zugleich suche ich für sie einen Platz in einem geordneten System ; und wenn dieser Platz nicht zu finden ist, wird man suchen müssen, wo der Fehler liegt, — im System oder bei den Belegen.

M. Skutsch : I believe that a large number of *-ai* endings are found at the end of the line and that, if this is taken into account, the disproportion between *-ai* and *-ae* disappears.

M. Untermann : Solange für *Lunai* am Versanfang (*Ann.* 16) keine Motivierung gefunden ist, möchte ich dem Vorschlag von Herrn Skutsch noch nicht folgen.

M. Jocelyn : I am suspicious of attempts either to « normalise » or to « systematize » Ennius' usage too much. The categories of modern linguistics derive from spoken languages, not artificial poetic languages like that which Ennius constructed for his

Annals. The language of Homer's *Iliad*, which obviously much affected Ennius' construct, must have seemed much more disorderly and full of inexplicable irregularity to ancient students than it does to modern linguists.

Ennius was surely aware of the Greek grammarians' theories about language in general and the language of Homer in particular (whether he or another " Ennius " was the professional *grammaticus* referred to by Suetonius and the *Anecd. Paris.* is another question). What theory he followed, if any, in constructing a Latin epic language is, however, quite unclear. Some later Romans certainly felt that his sense of what could be generated by ordinary Latin speech and of what could not was faulty. Is it not sufficient to say that Ennius observed great variety in phonology, morphology etc. in the *Iliad* as in other Greek poems of the higher styles and imitated this variety in the Latin of his *Annals*? The language of Roman comedy and tragedy already contained a degree of morphological oscillation which must have been absent from spoken Latin. Must one expect to find a conscious literary motive behind every particular variation by Ennius from the " norm " or the " system "?

M. Badian: Ennius was interested in linguistic theory: certainly the duplication of consonants, possibly (if it was he) the spelling and etymology of *erumna*; cf. also *Varia* 59 (*Proserpina*). Hence, when he did opt for variety, we are entitled (as Professor Untermann says) to look for the reasons he may have had, in each case, for making the choice he did.

M. Skutsch: Metrical categories must always be kept in mind in linguistic questions. When Ennius uses *praecipe casu* at the end of the line in *Ann.* 399, it seems clear to me that he has created this form for the sake of the metre, on the analogy of *principe*.

M. Badian: Would you say that Ennius shows signs of the kind of " analogist " (as opposed to " anomalist ") theory that we find in the first century? I am thinking of such forms as *ueter* (for *uetus*), *Anionem* (for *Anienem*); and others that you have mentioned could be explained in that way.

M. Untermann: Gewiss können Änderungen wie *praecipite* zu *praecipe* unter dem Zwang des Metrums vorgenommen worden sein; aber die Grenzen, innerhalb derer sich der Dichter solche Änderungen leisten kann, ohne unverständlich zu werden, können und müssen doch in einer Grammatik ermittelt und beschrieben werden. *praecipe*, *lapi*, *itiner* und dergleichen war möglich, weil der Hörer oder Leser die darin vorliegende Vereinheitlichung des Paradigmas leicht nachvollziehen konnte.

Zur Frage von Herrn Badian: auch ich bin der Überzeugung, dass Ennius seine Eingriffe in die lateinische Sprache nicht ohne Zusammenhang mit grammatischen Theorien seiner Zeit durchgeführt hat, und es wäre sicher wertvoll, wenn ein Spezialist hierüber genauere Untersuchungen anstellen würde.

M. Suerbaum: Dem Argumentieren mit metrischen Zwängen zur Erklärung bestimmter Wortformen stehe ich weitgehend skeptisch gegenüber. Ennius war weniger als etwa Homer, hinter dem eine rhapsodische Tradition steht, auf die Verwendung bestimmter Wörter festgelegt. Er hätte ja statt eines metrisch unbequemen Wortes, insbesondere eines Adjektivs, ohne weiteres ein Synonym wählen können. Für die Verwendung von *ueter* statt *uetus* versagt auf jeden Fall eine metrische Erklärung.

M. Skutsch: I did not mean to imply that metrical categories are the only ones capable of producing new forms.

M. Waszink: Ich bin fest überzeugt, dass Formen wie *lapi* statt *lapide* und *praecipe* statt *praecipite*, die an sich vom Lateinischen aus unmöglich sind, durch den Einfluss, oder besser als direkte Imitation von homerischen Dublettformen zu erklären sind. Ich denke an Formen wie πρόμος neben πρόμαχος, wo Ennius einfach Auslassung einer Silbe gesehen haben muss. Er folgt ja auch Homer, wenn er *do* statt *domum* schreibt (*Ann.* 576).

M. Untermann : Ich bin ohne Weiteres geneigt, damit zu rechnen, dass Ennius Begriff und Ausmass grammatischer Lizenzen aus seinem Umgang mit griechischer Dichtung gewonnen hat ; ich wiederhole aber noch einmal, dass er seine Änderungen doch im Rahmen bestimmter, vom Hörer nachvollziehbarer grammatischer Grenzen halten musste ; und die Beschreibung dieser Grenzen ist Gegenstand einer Enniusgrammatik.

M. Wülfing : Man muss berücksichtigen, dass selbst die äusserst bewusste Epensprache eines Kallimachos Varianten beibehält (οὔνομα-ὄνομα, ἕταιρος-ἕταρος) und zwar ungefähr in derselben Relation zueinander, wie sie in den homerischen Epen galt. Das machte « episch ». Also könnte ein Teil ennianischer Doppelformen ebenso zu erklären sein.

M. Skutsch : Ennius has *ted* once in *Sc.* 177, and *med* once in the *Epicharmus*, 45. I have tried to introduce *ted* by conjecture in *Ann.* 52, but the matter is somewhat uncertain, and Ennius may have admitted these forms in certain types of composition and excluded them from others.

M. Suerbaum : Über die Epitheta bei Homer und Vergil und auch bei Ennius hat eindringlich F. W. Worstbrock, *Elemente einer Poetik der Aeneis*, Münster 1963, 168 ff. gehandelt. Besonderes Interesse verdient die Entwicklung im Hinblick auf den Gebrauch des sog. *epitheton constans.* Bei Vergil zeichnet sich die Tendenz ab, die Epitheta bewusster, situationsgerechter zu verwenden, auch wenn z.B. ein achtmaliges *infelix Dido* dagegen zu sprechen scheint. (Solche *epitheta constantia* betonen den Grundzug des Wesens, hier die « tragische Existenz ».) Eine parallele Erscheinung zeigt sich in der nachhomerischen Gleichnistechnik. Während es in homerischen Gleichnissen die berühmten « überschiessenden Züge » gibt, streben die späteren Dichter — u.a. auch Ennius — danach, eine möglichst enge Parallelität des Gleichnisses zur zu illustrierenden Handlung herzustellen.

M. Wülfing: Das *epitheton constans* ist im Grunde nach *Ilias* und *Odyssee* tot. Die Bedingungen der mündlichen Rhapsodendichtung liegen schon bei Hesiod nicht mehr vor. Von da ab muss man stets mit reflektiertem Gebrauch der Epitheta rechnen, wenn auch manches Epitheton mitgeschleppt wurde, um zu « homerisieren », d.h. um in der Epensprache zu bleiben.

M. Skutsch: Further inquiries into the frequency and the order of attributes are required. *Ann.* 514-518 seems to me extremely clumsy, compared to later poetry.

VI

PETER WÜLFING-VON MARTITZ

Ennius als hellenistischer Dichter

ENNIUS
ALS HELLENISTISCHER DICHTER

Entretiens mehrerer Ennius-Fachleute über das Thema Ennius haben doch wohl den Sinn, dass ein jeder die übrigen von seinem Standpunkt aus befragt. Man rechnet darauf, dass durch die Vielfalt der Fragestellungen neue Perspektiven, neue Möglichkeiten der Beantwortung erschlossen werden. Jede Frage geschieht von einem Standpunkt aus, setzt Dinge — wenigstens vorübergehend — als bekannt voraus und stellt andere als fragwürdig hin. So ist uns hier der Ennius-Text in seinem fragmentarischen Zustand fragwürdig gewesen, die Einzelstellen, die grösseren Zusammenhänge, ihre Einordnung in das Gesamtwerk, von dem wir uns mosaikartig ein Bild zusammensetzen. Jedesmal werden Dinge als feststehend vorausgesetzt, die es eigentlich nicht sind. Es wird z.B. vorausgesetzt, dass unsere Quelle stimmt, dass sie den ennianischen Wortlaut bietet, oder dass er aus dem Gegebenen herstellbar sei, dass wir also die philologischen Methoden richtig angewendet haben. Wir schreiten dann weiter, setzen voraus, dass der Wortlaut richtig hergestellt sei und erschliessen daraus den Zusammenhang, in den er gehörte. Wieder ändern wir den Standpunkt und etablieren ein anderes Fragment mit Hilfe gerade des eben erst erschlossenen Zusammenhangs, diesen als gesichert voraussetzend. Dies ist eine schwierige Prozedur, — aber die einzige, die wir anwenden können. Generationen von Gelehrten haben an ihr bereits gewirkt. Ständiges Wechseln des Standpunkts, von dem aus das Material betrachtet wird, führt zu ständiger Überprüfung vorher ermittelter Ergebnisse, bis ein Gewebe widerspruchsfreier — oder wenigstens widerspruchsarmer — Beziehungen entsteht, das wir dann als gültiges Ergebnis der Forschung ansehen können.

Der Sinn dieser Zusammenkunft liegt also in der Erweiterung der Zahl der Standorte und in der Erweiterung der Zahl von Antworten, die auf neue Fragestellungen gegeben werden können.

Die Lückenhaftigkeit der Überlieferung — ich spreche im Folgenden von Ennius' *Annalen* allein — die oft verzweifelte Schwierigkeit, das Überlieferte zu verstehen, kann unter e i n e m Aspekt vergessen werden: wenn wir nach der Tradition fragen, in welcher Ennius' Epos stand und wenn wir bemerken, dass innerhalb jenes Zweiges der hellenistischen Dichtung, den wir als historisches Epos bezeichnen, Ennius der bestbezeugte Autor weit und breit ist. Von dem Wissen über seine *Annalen* aus würde man gerne rekonstruieren, wie das hellenistische historische Epos beschaffen war. Man wird also wenigstens für einige Augenblicke die Textprobleme so behandeln, als seien sie geklärt und von dem aus, was wir von diesem Autor der frühesten Periode lateinischer Literatur besitzen, auf eine Entwicklung zurückschliessen, die wir aus eigenen Zeugnissen kaum kennen. — Allerdings wird dann sehr schnell die Ennius-Problematik wieder auf uns zurückfallen; denn nur aus intimer Kenntnis des Ennius-Textes werden gültige Antworten zu gewinnen sein. Deshalb halte ich es für sinnvoll, Fragen an diesen Kreis von Kennern zu richten, wozu ich die Berechtigung aus der Hoffnung herleite, dass von meiner Fragestellung her ein Zuwachs an Klarheit auch über Ennius' Eigenart und persönliche Leistung eintreten wird.

Ennius als Dichter der *Annalen* ist Epiker. Er ist ein hellenistischer Epiker. Die Frage ist, was das eigentlich bedeutet. Es bedeutet doch nicht nur jene Selbstverständlichkeit, dass Ennius in der Zeit des Hellenismus wirkte, der Epoche zwischen Alexander und Augustus, nicht nur jene Grundvoraussetzung aller römischen Literatur, dass diese von der griechischen her entsteht und sich stets auf griechische Vorbilder bezieht, sich als griechische Literatur im Gewand der lateinischen Sprache begreift. Sondern es impliziert eine spezifische Einstellung zum eigenen Tun, welche die Römer von Anfang an von den Griechen ihrer Zeit übernommen haben. In Griechenland beginnt mit dem Hellenismus das Bewusstsein vorzuherrschen, dass die meisten Dinge vorher schon gesagt worden sind, dass bestimmte Literaturgattungen erschöpft seien, wenigstens in der Form, wie sie bis dahin gepflegt wurden. Hierzu gehörte an erster Stelle bekanntlich das Grossepos homerischer Prägung. Es beginnt ein bewusstes Experimentieren im Formalen wie im Inhaltlichen, mit dem Ziel, den Konsequenzen zu entgehen, welche sich aus der Einsicht in die Krise der Dichtung ergeben hatten. Ein hoher Grad von Bewusstheit ist charakteristisch. Der Hellenismus leitet eine Epoche programmatischer Selbstaussagen und mancher Polemik in der Dichtung ein.

Dieses Erbe treten die Römer an. Bei ihnen fiel schon immer die Bewusstheit vom eigenen Tun auf, die für ihre gesamte Literatur, und sogleich von den Anfängen an gilt. Ennius ist dafür ein hervorstechender Zeuge.

Für die beschriebene Geisteshaltung des hellenistischen Dichters ist Kallimachos geradezu ein Inbegriff geworden, mit seinem Programm, in seinen Werken und in der Wirkung auf seinen Kreis. Funde der letzten Jahrzehnte liefern uns heute ein sehr verdeutlichtes Bild seiner programmatischen Ausführungen. Die vielen Unklarheiten, welche bleiben, lasse ich wieder dahingestellt. Kallimachos hat zweifellos einen starken Einfluss auf seine Zeit ausgeübt. Zwei Umstände haben sogar das Entstehen der Ansicht begünstigt, es sei, nachdem Kallimachos sein Programm verkündet habe, nur noch in dessen Sinn gedichtet worden : der Umstand, dass uns die griechische Literatur der drei Jahrhunderte nach Aristoteles überhaupt schlecht überliefert ist, zumal die epische Dichtung ; und der Umstand, dass das kallimacheische Programm unter den besonderen Bedingungen der frühaugusteischen Zeit auf römische Dichter einen kaum zu überschätzenden Einfluss hatte. Von dem Verlorenen war man geneigt zu glauben, es habe sein Schicksal verdient. Dieser Ansicht ist Konrat Ziegler in seiner Abhandlung von 1934 über das hellenistische Epos leidenschaftlich entgegengetreten. Er sprach von einem 'vergessenen Kapitel griechischer Dichtung' [1]. Einen raschen Erfolg hatte Zieglers Buch nicht, aber doch einen gesicherten ; es fällt uns heute weniger schwer, eine breite Produktion umfangreicher Epen während der hellenistischen Epoche in Rechnung zu stellen. Jedoch gibt uns die fehlende oder ganz trümmerhafte Bezeugung dieser Epik viele kaum lösbare Aufgaben auf.

Da ist es gerade Ennius, dessen *Annalen* immerhin in Umrissen, dessen epischer Stil relativ gut kenntlich sind. Um seine Stellung innerhalb der hellenistischen Traditionen zu bestimmen, bedarf es einer Reihe von Überlegungen, die das Problem einkreisen.

Man wird zunächst allgemein fragen : was ist Ennius' eigene Leistung ? Wie weit wirken Traditionen auf ihn ? Es ist z.B. undenkbar, dass seine römischen Vorgänger, hier besonders Naevius, ohne Wirkung geblieben wären. Gegen Naevius, wie gegen einige andere, richtet sich eine Polemik zu Beginn des 7. *Annalen*buchs, v. 213 ff., — aber gegen niemand polemisiert man rückhaltloser als gegen denjenigen, dem man etwas verdankt. Dieser Überlegung steht wiederum das Selbstzeugnis gegenüber, dass Ennius sich als wiedergeborenen Homer sah.

Ich versuche, aus den sich überschneidenden Gedanken eine geordnete Folge von Fragen an die Ennius-Überlieferung heranzutragen :

Wenn Ennius ausdrücklich an Homer anknüpft, so müssen wir zunächst ganz einfach fragen : wie weit geht

[1] Der 2. Auflage, 1966, hat K. ZIEGLER einen Anhang « Ennius als hellenistischer Dichter» hinzugefügt. An das dort Begonnene knüpfen die folgenden Überlegungen an.

Homerisches bei Ennius? Sodann aber kompliziert sich das Problem. Wir müssen zu interpretieren versuchen, was Ennius damit ausdrücken wollte, dass er seine *Annales* als Gedicht eines wiedergeborenen Homer hinstellte.

Allein die Tatsache, dass Ennius ein solches Bekenntnis formuliert, trennt ihn von homerischer Epik, macht ihn zum hellenistischen Dichter, der Rechenschaft über seine Poetik ablegt. Ein berühmtes Beispiel eines solchen Bekenntnisses liegt uns bei Kallimachos vor. — Ist Ennius Kallimacheer? Wie weit geht Alexandrinisches bei Ennius? [1]

Wir können erwarten, auf nicht wenige Elemente zu treffen, die weder dem einen noch dem anderen Einfluss vernünftigerweise zugerechnet werden können. Kommt für diese auch römisch-italischer Einfluss nicht in Frage, ebensowenig das persönliche Wollen und Können des Dichters, so können wir eine hellenistische, ausseralexandrinische Tradition ansetzen, eine hellenistische Epik, die Geschichte bis zur Zeitgeschichte als Gegenstand wählte. — Hellenistisches historisches Epos bei Ennius?

Wir wissen von dem Vorhandensein dieser Gattung, können uns aber von ihrer Eigenart nur eine sehr ungefähre Vorstellung machen. Aus Ennius dafür Zeugnisse hinzugewinnen zu wollen, könnte auf eine *petitio principii* hinauslaufen. Es wird also genau darauf zu achten sein, dass bei

[1] Schon von jeher unterscheidet man aus sachlichen Gründen eine frühhellenistische Periode (3. und 2. Jh. v. Chr.) von späterem und spätem Hellenismus. Die einseitig zeitbezogene Unterscheidung lässt jedoch unberücksichtigt, dass verschiedene literarische Tendenzen nebeneinander und gleichzeitig wirksam waren. Deshalb benutze ich (was dem gegenwärtigen Sprachgebrauch nicht widerstreitet) 'hellenistisch' für die nachklassische griechische Literatur im ganzen; für die besondere Entwicklung der Schule um Kallimachos wähle ich die Bezeichung 'alexandrinisch' und für deren spezielle Ausprägung im 1. Jh. v. Chr. 'neoterisch'. Die drei literarhistorischen Tendenzen mag man zeitlich noch in 'früh-' und 'spät-' unterteilen; wichtig ist jedoch hier, dass die Bezeichnung 'hellenistisch' zunächst frei bleibt von Festlegungen auf ein bestimmtes literarisches Programm.

dem angewendeten Subtraktionsverfahren keine Instanz übergangen wird.

In dem Fall, dass wir sowohl homerischen als auch alexandrinischen Einfluss fernzuhalten berechtigt sind, werden wir erst römischen Einfluss und ennianische Neuschöpfung ausschliessen müssen, ehe wir eine Tradition hellenistischer historischer Epik ansetzen dürfen. Darüberhinaus muss auf sie eine innere Wahrscheinlichkeit hindeuten.

Solche Überlegungen möchte ich an einigen Beispielen demonstrieren, an Beispielen verschiedenster Art, von der Hexametermetrik bis zur Gedankenwelt des Ennius reichend. Die Frage, wohin ein jedes dieser Elemente einzuordnen sei, wird jeweils verschieden zu beantworten sein. Das Augenmerk richte ich natürlich besonders darauf, ob für die ausseralexandrinische, hellenistische Epik Hinweise 'übrigbleiben'.

1. Ennius' folgenreichste Entscheidung war die Einführung des Hexameters in die lateinische Literatur. Was er einführte, war der Hexameter der homerischen Epen, jedenfalls eher dieser als der feingliedrige, in vieler Hinsicht strenger geregelte Hexameter des Kallimachos. Und doch unterscheidet sich seine Metrik von der homerischen. Sein Vers ist reicher an Spondeen. Als Mittelzäsur überwiegt ganz entscheidend die männliche Penthemimeres. Die sog. Hermann'sche Brücke wird nicht beachtet, Wortschluss nach dem vierten Trochäus ist frei.

Die Tendenz ist der alexandrinischen Strenge entgegengesetzt; was die Mittelzäsur betrifft, so bevorzugten die Alexandriner gerade die weibliche nach dem dritten Trochäus. Man braucht nicht zu zögern, die Abweichungen von griechischer Metrik durch die Schwierigkeiten zu erklären, die in dieser Frühzeit lateinischer Dichtung überwunden werden mussten. Doch kann das allein nicht als Erklärung genügen. Wenn ich recht sehe, ist bisher Kurt Witte mit seiner Abhandlung über den Hexameter des Ennius [1] am weitesten vorgedrungen. Er hat festgestellt, dass Wortende im allgemeinen nach der Arsis bevorzugt wird und hat Parallelen zur Rhythmik des saturnischen Versmasses gezogen. Aber an diesem Punkt kommt man schon nicht mehr weiter.

Vorläufiges Fazit: Die Basis ennianischer Hexameter-Metrik können wir als homerisch bezeichnen. Der alexandrinischen steht sie offensichtlich ferner. Einflüsse von römisch-italischer Tradition sind möglicherweise anzuerkennen. Auf jeden Fall muss die Verschiedenheit der sprachlichen Bedingungen in Rechnung gestellt werden. Merkwürdigerweise ist es nicht gelungen, diese mehr als global zu formulieren, etwa, dass das Lateinische weniger kurze Silben aufweise als das Griechische. Und doch vermochte Ennius eine erstaunlich grosse Zahl von daktylischen Metren zu bilden [2]. Kaum möglich scheint es, einen ausseralexandrinischen, hellenistischen Hexameter-Typ abzugrenzen.

2. Einige auffallende Merkmale müssen wir jedoch berücksichtigen. Da ist zuerst die scharfe Einschränkung von Elisionen gegenüber Ennius' eigenen Gewohnheiten in den szenischen Dichtungen, sowie die weitgehende Meidung des Hiats. Hier kündigt sich doch eine Tendenz zu strengeren Regelungen an.

3. Im Zusammenhang damit steht, wie Ennius den Sinneseinschnitt im Vers behandelt. Wir wissen, dass im neoterischen Hexameter Sinneseinschnitt und Versende fast stets zusammenfallen. Ennius hat diese Tendenz noch nicht. Bei

[1] *RhM* 69 (1914), 205-232. Nicht zugänglich war mir A. Bartalucci, « La sperimentazione enniana dell'esametro ... » *SCO* 17 (1968), 99-122. Nach dem Kurzreferat im 'Marouzeau' für 1969 rechnet der Verfasser mit Einfluss des Saturniers.

[2] Man vergleiche die Ausführungen Franz Skutschs, *RE*-Artikel Ennius, Sp. 2623 und F. Leos in seiner *Geschichte der römischen Literatur*, S. 186.

ihm, wie bei Lukrez, ist schwere Interpunktion im Versinnern zugelassen. Bis zu einem gewissen Grad gilt für ihn wie für *Ilias* und *Odyssee*, dass der Satzinhalt über die Versgrenzen hinwegfliesst. Das entspricht auch noch der frühalexandrinischen Versbehandlung. Erst die jüngeren Alexandriner und erst recht die Neoteriker suchten, die Interpunktionen am Versende, höchstens noch an der Mittelzäsur, zu konzentrieren [1].

Die Versbehandlung des Ennius steht also auf einem Stand, der, vorsichtig ausgedrückt, auch noch nachhomerisch gegolten hat, auch noch bei den ersten alexandrinischen Dichtern.

4. An bestimmten Einzelheiten erkennen wir aber, dass Ennius auch neueren Entwicklungen gefolgt ist. Ein Beispiel : das alte griechische Epos, reich an direkten Reden, benutzte meist versfüllende Formeln, um solche Reden einzuführen. Die direkte Rede begann in jedem Fall mit dem Anfang des folgenden Verses. Ausnahmen sind noch sehr selten ; zwei finden sich bei Kallimachos, *H.* IV 150 und 162, einige mehr bei Theokrit [2]. Bei Ennius haben wir

v. 394 *infit* : « *o ciues, quae me fortuna* . . . »

und in v. 44 f. eine Rede innerhalb der Rede. In der Traumerzählung der Ilia werden die prophetischen Worte des Vaters als direkte Rede so eingeführt :

exim compellare pater me uoce uidetur
his uerbis : « *o gnata, tibi sunt ante gerendae*
. . .

[1] H. Patzer, « Zum Sprachstil des neoterischen Hexameters », *Mus. Helv.* 12 (1955), 77-95. Die Untersuchung knüpft u.a. an Ed. Norden, *Aeneis* VI, Anhang II, S. 386 ff. an.

[2] Ed. Norden zu *Aeneis* VI, v. 45 ff. unter Benutzung von J. Kvičala, *Neue Beiträge zur Erklärung der Aeneis*, Prag 1881.

Man wird auch 360 f. anführen dürfen, wo möglicherweise eine Verwünschung des Cato gegen seine Gegner zitiert wird:

> ... « *malo cruce* », *fatur*, « *uti des*
> *Juppiter*, ... »

Sonst findet man die kurze Redeeinleitung durch *inquit* und *ait* erst bei Vergil, doch darf man *infit* aus Ennius, *Ann.* 394, und *fatur*, 360, als ebenfalls kurze, beiläufige Einleitungen direkter Rede dem zur Seite stellen.

Im übrigen bedarf es keiner langen Ausführungen darüber, dass Ennius die sprachlichen Gepflogenheiten der nachhomerischen und hellenistischen Dichtung ererbt hat. Formelhaft ist seine Sprache nur an wenigen Stellen; schliesslich sind die Voraussetzungen, die für eine mündlich geformte Versepik galten, längst entfallen und die Entwicklung der griechischen Epik war über diese Form des Homerisierens inzwischen hinausgekommen.

5. Anaphern hat Ennius andererseits reichlicher gebraucht und die spielen bei Homer noch eine ganz verschwindend kleine Rolle. Um nicht grosse Listen geben zu müssen, erwähne ich hier nur die besonders auffällige Sonderform des Polyptoton, die sichere hellenistische Vorbilder hat[1], z.B.

457 f.: *Juppiter hic risit, tempestatesque serenae*
riserunt omnes risu Jouis omnipotensis.
493: *qui uincit non est uictor nisi uictus fatetur*
<scil. *se uictum esse*>

6. Alliterationen mögen vielleicht italischen Sprachbedingungen entstammen, jedoch ist Ennius' bewusste Sprachbeherrschung besser noch an ausgesprochenem Spiel mit Wortformen abzulesen, wie sie hellenistischer Übung entspricht:

[1] Über Polyptota bei Kallimachos vgl. F. Lapp, *De Callimachi tropis et figuris*, Diss. Bonn 1965, S. 65.

309 : *nauibus **ex**plebant sese terrasque **re**plebant.*
105 : *... sues **stolidi soliti** sunt.*
252 : *alter **nare** cupit, alter **pugnare** paratust.*
183 ff. : *proletarius publicitus scutisque **fero**que*
*ornatur **ferro**, muros urbemque **forum**que*
excubiis curant.

7. Grössere Klarheit können die Fragmente grösseren Umfangs erbringen, weil sie thematisch eine Einheit bilden. Sie können sowohl nach Inhalt als auch nach Ausdruck verglichen und interpretiert werden. Ich führe hier nur ein paar Beispiele an. Die Interpretationen liegen z.T. schon seit langer Zeit vor [1]. Zunächst zwei, die auf homerische Vorbilder zurückgehen.

187-191 : *incedunt arbusta per alta, securibus caedunt,*
percellent magnas quercus, exciditur ilex,
fraxinus frangitur atque abies consternitur alta,
pinus proceras peruortunt : omne sonabat
arbustum fremitu siluai frondosai.

Von Makrobius zitiert, um *Aen.* VI 179 ff. dagegen zu stellen. Aber für diesen Zusammenhang ist es noch interessanter, dass *Ilias* XXIII 114-120 Vorbild gewesen ist :

οἱ δ' ἴσαν ὑλοτόμους πελέκεας ἐν χερσὶν ἔχοντες
σειράς τ' εὐπλέκτους· πρὸ δ' ἄρ' οὐρῆες κίον αὐτῶν.
πολλὰ δ'ἄναντα κάταντα πάραντά τε δόχμιά τ' ἦλθον·
ἀλλ' ὅτε δὴ κνημοὺς προσέβαν πολυπίδακος Ἴδης,
αὐτίκ' ἄρα δρῦς ὑψικόμους, ταναήκεϊ χαλκῷ
τάμνον ἐπειγόμενοι· ταὶ δὲ μεγάλα κτυπέουσαι
πῖπτον· ...

Der Unterschied liegt in der Betonung ganz verschiedener Aspekte bei Homer und bei Ennius. Bei Homer : Bewegung

[1] z.B. bei F. Leo, *Literaturgeschichte*, S. 176 ff.

aus vielen Richtungen zum Bergwald hin. Maultiere, Eichenbäume, die in eiliger Tätigkeit gefällt werden. Mit grossem Lärm fallen sie zu Boden.

Bei Ennius dieselbe Einleitung : οἱ δ' ἴσαν entspricht *incedunt*. Derselbe Schluss : Lärm fallender Bäume. Das Bild der Massenhaftigkeit wird aber auf ganz andere Weise gegeben. Er erwähnt nicht allein Eichen, sondern zählt viele Baumsorten auf : Kumulation der Nomina und der Verba mit allen Mitteln der *variatio*, die als Stilprinzip hellenistischer Dichtkunst [1] zu gelten hat. Herr Skutsch hat sie gerade wieder hervorgehoben. Hier formuliert Ennius also anders als Homer ; jedoch auch bei Kallimachos wird man diese Form der Kumulation nicht finden [2]. Sollte sie römisch sein? Entspricht sie dem, was man bei Plautus als 'Fülle des Ausdrucks' bezeichnet? Man vergleiche die Kumulationen, mit denen Plautus, *Cist.* 206 ff., Liebesschmerz zu beschreiben wusste :

iactor, crucior, agitor, stimulor, uorsor
in amoris rota, miser exanimor,
feror, differor, distrahor, diripior ... etc.

8. Oder ein Stück, das mit einem gleich zu besprechenden Enniusfragment verwandt ist durch den εἰκονισμός, der Aufzählung von konkreten Eigenschaften, statt abstrakter Zusammenfassung : *Persa* 417 ff. :

uir summe populi, stabulum seruitricium,
scortorum liberator, suduculum flagri,
compedium tritor, pistrinorum ciuitas
perenniserue, lurcho, edax, furax, fugax.

Eine solche Kumulierung haben wir auch in der Beschreibung des '*ideal companion*' (234-251 Vahlen). Nach den er-

[1] So ist L. Deubners Aufsatz überschrieben, *Neue Jahrbücher* 1921, 361 ff.

[2] Am nächsten mag noch der viergliedrige Ausdruck kommen, mit dem, *H.* VI 66 f., der Hunger des Erysichthon beschrieben wird.

schöpfenden Untersuchungen über das spezifisch Hellenistische dieser Stelle, die Friedrich Leo (*Literaturgeschichte* 178), die Herr Skutsch (*Studia Enniana* 92 ff.) dieser Stelle gewidmet haben, nachdem Konrat Ziegler im Anhang der 2. Auflage seines *Hellenistischen Epos* S. 63-65, gerade das Typische einer Herrscher-*Confident*-Verbindung in den hellenistischen Fürstentümern hervorgehoben hat, brauche ich keine weitere Interpretation den früheren hinzuzufügen. Herr Skutsch hat erstens ein Menanderzeugnis : Terenz' *Eunuchus* 401 ff. angezogen, worin ein *miles gloriosus* namens Thraso (eine Figur aus Menanders *Kolax*, von Terenz in den *Eunuchus* hineingenommen) sich seiner vertrauten Beziehung zum König rühmt. Damit wird in komischer Form und gleichsam aus der Froschperspektive des eitlen Angebers eine vergleichbare Situation beschrieben. Herr Skutsch hat zweitens einen hellenistischen Text zitiert, der inhaltlich demjenigen der ennianischen Darstellung entspricht : auf einem Papyrus des 3. Jahrhunderts v. Chr. (*Select Papyri* III, ed. D. L. Page, no. 111) findet sich diese Beschreibung eines « Offiziers des königlichen Hofes von Alexandria » (Page, dem Skutsch zustimmt, vgl. aber Momigliano bei Skutsch, *Studia* S. 101, Anm. 21) :

ἀγαπᾶτε ταῦτα πάντες ὅσ' ἔχει· τἀγαθὰ
ἅπαντ' ἐν αὐτῷ· χρηστός, εὐγενής, ἁπλοῦς,
φιλοβασιλεύς, ἀνδρεῖος, ἐν πίστει μέγας,
σώφρων, φιλέλλην, πραΰς, εὐπροσήγορος,
τὰ πανοῦργα μισῶν, τὴν δ' ἀλήθειαν σέβων.

Charakterisierung des ausserordentlich Eindrucksvollen durch Kumulation von einzelnen Eigenschaften, erscheint hier als eine hellenistische Form der Beschreibung, wenn auch in nicht-epischer Form. Solange wir weder für den Katalog der Baum-Arten, noch für die Personencharakterisierung e p i s c h e Beispiele beibringen können, müssen wir uns mit dem Hinweis auf die Ansätze in der griechischen

Tragödie und verwandten (?, der angeführte Papyrustext ist nicht einzuordnen) Texten begnügen, wobei wir das römisch-italische Bedürfnis nach Ausdruckfülle nicht übersehen sollten. Wir sind vielleicht in einer ähnlichen Lage wie gegenüber den Kumulationen in den Plautus-Komödien [1].

Es bedarf kaum eines Wortes, dass das onomatopoetische *taratantara* in v. 140 keine Parallele in griechischer Epik gehabt haben dürfte.

9. Noch ein Wort zu den homerischen Gleichnissen bei Ennius: aus ihnen greife ich das Pferdegleichnis, 514 ff. Vahlen, heraus. Darin lässt sich, gerade bei der Feststellung, wie sehr Ennius' Gedanken auf die *Ilias* gerichtet sind, ablesen, was bei ihm ganz anders ist. Nach den Untersuchungen von Johanna v. Kameke, *Ennius und Homer*, Diss. Leipzig 1926, und anderen hat M. v. Albrecht neuerlich das Pferdegleichnis mit den Vorlagen in der *Ilias* und bei Apollonios Rhodios sowie mit der Nachahmung bei Vergil verglichen (*Hermes* 97 (1969), 333-345). Wir erfahren aus dieser Analyse, dass Ennius sich einer Gleichnistechnik bedient, welche aus der homerischen weiterentwickelt ist. (Ich bemerke hier nur nebenbei: Gleichnisse homerischer Art sind bei Kallimachos ganz selten geworden. Zwei befinden sich im *Deloshymnos* 141-147 und 228-232. Das andere Material ist teils ganz unsicher, teils von einem komplizierten Aufbau, der mit homerischen Vergleichen fast nichts mehr gemein hat.)

Die Texte: *Ann.* 514-518:

514 *et tum sicut equus qui de praesepibus fartus*
uincla suis magnis animis abrupit et inde
fert sese campi per caerula laetaque prata,

[1] E. Fraenkel, *Plautinisches im Plautus*, 1922, bes. S. 361 ff. (= *Elementi Plautini* S. 343 ff.), H. Haffter, *Untersuchungen zur altlateinischen Dichtersprache*, 1934, 3. Kapitel.

— celso pectore saepe iubam quassat simul altam,
spiritus ex anima calida spumas agit albas —

Ilias VI 506-511 :

ὡς δ' ὅτε τις στατὸς ἵππος, ἀκοστήσας ἐπὶ φάτνῃ,
δεσμὸν ἀπορρήξας θείῃ πεδίοιο κροαίνων,
εἰωθὼς λούεσθαι ἐϋρρεῖος ποταμοῖο,
κυδιόων· ὑψοῦ δὲ κάρη ἔχει, ἀμφὶ δὲ χαῖται
ὤμοις ἀΐσσονται· ὁ δ' ἀγλαΐηφι πεποιθὼς
ῥίμφα ἑ γοῦνα φέρει μετά τ' ἤθεα καὶ νομὸν ἵππων·

Ich fasse aus v. Albrechts Aufsatz einige Ergebnisse zusammen. Zunächst kann nicht die geringste Rede davon sein, dass Ennius übersetzt, nicht einmal dass er imitiert, sondern er schafft ein neues Gleichnis unter Verwendung einiger Elemente des homerischen Vorbildes. Ennius' Wiedergabe ist im ganzen kürzer, sein Satzbau ist verhältnismässig straff, anders als die locker, assoziativ geführten Gedanken eines homerischen Gleichnisses, und auch des hier angezogenen. Bei Ennius entfallen einige überschiessende Ausmalungen. Z.B. στατὸς ἵππος wird einfach *equus*. Nebenelemente, wie das Bad im Strom, der Weideplatz der Stuten werden weggelassen. Wohin das Pferd läuft, ist bei Ennius im Gleichnis garnicht angedeutet, sondern es wird ein Bild der Weite gegeben, in welche hinein das Pferd ausbricht,

fert sese campi per caerula laetaque prata.

Ennius beschränkt also das Gleichnis auf das Wesentliche (wie wir unpoetisch sagen würden), auf das absolut Vergleichbare. Aus der Wiederaufnahme des Gleichnisses bei Vergil, *Aen.* XI 492-497 können wir schliessen, dass ein losstürmender Krieger der Gegenstand des Vergleichs war. Ennius zieht nur dieses Lostürmen, das Sich-Losreissen in Betracht, ohne auf dessen Ziel einen besonderen Wert zu legen. Diese Beschränkung steht in Übereinstimmung mit hellenistischer Theorie und Praxis des Gleichnisses, welche besagt, dass das Gleichnis statt der Verdeutlichung eines Vergleichspunktes mehr die Parallelität der Gesamtbewegung von Vergleich und Verglichenem anstreben soll [1].

Illustrativ ist in diesem Zusammenhang die Parallelstelle bei Apollonios Rhodios III 1259-1261 (vgl. v. Albrecht, 341 f.):

ὡς δ' ὅτ' ἀρήιος ἵππος, ἐελδόμενος πολέμοιο,
σκαρθμῷ ἐπιχρεμέθων κρούει πέδον, αὐτὰρ ὕπερθε
κυδιόων ὀρθοῖσιν ἐπ' οὔασιν αὐχέν' ἀείρει.

Apollonios spricht nicht, wie Homer, von einem Hengst, der zu den Stuten strebt, sondern von einem Kriegspferd, das zum Kampf eilt, wiehernd den Boden stampft mit emporgerichteten Ohren, den Kopf hoch erhoben.

Ennius verknappt so weitgehend nicht. Die hellenistische Nüchternheit der Vergleichung ist bei ihm nicht zu finden. Allerdings ist Vorsicht geboten; die Vergleichsobjekte sind keineswegs die gleichen: ein Krieger, der zum Kampf strebt bei Ennius (erschlossen aus Vergil), ein Waffentanz bei Appollonios.

'Mehr' als Homer hat Ennius in folgenden Zügen (vgl. v. Albrecht, S. 338 f.): er legt stärkeres Gewicht auf den inneren Zustand des Pferdes, z.B. 515 *suis magnis animis* und 518 *anima calida* (nach der Temperamentenlehre sind Stolz und Begeisterung warme Säfte); weiter treten hinzu die Adjektive *celsus* und *altus*, die nicht *epitheta constantia*, sondern auf die konkrete Situation gemünzt sind, sowie die Farbadjektive *albas* und *caerula*. Solche tauchen in keinem der Paralleltexte auf, weder bei Homer, noch bei Apollonios noch bei Vergil. Blaues Feld ist hier weites Feld. Von der

[1] A. Clausing, *Kritik und Exegese der homerischen Gleichnisse im Altertum*, Diss. Freiburg i. Br. 1913; vgl. dazu auch W. Suerbaum, *Untersuchungen*, app. 27.

Vielfalt der Farbadjektive bei Ennius handelte bereits Leo, S. 174 f.

Es ergibt sich eine bereits beträchtliche Eigenständigkeit des Ennius in den Gleichnissen. Anlehnung an Homer bleibt spürbar; aber ebenso deutlich sind die Abweichungen in Richtung auf die hellenistische Entwicklung, nur nicht bis hin zu ihrer schärfsten Ausprägung bei den Alexandrinern.

10. Ich brauche hier an Leos Ausführungen über die Traumszene der Ilia nur zu erinnern, S. 178 ff. Leo hebt das hellenistische Grundelement sehr umsichtig heraus: «Ennius ... gibt hier die homerische Weise auf und wendet eine neu der Natur abgelauschte an ... Obwohl er nicht der erste gewesen ist; in der hellenistischen Poesie finden wir auch vor ihm das wirklich geträumte Traumbild» (S. 179; sein wichtigstes Beispiel: Apollonios Rhod. III 616 ff., ebenda Anm. 2) [1].

Wir stellen also, jetzt im Hinblick auf das gesamte bisher Ausgeführte, fest: Anlehnung an Homer, aber durchaus nicht homerische Sprachbehandlung und Gedankenwelt, sondern Erbe des Hellenismus; 'Hellenismus' jedoch nicht im Sinne der kallimacheischen Kunsttheorie.

Und doch ist Ennius diese Herausforderung nicht unbekannt. Er ist sich ihrer voll bewusst und verleiht dem Ausdruck. Hellenistischer Dichter ist Ennius schon dadurch, dass er Aussagen über sein Dichten gemacht hat. Sein Traum-Proömium als solches rückt ihn bereits sehr nahe an Kallimachos' *Aitien*-Prolog heran und seine Polemik gegen die Dichter der *Fauni*- und *Vates*gesänge am Anfang des VII. Buches ebenso (Polemik dieser Art hat im Epos der Römer keine Nachfolge gefunden, Leo S. 164). Dort, 213-219, sagt Ennius auch etwas über seine Kunstbemühung, er

[1] Ergänzend dazu W. H. FRIEDRICH, *Philologus* 97 (1948), 288-291.

bezeichnet sich als *dicti studiosus* und spricht darüber, dass man *sapientia*, *sophia* besitzen muss, um in der Dichtung zu reüssieren. Er weist auf sein *studium* hin, womit wir bei alexandrinischen Programmwörtern sind, wie, *labor*, πόνος, *lima* usw. Mindestens soviel hat Ennius gesagt : *studium* muss vorausgehen, um *somnium* zu ermöglichen.

Zwei weitere Hinweise auf Ennius' Stellung zur Gelehrsamkeit mögen hier folgen :
1. Das Bewusstsein vom Vorhandensein fremder Sprachen war den Griechen weitgehend fremd [1]. Für die Römer wurde jedoch zumindest das Griechische von Anbeginn integrierender Bestandteil ihres Sprachbewusstseins. Bei Ennius findet das Ausdruck in mehreren Fragmenten, in denen er lateinische Wörter zu griechischen in Beziehung setzt [2]; die Verba *memorare* und *perhibere* spielen eine Rolle dabei [3].

2 : *Musas quas memorant, nosce nos esse Camenas*
148 : *uento quem perhibent Graium genus aera lingua.*
218 f. : *nec quisquam sophiam, sapientia quae perhibetur*
in somnis uidit ...
356 : *contendunt Graecos, Graios memorare solent sos,*
... lingua longos per,

oder um Benennungen als bei den Menschen gültig anzuführen : der Zusammenhang ist nicht erkennbar in

409 : *arcus subspiciunt, mortalibus quae perhibentur,*

[1] Davon handelt ein Aufsatz von J. Kakridis, der mir in der deutschen Übersetzung von W. Bauer zur Kenntnis gekommen ist : « Die alten Griechen und die fremden Sprachen », *Hellenika*, Bochum, 6. Jahrg. (1969), Heft 16/17, 5-15.

[2] Wie V. 503 : *Hispane, non Romane, memoretis loqui me* zu verstehen sei, vermag man nicht mit Sicherheit zu entscheiden ; ist ein Sprachgegensatz oder ein Interessengegensatz gemeint?

[3] Wie in Pacuvius' *Chryses*, Fr. 89 Ribb. *id quod nostri caelum memorant Grai perhibent aethera.*

eher in 23 : *est locus, Hesperiam quam mortales perhibebant.*

V. 25 *Saturnia terra* könnte in diesem Zusammenhang gestanden haben, vgl. Suerbaum Anm. 770.

Dass Götter andere Namen und Appellative benutzten als Sterbliche, ist in den homerischen Gedichten ein paarmal erwähnt, *Il.* I 403, II 813 u.a. ; zu vergleichen ist auch *Il.* XVIII 487 ἄρκτόν ϑ', ἣν καὶ ἅμαξαν ἐπίκλησιν καλέουσιν, wo die Namen (grosser) Bär und Wagen für das Sternbild nebeneinander erwähnt werden ; jedoch haben wir es ja nicht mit diesem Phänomen allein zu tun, sondern in den zuerst zitierten Beispielen mit dem quasi-philologischen Interesse des Ennius, genaue Angaben über die Herkunft eines Begriffs zu machen. Dies scheint mir mit einer typisch hellenistischen Haltung übereinzustimmen. Bei den Griechen äusserte sie sich, wie ich vorhin bemerkte, nicht als Betonung von Muttersprache im Gegensatz zu einer fremden Sprache. Besonders die hellenistischen Dichter liebten es aber, ältere oder seltener gebrauchte Zweitnamen, die sie entdeckt hatten, sorgfältig zu verzeichnen und als gelehrte Anmerkung in erlesener poetischer Sprache zu formulieren. Bei Kallimachos findet man etwa den Typus fr. 601 : ἐν Δίῃ· τὸ γὰρ ἔσκε παλαίτερον οὔνομα Νάξῳ, vgl. *H.* III 47 f., IV 49 u.v.a., bei Apollonios Rhodios z.B. I 624, II 296 f. Es ist das Spiel des Dilettanten mit der Pedanterie.

Für Ennius haben die Angaben vom Typus *quod ... perhibent* ein anderes, schwereres Gewicht, aber als Formulierungstypus im Genus des Epos ist es bei hellenistischen Dichtern vorgeprägt und sollte bei ihnen stets den Eindruck von hoher Bildung und Genauigkeit hervorrufen ; die gesuchte Wirkung war nur durch *studium* und *sapientia* zu erzielen.

2. Ein Dokument von Ennius' bewusster Formulierungskunst ist der Satzbau des Verses 197 f. :

uosne uelit an me regnare era quidue ferat Fors
uirtute experiamur [1]

Die Wortfolge in Prosa wäre vielleicht *uirtute experiamur uosne an me regnare Fors era uelit quidue ferat.* Die Formulierung erhält dadurch ihre Besonderheit, dass *Fors,* wozu *era* Apposition ist, erst nach derselben, in einem anderen Satzteil nachgetragen wird. Die frühesten Beispiele, bei Kallimachos *H.* IV 304 f. und fr. 519 Pf. hatte schon Leo gesehen. Sie gehören mit anderen Formen kunstreicher Hyperbata zusammen. R. Pfeiffer hat mehrere Kategorien unterschieden und zu fr. 6 zusammengestellt (dazu die Addenda in Band I seiner Ausgabe). Für diesen Appositionstypus findet sich kein weiteres Beispiel, jedoch scheint mir der Typus '*substantivum in relativae enuntiationis partem reicit poeta*' sehr nahe zu kommen : *H.* II 112, IV 156, fr. 68, 519, 550 [2].

Dieses, wohl nur infolge der Überlieferungslage vereinzelte [3], Beispiel scheint mir zu zeigen, dass Ennius gesuchte Effekte der alexandrinischen Dichtkunst kannte und zu erzielen wusste : das ist seine *sophia.*

Also nähert sich Ennius' Kunstauffassung und dichterische Praxis dem alexandrinischen Programm? Auf dieses scheint er doch auch in seinem Musen-, Quellen- und Traumproömium Bezug zu nehmen.

Kein Zweifel, sein Proömium klingt in manchem an dasjenige der *Aitia* des Kallimachos an. Nur eine Kleinig-

[1] F. Leo hat diesen Vers in den *Analecta Plautina* I, S. 20 (= *Ausgew. Kleine Schriften* I, S. 91) behandelt, weil ein solcher Typus bei Plautus noch nicht begegnet, sondern in der Latinität erst hier.

[2] Den Eingang solcher Hyperbata in die augusteische und spätere Dichtung haben F. Leo, *a.a.O.* und F. Vollmer, Zu Horaz epod. 15.15, *Sitzber. Bayr. Akad.* 1918, 4, S. 3-7 behandelt.

[3] Andere Beispiele preziöser Wortstellung hat er durchaus, z.B. 247 f. : ... *sepulta uetustas/ quae facit,* oder 294 : *aut occasus ubi tempusue audere repressit.*

keit passt nicht ins Bild: die Figur Homers. Der wäre bei einem Kallimacheer Ennius nicht vorgekommen. Die Dinge liegen eben anders. Es war angesichts des alexandrinischen Programms eine schwerwiegende Entscheidung, dass Ennius sich für sein Vorhaben auf Homer beruft. Da sein Proömium — wie dessen einzelne Formulierungen auch gelautet haben mögen — die *Aitia* des Kallimachos 'zitiert', muss darin doch geradezu eine Antwort auf Kallimachos' Herausforderung liegen. Mit den Anklängen wurde erst deutlich, wogegen sich seine Entscheidung richtete, wovon er sich distanzierte. Leo hat, S. 166, in der Nennung Homers lediglich ein Bekenntnis zum höchsten denkbaren Standard der Dichtung sehen wollen: « Homer ist sein Vorgänger nur weil er unbestritten der grösste ist. » Das dürfte in keiner Weise genügen. Wir kommen hier vielmehr zu der Erkenntnis, dass Ennius das alexandrinische Programm vor Augen hat. Er leistet ihm nicht Folge, sondern schliesst sich gerade der Epen-Tradition an, welche Kallimachos und sein Kreis für erschöpft hielten, einer Tradition epischer Dichtung, die niemals die Nachfolge Homers (der *Ilias*) abgeleugnet hatte, dem historischen Epos. Bezugnahme auf das alexandrinische Programm, jedoch in der Weise der Erwiderung sieht auch O. Skutsch, wenn er, *Studia* S. 9, betont, Ennius spreche von Seelenwanderung, weil er der problematisch gewordenen Vorbild-Nachfolge-Beziehung entgehen will. Homer-Nachfolge war durch die *Aitia* eben doch versperrt.

Es bestätigt sich damit, was wir an einer Reihe von Einzelzügen erkannten: Ennius ist sich alexandrinischer Theorien und Verfeinerungen wohl bewusst. Manches interessiert ihn daran, aber er weiss genau, dass für sein Vorhaben eine andere hellenistische Tradition massgebend ist, die des historischen Epos, die sich weiterhin auf Homer berief, sich in Ausdrucksformen und sprachlichen Eigenschaften aber notwendigerweise von Homer fortentwickelt hatte und sich von den Alexandrinern entfernt hielt.

Auf unsere eingangs erhobenen Fragen sind somit einige Antworten möglich: Homerisches im Ennius? — Unleugbar, aber an welcher Stelle wir auch immer ansetzen, bei der Metrik, der Sprachbehandlung, den Bildern und Gleichnissen, es ist immer nur halbwegs homerisch. Was bedeutet das? — Diese Epik hatte sich in den homerischen Geleisen zwar, aber doch von der alten Epik fort entwickelt.

Ennius ein Alexandriner? Es gibt dafür eine Reihe von Hinweisen, aber es gibt ebensoviele ausgesprochene Warnungen, Ennius allzu nahe dorthin zu rücken. Was bedeutet das? — Es gab hellenistische Traditionen, die von den Alexandrinern wenig berührt waren. D.h. hellenistische Dichtung gab es nicht nur in der Gestalt, welche die Alexandriner ihr geben wollten. Wir müssen uns vergegenwärtigen, was unternahm der Dichter der *Annales* tatsächlich?

1. Er schuf ein Epos, dessen Thema die Taten der Römer waren. Die Erzählung geht von den Ursprüngen der Stadt in die historisch überlieferte Zeit hinüber und reicht schliesslich bis in die Gegenwart der Abfassung.

2. Als ein Mittel seiner Darstellung benutzte er den Götterapparat, Erbe der altgriechischen Epik. Gerade für das griechische historische Epos nehmen aber manche an, es habe ihn nicht gehabt (auf diese Frage komme ich zurück).

3. Er nannte dieses Werk *Annales*, stützte sich auf amtliche Aufzeichnungen und Kalenderdaten, direkt oder indirekt. Er wich damit ab von der hellenistischen Tradition, nach welcher sein Werk *Romaïs* hätte heissen können (allerdings gab es auch im griechischen Raum Werke mit dem Titel ὧροι).

Können wir das alles römisch nennen? Wir müssten dann sagen, dass Naevius derjenige war, der die Zeitgeschichte als Thema des Epos erfand und auf die Idee kam, die homerische Götterkonstruktion in diese zeitgeschichtliche Epik zu übernehmen. Auf die Frage: gab es Römisches, oder ganz Persönliches bei Ennius, werden wir zustimmen, was den Titel *Annales* angeht, was manchen Wortgebrauch und genuin römische Vorstellungen angeht. Zweifellos hat Ennius einen nachhaltigen Eindruck durch die Tatsache empfangen, dass Naevius römische Zeitgeschichte episch bearbeitete. Aber dass Naevius der erste war, der das historische Epos so weit führte, das zuzugeben werden wir zögern, wenn wir auch keine handfesten Beweise für das Gegenteil haben. Uns fehlt, wie K. Ziegler betont hat, ein wichtiges Kapitel der griechischen Literaturgeschichte. Wir wissen, dass es eine Epik gab, die wir unter dem Namen historisches Epos zusammenfassen. Wir wissen, dass am Ende des 5. Jh. Choirilos von Samos ein Epos von den Perserkriegen schuf, für ihn keineswegs mehr Zeitgeschichte, sondern 'grosse' Vergangenheit, welche dem heroischen Mythos gleichzustellen schon lange vor ihm Aischylos unternommen hatte. Wie wissen, dass es eine Gattung von Regionalepen gab, als Beispiel nehme ich den einzigen nicht gänzlich unbekannten Rhianos, welcher *Messeniaka* dichtete. Nach allem, was wir über ihn wissen, jetzt besonders aus der Kölner Dissertation von R. Misgeld, *Rhianos von Bene und das historische Epos im Hellenismus*, 1968, war auch bei ihm die grosse Vergangenheit des Landes Gegenstand der Darstellung. Wir wissen schliesslich, dass es eine Epik um Alexander den Grossen und die Diadochenfürsten gegeben hat. Es ist kaum mehr, was wir wissen. Wenig sinnvoll wäre es, hier einen Abriss des nicht Bekannten zu geben [1]. Auch unter den Papyrusfunden taucht selten einmal etwas auf, was man dem historischen Epos zuordnen könnte, es sei denn einige Stücke der späteren römischen Kaiserzeit, die immerhin das Fortbestehen der Gattung bezeugen, z.B. *Greek*

[1] Ich verweise auf die nicht gerade reiche Spezial-Literatur zum Thema : W. Kroll, Das historische Epos, *Sokrates* 4 (1916), 1-14 ; K. Ziegler, *op. cit.*, bes. S. 15 ff. ; K. Thraede, Artikel « Epos » im *RAC* V 1962, bes. S. 988 ff. sowie die genannte Dissertation von R. Misgeld, die das Verdienst hat, Aristoteles und die epische Theorie der *Poetik* für die Rekonstruktion auszuwerten. Schliesslich vgl. noch W. Suerbaum, *Untersuchungen*, S. 14 f.

Literary Papyri no. 142 (= Heitsch, *Griechische Dichterfragmente der römischen Kaiserzeit* no. 32), 132, (Heitsch 28), 144 (Heitsch 34). In den letzten Jahren sind in *POxy*. 30, 1964, no. 2520 ein episches Gedicht auf Philipp v. Mazedonien und *POxy*. 37, 1971, no. 2814 über einen Krieg zwischen Griechen und Persern publiziert worden. Bei letzterem zieht Lobel sogar als Verfasser, allerdings unter fast widerrufenden Einschränkungen, Choirilos von Samos in Erwägung. Es war sicherlich zunächst einmal diese Gattung von Epik, welche Kallimachos für unergiebig und für ästhetisch verbraucht hielt. Auch Aristoteles hatte eine Darstellung von Handlungen, die lediglich durch einen gemeinsamen Zeitraum zusammenhängen, für unkünstlerisch erklärt (*Poetik* 23. 1459 a 21 ff., vgl. R. Misgeld, *a.a.O.* S. 34 ff.). Und obwohl er demgegenüber die *Ilias* wegen ihrer kompositorischen Einheit gelobt hatte, knüpfte das historische Epos offensichtlich an die *Ilias* an, die es für seinesgleichen hielt.

Wenn Ennius sich zu Homer bekannte, so konnte das zu seiner Zeit nichts anderes bedeuten, als dass er sich zum historischen Epos bekannte, so wie er es in Magna Graecia kennengelernt hatte und wie er es in Rom fortsetzen wollte ; denn Ennius sah offensichtlich, dass Naevius' Weg, einen altlateinischen Vers zu benutzen, eine Sackgasse war, dass der Saturnier keine Zukunft hatte.

Auf einige Aspekte des ennianischen Epos, die, wie ich vermuten möchte, auch charakteristisch für historische Epik gewesen sind, möchte ich nun eingehen. Wir sahen oben, dass Ennius' Epik gleichermassen von Homer wie von den Alexandrinern entfernt ist. Das gilt auch für die Selbstaussage, welche Herr Suerbaum in seinen *Untersuchungen* in allen Einzelheiten erörtert hat. Sie trennt Ennius selbstverständlich von den Gepflogenheiten des altgriechischen Epos. Ebensowenig findet sich andererseits bei ihm irgendeine Exklusivität, jene Haltung, die sich nur an den hochzivilisierten Zirkel zu wenden vorgibt, der die Feinheit der Dichtung zu goutieren weiss. Vielmehr glaubt Ennius, einen Auftrag an die Römer zu erfüllen. Wir sehen dies an den Fragmenten, in denen sich der Dichter mit dem römischen Leser zu identifizieren scheint. Sein Publikum ist die Öffentlichkeit des *populus Romanus Quiritium*. In einigen Fragmenten bleibt dies fraglich, weil es sich auch um Stücke aus direkter Rede handeln kann, z.B. in 370

unus homo nobis cunctando restituit rem,

dessen Zuweisung immer noch kontrovers ist. Wenn schon keine Sicherheit darüber zu gewinnen ist, dass es sich um des Dichters eigene Worte handelt, so darf es doch jedenfalls als eine Möglichkeit ernsthaft erwogen werden. Es könnte sich um eine ähnliche Identifikation mit dem Leser handeln, wie des Dichters Anrede an seine Mitbürger, *ciues* in v. 16 [1].

Ich neige dazu, in der Einbeziehung des Lesers (nicht gleichzustellen mit der Aussage des Dichters über sich selbst) einen Zug gerade des historischen Epos zu erkennen, welches ja eine politische Funktion erfüllt, Bewusstsein von einer verpflichtenden Vergangenheit zu erzeugen oder zu pflegen und würde

v. 587 : ... *nostri cessere parumper*

und

v. 128 : *et simul effugit speres ita funditus nostras*

noch dazustellen.

Für Reflexionen, die eine politische Dimension haben, gibt es noch andere Zeugnisse bei Ennius: Reflexionen über Macht und Geist, über Krieg und Frieden und über den Sieg.

[1] Starke Argumente für die Zugehörigkeit dieser Verse zum Beginn der *Annalen* bei W. SUERBAUM, S. 50 ff. Housmans Argument, es sei schlechthin unepisch, dass der Leser angeredet werde, operiert mit etwas, was wir nicht wissen : mit den Usancen historischer Epik.

Ihren schönsten Ausdruck findet die Verbindung Macht und Geist in den Versen vom '*ideal companion*', deren hellenistischen Hintergrund K. Ziegler, *a.a.O.* S. 64 f., herausgearbeitet hat. Von der Verbindung 'ziviler' und militärischer Fähigkeiten spricht auch

222: *quantum is consiliis quantumque potesset in armis*,

Reflexion gilt aber auch dem Gegensatz zwischen Macht und Geist, *sapientia* und *uis*, in den bekannten Versen vom Ausbruch des hannibalischen Krieges,

268 : *pellitur e medio sapientia, ui geritur res*
spernitur orator bonus, horridus miles amatur.

und weiter stehen dann im Gegensatz v. 270 : *haut doctis dictis* ... *nec* (oder *sed*?) *maledictis*, 272 : *non ex iure* ... *sed* ... *ferro*, 273 : ... *solida ui*, vgl. noch die Worte v. 582 f.: *oratores/doctiloqui.*

Ähnliche Gedankengänge kommen zum Ausdruck in

134 : *ferro se caedi quam dictis his toleraret*,

wo *dicta*, als *maledicta*, schwerer erträglich sind als Verwundung durch die Waffe oder in 180 f., die Angehörigen des *stolidum genus Aeacidarum* sind *bellipotentes magis quam sapientipotentes*. Und das Wort *stolidum* führt zu

105 : *nam ui depugnare sues stolidi soliti sunt.*

Der Gedanke, dass friedliche Lösung der Konflikte dem Krieg vorzuziehen sei, ist, wie jüngst H. Fuchs [1] hervorhob, aus griechischem Denken belegbar. Aber mindestens für den letzterwähnten Vers hat Herr Skutsch (*Studia* S. 46 ff.) als viel wahrscheinlicher erwiesen, dass die Anwendung von Kriegslist gemeint sei, im Gegensatz zu unüberlegter Kraftanwendung. In diesem Sinn konnte er auch v. 98 herstellen :

[1] *Mus. Helv.* 12 (1955), 202-205.

astu non ui summam seruare decet rem.

Es bleibt aber die Tatsache, dass geistige Mittel den physischen gegenübergestellt und als überlegen bezeichnet werden. In diesen Zusammenhang fügt sich, wenn auch lose, die Formulierung des 'Pyrrhussiegs', die eine Reflexion auf das Problematische eines Sieges auf dem Schlachtfeld voraussetzt. Von dem 'Epigramm', das seinen Ursprung epischer Dichtung, also wohl Ennius, verdanken dürfte (O. Skutsch, *a.a.O.* 88 ff.) zitiere ich nur

v. 193 : *hos ego ui* (O. Skutsch nach Speijer ; *in* codd.)
pugna uici uictusque sum ab isdem.

Und wie abhängig ein 'Sieg' sein kann von der Interpretation, welche die Lage vielleicht erst nachträglich erhält, ist in einem bemerkenswerten Satz ausgesprochen,

v. 493 : *qui uincit non est uictor nisi uictus fatetur*
<scil. *se uictum esse.*>

Dies alles sind Reflexionen, einer Gattung angemessen, die das Geschichtsbewusstsein eines Volkes, einer Stadt zu erwecken oder zu pflegen zur Aufgabe hatte und damit die politische Haltung ihrer Bürger ausdrückte, womöglich beeinflusste.

Abschliessend behandle ich eine Stelle, die in diesen Zusammenhang gehören könnte, wenn sie auch nicht eindeutig ist. Unter den Eigenschaften des '*ideal companion*' werden neben seiner Umgänglichkeit und Diskretion seine Kenntnisse gelobt. Hier fällt auf

v. 248 : . . . *et mores ueteresque nouosque tenentem.*

Er kennt alte und neue Sitten (vielleicht Gebräuche, vielleicht Satzungen). Hervorgehoben wird merkwürdigerweise auch die Kenntnis n e u e r Institutionen. Über die Schwierigkeiten des Zusammenhangs darf man sich nicht täuschen, wobei ich von dem Konstruktionswechsel ganz absehe.

Vorausgeht

247 f.: ... *multa tenens antiqua, sepulta uetustas*
quae facit

und es folgt

249: *multorum ueterum leges diuumque hominumque.*

Falls uns nicht die Überlieferung täuscht, müssen wir diese Reihe doch wohl so verstehen: es handelt sich um Kenntnisse
1. die durch ihr hohes Alter sonst vergessen sind,
2. um alte und junge *mores,*
3. um die alten Gesetze der Menschen, die ihnen mit den Göttern gemeinsam waren.

Der mittlere Teil, der auch die *nouos mores* enthält, ist also fast erdrückt von den umgebenden Sätzen, die nur die Traditionen hervorheben.

Man ist natürlich in Gefahr, zuviel in dem Gegensatz veteres-novos zu sehen. Schliesslich ist es ein μερισμός, um zu sagen « alle *mores* kannte er ». Die Aufgliederung der Gesamtheit geschieht jedoch mit Hilfe der zeitlichen Kategorie und mir scheint es ein wichtiger Gedanke, welcher zur klassischen *mos maiorum*-Ideologie im Gegensatz steht, im Gegensatz auch zu den Worten, die Ennius einem strafenden Vater (O. Skutsch, *a.a.O.* 51 ff.) in den Mund gelegt hat,

v. 500: *moribus antiquis res stat Romana et uiris,*

dass hier jemand beschrieben wird, dessen Verdienste auch in der Beobachtung und Kenntnis 'neuer Entwicklungen', des Zeitgenössischen, liegen.

Vielleicht verrät sich in dieser kleinen Zeile der Geist des zeitgeschichtlichen Epos, das, wie man nicht verkennen sollte, e i n e der möglichen Formen historischer Epik ist. Choirilos' Epos von den Perserkriegen, Rhianos' *Messeniaka* handelten von Ereignissen, die einige Generationen vom Autor entfernt waren. Vielleicht darf man bei ihnen zeitgeschichtliche Anspielungen vermuten von der Art wie die Schildbeschreibung in der *Aeneis*, vielleicht Weissagungen, die ja ein vorzügliches Mittel waren, Geschehnisse der eigenen Zeit aufzuwerten als etwas, was längst im Ratschluss der Götter beschlossen ist und was die eigene Zeit mit der heroischen Vergangenheit verkettet. Das war immerhin leichter als das Heroische bis in die eigene Gegenwart zu verlängern. Direkt zeitgeschichtlich ist wahrscheinlich die Epik der Alexanderzeit gewesen. Und die dürfte von dem Mittel, durch θαυμάσια aller Art die Gegenwart aufzuhöhen, umfassenden Gebrauch gemacht haben. Schliesslich hatte Aristoteles, *Poetik* 24, 1460 a 11 ff., den Gebrauch des θαυμαστόν und des ἄλογον als dem Epos besonders zukommend und erfolgreich anerkannt, und doch wohl auch von der Epik seiner Zeit aus geurteilt. Wenn ich in den vorgelegten Einzelbeobachtungen einen modernen, philosophischen, nüchternen Geist aus den *Annalen* herausheben wollte, so soll dadurch nicht verdeckt werden, dass Ennius auch mit hochpathetischen Schilderungen von Massenkämpfen (Stellen bei K. Ziegler, S. 71) und *portenta* wie der Kriegsfurie in hellenistischer Tradition stand. Dem Grausamen weiss er pathetischen Ausdruck zu verleihen. Zwei Beispiele für viele : das abgeschlagene Haupt dessen halb verloschene Augen noch das Licht dieser Welt suchen 472 f., oder die Tuba, die das Signal vollendet, nachdem des Bläsers Haupt schon zu Boden rollte, 519 f.

Das führt zu einer oft diskutierten Frage, die ich am Schluss noch berühren will, ohne dass ich mehr als ein Postulat aufstellen könnte. Welche Rolle hat der Götterapparat im historischen Epos der Griechen gespielt? Wir sind mit der Tatsache konfrontiert, dass Ennius wie Naevius von diesem Vehikel epischer Dichtung Gebrauch gemacht haben, obwohl sie zeitgenössische, jedenfalls 'historische' Epen schreiben. So haben viele geglaubt, die aufgeklärten Griechen hätten längst auf die göttliche Erzählungsebene verzichtet, die in der *Ilias* die irdischen Handlungen begleitet. Insbesondere — so meint K. Ziegler, S. 25 — könne man doch kaum glauben, dass Choirilos von Samos derartiges in sein Perserkriegs-Epos eingedichtet habe. Auch R. Misgeld gelingt es nicht, aus den wenigen Zeugnissen für die *Messeniaka* etwas zu gewinnen, was auf eine göttliche Ebene der epischen Erzählung schliessen lässt, vgl. *a.a.O.* S. 90 f. K. Ziegler vermutet eher, die Zeit der Alexander- und Diadochenepik könnte die Hofepiker dazu veranlasst haben, auf das homerische Relikt zurückzugreifen, sozusagen als Instrument der Schmeichelei.

Ich kann dem nicht zustimmen. Wenn Ennius, wenn auch Naevius aufgrund ihrer Vorbilder die Wahl gehabt hätten, den Götterapparat zu verwenden oder nicht, warum entschlossen sie, die mit ihrer Darstellung der eigenen Zeit besonders nahe kamen, sich dann für ihn? Sollte man nicht eher annehmen, dass eine Wahl garnicht bestand, sondern eine ununterbrochene Tradition in diesem Zweig des hellenistischen Epos gewahrt blieb? Der Götterapparat hatte seine Funktion, gerade im historischen Epos mit seiner politischen Aufgabe. Er gab Gelegenheit, göttlichen Willen, wirkend in der Entwicklung eines Volkes oder Staates, darzustellen, eine Art 'Sinn der Geschichte' zu formulieren. Von der poetischen Technik aus gesehen, war er ein Instrument der Komposition.

Als Lukan für sein *Bellum civile* auf dieses Darstellungsmittel verzichtete, erntete er schärfste Kritik, formuliert bei Petron, *Sat.* 118 und bei anderen, welche ihn eines schweren Verstosses gegen die Regeln des Genus ziehen [1]. Selbst n a c h Lukan dauerte es wieder ein halbes Jahrtausend, bis sich ein weiterer Epiker entschloss, auf das 'Beiwerk' eines Götterapparates zu verzichten [2].

[1] W. Kroll, *a.a.O.*; H. Stubbe, *Philologus-Suppl.-Band* 25 (1933), 61-64.

[2] Corippus, vgl. Fr. Skutsch, *RE* IV Sp. 1239 25 und 1242 20 ff.

DISCUSSION

M. Suerbaum: Wenn schon zur Rekonstruktion bestimmter Züge des hellenistischen Epos notgedrungen auf nichtepische Gattungen zurückgegriffen wird (was ja jedesmal der Fall ist, wenn der Name Kallimachos erwähnt wird ; auch die Parallelen zur Charakteristik des '*good companion*' sind ja nicht-episch), sollte man auch nicht darauf verzichten, die hellenistische Historiographie zu berücksichtigen (vgl. meine *Untersuchungen*, S. 17 ff.). Ein solches Vorgehen ist bei der sich im Hellenismus abzeichnenden Kreuzung der Gattungen, über die W. Kroll, *Studien*, Stuttgart 1924 = Darmstadt 1964, 202 ff., gehandelt hat, allgemein gesehen methodisch gerechtfertigt. Im Hinblick auf charakteristische epische Züge aber, wie einer etwa die Verwendung von Gleichnissen ist, sollte man Argumente nur aus dem einen literarischen Genus des Epos ableiten und z.B. mit Ennius' Praxis nicht die Häufigkeit und Technik der Gleichnisse bei Kallimachos, sondern bei Apollonios Rhodios vergleichen.

M. Wülfing: Das ist richtig, und so auch oben gehandhabt. Mit Kallimachos wollte ich lediglich den extremen Gegenpunkt bezeichnen. Apollonios Rhodios ist notwendigerweise « epischer » als Kallimachos. Allerdings gehören die *Hymnen* des Kallimachos, unter denen schliesslich einer in elegischen Distichen steht, und die *Aitia* doch zum selben Genus und zwar zum epischen.

M. Skutsch: I would consider it possible that Ennius introduced the idea of the migration of souls in order to be able to escape from Callimachus' ban on the imitation of Homer. He was not an imitator of Homer but Homer re-born.

M. Suerbaum : Man würde, glaube ich, den Einfluss des Kallimachos auf Ennius überschätzen, wenn man Ennius' *Homerus-rediuiuus*-Konzeption gewissermassen als Umgehung des kallimacheischen Verbots auffasst, Homer nachzuahmen. Die *Annales* sind als Ganzes betrachtet ein durchaus unkallimacheisches Werk. Die ennianische Homer-Metempsychose enthält ein anti-kallimacheisches Programm und bedeutet eine literarkritische Selbstbeurteilung. Die Form des *Somnium Ennii* halte ich für von Kallimachos beeinflusst, der Geist ist un-kallimacheisch.

M. Jocelyn : Is there any more than an accidental similarity between Ennius' dream and that of Callimachus ? After all the *Aitia* was an elegy with a consciously irreverent attitude to epic and themes of epic like revelatory dreams. Ennius described his dream with a certain earnestness of intent. He wanted his readers to think of the dreams described in serious poetry and neo-Pythagorean treatises, perhaps even of those recorded by the Roman *pontifices.* The versified literary criticism of Callimachus' *Aitia* belonged to a different world.

M. Wülfing : Das Proömium scheint so formuliert gewesen zu sein, dass ein erheblicher Abstand zu Homer wie zu Kallimachos erkennbar war. Die Entscheidung für die Metempsychosis statt eines anderen Symbols (z.B. Stabüberreichung) muss von uns interpretiert werden. Eine solche Interpretation legt uns Herr Skutsch vor.

Vielleicht hat man früher den Effekt des kallimacheischen Verdikts überschätzt. Doch darf man jetzt nicht zu weit in der Gegenrichtung gehen. Mir scheint es undenkbar, dass ein Dichter, sofern er überhaupt Stellung nimmt zu seinem epischen (!) Dichten, an Kallimachos vorbeigehen konnte, als ob dieser nichts über das Grossepos gesagt hätte. Dass Ennius' Traumproömium dem des Kallimachos besonders eng verwandt gewesen sein müsse, ist damit nicht gesagt. — Schliesslich dürfte es vor Ennius eine grosse Zahl anderer Inspirationsproömien gegeben haben, von denen wir nichts wissen.

M. Waszink: Herr Wülfing hat über Götterversammlungen gesprochen, die den Sinn der Geschichte klarlegen sollen. Wenn ich recht sehe, gehörte zu dieser Kategorie die Götterversammlung am Anfang des *Bellum Punicum* des Naevius, in der der zukünftige Konflikt zwischen Rom und Karthago vorbereitet wurde. Die Götterversammlung am Ende des ersten Buches der *Annalen* ist anderer Art : dort handelt es sich nur um die Apotheose des Romulus. Dagegen ist anzunehmen, auch wenn man nicht in allen Einzelheiten Nordens Ausführungen in *Ennius und Vergilius* beipflichten will, dass Ennius bei Anlass des *zweiten* Punischen Krieges eine Götterversammlung eingelegt hat, in der, wie bei Naevius, der Verlauf der Geschichte bestimmt wurde.

M. Badian: I cannot see any clear evidence for a *concilium deorum* after the first one (concerning Romulus). I suspect the divine machinery tended to fade out in the events of Ennius' lifetime. Jupiter promising the destruction of Carthage (*Ann.* VIII, fr. XV) may well have appeared in a dream : compare Hannibal's famous vision of the devastation of Italy in Livy. (Since Carthage was not destroyed in 201, the actual wording of Servius is in any case misleading.) That Juno was placated and began to favour Rome (*Ann.* 291 — again a report, not a quotation, by Servius) may refer to no more than the result of a religious rite : compare the *carmen* written by Livius Andronicus in 207. For there is no doubt that the Romans, on the whole, believed in their religion and that Ennius, like Livy, would report that belief. But I do not see that this adds up to 'divine machinery', any more than we would speak of 'divine machinery' in Livy ; though (of course) I do not want to suggest that the *Annales*, even for Ennius' lifetime, showed the spirit of Lucan. But the idea of Ennius' awkwardly introducing divine colloquies into events of his own generation rests (I think) only on overinterpretation of a late (and demonstrably inaccurate) source.

M. Skutsch : Ann. 175 *tum cum corde suo diuum pater atque hominum rex effatur* is certainly a soliloquy, and not part of a council of the gods. *Cum corde suo* is the equivalent of *secum*.

M. Suerbaum : Wenn Servius zu *Aen.* I 20 *(Iuno) audierat* kommentiert : *et perite « audierat » ; in Ennio enim inducitur Iuppiter promittens Romanis excidium Carthaginis* (=Enn. *Ann.* VIII fr. XV) geht daraus eindeutig hervor, dass bei Ennius Iupiter mit Iuno ein Zwiegespräch gehalten hat. Dass Iupiter wirklich als handelnde Person, und nicht nur in einer Traumerscheinung, aufgetreten ist, wird auch schon durch das typische *inducitur* c. Partic. nahegelegt. Wenn ausserdem noch berichtet wird *bello Punico secundo, ut ait Ennius, placata Iuno coepit fauere Romanis* (*Ann.* 291), ergibt sich eindeutig, dass in *Ann.* VIII wirklich eine Götterszene gestanden hat, an der wohl nicht das ganze *concilium deorum*, sondern nur Iupiter und Iuno beteiligt waren (ähnlich wie gegen Ende der *Aeneis*). Das hat Ed. Norden, *Ennius und Vergilius*, Leipzig-Berlin 1915, 167 ff. überzeugend nachgewiesen. Bei dieser Gelegenheit muss Iupiter den Sieg der Römer (*excidium Carthaginis* konnte der vor dem 3. Punischen Krieg gestorbene Ennius in der Tat nicht voraussehen) angekündigt haben, gleichzeitig aber auch Iuno in irgendeiner Weise zufriedengestellt worden sein. Wir haben also nicht nur in *Ann.* I, also im eher mythischen Teil, ein *concilium deorum*, sondern nachweislich noch mindestens eine weitere Götterszene, eben das Zwiegespräch Iupiter/Iuno im rein historischen Teil der *Annalen* (über diese Götterszenen handelt, in Auseinandersetzung besonders mit Nordens bekannter These eines *concilium deorum* in *Ann.* VII, eindringlich F. Klingner, *Virgil*, Zürich-Stuttgart 1967, 568 ff. 579 ff.), dazu noch mindestens ein Selbstgespräch Iupiters, innerhalb des Pyrrhus-Buches (*Ann.* 175 f.), auf das Mr. Skutsch aufmerksam gemacht hat.

An der Verwendung des « Götterapparates » lassen sich aufschlussreiche Beobachtungen für die kompositorische Gestaltungskraft der beiden frühen historischen Epiker Roms treffen. Naevius hat gewissermassen eine epische Monographie geschrieben, mit dem 1. Punischen Krieg einen einzigen Geschehniszusammenhang dargestellt. Er konnte sich deshalb damit begnügen, gegen Beginn seines Werkes im «Prologo in cielo» (M. Barchiesi, *Nevio epico*, Padova 1962, 330 ff.) eine einzige Götterszene — ein von Vergil in *Aeneis* I nachgeahmtes Zwiegespräch Iupiter/Venus — zu bieten, die das ganze im Werk dargestellte Geschehen überschaute. Ennius dagegen hat in einem kompositorischen Missgriff ein reihendes Epos geschrieben, das gewissermassen keine Mitte und kein Ende hat (und von Ennius in der Tat offenbar mehrfach über das zunächst anscheinend den Abschluss bildende XV. Buch hinaus «verlängert» worden ist) und das bestenfalls aus Teileinheiten (z.B. Buch VII-IX, 1. und 2. Punischer Krieg) besteht. Er konnte nicht am Anfang Iupiter auftreten und z.B. den Triumph des M. Fulvius Nobilior 187 v. Chr., mit dem das XV. Buch vielleicht geschlossen hat, voraussagen lassen. Er war gezwungen, gewissermassen kurzatmigere Götterszenen zu gestalten, die nur jeweils einen Teil der Zukunft bestimmen konnten. Deshalb ist es nur natürlich, wenn auch künstlerisch eher misslich, dass bei Ennius mehrere Götterszenen (nicht unbedingt immer *concilia deorum*) vorgekommen sind.

M. Wülfing: Für mich stellt sich die Frage, ob für das historische Epos, angefangen bei Choirilos von Samos bis zu den Epen der ennianischen Zeit, göttliche Interventionen als dichterisches, oder wie Herr Suerbaum hervorhebt, kompositorisches Mittel postuliert werden dürfen. Ich möchte lieber an eine Kontinuität glauben, die erst mit Lucan geendet hat, als an einen Neuanfang in der Zeit der Alexanderepik: «In der Atmosphäre des hellenistischen Herrscherkultes war es auch ganz natürlich, den homerischen Götterapparat in das historische Epos einzuführen, der in Choirilos' Epos über die Perserkriege und in seinen und anderer Epiker Gedichten über die Taten Lysanders ... gefehlt haben dürfte.» (K. Ziegler, *Das hellenist. Epos*², S. 67). In diesem Zusammenhang scheint mir der Götter*rat*, der eine einmalige Interpretation des Geschehens bot und in die göttlich-heroische Frühzeit verlegt werden konnte (im Gegensatz zum immer wieder intervenierenden Götter*apparat*), eine Form zu sein, deren Vorhandensein auch bei Choirilos oder Rhianos von Bene (vgl. Diss. R. Misgeld, S. 29 f., der die Möglichkeiten göttlicher Interventionen bei Rhianos skeptisch beurteilt; das Material erlaubt keine Entscheidung) usw. glaubhaft ist; wir kennen sie bei Naevius und Vergil, um die Nächstliegenden zu nennen. Wäre die m e h r f a c h e Intervention bei Ennius entweder zu bestreiten oder als Notlösung kompositorischer Misslichkeiten zu erklären, wäre auch er, mindestens nach seiner ursprünglichen Absicht, hier einzureihen.

VII

WERNER SUERBAUM

Ennius bei Petrarca

Betrachtungen zu literarischen Ennius-Bildern

ENNIUS BEI PETRARCA

Betrachtungen zu literarischen Ennius-Bildern

Ennius als Person, als handelnde Person, von der erzählt wird, die nicht nur Objekt der Reflexion ist, kommt — abgesehen von einigen kurzen Anekdoten wie etwa der von Cicero *De orat.* II 276 im Kapitel über den Witz erzählten — in der Literatur nur dreimal vor: Ende des 1. Jh.n.Chr. bei Silius Italicus in einer Episode seiner *Punica* (XII 387-419), um 400 bei Claudian in der Einleitung zu einem Preisgedicht auf Stilicho (*Carm.* 23 = *De cons. Stilichonis* lib. III praef.) und Mitte des 14. Jh. in Petrarcas Epos *Africa*. Bei Petrarca erhält die Person des Dichters Ennius eine Bedeutsamkeit, die in seinem gesamten literarischen Nachleben [1] einmalig ist. Deshalb soll dieses reiche Enniusbild Petrarcas im Mittelpunkt meiner Betrachtungen stehen und vor allem durch eine Würdigung der Ennius-Partie bei

[1] Das Material ist vorgelegt in J. Vahlens *Historia Ennii* in der 2. (noch nicht in der 1.) Auflage seiner Ennius-Ausgabe Leipzig 1903. Ergänzend hinzu treten — vor allem für die Rolle des Ennius im Mittelalter (für die die sporadischen Hinweise Vahlens p. cxxix sq. und der unzulängliche Aufsatz von C. Pascal, Ennio nel medio evo, *Athenaeum* 1 (1913), 373-381 überholt sind) — die wertvollen Beiträge M. Barchiesis, *Nevio epico*, Padova 1962, bes. S. 118-136, der auch erstmals S. 140 ff. die Ennius-Kenntnis der Humanisten behandelt, u.a. (noch im Kapitel ‘ Mittelalter ’) die Petrarcas, S. 136-139. — Zwar meint Barchiesi 144 f., « per certi aspetti il Boccaccio rappresenti il culmine della sua (d.h. des Ennius) fortuna medioevale », doch rechtfertigt der Hinweis auf einige Stellen in Boccaccios *Genealogie deorum gentilium* (a cura di V. Romano, 2 vol., Bari 1951) bei näherer Nachprüfung dieses Urteil, wenn man die Rolle des Ennius in Petrarcas *Africa* vergleicht, nicht (noch am stärksten wirkt *Geneal.* XIV 29 p. 740, 24 ff.). — Über Petrarca greife ich sonst nicht hinaus, obwohl z.B. Poliziano in seiner *Sylva Nutricia* (1486) einen langen wichtigen Abschnitt über Ennius bietet (vgl. Barchiesi, 155 ff.) und auch der einflussreiche Hieronymus Vida ihm in seiner *Poetik* von 1527 einige Verse widmet. Interessante Aspekte würden übrigens m.E. noch die Glückwunschadressen zum Erscheinen von P. Merulas Ennius-Ausgabe Leiden 1595 beitragen.

Silius ergänzt werden. Bei einer solchen Beschränkung [1] können nicht alle Züge des Ennius-Nachlebens erfasst werden. Aber jene Züge im literarischen Bild des Ennius verdienen besondere Beachtung, die so gewirkt haben, dass sie die Phantasie gestaltender Künstler wie eben Silius, Claudian, Petrarca zu bewegen vermochten. Untersuchungen zum Nachleben eines Dichters wollen nicht Beiträge zu seiner historischen Gestalt geben, ' wie er wirklich gewesen ist ' ; sie wollen und können nur zeigen, wie er aufgefasst wurde.

I

Zunächst sei ein Überblick über das Enniusbild in Petrarcas *Africa* [2] gegeben.

[1] Die vorliegende Druckfassung bietet nur etwa die Hälfte meines Genfer Originalvortrages. Unter dem weitergreifenden Titel ' Petrarcas Africa und das Nachleben des Ennius ' waren dort über die unmittelbaren Vorlagen Petrarcas hinaus Schwerpunkte und Konstanten im Enniusbild der ganzen Antike und des Mittelalters herausgearbeitet worden. Bei der drastischen Kürzung für die Druckfassung habe ich mich im wesentlichen auf das Enniusbild Petrarcas und dessen Quellen beschränken müssen, auch wenn dadurch die Darstellung in Teil III etwas skelettartig wirken mag. Ich hoffe jedoch bei anderer Gelegenheit über diese ' Konstanten im Nachleben des Ennius ' handeln zu können. Vgl. ferner S. 308, Anm. 1 ; S. 319, Anm. 1 ; S. 331, Anm. 2 und 4 ; S. 335, Anm. 1 ; S. 345, Anm. 1.

[2] Die *Africa* wird zitiert nach der kritischen Ausgabe von N. Festa, Firenze 1926 (Ed. Naz. delle Opere di F. Petrarca I), vgl. zu ihr jedoch die Einwendungen von E. Fraenkel, *Gnomon* 3 (1927), 485-494. Ein Teil der Ennius-Partien ist auch in der zweisprachigen komm. Auswahl enthalten, die G. Martellotti in *F. Petrarca, Rime, Trionfi e poesie latine*, a cura di F. Neri u.a., Milano-Napoli 1951 (La letteratura ital., Storia e testi vol. 6), S. 626-703 gibt. Gerade für Ennius enthält wichtige Quellenangaben und Parallelstellen aus Petrarcas Werken die ältere lateinisch komm. *Africa*-Ausgabe von F. Corradini, in *Padova a F. Petrarca nel quinto centenario della sua morte*, Padova 1874, 77-474, bes. S. 422 f. zu *Afr.* II 445. — Der darstellende Teil I des folgenden Vortrages fusst auf meinem Beitrag zur ungedruckten Festschrift für F. Beckmann, Münster i.W. 1965, 1-9. 70-77 « Literarischer Ruhm : Petrarcas *Africa* und Ennius ». Der Anstoss zu jenen Betrachtungen ging aus von der offenbar einzigen jemals ausserhalb Italiens veröffentlichten

Petrarca hat sich mit der *Africa*, die in seinen Augen — nicht aber in denen der modernen Beurteiler — sein Hauptwerk ist, seit 1338/39 immer wieder beschäftigt. Bei seiner Krönung zum *poeta laureatus* Ostern 1341 auf dem Kapitol waren vielleicht nur die ersten Bücher vollendet. Bei seinem Tode 1374 lagen neun Bücher vor, die aber vor allem nach dem IV. Buch und auch an einer uns näher interessierenden Stelle im IX. Buch noch Lücken aufwiesen. Petrarca hat das Werk nicht als vollendet betrachtet und darum auch nicht selbst herausgegeben.

Die *Africa* ist ein Epos zur Verherrlichung des älteren Scipio Africanus. Seine Taten im 2. Punischen Krieg werden vom Jahre 206, als der Kriegsschauplatz nach Afrika selbst verlegt werden soll, bis zu seinem Triumphzug i.J. 201 vor-

Monographie über die *Africa*: A. S. BERNARDO, *Petrarch, Scipio and the 'Africa'. The birth of humanism's dream*, Baltimore 1962 (dort S. 185 ff. Übersicht über die moderne Literatur seit 1878). Das an sich sehr gehaltvolle Buch (u.a. auch für die Rolle des Ennius in der *Africa* und zugehörigen Werken Petrarcas) ist allerdings für die Beziehungen der *Africa* zum Klassischen Altertum enttäuschend. W. P. MUSTARD, Petrarch's Africa, *AJPh* 43 (1921), 97-121 interessiert in unserem Zusammenhang nicht, da er, abgesehen von Quellenhinweisen, im wesentlichen eine paraphrasierende Inhaltsanalyse gibt. Wichtig ist aber G. MARTELLOTTI, Sulla composizione del 'De viris' e dell' 'Africa' del Petrarca, *Ann. Scuola Norm. Sup. di Pisa*, Lett., storia e filos. Ser. 2, vol. 10 (1941), 247-262, da dort gerade die prominente Rolle des Ennius im IX. Buch der *Africa* und auch in der jüngsten Redaktion α der *Vita Scipionis* Petrarcas, die von den relativ negativen Ennius-Erwähnungen in den Büchern II und IV der *Africa* bzw. von deren völligem Fehlen in den beiden älteren Redaktionen γ und β der *Scipio-Vita* absticht, als wichtiges Moment für die Schichtenanalyse sowohl der *Africa* wie der *Scipio-Vita* benutzt wird (vgl. MARTELLOTTI, bes. S. 258 ff.). — Bei der Zitierung anderer Werke Petrarcas konnte ich die kritischen Ausgaben der *Ed. naz. delle opere di F. Petrarca*, Firenze, für *Fam.* (ed. V. ROSSI, 4 Bde. 1933-1942), *Rer. mem.* (ed. G. BILLANOVICH, 1955) und *Vir. illustr.* (ed. G. MARTELLOTTI, 1964) benutzen, musste aber manchmal — zumal für die *Epist. metr.* und teils auch das *Buc. Carm.* — in Ermangelung der Ausgabe von D. ROSSETTI, *F. P., Poemata minora*, 3 Bde., Mailand 1831-34, auf die Gesamtausgabe der *Opera*, Basileae 1554 (Neudruck Ridgewood, New Jersey 1965) zurückgreifen; etwaige genauere Versangaben bzw. andere Lesarten sind der Sekundärliteratur (bes. BERNARDO) entnommen.

wiegend nach Livius geschildert. Scipio spielt bei Petrarca nicht nur in der *Africa*, sondern auch in anderen Schriften, nicht zuletzt in einer umfangreichen eigenen *Vita Scipionis*, eine ganz bedeutsame Rolle. Eine blosse historische Würdigung des grossen Feldherrn weit hinter sich lassend, spiegelt Petrarca in der *Africa* in dem Verhältnis Ennius/Scipio die Beziehung zwischen dem Dichter und seinem Helden schlechthin.

Ennius wird in der *Africa* in zwei Partien erwähnt, nämlich :

1. innerhalb des Traumes des Africanus im II. Buch, und
2. in der Rede des Laelius im IV. Buch.

Als handelnde Person tritt Ennius auf

3. im IX. Buch, das er allerdings als Hauptfigur geradezu beherrscht. Sein Dialog mit Scipio enthält einen Bericht über eine Homervision ; mit Scipio zusammen wird er auf dem Kapitol mit dem Lorbeerkranz gekrönt.

Nur beiläufig sei erwähnt, dass das Enniusbild innerhalb der *Africa* nach der weithin akzeptierten Theorie G. Martellottis schichtenweise entstanden sein soll. Die beiden Belege 1 und 2 sollen — wie ein Vergleich mit drei verschiedenen uns noch fassbaren Redaktionen der *Vita Scipionis* Petrarcas zeige — einer früheren Schicht angehören als die Figur des Ennius im IX. Buch [1].

[1] Vgl. dazu den grundlegenden Aufsatz MARTELLOTTIS von 1941 (referiert u.a. bei BERNARDO, *Petrarch* 103 ff.) und die entsprechende Introduzione seiner *Viris-illustribus*-Ausgabe von 1964 (darin die *Scipio-Vita* S. 156-313) bzw. seiner früheren Spezialausgabe *F. Petrarca, La vita di Scipione l'Africano*, Milano-Napoli 1954. Auf MARTELLOTTI fussen die Späteren, z.B. U. Bosco, *Francesco Petrarca* [3], Bari 1965, 291. 298 f. Wichtige Einwendungen macht jedoch BILLANOVICH in der Introduzione LXXXVI adn. 2 seiner *Rer.-mem.*-Ausgabe von 1955 : er weist mit Recht auf das Schillern der Ennius-Bewertung bei Petrarca hin, der zur gleichen Zeit positive und negative Elemente nebeneinander vorbringen konnte ; vgl. dazu unten meinen Abschnitt II 3. — Wenn MARTELLOTTI in seinem Aufsatz von 1941, 259 schreibt, dass in den beiden älteren Redaktionen γ und β der *Scipio-Vita* « Ennio è,

I 1

Fast das ganze Buch I und II der *Africa* werden von einem Traum eingenommen, den nach Petrarcas Darstellung der ältere Scipio Africanus an den Säulen des Hercules vor dem Übersetzen nach Afrika zum Angriff auf Karthago hatte. In ihm erscheint der 211 gefallene P. Cornelius Scipio zusammen mit seinem Bruder Gnaeus seinem Sohne und eröffnet ihm die Zukunft, u.a. seinen entscheidenden Sieg über Hannibal. Dass hier eine Nachahmung des durch Macrobius' Kommentar erhaltenen weitberühmten *Somnium Scipionis* (minoris) Ciceros vorliegt, ist offenkundig. Ganz im Stile Ciceros *Rep.* VI 20 ff. enthält auch die Rede des Vaters des Träumenden bei Petrarca eine Partie über die Beschränktheit des menschlichen Ruhmes (II 350-500). In sie ein-

al solito, ricordato come rozzo cantore d' un eroe che sarebbe degno di Omero», so verstehe ich das nicht: Ennius kommt überhaupt erstmals in der jüngsten Redaktion α vor. — Martellotti nimmt an, dass die Gestaltung des IX. Buches der *Africa* und die Erweiterung des XI. Kapitels der *Scipio-Vita* in der Fassung α erst nachträglich unter dem Eindruck der Lektüre Claudians entstanden sei. Wenn Petrarca die Claudian-Partie *De cons. Stil.* III praef. schon früher gekannt hätte, wäre nicht einzusehen, warum nicht mindestens schon in der Redaktion β (von 1342) der *Scipio-Vita* die Freundschaft zwischen Ennius und Scipio erwähnt wäre. Dass das *Somnium Ennii* ein relativ junges Stück ist, scheint mir (mit Corradini zu IX 280-283 und I 19-39 und Billanovich, *a. a. O.*) über Martellotti hinaus aus IX 263 ff. hinreichend deutlich hervorzugehen. — Nachträglich wird mir in Gestalt der schwer zugänglichen Rede Petrarcas bei Gelegenheit seiner Lorbeerkrönung i.J. 1341 (erste und offenbar einzige Edition in: *Scritti inediti di F.P.*, pubbl. ed ill. da A. Hortis, Trieste 1874, S. 312-328 ; engl. Übers. von E. H. Wilkins, *PMLA* 68 (1953), 1241-1250) ein schlüssiger Beweis gegen die Behauptung Martellottis bekannt (S. 260), Petrarca habe die Claudian-Partie über die Lorbeerkrönung des Ennius erst nach 1343 kennengelernt (die angeblichen Claudian-Reminiszenzen, die W. P. Mustard, *AJPh* 42 (1921), 120 f. in älteren Partien der *Africa* finden will, sind dagegen m.E. nicht beweiskräftig). Siehe dazu S. 317, Anm. 2. Diese *laureatio*-Rede von 1341 zeigt überdies eine ganze Reihe von Zügen, die sich später im IX. Buch, aber auch in früheren Partien der *Africa* finden (vgl. dazu S. 299, Anm. 1 ; S. 303, Anm. 1 ; S. 305, Anm. 1 ; S. 345, Anm. 3). Das spricht für die Konstanz im Denken Petrarcas, der gegenüber chronologische Untersuchungen darüber, wann einzelne Passagen geschrieben sein mögen, wenig bedeuten.

gelegt ist jedoch ein Abschnitt [1], der kein Vorbild in Ciceros *Somnium* hat : der Hinweis auf einen erst in kommenden Jahrhunderten erstehenden jungen Dichter aus Etrurien (sprich : Petrarca), der als zweiter Ennius (*uelut Ennius alter* II 443) die Taten des älteren Africanus besingen wird. Dem Sprecher, dem Vater Scipios, sind beide lieb, Ennius wie Petrarca, denn beide leisten (allgemein gesehen :) für die musische Kultur und (im besonderen :) für die Verherrlichung der Scipionen einander Entsprechendes : Ennius hat mit seiner rohen Dichtung die noch kunstlosen Musen in Latium eingeführt, Petrarca aber wird durch seine Dichtung die Musen, die Italien schon verlassen wollen, zum Einhalten bewegen. Beide werden die Leistungen der Scipionen in unterschiedlichem Stile besingen und danach streben, ihnen das kurze Leben zu verlängern. Petrarcas Lob aber

[1] *Africa* II 441-454

Cernere iam uideor genitum post secula multa
442 *finibus etruscis iuuenem qui gesta renarret,*
nate, tua et nobis ueniat uelut Ennius alter.
444 *Carus uterque michi, studio memorandus uterque :*
iste rudes Latio duro modulamine Musas
446 *intulit ; ille autem fugientes carmine sistet ;*
et nostros uario cantabit uterque labores
448 *eloquio, nobisque breuem producere uitam*
contendet ; uerum multo michi carior ille est
450 *qui procul ad nostrum reflectet lumina tempus.*
In quod eum studium non uis pretiumue mouebit,
452 *non metus aut odium, non spes aut gratia nostri ;*
magnarum sed sola quidem admiratio rerum,
454 *solus amor ueri. Sed quid tamen omnia prosunt ?*

Dieser Einschub mit dem Hinweis auf Ennius steht übrigens in einem gewissen Widerspruch zu der Tendenz der Redepartie, in die er eingelegt ist : das zeigt gerade die bemühte Überleitung (454) : und doch — was nützt selbst eine solche Verherrlichung ? Der vorhergehende Abschnitt II 428-432 hatte nämlich bereits gezeigt, dass dem Menschen nach seinem natürlichen Tod noch ein zweiter, die Zerstörung seines Grabes und dessen Aufschrift, drohe, und im Anschluss an die ausgeschriebene Stelle wird darauf hingewiesen, dass schliesslich ein dritter Tod, der Untergang der ihm gewidmeten Bücher, unausweichlich sei : nach der Traumverkündigung Scipios ist also selbst durch Verherrlichung in der Literatur kein ewiges Andenken zu sichern.

wird als wertvoller empfunden, da er — natürlich ist zu verstehen : im Gegensatz zu Ennius — *sine ira et studio* dichten wird. Sein Motiv zur Verherrlichung Scipios wird nur in der reinen Bewunderung grosser Taten und in der Liebe zur Wahrheit bestehen, nicht etwa in Furcht und Hass oder Dankbarkeit und Hoffnung auf Belohnung [1].

I 2

Die zweite Enniuserwähnung, wieder innerhalb einer Rede, erfolgt zu Beginn des IV. Buches. Laelius, der engste Freund des älteren Scipio, versucht den Numiderkönig Syphax als Bundesgenossen zu gewinnen. Auf Bitten des Königs entwirft Laelius ein Portrait Scipios, das das ganze IV. Buch ausfüllt. Laelius beginnt seine grosse Charakterschilderung Scipios mit dem Exordialtopos der affektierten Bescheidenheit [2]. Um der Bitte des Syphax nach einer

[1] Aufschlussreich ist Petrarcas analoge Selbstcharakterisierung in der ältesten Fassung γ seiner *Scipio-Vita* cap. XI (ed. G. Martellotti 1954, S. 221 = 1964, S. 350) zur Begründung von deren unverhältnismässiger Breite : *nec moleste ferant si michi historico in opere* [d.h. in *De uiris illustribus*] *librum unum Scipio meus tenet, qui in pyerio* [d.h. in der *Africa*] *tenet omnes ; notus ut arbitror ad hunc ducem amor est meus, non ex conuictu* [d.h. wie im Falle des Ennius], *non ex nexu sanguinis neque ex beneficiis acceptis aut obsequio aut spe ulla sed ex auctorum testimoniis rebusque et moribus uiri ortus.* Petrarca lässt sich also in der *Africa* II 451 ff. dieselben Motive für seine Scipio-Verehrung zusprechen, die er in der etwa gleichzeitig entstandenen Fassung γ der *Scipio-Vita* direkt zum Ausdruck gebracht hat. Die *sine-ira-et-studio*-Erklärung Petrarcas stammt, wie der ausdrückliche Verweis auf Cicero in ähnlichem Kontext am Schluss der *laureatio*-Rede Petrarcas von 1341 (p. 328 Hortis) zeigt, aus Cic. *Marcell.* 29.

[2] *Africa* IV 34-42

34 *Incipit : « Heu quanto tam grandia iussa sequenti*
est opus eloquio ! Michi non facundia torrens
36 *largaque Cecropie contingit gratia lingue.*
Maximus insano iuueni uigilavit Homerus :
38 *rusticus egregio uigilat nunc Ennius. Atqui*
dignus est hic Graio ; sic dignior ille Latino

Würdigung Scipios wirklich Genüge tun zu können, bedürfte es der hinreissenden Beredsamkeit eines Griechen. Einem rasenden jungen Mann (Achill) hat der grosse Homer sein dichterisches Werk gewidmet ; für einen so hervorragenden Mann wie Scipio arbeitet jetzt ein Ennius, ein wahrer Bauer. Und doch hätte Scipio verdient, von Homer gefeiert zu werden, so wie umgekehrt Achill eines Sängers wie Ennius wert war ; allerdings bedarf Scipio im Gegensatz zu Achill nicht unbedingt literarischer Verherrlichung. Sein Ruhm wächst auch ohne literarische Darstellung von Tag zu Tag [1].

Laelius beteuert also einleitend, er werde der Grösse Scipios in seiner Rede nicht gerecht werden können, dazu wäre allein ein Homer fähig. Leider ist Scipio nicht so glücklich wie Achill, einen neuen Homer gefunden zu haben ; er hat nur Ennius, einen unzulänglichen Dichter [2].

I 3

Das IX. Buch der *Africa* steht weitgehend im Zeichen des Ennius, der nach seinen beiden Erwähnungen jetzt erstmals persönlich auftritt.

Gleich der Beginn des Buches könnte eine Ennius-Reminiszenz sein : er schildert die Ruhe des Meeres bei der Rückfahrt Scipios von Afrika nach Italien (IX 1-7). Eine ähnliche Szene aus dem *Scipio* des Ennius (*var.* 9-12) konnte

40 *uate fuit. Precone autem fortassis Achilles*
indiget ; hic nullo. Surgit sua fama sine ullis
42 *artibus, inque dies crescunt preconia. ...*

[1] Dieser Topos ' Ruhm ohne Dichtung ', der am ausgeprägtesten in dem ps.-verg. *Panegyricus auf Messalla* (*Catal.* 9,57 f.) vorliegt, wird auch von Val. Max. 8, 14, 1 als Überzeugung des älteren Scipio unterstellt, der jedoch daneben den Wert seiner Verherrlichung durch Ennius zu würdigen wusste.

[2] Diese Kritik des Laelius ist nur als *uaticinium ex euentu* verständlich. Dass nämlich Laelius schon in diesem Stadium der Ereignisse die literarische Leistung des Ennius beurteilen konnte, ist unglaubwürdig.

Petrarca bei Macrobius lesen, allerdings auch bei dem von ihm ausgiebig benutzten Livius (XXIX 27, 13 ff.) [1].

Den Hauptteil des Buches bildet die grosse nächtliche Unterhaltung zwischen Scipio und Ennius auf dem Flaggschiff der römischen Flotte [2]. Ennius, der ständige Begleiter Scipios und Zeuge seiner Taten (IX 11 *Ennius assiduus rerum testisque comesque*), sitzt meditierend da, als ihn Scipio auffordert, sein Schweigen zu brechen, indem er ihn an seine Musenweihe erinnert (IX 18-22).

In seiner Entgegung [3] spricht Ennius vor allem über den künftigen Ruhm Scipios, der nach dessen Tode noch grösser als schon zu seinen Lebzeiten sein werde. Seine

[1] N. Festa, *Saggio sull' ' Africa ' del Petrarca*, Palermo-Roma 1926, 79 nennt den Dialog oder das Selbstgespräch auf einer Seefahrt ein oft wiederholtes Motiv der *Africa*.

[2] Zu diesem Dialog zwischen Ennius und Scipio vgl. auch das Kapitel ' Storia e poesia dell' 'Africa ' bei Festa, *Saggio*, bes. S. 82 ff. Martellotti in seinem Aufsatz von 1941, 260, spricht von « l'episodio forse più originale dell' *Africa* ».

[3] *Africa* IX 45 b-64

Sed nostra peritia fandi
nondum propositam ualuit contingere metam,
nuper ab exiguis radicibus orta, nec ante
cognita per Latium, argolicis contenta colonis.
Hoc igitur mecum indignans sub mente mouebam,
precones meritos tua quod notissima uirtus
non habitura foret. Macedum rex magnus amici
forte uidens saxum Eacide titulosque sepulcri,
« Fortunate » inquit « iuuenis, cui nominis illum
preconem reperire fuit ! » Non parua profecto
est claris fortuna uiris habuisse poetam
altisonis qui carminibus cumulare decorem
uirtutis queat egregie monimentaque laudum.
At tibi, summe ducum, claro quo nullus Homero est
dignior, in reliquis blanda inque hoc durior uno,
me solum fortuna dedit. Currentibus annis
nascetur forsan digno qui carmine celo
efferat emeritas laudes et fortia facta
et cui mellifluo melius resonantia plectro
Calliope det fila lire uocemque sonoram.

eigene Kunst (IX 45 *nostra peritia fandi* — vielleicht ist auch zu verstehen : die römische Literatur) betrachtet jedoch Ennius als der grossen Aufgabe, Scipio zu verherrlichen, noch nicht gewachsen. Die römische Literatur ist ja eben erst aus ärmlichen Wurzeln entstanden. Bisher gab es Literatur nur in den Griechenstädten (IX 48). Aufgrund dieser Überzeugung bedauert er es, dass Scipios Leistung keine würdigen Herolde haben wird. Als Parallele zitiert Ennius die bekannte Anekdote, Alexander habe Achill glücklich gepriesen, weil er in Homer einen würdigen Künder seines Ruhmes gefunden habe. Es ist nichts Kleines, betont der Ennius Petrarcas, wenn grossen Männern grosse Dichter zuteil werden, die ihr Lob singen können. Dem Scipio jedoch, der wie kein anderer eines Homers würdig sei, habe das Schicksal nur ihn selbst (60 *me solum*) gegeben. « Vielleicht » aber werde dereinst auch dem Scipio ein würdiger Lobredner erstehen (60-64) — ein Vorverweis nicht etwa auf Silius Italicus, sondern auf Petrarca.

Scipio weist diese Bescheidenheit des Ennius zurück (65-77) : für ihn sind selbst Homer und Euripides nicht grösser als Ennius ; er beteuert, mit Ennius vollauf zufrieden zu sein [1]. — Nach diesem Kompliment legt Scipio dem Ennius zwei bestimmte Fragen über die Dichtung vor : das Problem der Wahrheit der Dichtung bzw. der poetischen Freiheit und die Frage, warum der Lorbeer in gleicher Weise hervorragenden Feldherrn wie auch verehrungswürdigen Dichtern zukomme (73 f. *quid laurea signet | tam ducibus claris quam uatibus addita sacris*). Aus der Entgegnung des Ennius hat uns der an sich für die poetischen Anschauungen

[1] *Africa* IX 65-69 a

Parce, precor, uerbis : tibi non, me iudice, uates
meonius nec iure tibi preponitur altus
Euripides aut quos claro cognomine Grai
concelebrant. Alio nolim me carmine dici,
si dicendus ero.

Petrarcas sehr wichtige Abschnitt über die Wahrheit der Dichter (90-107) [1] in unserem Zusammenhang nicht zu interessieren: wohl aber der Abschnitt über den Lorbeer (108-123). Der Lorbeer, an dem ihm Scipio ein wenig Anteil vergönnen möge, stehe dem Dichter deshalb genauso wie dem Feldherrn zu, weil Ruhm ebenso gut aus dem *ingenium* wie aus dem *bellum* fliesse. Das unvergängliche Grün des Lorbeers deute auf den unsterblichen Ruhm sowohl der Dichter wie der Feldherrn hin [2]. Der Lorbeer stehe unter Apolls und Jupiters Schutz (119-123).

Nach einer Zwischenfrage Scipios schildert Ennius neu anhebend seine Verehrung für die grossen Männer der Vergangenheit, die er wie Väter verehrt, vor allem Homer. Homer steht ihm Tag und Nacht vor Augen. Petrarca gibt in einem längeren Abschnitt (146-159) eine poetische Umschreibung jener rationalistischen Deutung, die der jüngere Scipio bei Cicero *Rep.* VI 10 für die Homererscheinung des originalen Ennius anführt: Homer sei dem authentischen Ennius im Schlaf deshalb erschienen, weil dieser sich im Wachen so intensiv mit ihm beschäftigt habe. Auch der Ennius Petrarcas will mit der breiten Schilderung seines engen Verhältnisses zu Homer die Homererscheinung, von der er anschliessend (ab 160) sprechen wird, vorbereiten und motivieren.

[1] Wenig bekannt ist, dass Petrarca auch in seiner *laureatio*-Rede von 1341 (s.o. S. 297, Anm.), p. 320 HORTIS ausführlich auf dieses Thema eingeht. In dieser Rede findet sich auch ein weit umfangreicheres Analogon (p. 323 sqq.) zu dem in der *Africa* folgenden *laurus*-Abschnitt, vgl. unten, S. 319, Anm. 3.

[2] *Africa* IX, 108-113

108 *Laurea restat adhuc: cuius dignare parumper*
participes nos esse tibi. Si gloria bello,
110 *nec minus ingenio constat, patiere uirenti*
fronde duces uatesque simul sacra tempora cingant.
112 *Immortale decus uiror immortalis utrisque*
indicat et longe promittit temporat uite.

Ennius erzählt, Homer sei ihm in der schlaflosen Nacht vor der Entscheidungsschlacht bei Zama erschienen (160-166 ; cf. 213 f., 286-289). Es war eigentlich kein Traum — deshalb ist die übliche Bezeichnung unserer Partie als *Somnium Ennii* nicht ganz korrekt —, sondern eine Art Vision (159 f.). Bei seinem Erscheinen stellt sich der deutlich als Blinder erkennbare Homer gleichsam vor : *aspice qualis erat quondam dum uixit Homerus* (IX 175) [1]. Er erklärt, dass er aus dem Hades komme. Als Ennius ihm die Füsse küssen will, wehrt es Homer ihm mit der Begründung, Ennius stehe mit ihm doch auf gleicher Stufe (*ex aequo* 180 f.).

Die erste Frage des Ennius an Homer bezieht sich auf die Blindheit des Dichters, der die Menschen doch erst die Welt habe sehen lehren (183-199). Homer antwortet darauf, dass er anstatt der irdischen Augen andere habe, mit denen er die Geheimnisse der Zukunft schauen könne (200-214).

Damit bricht der Text mitten im Vers IX 215 ab. Offensichtlich hat Homer den Ennius mit auf eine Wanderung — man weiss nicht recht, ob durch die Unterwelt oder durch die Jahrhunderte der Zukunft — genommen [2] ; denn

[1] Dies ist übrigens m.W. der einzige Vers aus der *Africa*, der gelegentlich von Ennius-Interpreten (so E. M. Steuart, *The Annals of Quintus Ennius*, Cambridge 1925, S. 98 zu ihrem fr. 3 libri I) herangezogen wird, weil er sich nämlich eng mit dem Ausruf des Aeneas bei Verg. *Aen.* II 274 berührt : *Ei mihi qualis erat, quantum mutatus ab illo / Hectore.* Servius vermerkt z.St. *Ennii uersus* (= *Ann.* 7, doch bezieht ihn H. D. Jocelyn, *CQ* 15 (59), 1965, 142 f. eher auf Ennius' *Alexander*, während er ihn in seiner Ausgabe *The tragedies of Ennius*, Cambridge 1967, S. 87 als Parallele zu einer *Andromache*-Stelle notiert). Petrarca, der einen eigenen Servius-Kodex besass, hat vielleicht absichtlich diese Ennius-Reminiszenz in s e i n e m *Somnium Ennii* einfliessen lassen. Vgl. Petrarca *Ecl.* X 65 ff. *cecumque senem, sed multa uidentem | conuenio. isque, italo missum ut cognouit ab orbe, | prosiluit dextramque dedit* und dazu die kommentierte zweisprachige Spezialausgabe *F. Petrarca, Laurea occidens. Bucolicum Carmen X*, von G. Martellotti, Roma 1968 (Note e discussioni erudite 12), S. 46 f. z.St.

[2] Festa, *Saggio*, S. 86 glaubt (gegen Corradini zu *Africa* IX 216) nicht, dass Petrarca in der Lücke « la sede ultramondana delle anime destinate a incarnarsi » habe geben wollen, denn das hätte die für Petrarca unmögliche An-

nach der Textlücke bittet Ennius Homer um Auskunft über einen jungen Mann, den er *clausa sub valle* (natürlich ein Hinweis auf Vaucluse, den Lieblingsaufenthalt Petrarcas) sich einen Lorbeerkranz ins Haar flechten sieht (216-221). Homer eröffnet ihm, dass dies Franciscus (Petrarca) sei, der dereinst wieder die flüchtigen Musen vom Helikon zurückführen (230) und die grossen Taten, deren Zeuge Ennius gewesen sei, in einem umfassenden Gedicht *Africa* darstellen werde [1]. Nach weiteren Hinweisen auf diesen Dichter

erkennung der Metempsychosis-Theorie vorausgesetzt (vgl. dazu unten S. 330) und zudem eine Dublette zur Vision der Seelen in den beiden ersten Büchern (wo jedoch im futurischen Teil nicht von Seelen die Rede ist, sondern eine Prophetie gegeben wird) und zur Unterweltsszene im Buch VI dargestellt. Festa meint vielmehr, Petrarca habe « un viaggio non solo attraverso lo spazio, ma anche attraverso gli secoli venturi » imaginiert. In dem (ausgefallenen) *Somnium Ennii* vermutet ein « literarhistorisches Pendant » zur politisch-historischen Prophetie im *Somnium Scipionis* von I/II K. Borinski, *Die Antike in Poetik und Kunsttheorie*, Bd. I, Lpz. 1914 (Das Erbe der Alten IX), S. 131 (in dem Abschnitt « Poetik der Africa »).

[1] Dieser erneute Vorverweis auf Petrarca, wiederum innerhalb einer Vision, stellt offensichtlich eine Dublette zu der verwandten Partie *Afr.* II 441-454 dar. Selbst wenn man darin zur Not eine Art Ringkomposition sehen könnte, möchte ich hoffen (diese Erwartung ist m.W. noch nicht deutlich ausgesprochen worden — A. Carlini bei Martellotti 1941, 258, bezeichnet die Szene in Buch IX nur als « manifesto ampliamento » von II 441 ff.), dass Petrarca bei einer abschliessenden Redaktion der *Africa* die ästhetisch und nicht zuletzt menschlich unbefriedigende Wiederholung (die Partie in Buch II und auch in Buch IV würdigt Ennius, den Vorgänger, unnötig stark herab) beseitigt hätte, natürlich zugunsten der Beibehaltung der jüngeren Fassung des IX. Buches. Übrigens ist mir zu der Erscheinung, dass der Autor innerhalb seines Epos einen « Vorblick » auf die Konzeption eben dieses Epos gibt, keine Parallele bekannt; der Appendix XIV ad lib. VI '*Futurarum rerum praedictiones in epico carmine*', in der auch eine Reihe von Epen der beginnenden Neuzeit besprochen werden, in Ch. G. Heyne (4. Aufl. von G. Ph. Wagner)s *Vergil-Kommentar*, Bd. II, Lpz. 1832, S. 1036-1041, ist nichts Vergleichbares zu entnehmen. Dieses Hervorheben der eigenen Person und der eigenen Leistung wird nicht jedermanns Beifall finden. Verhältnismässig milde urteilt M. von Albrecht, *Silius Italicus*, Amsterdam 1964, 129 Anm. 27: « Petrarca redet von seiner eigenen Grösse mit ciceronischer Unbekümmertheit, vgl. IX 216 ff., I 19 ff., 61 ff., II 441 ff., so dass wir versucht sind, mit Petrarcas Ennius auszurufen: *ingenii fiducia quanta* (IX 256). — In seiner Zurückhaltung in diesem Punkt erscheint Silius dagegen als echter

— natürlich autobiographischen *uaticinia ex euentu* —, insbesondere auf seine Dichterkrönung mit dem Lorbeerkranz auf dem Kapitol (237 f.), wird Ennius plötzlich durch die Trompetensignale am Morgen der Schlacht von Zama aus der Vision aufgeschreckt (286-289). Damit endet die Erzählung des Ennius, doch schildert noch eine längere Partie (290-308) den Eindruck seiner Rede.

Ennius tritt wieder auf im eigentlichen Schluss der *Africa* [1] bei der Schilderung des Triumphzuges Scipios. Dort heisst es IX 398-402 : er selbst (Scipio), bekränzt mit grünendem Lorbeer, schritt froh durch die ganze Stadt, vom tarpeischen Felsen zurückkehrend. Ennius zur Rechten des Siegers, die Schläfen mit gleichem Laube kränzend, feierte unter einem so bedeutenden Schirmherrn den ehrenvollen Triumph geistiger Arbeit und holder Poesie [2].

Aus dieser Nacherzählung der drei Enniuspartien in der *Africa* möchte ich neun Punkte stichwortartig herausheben, die mir für Petrarcas Enniusbild charakteristisch zu sein

Vergilianer. » Übrigens lässt sich Petrarca in seiner *laureatio*-Rede in ganz ähnlichem Zusammenhang wie in der *Africa* IX 236 von einem fingierten Interlocutor fragen : *unde tibi ista tanta fiducia*? (p. 315 Hortis).

[1] Die später noch folgenden Verse begründen einmal, warum Petrarca die Schicksale Scipios nach seinem Triumph nicht mehr behandelt (IX 410-420), und enthalten zum andern einen Nachruf auf den König Robert von Sizilien (IX 421-477) ; IX 478-483 ist ein versprengtes Stück.

[2] *Africa* IX 398-409

398 *Ipse coronatus lauro frondente per urbem*
letus iit totam Tarpeia rupe reuersus.
400 *Ennius ad dextram uictoris, tempora fronde*
substringens parili, studiorum almeque Poesis
402 *egit honoratum sub tanto auctore triumphum.*
Post alii atque alii studio certante secuti.
404 *Ipse ego ter centum labentibus ordine lustris*
dumosam tentare uiam et uestigia rara
406 *uiribus imparibus fidens utcumque peregi,*
frondibus atque loco simul et cognomine claro
408 *heroum ueterum tantos imitatus honores,*
irrita ne Grai fierent presagia uatis.

scheinen. Die Quellen und Motive Petrarcas werde ich dann im Hauptteil meines Vortrages (III) betrachten.

1) Ennius ist der lorbeerbekränzte Dichter, der auf dem Kapitol zusammen mit Scipio, dem Sieger im Kampf gegen die Punier, einen Triumph feiert, einen Triumph des Geistes : *poeta laureatus et triumphans*.

2) Der Lorberkranz wird Ennius deshalb zuteil, weil er seinen Helden Scipio preist und dessen Ruhm verewigt : *praeco virtutis*.

3) Ennius ist nicht nur der Lobredner Scipios, er ist auch der Zeuge seiner Taten und sein ständiger Begleiter : *assiduus rerum testisque comesque*.

4) Ennius ist ein glühender Verehrer Homers. Homer ist ihm im Traum erschienen und hat ihm Enthüllungen gemacht : Stichworte wie *Somnium Ennii* und *alter Homerus* bieten sich an.

5) Ennius steht am Anfang der römischen Literatur ; er hat die Musen in Latium heimisch gemacht : *poeta primus*.

6) Ennius ist als Kind von den Musen zum Dichter geweiht worden.

7) Nach Scipios Urteil ist Ennius Homer und allen griechischen Dichtern überlegen.

8) Nach anderer Deutung aber ist Ennius ein unzulänglicher Dichter, dessen Gesang noch roh ist : *poeta rudis*.

9) Ennius' Leistung für Scipio wird mit der Homers für Achill verglichen und auf diesem Hintergrund abgewertet. Damit ist das Stichwort ' Alexander-Anekdote ' gegeben.

Bevor diese Einzelzüge im Bilde des Ennius näher betrachtet werden, seien einige a l l g e m e i n e B e m e r k u n g e n vorausgeschickt.

II 1

Wenn antike Traditionen das Enniusbild der Nachwelt und insbesondere Petrarcas geformt haben [1], dann sind es vor allem *iudicia* über Ennius gewesen, keine Enniuszitate [2]. Deshalb ist grundsätzlich zu all meinen Belegen zu sagen, dass ich Testimonia für Ennius anführe [3], keine Zitate. Da Grammatiker in der Antike — und vielleicht nicht nur damals — selten oder gar nicht urteilen, wird deshalb bei mir z.B. von Festus, Nonius, Charisius, Servius oder Priscian so gut wie nie die Rede sein. Zwar soll man den Einfluss der Grammatiker auf die Folgezeit für die (zumal namentliche) Bekanntheit eines Autors nicht unterschätzen, aber wenn sie nur Beispielsätze bringen oder einzelne Worte mit einem vorgesetzten *Ennius* bzw. *Ennius in annali primo* o.ä., dann kann dadurch keine Vorstellung, kein Bild vermittelt werden. Bilder von Menschen werden durch Nachrichten und Urteile erzeugt und durch inhaltlich aussagekräftige Fragmente, durch etwas, was die Vorstellung anregt. Belege dafür, dass Ennius *sos* statt *eos* gebraucht hat, sind bestenfalls dazu geeignet, das Bild eines archaischen Stilisten zu evozieren; die Nachricht jedoch, dass er auf Sardinien gewesen ist, oder die Beziehungen seines Werkes auf den älteren Scipio

[1] Auf die Nachweise aus der gesamten antiken Tradition (über die unmittelbaren Quellen Petrarcas hinaus) für diese charakteristischen Züge im Nachleben des Ennius, die im Genfer Originalvortrag gegeben waren, ist hier in der Druckfassung weitgehend verzichtet worden; vgl. S. 294, Anm. 1.

[2] Noch weniger als Zitate können Ennius-Imitationen aus der Antike auf Petrarca gewirkt haben. Solche Ennius-Imitationen zeigen zwar, dass Ennius in der betr. Zeit gelesen und offenbar auch geschätzt wurde; wenn und weil sie aber den Namen des Ennius nicht bieten, konnte ein späterer Autor wie etwa Petrarca, der keine direkte Ennius-Kenntnis mehr besass, sie nicht unmittelbar als Ennius-Imitationen identifizieren.

[3] Man überschaut sie bequemer als bei VAHLEN in der *Ennius-Ausgabe* von L. MUELLER, St. Petersburg 1884, S. 145-154 und (weniger vollständig) auch in der zweisprachigen *Annalen-Ausgabe* von R. ARGENIO, Torino 1968 (Testi classici commentati 3). S. 5-8.

haben die Phantasie Späterer in Bewegung gesetzt. Gerade bei Untersuchungen über das Nachleben kann das Werk eines Dichters nicht als ein ein für allemal abgeschlossenes Artefakt betrachtet werden, sondern eine andere Seinsweise von Literatur tritt in den Vordergrund: Dichtung als Erlebnis des Lesers [1].

II 2

Quellen- oder Imitationsuntersuchungen wirken immer dann enttäuschend, wenn sie für einen bestimmten Autor Vorbilder oder Parallelen ermitteln — und es damit bewenden lassen. Dabei bieten die nachgewiesenen Quellen nur erst das Material für eine Würdigung des betreffenden Autors, für die Interpretation der Ziele oder Wirkungen, die er mit der Verwendung dieses Materials innerhalb seines, innerhalb dieses neuen Zusammenhanges angestrebt oder erzielt hat. Vorbildlich in dieser Hinsicht hat M. von Albrecht das Verhältnis des Silius Italicus zu Vergil untersucht. M. von Albrecht ist auch einer der ganz wenigen klassischen Philologen, die näher auf Petrarcas *Africa* eingegangen sind [2]. Er hat mit Recht einen Vergleich zwischen Silius' *Punica* und Petrarcas *Africa* deshalb für fruchtbar angesehen, weil man hier « dem silianischen Epos ein inhaltlich und gattungsmässig nahestehendes Werk gegenüberstellen » kann. Dabei handelt es sich um zwei Werke, die unabhängig voneinander

[1] Vgl. dazu R. Wellek-A. Warren, *Theorie der Literatur*, Ullstein-Buch Nr. 420/421, in dt. Übers.v. E. und M. Lohner, Frankfurt/Main-Berlin 1963, S. 121 ff.

[2] Das *Silius-Buch* M. von Albrechts mit dem bezeichnenden Untertitel *Freiheit und Gebundenheit römischer Epik* (Amsterdam 1964) enthält ein eigenes Kapitel « Silius und Petrarca », S. 118-144, vgl. auch S. 22 f. u.ö., dazu eine kleine *Africa*-Bibliographie, S. 236 f. Die folgenden Zitate stammen aus von Albrecht S. 121. Ausser von Albrecht hat sich offenbar nur R. T. Bruère, Lucan and Petrarch's Africa, *ClPhil* 56 (1961), 83-99 mit dem Verhältnis der *Africa* zu einem klassischen Autor beschäftigt.

entstanden sind. Denn so überraschend es klingen mag: Petrarca, der mehrfach in seiner *Africa* betont, dass er mit seinem Epos das ungenügende Werk des Ennius zum Ruhme Scipios ersetzen will, weiss nicht, dass er darin bereits in Silius Italicus eine Art Vorläufer gehabt hat. Er hat das Werk des Silius Italicus nicht benutzt, scheint nicht einmal dessen Namen gekannt zu haben [1]. Das macht den Vergleich der *Punica* mit der *Africa* nur noch reizvoller. « Beide Epen behandeln denselben Stoff, beide Dichter sind Verehrer des Livius und Schüler Vergils, beide blicken aus einer als Spätzeit empfundenen Gegenwart zurück auf die grosse Vergangenheit. » Und — so möchte ich hinzufügen — in beiden Epen spielt Ennius als Person eine Rolle. Die unterschiedliche Rolle, die beide Epiker dem Ennius in ihren Dichtungen zuteilen, ist in erster Linie bestimmt von den je verschiedenen und ganz persönlichen poetischen Zielen des Silius oder des Petrarca.

[1] Diese erstaunliche Tatsache ist oft bestritten worden (man hat Petrarca sogar schon verdächtigt, das Werk des Silius gekannt und benutzt, aber wohlweislich unterdrückt zu haben), aber nicht zu bezweifeln. Vgl. etwa das Sonderkapitel in L. Pingauds *Africa-Ausgabe*, Paris 1872, 26-33; P. de Nolhac, *Pétrarque et l'humanisme*, Paris 1892 / Neuausgabe Paris 1907 (= Turin 1959), 159/193; von Albrecht, S. 119 Anm. 2; zur Silius-Kenntnis im Mittelalter auch O. Zwierlein, *Antike und Abendland* 16 (1970), 157 A 31. — Silius figuriert z.B. auch nicht unter den etwa 120 griechischen und römischen Dichtern, auf die Petrarca verschlüsselt in seiner X. *Ekloge* (vgl. den Index in der Spezialausgabe *Laurea occidens* von G. Martellotti, Roma 1968) anspielt. Nach der ältesten Fassung der *Scipio-Vita* (in Martellottis Ausgabe 1954, 221; 1964, 350) ist allerdings Scipios Ruhm *per omnes fere libros, non tantum historicos sed poeticos et morales* verbreitet, doch wird bei den *poetici libri* nur an Ennius gedacht sein. Vgl. auch *Fam.* X 4, 34 *cultior tamen de illis (sc. Scipionis) rebus liber metricus non apparet*, und dazu unten S. 344. — Es gibt jedoch einige Fälle, bei denen Petrarca und Silius unabhängig voneinander in ähnlichem Zusammenhang auf dasselbe Motiv verfallen sind; vgl. neben den beiden von M. von Albrecht, 139 Anm. 48 und 142 (dazu unten S. 312, Anm. 2) notierten Zügen auch die gleichartige Verwendung der Alexander-Anekdote Silius XIII 793 ff. und Petrarca *Africa* IX 51 ff. (vgl. dazu unten III 9).

Das Verhältnis des Silius und Petrarca zu Ennius ist methodisch gesehen gleich oder doch vergleichbar. Beide besassen bestimmte Nachrichten über Ennius. Beide wussten insbesondere, dass Ennius im 2. Punischen Krieg lebte und Beziehungen zu Scipio Africanus besessen haben muss. Aber beide Dichter haben von diesem vergleichbaren Ausgangspunkt her die Figur des Ennius unabhängig voneinander ganz verschieden entwickelt. Dabei ähneln sich die beiden Dichter insofern, als sie mit Ennius nicht einfach so frei schalten, wie es ein moderner Autor mit einer völlig fiktiven Romanfigur tut. Beide Dichter fühlen sich ja als historische Epiker (gerade seinen Ennius lässt Petrarca IX 90 ff. über die Wahrheit der Dichter sprechen) und schaffen deshalb einen Ennius, der Verbindungen zum historischen Ennius aufweist, bzw. genauer genommen zu dem Bild des Ennius, das Silius und Petrarca aus den ihnen bekannten Nachrichten gewinnen mussten. Dass bei dem Bemühen, einer handelnden Figur der Dichtung Profil zu geben, dann doch wieder neue Züge, weiterentwickelte Züge entstehen, ergibt sich geradezu mit Notwendigkeit aus dem Wesen epischen Erzählens.

II 3

An sich war weder Silius noch Petrarca gezwungen, Ennius innerhalb ihrer quasi-historischen Dichtungen überhaupt zu erwähnen. Livius, die Hauptquelle beider, berichtet nichts von irgendeiner Teilnahme des Ennius am 2. Punischen Krieg [1]. Selbst wenn Silius in Ennius' *Annalen* einen Hinweis auf seine aktive Teilnahme als Soldat am 2. Punischen Krieg

[1] Livius erwähnt Ennius nur zweimal: XXXVIII 56, 4 im Hinblick auf die Aufstellung seiner Statue im Scipionengrab; XXX 26, 9 als Autor des Cunctator-Elogiums.

gefunden haben sollte [1], dann kann diese soldatische Tätigkeit des Ennius doch auf gar keinen Fall so bedeutsam gewesen sein, dass sie unbedingt in einer Darstellung des 2. Punischen Krieges hätte berücksichtigt werden müssen. Und selbst wenn Petrarca etwa von einer Teilnahme des Ennius am Triumphzug des Scipio gelesen hat (was, wie wir noch sehen werden, tatsächlich der Fall ist), so hätte diese Einzelheit nicht unbedingt Erwähnung finden müssen [2]. Aber Petrarca befand sich in der *Africa* gegenüber der Person des Dichters Ennius in einer Art Zwangslage. Zu seinen poetischen Zielen in der *Africa* gehörte unverkennbar das Bestreben, in ihr seine Vorstellungen von dem Wesen und auch der Würde des Dichters und der Poesie zum Ausdruck zu bringen. Um nun innerhalb einer Darstellung des 2. Punischen Krieges seine eigenen humanistischen poetischen Ideale spiegeln zu können, bedurfte Petrarca dafür einer geeigneten Figur. Er konnte jedoch nicht eines der sonst von ihm so verehrten *tria lumina Romani ingenii* (Cicero,

[1] Es ist sogar umstritten, ob Silius die *Annalen* des Ennius überhaupt gelesen hat (ältere Literatur zu Silius / Ennius bei SCHANZ-HOSIUS, *Röm. Literaturgesch.* II (1935), 529). Die Skepsis von G. FÜRSTENAU, *De Sili Italici imitatione quae fertur Enniana*, Diss. Berlin 1916 in dieser Hinsicht und seine Behauptung, dass Ennius im 1. Jh. n.Chr. nicht einmal ausnahmsweise zur Lektüre eines römischen Gebildeten gehört habe, scheint mir zu weit zu gehen (trotzdem bleibt die Übersicht FÜRSTENAUS über die Ennius-Geltung im 1. Jh. n.Chr., S. 8 ff. wertvoll). E. HECK, *WSt* 83 (1970), 172 ff. folgt von ALBRECHTS (*Silius*, 161 ff.) *non liquet* im Hinblick auf eine direkte Ennius-Lektüre des Silius. Wenn aber ein späterer Autor weiss, dass ein berühmter älterer Dichter denselben Gegenstand wie er behandelt hat, wird er doch kaum darauf verzichten, dessen Darstellung (also 2 einschlägige Bücher in Ennius' *Annalen*) nachzulesen.

[2] Immerhin wäre die Aufnahme dieses Einzelzuges bei Petrarca schon eher zu erwarten, denn Petrarca bietet auch die beiden anderen Details, die Livius (XXX 45, 3-5) als einzige aus dem Triumphzug Scipios erwähnt, nämlich die Beteiligung eines aus punischer Versklavung befreiten römischen Senators Terentius und die in ihrer Faktizität umstrittene Aufführung des Königs Syphax, bei der Petrarca — übrigens bezeichnenderweise (vgl. dazu von ALBRECHT, *Silius*, 142 mit Anm. 53) übereinstimmend mit Silius — von der von Livius ausdrücklich gegen Polybios vertretenen Version abweicht.

Varro, Vergil) wählen [1]; als Sprachrohr bot sich nur Ennius an, der einzige Dichter, von dem ihm bekannt war, dass er am 2. Punischen Kriege teilgenommen hatte.

Doch zeigt sich in der Konzeption des Ennius innerhalb der *Africa* ein geradezu notwendiger Zwiespalt. Einerseits sollte Ennius als Präfiguration, als Vorgänger im Sinne eines Vorbildes für Petrarca dienen. Deshalb ist es verständlich, dass Petrarca an seinem Ennius Züge herausgearbeitet, insbesondere überlieferte Züge verstärkt hat, die die Würde, die Würdigung, die Ehrung des Dichters betreffen. Für die soziale Stellung des Dichters, für sein Verhältnis zu den Grossen seiner Zeit und für die Anerkennung, die der Grösste seiner Zeit ihm gezollt hat, war die Figur des Ennius für Petrarca ein Vorbild, Vorwegnahme dessen, was Petrarca selbst erstrebte, teils schon erreicht hatte und — eben durch die Aufstellung eines Ideals, das schon in der Antike verwirklicht worden sei — verteidigen wollte.

Das ist die positive Seite des Enniusbildes bei Petrarca. Es gibt aber, und wiederum mit einer inneren Notwendigkeit, auch eine negative Seite desselben Ennius bei Petrarca. Petrarca konnte wohl kaum die ihm bekannten, in der Antike vielfach belegten Abqualifizierungen des Ennius als Dichter einfach ignorieren [2]. Diese negativen Urteile zu benutzen, wurde ihm darüber hinaus durch ein persönliches

[1] Auch wenn Ennius in Petrarcas *Africa* der einzige Dichter und im IX. Buch sogar die beherrschende Figur neben Scipio ist, darf man nicht glauben, in Petrarcas Augen sei Ennius der grösste Literat Roms überhaupt. An Ennius hat Petrarca keinen seiner (im XXIV. Buch der *Familiari* gesammelten) Briefe an grosse Autoren des Altertums gerichtet, wohl aber an Cicero, Seneca, Varro, Quintilian, Livius, Asinius Pollio, Horaz, Vergil und auch an Homer. — Zum Dreigestirn der römischen Literaten vgl. z.B. im *Trionfo della Fama* III nach der Erwähnung Vergils und Ciceros (16 ff.) als den occhi de la lingua nostra (21) : Varrone, il terzo gran lume Romano (III 38 in : *Petrarca, Rime*, 1951, S. 544). In seiner *laureatio*-Rede nennt Petrarca Vergil *poetarum pater* (p. 314) und *illustrissimus et omnium maximus poeta* (p. 311), Homer *poetarum princeps* (p. 323 Hortis).

[2] Vgl. den Abschnitt III 8 über Ennius als *poeta rudis*.

Motiv nahegelegt, das durch die Konzeption der *Africa* gegeben ist. Petrarca wollte in der *Africa* ein exemplarisches, ein wahrhaft würdiges Epos zum Ruhm des grossen Scipio Africanus schreiben. Das aber wäre ja ein — wenigstens in den Augen der Mitwelt — unnötiges Unterfangen gewesen, wenn Scipio bereits in einem früheren panegyrischen Epos, eben dem des Ennius, eine gültige Würdigung erfahren hätte. Deshalb musste Petrarca betonen, dass er zwar in Ennius einen Vorgänger gehabt habe, dass dessen Leistung aber nicht ausreichend gewesen sei [1]. Silius dagegen hat Ennius zwar nicht nur als Soldaten, sondern auch als künftigen Dichter des 2. Punischen Krieges gewürdigt [2]; aber er hat Ennius nicht in der Weise wie Petrarca zu einer Vorgängerfigur aufstilisiert. Ein persönliches Messen seiner eigenen Leistung an der des Ennius hat Silius vermieden. Petrarca hingegen, dessen erklärtes Ziel es war, Ennius zu übertreffen, musste daran gelegen sein, die Leistung des Ennius für Scipio zu drücken. Petrarca will mehr als ein *Ennius alter* sein, auch wenn sich so II 443 apostrophieren lässt. Deshalb nutzt Petrarca die Chance, die ihm abfällige antike Urteile über Ennius ohnehin an die Hand gaben, mehrfach innerhalb der *Africa* aus.

So ergibt sich der Zwiespalt der Enniusgestalt bei Petrarca. In sozialliterarischer Hinsicht, im Hinblick auf die Funktion des Dichters in der Gesellschaft und seine Anerkennung durch die Gesellschaft, ist Ennius für Petrarca ein Vorgänger im Sinne eines Vorbildes. Seine poetischen Absichten (nämlich mit seiner Dichtung dem Ruhm eines grossen Mannes zu dienen) entsprechen genau denen, die

[1] Ein Hinweis auf die äussere Tatsache, dass von Ennius' Scipio-Verherrlichung zur Zeit Petrarcas so gut wie nichts mehr vorhanden war, hätte nicht ausgereicht — auch wenn ein solcher Überlieferungsbefund durch ein abschätziges Werturteil der Nachwelt über Ennius bedingt sein mochte.

[2] Innerhalb der bei Vahlen p. lxxvi sq. abgedruckten Partie Sil. XII 387-419, bes. vs. 410 ff.

auch Petrarca selbst vertritt. Als Künstler dagegen (wenn man so will: bei der Durchführung der richtigen poetischen Ziele) hat Ennius in Petrarcas Augen weitgehend versagt. In artistischer Hinsicht ist Ennius für Petrarca keineswegs das Vorbild, das er im Hinblick auf Gesinnung und Stoff für ihn darstellt. Um das Verhältnis Petrarcas zu Ennius, um das Enniusbild Petrarcas in der *Africa* epigrammatisch zusammenzufassen: für Petrarca ist Ennius der *poeta laureatus* und der *poeta rudis* oder, um zwei andere Chiffren zu benutzen, die Petrarca allerdings nicht verwendet: Ennius ist sowohl der *alter Homerus* wie der *alter Choerilus*.

III 1

Die Gleichstellung des Dichters Ennius in Petrarcas *Africa* (IX 398-409) mit dem Triumphator Scipio, wobei beide mit dem Lorbeer gekrönt werden, die Vorstellung also des *poeta laureatus et triumphans* [1], ist natürlich unhistorisch.

Das erste und bei weitem wichtigste Motiv der Erfindung darf man in dem Bestreben Petrarcas sehen, die Ehre der Dichterkrönung, die ihm selbst im Jahre 1341 in Rom zuteil geworden ist, in jene Zeit, in der sein Epos spielt, zurückzuspiegeln und ihr damit die Weihe der Tradition zu geben. Er stellt sich, auch im Hinblick auf diese Dichterkrönung, ausdrücklich als Nachfolger des Ennius hin, als einen derjenigen *alii atque alii* (IX 402), die seither dem Ennius im Ringen um den dichterischen Lorbeerkranz gefolgt sind. Aber bei all seinem verständlichen Streben, in dem Dichter der fernen Vergangenheit sich selbst zu spiegeln und durch das Medium des historischen Epos trotzdem

[1] Weitere Belege für diese Vorstellung bei Petrarca in *Epist. metr.* II 9 (Edit. Basil. 1554, p. 1350 a) und *Ecl.* III 152 ff. (p. 1260 b) sind unten S. 342 u. 344 zitiert.

seine eigenen Anschauungen über das Wesen und die Würde der Poesie zum Ausdruck zu bringen, hätte Petrarca es dennoch wohl kaum gewagt, Ennius in dieser Rolle als *poeta laureatus et triumphans* auftreten zu lassen — wenn er für diese Auffassung nicht Stützen oder gar einen Beleg in der Tradition vorgefunden hätte. Denn die äusseren Züge, die der Enniusfigur in der *Africa* gegeben sind, sind — wie wir immer wieder sehen werden — kaum einmal frei erfunden, sondern aus antiker Überlieferung entnommen. Ähnlich steht es mit dem Bericht von der triumphalen Lorbeerkrönung des Ennius auf dem Kapitol beim Triumph Scipios. Petrarcas Quelle in diesem Punkt ist wohlbekannt ; er nennt sie nämlich selber ausdrücklich in jener *Scipio-Vita*, die in ihren verschiedenen Phasen in engem Zusammenhang mit der schichtenweisen Ausformung der *Africa* selber entstanden ist. Zu den Erweiterungen in der jüngsten, dritten Redaktion der *Scipio-Vita* (der sog. Redaktion α), die offenbar zwischen 1351 und 1360 entstanden ist [1], gehört auch ein längerer Abschnitt über die Begierde Scipios nach Ruhm und seine daraus resultierende Liebe für die Dichter seiner Zeit. Als Quelle zitiert Petrarca hier in der *Vita Scipionis* XI 12 ausdrücklich einige C l a u d i a n-Verse (*Cons. Stil.* III praef. 1-4), die von der Vereinigung von Kriegshandwerk und musischen Interessen beim älteren Scipio sprechen, und referiert dann, unter nochmaliger Berufung auf Claudian, dessen weitere Darstellung, dass Scipio den Dichter Ennius auf allen seinen Feldzügen ständig um sich gehabt und ihn schliesslich im Triumphzug lorbeerbekränzt mit sich auf das Kapitol geführt habe :

cap. XI

(12) *hoc de fonte prodiit quod poetas sui temporis coluit ac dilexit* (*sc. Scipio*) *; cuius rei Claudianus meminit his uersibus :*

[1] Vgl. dazu die Untersuchungen Martellottis, oben, S. 294, Anm. 2 und S. 296, Anm. 1.

Maior Scipiades Italis qui solus ab oris
in proprium uertit Punica bella caput,
non sine Pieriis exercuit artibus arma,
semper erat uatum maxima cura duci.

Antes omnes Ennium poetam carum habuit, quem bellis omnibus comitem suarumque testem rerum lateri semper habuit herentem. (13) *Denique triumphi die, «gemina Carthagine uicta», ut testatur idem* (*sc. Claud. vs.* 15), *in Capitolium ascendens coronatus uictor, laureatum secum illum retulit* ... [1].

In der *Africa* konnte Petrarca dem literarischen Genos entsprechend nicht, wie hier in dem biographisch-historischen Werk, eine Quellenangabe machen; aber seine Abhängigkeit auch im Epos von Claudian [2] ist evident.

[1] Die Fortsetzung dieser Partie *Vita Scipionis* XI 13 ist unten, S. 342, Anm. 1 zitiert.

[2] Der Text von Claudian, *Cons. Stil.* III praef. 1-20 ist bei VAHLEN p. CXXI abgedruckt. Petrarca kannte diese Claudian-Partie bereits i.J. 1341: das zeigt seine *laureatio*-Rede (s.o. S. 297, Anm.), in der er ausdrücklich (p. 322 f. HORTIS) als Beleg für die Wertschätzung grosser Feldherrn für Dichter die Claudian-Verse 5/6 *gaudet enim uirtus testes sibi iungere Musas;* | *carmen amat quisquis carmine digna gerit* zitiert. Anschliessend kommt Petrarca ausführlich auf den Lorbeer zu sprechen (p. 323 ff.) und betont immer wieder, dass er nicht nur Caesaren, sondern auch Dichtern zukomme. Es ist nun aber sehr auffällig, dass im Anschluss an diese Argumentation, in der es zunächst nur um das *conuenire* geht, als Beleg für die Tatsache, dass eine solche Lorbeerkrönung wirklich jemals Dichtern zuteil geworden ist, von (angeblich) *innumerabilibus testibus* nur Statius (p. 327) mit Hinweis auf *Theb.* I 32 f. und *Ach.* I 15 f. genannt wird (wo aber nur metaphorischer Gebrauch vorliegt), nicht aber auch Ennius, von dessen Lorbeerkrönung Claudian doch anschliessend spricht. Ennius wird von Petrarca in der Rede nur einmal (p. 312) innerhalb eines Zitats aus Ciceros *Archias-Rede* 18 für die Bezeichnung der Dichter als *sancti* erwähnt. Als letzten Vorgänger für eine Lorbeerkrönung, die schon mehr als 1200 Jahre zurückliege, nennt Petrarca (p. 316) ausdrücklich Statius. Dass Petrarca erst in der *Africa* die Ennius-Erwähnung bei Claudian ausgewertet hat, nicht schon in der *laureatio*-Rede, mag daran liegen, dass er hier an die jüngste Tradition — also an Statius z.Zt. Domitians — anknüpfen und nicht auf ein noch etwa weitere 3 Jahrhunderte zurückliegendes Beispiel zurückgreifen wollte. In der *Africa* aber bot sich die Claudian-Stelle zur Übernahme geradezu an.

Nur die beiden wichtigsten Entsprechungen seien hervorgehoben: einmal ist Ennius bei Claudian (*Cons. Stil.* III praef. 11 f. *haerebat doctus lateri castrisque solebat* | *omnibus in medias Ennius ire tubas*) und in praktisch wörtlicher Übereinstimmung bei Petrarca (*Vita Scip.* XI 12 *quem* [*sc. Ennium*] *bellis omnibus comitem suarumque testem rerum lateri semper habuit herentem; Africa* IX 11 *Ennius, assiduus rerum testisque comesque*) der ständige Gefolgsmann Scipios auf seinen Feldzügen. Zum anderen zeigt Claudian (vs. 19/20) in der Tat Ennius als lorbeergekrönten Dichter: (beim Doppeltriumph über das spanische und das afrikanische Karthago) führte die Siegesgöttin die Musen wieder heim, und der Kriegslorbeer war der Kranz des Sängers: *aduexit reduces secum Victoria Musas* | *et sertum uati Martia laurus erat.* Hieraus hat Petrarca in der *Scipio-Vita* XI 13 und in der *Africa* IX 398 ff. sein Bild vom lorbeergekrönten Ennius übernommen. Wenn man es allerdings genau nimmt, erhält Ennius bei Claudian nicht den Lorbeer des Dichters, sondern den des Mitkämpfers, so wie alle Teilnehmer am Triumphzug lorbeerbekränzt waren. Aber Ennius ist eben gleichzeitig doch auch Dichter (*uates*), so dass die beiden Vorstellungen triumphierender Dichter | triumphierender Soldat auch bei Claudian fast zusammenfliessen. Es ist somit nur noch ein kleiner, wenn auch bedeutsamer Schritt, wenn Petrarca in der *Africa* den Ennius ausdrücklich als Dichter mit dem Lorbeer gekrönt sein lässt [1].

[1] Dass es, genau besehen, bei Claudian der Lorbeer des Triumphators und damit auch seiner Soldaten ist, der den Mitkämpfer Ennius zum *poeta laureatus* macht, wurde in der Diskussion (unten S. 348 ff. nicht referiert) von Mr. Badian unterstrichen. Aber Ennius ist bei Claudian auch als Soldat bereits Dichter, nicht nur — wie bei Silius — zukünftiger Dichter: das zeigt einmal der Auftakt der Partie (*Cons. Stil.* III praef. 1-6), dann aber auch Worte wie *doctus* (11), *canenti* (13), *uati* (20). Deshalb darf man mit gewissen Vorbehalten auch schon bei Claudian von einem *poeta laureatus et triumphans* sprechen. Petrarca lässt den Ennius ausdrücklich einen *studiorum almeque poesis triumphum* (IX 401 f.) feiern, obwohl kaum vorstellbar ist, dass Ennius zu dieser Zeit sein Preisgedicht auf Scipio, geschweige denn sein Epos, schon vollendet haben konnte. Aber gerade darin liegt eine eigenartige Parallelität zu

Mit dem Nachweis, dass Claudian die Quelle Petrarcas für die Vorstellung von Ennius als einem triumphierenden lorbeergekrönten Dichter ist, ist unsere Frage, wie es zu dieser Vorstellung gekommen ist, allerdings nur um eine Schicht, immerhin um fast ein Jahrtausend, verschoben. Der Entwicklung dieses Bildes vom *poeta laureatus et triumphans*, insbesondere im Hinblick auf Ennius, bin ich nachgegangen, doch ist das Material an anderer Stelle vorzulegen [1]. Überraschenderweise hat sich kein eindeutiger Beleg für eine reale Dichterkrönung mit Lorbeer in der lateinischen Literatur finden lassen. Als allerdings die Humanisten im 14. Jh. den Brauch der Krönungen von Dichtern mit Lorbeerkränzen einführten (schon vor Petrarcas epochaler Krönung von 1341 hat es dafür zwei weniger bekannte Beispiele gegeben [2]), glaubten sie damit eine antike Institution zu erneuern. Dafür gibt es gerade bei Petrarca, der mehrfach und sehr ausführlich über den Lorbeer, vor allem im Zusammenhang mit seiner Dichterkrönung, gehandelt hat, eine ganze Reihe von Belegen. Erwähnt sei [3] ein ganz unscheinbares, aber umso

Petrarcas eigener Situation : wie Petrarca den Ennius schon in einem Augenblick seinen literarischen Triumph feiern lässt, wo er noch an seinem Werk arbeiten wird, so ist Petrarca selber die Erhöhung zum *poeta laureatus* Ostern 1341 gewissermassen im Vorgriff auf die Vollendung der *Africa* zuteil geworden, von der damals höchstens die Bücher I-IV vollendet, aber nicht einmal publiziert (nur König Robert von Sizilien vorgelesen) waren.

[1] Die Untersuchung der Idee vom *poeta laureatus et triumphans* bildete einen Schwerpunkt meines Genfer Originalvortrags. In der vorliegenden Druckfassung habe ich diese zusammenhängende Erörterung weglassen müssen, hoffe jedoch, sie an anderer Stelle vorlegen zu können.

[2] Zu den Dichterkrönungen seit der Renaissance vgl. T. DOHRN, *Röm. Mitt.* 69 (1962), 83 ff. mit Literatur S. 84, Anm. 26 ; ferner J. EBERLE, Poeta laureatus — Dichterkrönungen, *Attempto (Nachr. f. Freunde der Univ. Tübingen)* 12 (1963), 11-16 (ohne exakte Quellenangaben ; zu Petrarca, S. 12 f.). — Die vorzügliche Darstellung von E. H. WILKINS, The coronation of Petrarch, *Speculum* 18 (1943), 155-197 (mit Untersuchung der 'Quellen' Petrarcas S. 158 ff.) ist mir erst nach Abschluss des Manuskripts bekanntgeworden.

[3] Vgl. DE NOLHAC, *Pétrarque*, 125 Anm. 2 / 149 Anm. 2, der noch auf *Epist. metr.* II 11, 20 ff. (Edit. Basil. 1554, p. 1350 b) verweist : *Florea uirginibus,*

bezeichnenderes Zeugnis : im Servius-Kommentar zu Vergils *Ecl.* VIII 12, wo allegorisch vom Lorbeer des Triumphators Pollio und vom Efeu des Dichters Vergil gesprochen wird, findet sich die Erklärung : *nam uictores imperatores lauro, hedera coronantur poetae.* Dazu hat nun Petrarca in seiner Servius-Handschrift, die wir heute noch besitzen, in einer Randbemerkung eine Korrektur angebracht. Er schreibt nämlich : *laurus Cesarum atque uictorum est, hedera poetarum, sed et laurus.* Für Petrarca ist also nicht nur der Efeu das Abzeichen der Dichter, « sondern auch der Lorbeer ». Wie nicht anders zu erwarten, weist auch die Urkunde, die Petrarca nach seiner Lorbeer-Dichterkrönung 1341 durch den römischen Senator Graf Orso dell'Anguillara überreicht wurde, darauf hin, dass der Lorbeer Kaisern und Dichtern zukomme : Kaisern, Feldherrn und Siegern, wie es in diesem sog. *Priuilegium laureae* heisst, *post labores bellorum*, Dichtern *post labores studiorum* [1].

sunt laurea serta poetis | Caesaribusque simul parque est ea gloria utrisque. — In *secret.* III (*F. Petrarca, Prose,* a cura di G. Martellotti u.a., Milano-Napoli 1955, La letteratura ital., Storia e testi, vol. 7, S. 158) lässt sich Petrarca vorhalten : *quam ob causam tanto opere siue cesariam siue poeticam lauream, quod illa (sc. Laura) hoc nomine uocaretur, adamasti ; ex eoque tempore sine lauri mentione uix ullum tibi carmen effluxit* (also einen *laurea*-Kult wegen seiner Laura-Verehrung). Vgl. auch die *De sumenda atque recepta laurea poetica ad amicos consultatoriae epistulae*, Edit. Basil. 1554, p. 1251 ff. (= *Fam.* IV 4-8, mit Richtigstellung der Adressaten), bes. *Fam.* IV 7, 2 (an König Robert von Sizilien) *Lauree morem, non intermissum modo tot seculis, sed ibi iam prorsus obliuioni traditum, aliis multum diuersis curis ac studiis in republica uigentibus, nostra etate renouatum te duce me milite.* — Die ausführlichste, aber offenbar am wenigsten bekannte Behandlung des Lorbeerthemas bei Petrarca (nicht unter den zahlreichen Erwähnungen von ' Laurel ' und ' Crown of laurel ' bei Bernardo, *Petrarch*), zugleich die für unsere Betrachtung wichtigste, findet sich in Petrarcas *laureatio*-Rede (s.o. S. 297, Anm.), von 1341, p. 323 ff. Hortis.

[1] Dass das *Privilegium Laureae* (Zitat aus der Edit. Basil. 1554, p. 1255, 1. Zeile) unter dem Einfluss Petrarcas verfasst sein wird, zeigt die enge Berührung nicht nur in diesem Punkte mit seiner *laureatio*-Rede. (Dort wird p. 324 H. der Lorbeer ebenfalls den Caesaren *post bellorum*, den Dichtern *pro laboribus studiorum* zuerkannt.)

III 2

Die bei Petrarca mehrfach (besonders *Africa* IX 49 ff.) belegte Auffassung des Ennius als *praeco uirtutis* ist nicht Ennius allein vorbehalten; diese Betrachtungsweise hat seit alters her in der Antike für den panegyrischen Dichter schlechthin Gültigkeit [1]. Und selbst der Dichter eines Heldenepos, in dem nicht ausdrücklich ein einziger Mann im Mittelpunkt steht, kann einseitig als ein solcher *praeco uirtutis* aufgefasst werden. Das gilt par excellence für Homer, wie am deutlichsten jener berühmte, auch von Petrarca zitierte Ausspruch Alexanders am Grabmal Achills in Troja zeigt, in dem er den Achill glücklich pries, weil er in Homer den Lobredner seiner Taten gefunden habe. Auf diese Anekdote werde ich in Abschnitt III 9 zurückkommen.

Ein Dichter als *praeco uirtutis* hat innerhalb der Gesellschaft eine wichtige soziale Rolle. Innerhalb der römischen Literatur wird — das kann man besonders an der *Archias-Rede* Ciceros ablesen — gerade von dieser Funktion her, von der Leistung der Dichter für die tragende Schicht der Gesellschaft und darüber hinaus direkt oder indirekt auch für den Staat, der Anspruch abgeleitet, dass auch die Dichter selber innerhalb der Gesellschaft einen geachteten Platz einnehmen müssen. Der Anspruch auf Geltung und Ruhm aufgrund einer rein artistischen Leistung ist dagegen erst sekundär.

Was nun Ennius persönlich angeht, so konnten die Späteren und auch noch Petrarca den *praeconium-uirtutis*-Charakter seiner repräsentativen Dichtungen, nämlich der *Annalen* und mit gewisser Einschränkung auch des *Scipio*, z.B. an den markanten Einzel-Enkomia berühmter Männer

[1] Zum Dichter als *praeco uirtutis* vgl. auch meine *Untersuchungen zur Selbstdarstellung älterer römischer Dichter. Livius Andronicus, Naevius, Ennius*, Hildesheim 1968 (Spudasmata 19), S. 198 ff. und S. 318.

ablesen, die teils, wie die Charakteristik des Fabius Maximus Cunctator, geradezu sprichwörtlich geworden sind [1]. Am prägnantesten bringt diesen *praeco-uirtutis*-Aspekt an der Gestalt und an der Dichtung des Ennius dessen Bildnis-Epigramm (*var.* 16), das Petrarca aus Cic. *Tusc.* I 34 kennen konnte, zum Ausdruck: *hic uestrum panxit maxima facta patrum.* Die ausführlichste Interpretation des Ennius in dieser Hinsicht gibt Cicero in seiner *Archias-Rede*. Auf Ennius und seine Verherrlichung des älteren Africanus bezieht es sich, wenn Cicero (22) sagt: *at his laudibus certe non solum ipse qui laudatur sed etiam populi Romani nomen ornatur*, und gleich darauf: *omnes denique illi Maximi, Marcelli, Fuluii non sine communi omnium nostrum laude decorantur.* Cicero kommt es hier darauf an zu erweisen, dass Ennius als der Lobredner römischer Grosser zugleich der Lobredner römischer Grösse ist.

Der Tendenz der ennianischen *Annalen* entspricht weniger der Auftakt der vergilischen *Aeneis*, wo durch *arma uirumque cano* der eine Mann in den Mittelpunkt gestellt

[1] Das Cunctator-Elogium (vgl. die Testimonia zu *Ann.* 170-172) ist eine der meistzitierten Stellen aus Ennius überhaupt. Unter anderem gehört es auch zu den relativ wenigen Enniuszitaten Petrarcas (*Famil.* XI 8, 27, wohl aus Cic. *Cato* 10 oder *Off.* I 84). Ferner zitiert Petrarca *Famil.* XXIV 12, 37 das ennianische Grabepigramm *Var.* 17 f. (auf das er ausserdem *Epist. metr.* I, ed. Basil. 1554, 1341 a, und III, p. 1365, d. h. III, 17, 15 ff. anspielt), das er insbesondere aus Cic. *Tusc.* I 34 kannte, und bezeichnet überdies *Famil.* III 12, 7 und XIII 5, 14 (auch *Senil.* XVI [XV] 1, edit. Basil. 1554, p. 1058) Verg. *Georg.* II 8 f. *qua me quoque possim tollere humo* richtig als ennianisch oder gar als Enniuszitat, offenbar aufgrund eigener Kombination, denn die antiken und Petrarca zugänglichen Vergilkommentare bieten zur *Georgica*-Stelle keinen Hinweis auf Ennius als Quelle. Schliesslich zitiert er *Rer. memor.* III, 46, 19 sieben Enniusverse aus dem *Telamo* über die Verspottung der *uates*, die er aus Cic. *Div.* I 88 und I 132 kombiniert hat — wiederum eine kleine philologische Leistung, der allerdings moderne Editoren (Vahlen, *Scen.* 394; 319-323; Jocelyn, *Tragedies* vs. 343 und 266-269) nicht folgen. — Auch bei Petrarca bestätigt sich also die Binsenweisheit, dass aus der Anführung von Enniuszitaten nicht unbedingt geschlossen werden darf, dass der zitierende Autor Ennius selbst gelesen hat. Zur angeblichen Ennius-Lektüre Petrarcas vgl. die Diskussion, unten S. 348 f.

wird, sondern eher der Anfang der *Punica* des Silius Italicus, der darstellen will: *quantosque ad bella crearit | et quot Roma uiros* (I 4 f.) [1]. Bei diesem, wenn man so sagen darf, kollektiven und nationalen Charakter der *Annalen* des Ennius tut Petrarca dem Ennius zwar nicht Unrecht, aber er stilisiert ihn einseitig, wenn er ihn vornehmlich als Lobredner Scipios hinstellt. Allerdings war die Auffassung der *Calabrae Pierides* des Ennius als Lobredners Scipios so fest, dass der Interpolator der Horazode IV 8 (vs. 17) und Porphyrio (zu Hor. *Sat.* II 1, 16) den falschen, den jüngeren Africanus als Objekt der ennianischen Dichtungen voraussetzen. Es ist anzunehmen, dass eine nahe Beziehung des Ennius zum älteren Scipio — die uns auch im folgenden Abschnitt III 3 beschäftigen wird — auch *per analogiam* aus der notorischen Freundschaft mit anderen römischen Grossen seiner Zeit, insbesondere mit den Fulviern, erschlossen wurde. Für Petrarca jedenfalls ist Ennius in erster Linie der *praeco uirtutis Scipionis*. Das ist verständlich, weil Petrarca als *Ennius alter* gerade eine solche Enniusgestalt als Vorgängerfigur in einem Epos wie der *Africa* brauchte, da auch er (die *Africa* beginnt mit einem wohl auf Ennius [2] verweisenden *et michi* ... *Musa uirum referes*) sich ja zur Aufgabe gesetzt hatte, einen einzigen Mann, denselben Africanus, zu verherrlichen.

III 3

Ennius ist nach Petrarca *Africa* IX 11 der *assiduus rerum testisque comesque* des älteren Scipio.

[1] Vgl. darüber M. von Albrecht, *Silius*, in seinem Kapitel S. 16 ff. ‘Das Proömium [nämlich der *Aeneis*, der *Punica* und der *Africa*] als Ankündigung des Ganzen’. Silius XII 411 charakterisiert Ennius’ Leistung mit *attolletque duces caelo*.

[2] Diese Möglichkeit der Beziehung des *Africa*-Auftakts *et michi* ... erwägt (neben zwei anderen) auch Festa, *Africa*-Ausgabe 1926 z.St.

Wir haben bereits bei der Besprechung des Punktes III 1 gesehen, dass die direkte Quelle für diese Auffassung Petrarcas jenes Claudiangedicht (*Cons. Stil.* III praef.) ist, nach dem der Dichter Ennius dem Scipio auf allen seinen Kriegszügen in Spanien und in Afrika gefolgt sei (gemäss dem Grundsatz Scipios: *gaudet enim uirtus t e s t e s sibi iungere Musas*: | *carmen amat*, *quisquis carmine digna gerit*, vs. 5/6) — die Voraussetzung für seinen späteren Triumph mit Scipio [1]. Hinter dieser Aussage steht letzten Endes das Bild des hellenistischen Hofdichters [2], der geradezu als eine Art Kriegsberichterstatter aufgefasst wird. Berichtet wird uns diese Erscheinung besonders für die Umgebung Alexanders des Grossen, wo vornehmlich der Dichterling Choirilos von Iasos sich unrühmlich hervorgetan hat.

Diese hellenistische Institution des Hofpoeten ist auch nach Rom übertragen worden und zum erstenmal zu belegen eben an der Gestalt des Ennius. Von ihm ist ja überliefert (Cic. *Tusc.* I 3), dass M. Fulvius Nobilior ihn mit auf den Feldzug nach Aetolien genommen hat und dass er später deshalb von Cato angegriffen wurde. In Catos Augen widersprach es offenbar dem Grundsatz, dass die Grossen Roms gewissermassen Beamte der *res publica* zu sein hätten, wenn sie sich eigene Dichter hielten, die ihren ganz persönlichen Ruhm künden sollten (vgl. Plut. *Cato* 19). Diese belegte Begleitung des Ennius beim Feldzug des Fulvius ist anscheinend — mit Sicherheit unhistorisch — auf das Verhältnis zu Scipio übertragen worden.

[1] Bezeichnenderweise bietet die *Africa* keinen Hinweis auf das (fiktive) Alter des Ennius. Am Schluss der III. *Ekloge* Petrarcas jedoch, wo ebenfalls vs. 152 ff. der Triumph Scipios und des Ennius gestreift wird, ist Scipio *iuuenis*, Ennius *rudis ille senex*. Wie Petrarca aus Hieronymus wissen konnte, ist das historisch gesehen unkorrekt: Ennius war im Jahre des Triumphes (201) 38 Jahre alt und nur etwa 5 Jahre älter als Scipio. Eine *senex*-Stilisierung würde die Ehrwürdigkeit eines Dichters unterstreichen; ein *senex* als *assiduus rerum comes* wäre nicht recht passend.

[2] Vgl. dazu meine *Untersuchungen*, S. 17 f.

Dabei hat gewiss auch die Erinnerung an den vertrauten Umgang anderer römischer Dichter mit römischen Adligen mitgewirkt [1]. Der Zeit des Ennius am nächsten steht der sog. Scipionenkreis, d.h. der Kreis von geistig und nicht zuletzt literarisch Interessierten um den jüngeren Scipio Africanus [2]. Als *assiduus rerum testisque comesque* wird man unter den Literaten um Africanus minor zwar nicht Terenz bezeichnen können, wohl aber Lucilius, der im Gegensatz zu den meisten älteren römischen Dichtern vornehmer Herkunft war und als Ritter im Numantinischen Krieg 134/133 unter Scipio diente und auch freundschaftlich mit ihm verkehrte. Wie wir Hor. *Sat.* II 1, 15/16 entnehmen können, hat Lucilius innerhalb seiner *Satirensammlung* Scipio verherrlicht. — Ein ähnliches Verhältnis ist für den Tragiker Lucius Accius zu D. Iunius Brutus Calaicus, dem Konsul von 138, belegt, der der Patron, Vertraute und Freund des Accius gewesen ist [3] (allerdings hat Accius wohl kaum an dem spanischen Feldzug seines Patrons teilgenommen).

Weitere, jüngere Beispiele für « Dichterpatronage in Rom » brauchen hier nicht angeführt zu werden, denn es soll nur verständlich gemacht werden, wieso der erste bedeutende lateinische Philologe und Grammatiker Aelius Stilo, der 150-70 v.Chr. lebte, auf den Gedanken kommen konnte, das berühmte Portrait des guten Gefährten, also die Charakterschilderung des Vertrauten eines römischen

[1] Vgl. dazu den vorzüglichen Artikel ' Dichterpatronage in Rom ' im *LAW*, Zürich 1965, 727-730 von M. von Albrecht.

[2] Die Entmythisierung des Scipionenkreises durch H. Strasburger, *Hermes* 94 (1966), 60-72 berührt das historisch gesicherte Verhältnis Scipio minor / Lucilius nicht. Im Hinblick auf Terenz z.B. kommt es in meinem Zusammenhang gerade auf den späteren Mythos an.

[3] Zum Verhältnis Accius / Decimus Brutus vgl. Schanz-Hosius I (1927), 132, ferner jüngst H. Cancik, Die Statue des L. Accius im Tempel der Camenen, in: *Silvae.* Festschrift E. Zinn, hrsg.v. M. von Albrecht und E. Heck, Tübingen 1970, 7-17, bes. S. 8.

Konsuls im 1. oder 2. Punischen Kriege [1], als Selbstbildnis des Ennius zu bezeichnen. Wer sich mit dem Nachleben des Ennius beschäftigt, wird hier nicht, wie es VAHLEN z.St. tut, die Leichtgläubigkeit oder den allzu grossen Scharfsinn dieses Interpreten hervorheben. Es handelt sich vielmehr um ein ganz bedeutendes Zeugnis für die Vorstellung, die man sich in varronischer Zeit, als man schon den Kreis um den jüngeren Scipio kannte und insbesondere die Beziehungen des Lucilius zu ihm, in Rückspiegelung auch von dem Verhältnis des Ennius zu den Grossen seiner Zeit gemacht hat.

Die Vorstellung von Ennius als dem Begleiter und Zeugen der Taten seines Helden könnte man auf die Formel bringen, die Tibull I 7, 9 für sein Verhältnis zu Messalla geprägt hat : *non sine me est tibi partus honos*. (Es folgt dann eine sechsgliedrige geographische *testis*-Anapher.) Tibull hat allerdings Messalla, dessen Triumph i.J. 27 v.Chr. er in diesem Geburtstagsgedicht feiert, offenbar nicht als Hofdichter in der literarischen *cohors* auf den Feldzug nach Aquitanien begleitet, sondern als Soldat. Auch im Zusammenhang mit einem anderen Zug Messallas gibt sich Tibull in seinem fingierten Grabspruch (I 3, 55 f.) nicht als Dichter, sondern als Gefolgsmann Messallas.

Es liegt auf der Hand, dass diese beiden an sich nicht identischen Funktionen, der Dichter als Freund des Feldherrn und der Soldat, der später auch Dichter sein wird, leicht kontaminiert werden. Für Ennius ist denn auch nicht nur die Beraterfunktion für einen römischen Feldherrn erschlossen worden (durch Aelius Stilo mit jener « Selbstportrait »-Interpretation) ; Ennius ist sogar direkt zum Soldaten stilisiert worden — nämlich noch vor Claudian [2] durch Silius

[1] Zur Plazierung dieses Fragmentes *Ann.* 234-251 im VII. oder VIII. Buch vgl. oben im Vortrag von Mr. BADIAN S. 162 ff.

[2] Dass Claudian Silius kannte, geht aus den von U. KEUDEL, *Poetische Vor-*

Italicus, einen Dichter aus jener Trias, die sich von der Person des Ennius zu erzählerischem Gestalten hat anregen lassen.

Der Ennius, der bei Silius (XII 393 ff.) innerhalb der Erzählung handelnd auftritt, ist nicht der Dichter, sondern der römische Soldat Ennius. Erst im Vorgriff, in einer durch Apoll gegebenen Zukunftsvision (XII 408 ff.), wird er auch als Dichter vorgestellt. Jetzt im Jahre 215 aber kämpft er auf Sardinien als Centurio unter Titus Manlius Torquatus im römischen Heer. Allerdings färbt Silius auch die Darstellung des Soldaten Ennius, der in diesem Augenblick — anders als der Ennius Claudians — offenbar noch kein Dichter ist, bereits jetzt mit den Zügen seines künftigen Dichtertums: der kämpfende Ennius wird mit dem kämpfenden Orpheus auf dem Argonautenzug verglichen (XII 398 ff.) [1].

läufer und Vorbilder in Claudians De consulatu Stilichonis, Göttingen 1970 (Hypomnemata 26) gesammelten Anspielungen usw. hervor. Mit Recht folgt KEUDEL 119 A. 3 VAHLENS Ansicht (CXX sqq.), dass Claudian Ennius wohl kaum benutzt hat.

[1] Die im *RE*-Artikel von K. ZIEGLER XVIII, 1 (1939) 1254 ff. zu überblikkenden Nachrichten bei Apollonios Rhodios, in den orphischen *Argonautika*, bei Valerius Flaccus usw. über ‘ Orpheus als Argonaut ’ erwähnen nirgends eine aktive Teilnahme des Orpheus an Kämpfen der Argonauten, insbesondere nicht beim Kampf gegen die Dolionen unter König Cycicus ; Silius hat diesen Zug also offenbar erfunden, um Ennius mit Orpheus parallelisieren und ihm so einen höheren Glanz verleihen zu können. Auf die Bedeutung dieser quasi-historischen Parallele, die als Gleichnis stilisiert ist, ist m.W. noch nicht hingewiesen worden ; M. von ALBRECHT, *Silius*, erwähnt es nicht in seinem einschlägigen Kapitel ‘ Die Welt der Gleichnisse ’ S. 90 ff., 192 ff., auch nicht in seinem Spezialaufsatz ‘ Gleichnis und Innenwelt in Silius’ Punica ’, *Hermes* 91 (1963), 352-374 (nach seinen Kriterien wäre es der Funktion ‘ Wesensschau ’ zuzuordnen). Orpheus spielt bei Silius eine grosse Rolle in dem Gesang des Teuthras vor Hannibal XI 459-480. — Dass der prophetische Ausblick Apolls XII 407-413 und auch der einleitende Musenanruf des epischen Erzählers XII 387-392 nebst dem auktorialen Vorgriff XII 397 Ennius als Dichter vorstellen, besagt noch nicht, dass er es in der Gegenwart ist. Wieso Ennius schon jetzt ein « getreuer Musendiener » (von ALBRECHT, S. 159) sein kann, wird nicht klar.

Man hat darüber gerätselt, welche Quellen Silius für die Ennius-Episode gehabt haben mag [1], für die er bei seiner Hauptquelle Livius (XXIII 40 f.) nichts finden konnte. Eine Verbindung des Ennius zu Sardinien ist uns bekannt aus der Nachricht des Nepos (*Cato* 1, 4), dass Cato ihn von dort i.J. 204 nach Rom gebracht habe [2]. Worauf Nepos seinerseits fusst, kann nur vermutet werden; letztlich dürfte eine originale Erwähnung bei Ennius zugrundeliegen, doch lässt sich nicht sagen, ob innerhalb der *Annalen* oder etwa in den *Satiren*. Vielleicht darf man das, was Gellius für Naevius berichtet, *quem M. Varro in libro de poetis primo stipendia fecisse ait bello Poenico primo idque Naeuium dicere in eo carmine quod de eodem bello scripsit* (XVII 21, 45), *mutatis mutandis* auf Ennius übertragen. Doch hat man mit Recht geschlossen [3], dass Silius für die Gestaltung seiner Episode sicherlich keine ausführlichere Selbstdarstellung des Ennius vor sich hatte. Denn wenn Ennius in seinen Annalen näher auf seine Taten in Sardinien eingegangen wäre, hätte Silius XII 391 f. wohl kaum von den *nota p a r u m magni ... facta uiri* gesprochen und eigens die Musen um Belehrung angerufen.

Bestenfalls eine Anregung also wird Silius bei Ennius oder möglicherweise in einer Darstellung *De poetis* für die Figur des Kämpfers Ennius gefunden haben. Sein Motiv für eine derartige Stilisierung ist nicht leicht zu erklären. Ich möchte am ehesten eine Art nationalen Motivs bei Silius vermuten: Silius selbst war bekanntlich kein blosser Schreibtischliterat und kein Nur-Dichter, sondern hatte es im öffentlichen Leben bis zum Konsulat gebracht. Da wird er geneigt gewesen sein, auch Ennius, den Künder römischer Grosstaten, nicht als blutleeren Literaten, der bestenfalls

[1] Vgl. z.B. FÜRSTENAU, *De Sili imitat. Enn.* 36 ff.; M. von ALBRECHT, *Silius*, 159 Anm. 38; meine *Untersuchungen*, S. 138 mit Anm. 440.

[2] Vgl. dazu den Vortrag von Mr. BADIAN, oben S. 149 sqq.

[3] FÜRSTENAU, *De Sili imitat. Enn.* 37.

ungefährdet im Stabe des Feldherrn bei Kämpfen zuschaut, zu stilisieren, sondern als einen Mann, der mitgekämpft hat, der sein Teil zum Aufbau Roms beigetragen hat.

III 4

Im Hinblick auf die ausführliche Erzählung des Ennius von seiner Homervision im IX. Buch der *Africa* (IX 131 ff., bes. 158-287) bietet sich als 4. Punkt das Stichwort *Somnium Ennii* bzw. *alter Homerus* an.

Hier ist zunächst für Petrarca festzustellen, dass er den wesentlichen Inhalt des originalen *Somnium Ennii* aus dem *Annalen*-Proömium nicht übernommen hat. In seinem *Somnium Ennii* findet sich nämlich kein Wort darüber, dass Ennius sich als *Homerus rediuiuus* oder *alter Homerus* gefühlt hat. Obwohl Petrarca die Homervision ganz in dem Stile vorbereitet, wie Cicero *Rep.* VI 10 die originale Homererscheinung in den *Annalen* des Ennius erklärt hat, nämlich durch Hinweis auf die intensive Beschäftigung des Ennius mit Homer, hat der in seinem *Somnium Ennii* auftretende Homer im Grunde keine nähere persönliche Beziehung zu seinem Verehrer Ennius [1]. Im originalen *Annalen*-Proömium hatte ja das *simulacrum Homeri* dem Ennius eröffnet, die *anima Homeri* sei in ihn eingegangen. Eine analoge Bemerkung fehlt bei Petrarca [2]. Mein anfänglicher Argwohn,

[1] Im Grunde ist die Figur Homers im *Somnium Ennii* bei Petrarca von der des Vaters Scipios im I. und II. Buch der *Africa* nicht wesentlich verschieden : Homer spielt eine Prophetenrolle. Da sich der Inhalt der jetzigen Eröffnungen im IX. Buch, von denen allerdings nur der letzte Teil von Petrarca ausgeführt worden ist, ausschliesslich auf den Dichter Petrarca bezieht, hat der Autor als Sprachrohr diesmal nicht einen Politiker, sondern eben den grössten Dichter gewählt.

[2] Sie kann auch nicht für die Ausfüllung der Lücke nach IX 215 geplant gewesen sein ; denn nach der Struktur der Handlung kann für die Lücke nur eine Aufzählung weiterer Literaten vorausgesetzt werden, die in Petrarca

Petrarca habe vielleicht zwar allgemein von den *somnia Pythagorea* (Hor. *Epist.* II 1, 52) des Ennius gewusst, jedoch keine detaillierte Kenntnis vom Inhalt des originalen *Somnium Ennii*, insbesondere von der Homer-Metempsychose besessen, weil die Hauptzeugen Scholiasten sind, hat sich nicht bestätigt. Er besass mit Sicherheit die pseudoacronischen Scholien [1], und die schaffen zu Hor. *Epist.* II 1, 51 über den Punkt, dass Ennius sich als *Homerus rediuiuus* ausgegeben hat, hinreichend Klarheit. Wir müssen also schliessen, dass Petrarca diese Vorstellung des originalen Ennius ausdrücklich, eben durch die Ignorierung, abgelehnt hat. Man kann nun vielleicht sagen, dass er als Christ die Metempsychosis-Lehre des Ennius zurückweisen musste, ähnlich wie sie von Lukrez trotz seiner Hochschätzung des Dichters Ennius verworfen wurde, weil sie mit der von ihm vertretenen epikureischen Philosophie unvereinbar war [2]. Dies theologisch-philosophische Motiv bei Petrarca vorauszusetzen, erscheint aber deshalb nicht überzeugend, weil Petrarca als Christ vermutlich auch nicht die Präexistenz der Seelen (aus dem VI. Buch der *Aeneis*) hätte übernehmen dürfen, wie er das offenbar aber im IX. Buch für seine eigene Person tut (IX 216 ff.). Gravierender scheint mir jedenfalls eine innerliterarische Überlegung zu sein : wenn Petrarca den originalen Ennius und auch seinen Ennius als

münden sollte. Nur der Höhepunkt dieser Reihe (Petrarca selbst) ist ausgeführt worden. Vgl. oben S. 304, Anm. 2.

[1] Das Standardwerk für Petrarcas Kenntnis antiker Autoren ist DE NOLHAC, *Pétrarque* (zu Ps. Acro dort S. 150/181 f.). Ein eigenes Kapitel über Petrarcas Lieblingsbücher von H. RÜDIGER findet sich in der *Geschichte der Textüberlieferung* Bd. I, hrsg.v. H. HUNGER, Zürich 1961, S. 526-537. Nicht gesehen habe ich G. BILLANOVICH, Petrarca e i classici, im Sammelband : *Petrarca e il petrarchismo*, Bologna 1961 (Atti del convegno petrarchesco 1959 Aix-en-Provence).

[2] Deshalb folgt auf das berühmte Lob des Lukrez, dass Ennius der erste wahre Dichter Roms gewesen sei (I 117-119), die Einschränkung : « wenn er auch daneben eine unsinnige Philosophie vertreten hat » (120 ff. *etsi praeterea...*). Zu Petrarcas Zukunftsvision vgl. oben S. 305 f.

Homerus rediuiuus, als *alter Homerus* akzeptiert hätte, hätte darin eine Anerkennung für die poetischen Qualitäten seines grossen Vorgängers gelegen, die er aber — wie wir noch (in III 8 und III 9) sehen werden — eben geleugnet hat.

Petrarca hätte sich bei seiner stillschweigenden Ablehnung des *Homerus-rediuiuus*-Anspruchs für Ennius in der Antike auf die Kritik bei Horaz *Epist.* II 1, 50 ff. an diesen *somnia Pythagorea*, vor allem aber auf Persius [1] berufen können, auf Vorgänger, die für die Ablehnung der Metempsychosis-Idee des Ennius bestimmte poetische Gründe hatten. Trotzdem lässt sich die Beobachtung machen (die durch jene negativen Reaktionen eher bekräftigt als widerlegt wird), dass Ennius mit diesem seinem *Homerus-rediuiuus*-Postulat eine sein Nachleben in literarkritischer Hinsicht geradezu bestimmende Selbstaussage gemacht hat [2].

Es ist ein charakteristischer Zug des ennianischen Nachlebens, dass man den *alter-Homerus*-Titel immer — von einer Ausnahme abgesehen [3] — gerade mit Ennius in Verbindung gebracht hat. An dem mit diesem Titel erhobenen Anspruch wurde er gemessen [4]. Ein solches Messen konnte natürlich zwei Ergebnisse haben : entweder akzeptierte man diesen Anspruch — und das hat man insbesondere in der ciceronisch-varronischen Zeit getan, wo Ennius unbestritten als der Höhepunkt der römischen Literatur galt — oder man

[1] Persius, *Prol.* 1 ff., kombiniert mit *Sat.* VI 10 f., vgl. auch V 7.

[2] Diese These habe ich im Genfer Originalvortrag weiter ausgeführt und dabei besonders die an sich naheliegende, aber selten belegte Idee betrachtet, dass sich der Dichter vom Geist eines grossen literarischen Vorbildes erfüllt wähnt. Wichtig ist in dieser Hinsicht das Proömium von *De raptu Helenae* des Dracontius.

[3] Hier. *Epist.* 121, 10, 5 ; *In Mich.* II 7, 5/7.

[4] Nur einmal, bei Silius XII 413, wird Ennius neben Hesiod gestellt ; vgl. dazu unten S. 338. Ausserdem glaubt G. Hafner, *Das Bildnis des Q. Ennius*, Baden-Baden 1968, bes. S. 36 und 42, in einer Kopenhagener Doppelherme sei Ennius mit Hesiod verbunden. Über diese Hypothese möchte ich in einem Essay über (wirkliche) Ennius-Bildnisse handeln.

erklärte, er sei diesem Anspruch nicht gerecht geworden — und diese Einstellung findet sich immer stärker seit der augusteischen Zeit. Das wird uns in Abschnitt III 8 und III 9 noch näher beschäftigen. Zunächst aber sind noch einige weitere vorwiegend positive Aspekte des Enniusbildes zu besprechen.

III 5

Ein zunächst auffälliger Zug in Petrarcas Enniusbild ist, dass Ennius nach eigener Erklärung (IX 45 ff.) am Anfang der noch kaum entwickelten römischen Literatur steht. Er hat die Musen in Latium heimisch gemacht (so wie umgekehrt Petrarca II 446 von sich sagt, dass er die Musen, die Latium schon wieder verlassen wollten, zum Einhalten bringt, oder aber IX 229 ff., dass er die Musen wiederum nach Latium zurückführt).

Wenn das hier so klingt, als ob Ennius der erste römische Dichter gewesen sei, so liegt das wohl nicht an einfacher Unkenntnis Petrarcas. (Auch moderne Gelehrte haben ja Ennius als « Vater der römischen Poesie » bezeichnet [1].) Petrarca besitzt nämlich z.B. einen Gellius und kennt damit auch das berühmte synchronistische Kapitel bei Gellius XVII 21 über die Chronologie der älteren römischen Dichter [2]. In der Tat wird denn in jener riesigen X. *Ekloge*,

[1] Vgl. dazu den Beginn des Vortrags von Mr. O. SKUTSCH, oben S. 3. Mir ist kein älteres Beispiel als die Formulierung von Bonaventura Vulcanius *uatum pater Ennius* in seinem Gedicht auf die Ennius-Ausgabe P. MERULAS (Leiden 1595) bekannt.

[2] Dass Petrarca einen vollständigen Gellius besessen hat, sollte man im Hinblick auf die Anspielung auf Gell. XVII 21, 45 in seinem *Buc. carm.* X 257 f. (dazu gleich S. 331, Anm. 1) nicht bezweifeln (vgl. auch BARCHIESI, *Nevio epico*, 136 Anm. 736 und 8 Anm. 18). Zur Kenntnis Petrarcas von der Chronologie der älteren römischen Dichter vgl. bes. seinen Briefwechsel (um 1345) mit dem Bologneser Juristen Giovanni d'Andrea, *Fam.* IV 15/16 (über diese ' scoperta ' des Naevius vgl. ein eigenes Kapitel bei BARCHIESI,

in der in Hunderten von Versen in verschlüsselten Anspielungen eine fast unendliche Reihe antiker Literaten vorgeführt wird, nicht nur auf Ennius (183-186), sondern auch auf Naevius (220 f.) und vor allem auf Livius Andronicus (226-228), und zwar auf diesen deutlich als den chronologisch ersten römischen Dichter, hingewiesen [1]. Der *poeta-primus*-Begriff, auf Ennius angewendet, ist deshalb nicht als chronologische Bestimmung aufzufassen, sondern als Wertung. — Dahinter steht eine gute antike Tradition, die schon auf Ennius selbst zurückgeht, der vor sich selber niemand als wahren *poeta* hat gelten lassen wollen : er sei der *primus* gewesen, der die Bereiche der Musen erschlossen habe (*Ann.* 213 ff.). Diese εὑρετής-Konzeption des Ennius ist später von anderen römischen Dichtern, die bestimmte Gebiete der

S. 6-11). Aufschlussreich für seine Einschätzung des Plautus und Naevius ist auch der Brief an Barbatus von Sulmona aus den *Variae* (edit. Basil. 1554, p. 1110 ; vgl. Barchiesi S. 138 Anm. 746) : Petrarca tadelt die Überheblichkeit ihrer (ihm aus Gellius I 24 bekannten) Grabsprüche und stellt fest : *et qui fuerint, scimus : ars exigua, mediocre ingenium, uiuax fama, magnus populorum fauor, rerum suarum extimatio immensa.* Petrarca dagegen will den Ehrentitel *rex poetarum* nicht annehmen : der sei schon vergeben : bei den Griechen an Homer, bei den Römern an Vergil.

[1] In der X. *Ekloge* (deren Hauptteil 1348 verfasst ist) ist Livius (seinen Namen Andronicus und seine griechische Herkunft scheint Petrarca auffälligerweise trotz z.B. Gell. XVIII 9, 5, Ps. Acro *Hor. Epist.* II 1, 62, Serv. *Verg. Aen.* X 636 nicht zu kennen, da ihm Ciceros *Brutus* und Suetons *De gramm.* noch fehlten) offensichtlich der chronologisch gesehen erste römische Dichter : *doceorque paternis* | *hunc* (*sc. grandeuum senem* = *Liuium*) *primum cecinisse modis* (vs. 227 f.). Ennius dagegen wird in derselben *Ekloge*, vs. 180-183 kritisiert ; vgl. dazu unten S. 341. Erwähnung verdient aus dieser *Ekloge* noch die Anspielung auf einen Dichter, *pennatas Musas qui martia traxit ad arma,* | *punica dum latio ferueret in orbe procella* vs. 257-8. Wie Martellotti in seinem Spezialkommentar (*Laurea occidens*, S. 74 ; vgl. auch schon Corradini zu *Africa* II 445, S. 423 f.) richtig erkannt hat, spielt Petrarca hier, auf Gellius XVII 21, 45 fussend (vgl. S. 332, Anm. 2 und S. 334, Anm. 2), auf Porcius Licinus an ; allerdings ist in der *Eklogen*-Stelle seltsamerweise die Aussage, die Porcius Licinus über den ersten römischen Dichter gemacht hat (wer gemeint ist, ist umstritten ; vgl. dazu zuletzt O. Skutsch, *Bull. Inst. Class. Stud. London* 17 (1970), 120 f.), auf ihn selber übertragen.

griechischen Literatur für Rom erschlossen, immer wieder übernommen worden [1].

Wie wir es schon häufig beobachtet haben, scheint auch diese Selbsteinschätzung des Ennius als *primus* auf spätere Kritiker eingewirkt zu haben. Jedenfalls ist es nicht ausgeschlossen, dass das berühmte Epigramm des Porcius Licinus von dem Einzug der kriegerischen Muse unter die noch wilden Römer zur Zeit des 2. Punischen Krieges auf Ennius zu beziehen ist [2]. Lukrez bezeichnet Ennius als denjenigen, *qui p r i m u s amoeno | detulit ex Helicone perenni fronde coronam* (I 117 f.). Ein Grammatiker wie Diomedes (*GL* I 484, 3 K.) erklärt bei seiner Besprechung des Epos korrekt, dass Ennius derjenige ist, *qui primus d i g n e epos Latinum scripsit*; aber ein Panegyriker des 3. Jh. nennt Ennius geradewegs *ille Romani carminis primus auctor* (*Paneg. Lat.* 3 [11], 16, 3) [3], wofür Silius XII 410 mit *hic canet illustri p r i m u s bella Itala uersu* eine Vorstufe bedeutet. Von Isidor von Sevilla wird Ennius — in seiner Chronik i.J. 615 — ebenfalls als *primus poeta Latinus* bezeichnet, und ebenso bei seinem ersten Auftauchen in einer mittelalterlichen Chronik, der um 1170 entstandenen *Historia Scholastica* des Petrus Comestor [4]. Hier macht sich der Einfluss des Hieronymus bemerkbar, der zwar Ennius nicht den *primus poeta Latinus* nennt, aber seine literarhistorischen Ergänzungen der Eusebianischen Chronik mit Ennius beginnt und erst dann

[1] Vgl. dazu A. Reiff, *Interpretatio, imitatio, aemulatio*, Diss. Köln 1959, S. 63 mit Anm. 100, und meine *Untersuchungen* an den im Index s.v. '*primus*-Begriff' genannten Stellen.

[2] Gellius XVII 21, 45 *Porcius autem Licinus serius poeticam Romae coepisse dicit, in his uersibus: Poenico bello secundo Musa pinnato gradu | intulit se bellicosam in Romuli gentem feram*; vgl. oben S. 333, Anm. 1.

[3] Zu den Ennius-Reminiszenzen dieses Claudius Mamertinus aus Trier (wo wenige Jahrzehnte zuvor das Monnus-Mosaik mit einer Darstellung des Ennius entstanden ist) vgl. A. Klotz, Studien zu den Panegyrici Latini, *RhM* 66 (1911), 513-572, bes. 533-540.

[4] Barchiesi, *Nevio epico*, S. 133 und 117.

Naevius, Plautus, Livius Andronicus anführt. Und es sei auch erwähnt, dass der erste Editor einer Ennius-Spezialausgabe, H. Columna, Neapel 1590, unter den drei Punkten, in die er die Bedeutung des Ennius zusammenfasst, an erster Stelle anführt: Ennius sei derjenige gewesen, *qui Musas primum in Italiam deduxit* [1].

III 6

In uns zunächst befremdender Weise erwähnt Scipio zu Beginn des IX. Buches (IX 18-22) [2] eine Legitimierung des Ennius als Dichter, die nicht — wie beim originalen Ennius — von der Homer-Metempsychose abgeleitet ist, sondern von einer Musenweihe in seiner frühesten Kindheit. Damals habe Apoll ihm sein *ingenium celeste* gegeben, damals habe ihn die Schar der Musen in der kastalischen Quelle eingetaucht und mit heiligem Wasser vom Helikon gebadet, ihn dann auf die Höhen (offenbar des Helikon) geführt und ihm dort das Emblem der Rohrflöte (*calamus*) und Mund und Geist des Dichters geschenkt.

[1] Der Brief H. Columnas (gest. 1586) an seinen Sohn Johannes ist in der Wiederholung seiner Ausgabe von F. Hessel, Amsterdam 1705, vor den *De Ennio ... Testimonia* (unpaginiert) abgedruckt. An Ennius rühmt Columna ferner: *hunc illum esse ..., quo Africanus, neque uiuus, neque mortuus carere potuit* (über diesen *praeco-uirtutis*-Aspekt ist im Abschnitt III 2 die Rede gewesen); *qui denique si non fuisset, Virgilium quidem tantum non haberemus* (das ist gewissermassen die Korrektur der *aurum-ex-stercore*-Anekdote, jenem zuerst bei Cassiodor *Inst. div.* I 8 belegten abfälligen Urteil Vergils über Ennius, über dessen Geschichte ich bei anderer Gelegenheit ausführlicher zu handeln gedenke; Columna hebt die wahre Bedeutung des Ennius für Vergil hervor).

[2] *Africa* IX 18-22

18 *si tibi nascenti, quo polles, summus Apollo*
ingenium celeste dedit, si turba dearum
20 *castalio infantem demersum gurgite lauit*
ex Elicone sacro, collesque eduxit in altos
22 *et calamum et uocem tribuit mentemque poete.*

Ich kann nun natürlich nicht etwa Petrarca als Stütze für die gelegentlich — z.B. von Herrn J. Waszink und auch von mir selbst — vertretene Auffassung beschwören, dass der originale Ennius neben der Homerszene auch noch eine Musenweihe geboten hätte [1]; als Quelle für Ennius-Rekonstruktionen ist Petrarca, der nur abgeleitete Ennius-Kenntnisse hat, natürlich unbrauchbar, und selbst als Zeuge für die (bestrittene) poetische Möglichkeit eines Nebeneinanders von Homer-Metempsychose und Musenweihe fällt Petrarca aus; denn die von Petrarca gestaltete Szene spielt in der frühen Kindheit des Ennius und ist keine Parallele, sondern ein Ersatz der Homerszene. Die Homerszene, die beim originalen Ennius die Funktion einer Dichterberufung hatte, ist von Petrarca im IX. Buch dieses Elementes entkleidet worden. Für die an ihre Stelle getretene Dichterweihe des Ennius durch die Musen auf dem Helikon hat sich Petrarca wahrscheinlich durch die entsprechenden metaphorischen Aussagen der ciceronisch-augusteischen Zeit [2], insbesondere des Lukrez (I 117 ff.), Vergils (*Ecl.* VI 64 ff.) und des Properz (III 3, 5 ff.), anregen lassen. Auf Properz weist die Rolle Apolls neben den Musen hin (18 f.); horazische Motive aus dem Musenlied *Carm.* IV 3 klingen in *tibi nascenti* (18) und *infantem* (20) an. Dass die Musen Ennius als Kind in der kastalischen Quelle geradezu gebadet haben sollen (19 f.), ist eine sonst m.W. nicht belegte Hyperbel; man darf wohl vermuten, dass hier christliche Taufvorstellungen mitspielen. An die Musenweihe des Gallus bei Vergil erinnert die Vorstellung, dass die Musen den in der Kastalia getauften Ennius zur Höhe des Helikon hinaufführen, ihm dort eine Flöte geben und ihn so zum Dichter weihen (22). So schildert es ja auch Vergil für Gallus, dem

[1] Vgl. dazu die Literaturangaben (und Stellungnahme) in meinen *Untersuchungen*, S. 46 ff.

[2] Vgl. dazu meine *Untersuchungen*, S. 55 ff., 74 ff.

ebenfalls — durch Linus, den Sprecher der Musen — eine Flöte, und zwar die Flöte des so zur Vorgängerfigur stilisierten Hesiod, überreicht wird.

III 7

Noch bevor bei Petrarca aus Ennius' einleitenden Worten zur Schilderung seiner Homervision hervorgeht, dass er sich als Bewunderer des *summus Homerus* fühlt (IX 144 ff.), erklärt Scipio, dass Ennius dem Homer, dem Euripides und allen anderen griechischen Dichtern überlegen sei, dass er von niemand anderem als Ennius besungen werden möchte (IX 65-69) [1].

Wenn es auch einigermassen überraschend ist, dass Ennius hier mit Euripides verglichen wird [2], so ist doch die Parallelisierung mit Homer für einen *alter Homerus* (auch wenn Petrarca selbst diesen Titel für Ennius offenbar nicht akzeptiert hat, kannte er ihn vor allem aus Hor. *Epist.* II 1, 50) nicht weiter verwunderlich. Allerdings gibt es wiederum — ähnlich wie bei dem Alleinanspruch des Ennius auf den *alter-Homerus*-Titel, der von Hieronymus [3]

[1] Der Text von *Africa* IX 65-69 a ist oben S. 302, Anm. 1 gegeben.

[2] Die Erwähnung des (Tragikers) Euripides mag zunächst befremden; sie ist aus der besonderen Wertschätzung Petrarcas für ihn zu erklären. *Ecl.* X 75-80 begegnet in der Reihe der (verschlüsselt dargestellten) griechischen Dichter nach Homer (X 64-74) als erster Euripides, worin allein schon ein Werturteil zu sehen ist (so auch Martellotti, *Laurea occidens* z.St.), auch wenn er nicht ausdrücklich *cunctis* (*sc. Homeri comitibus*) *sublimior unus* genannt wäre, dem *supremus hircus* als Preis der Tragödie zugefallen ist. Unter den von Martellotti z. St. notierten Parallelen für die Schätzung des Euripides (*Fam.* XVIII 2, 13; XXIV 12, 43) ist am aufschlussreichsten die Bezeichnung *alterum ab Homero poetice Graie lumen* (*De rem.* II, cap. 121). Von Euripides konnte Petrarca eine Reihe von Zitaten bei Cicero kennen. Der Inhalt seines Werkes wird *Ecl.* X 77 mit *fortunas casusque ducum regumque canebat* umschrieben — ein solcher Euripides bot sich denn auch wohl gegenüber einem Epiker wie Ennius zum Vergleich an.

[3] Vgl. oben S. 331, Anm. 3.

abgelehnt wurde — eine Ausnahme von der Regel, dass Ennius an Homer gemessen wird : Silius Italicus stellt ihn nicht neben Homer, sondern neben Hesiod. In jener Episode der *Punica* nämlich, in der wir Ennius als römischen Centurio auf Sardinien (s.o. III 3) kennengelernt haben, wird dem Ennius durch den Mund Apolls eine Huldigung dargebracht. Nach den Worten des Gottes ist Ennius ein *dignus Apolline uates* (XII 409). Er wird als erster (*primus*) im heroischen Versmass die Kriege Roms besingen und die römischen Führer zum Himmel erheben. Er wird den Helikon von lateinischer Dichtung erschallen lassen, und sein Ansehen wird Hesiod nicht nachstehen : *resonare docebit* | *hic Latiis Helicona modis nec cedet honore* | *Ascraeo famaue seni* (XII 411 ff.). Dieser Vergleich mit Hesiod ist im Lichte der sonstigen Urteile über Ennius befremdlich (jedenfalls noch nicht überzeugend geklärt), und man hat mit gewissem Recht durch Konjektur den Namen Homers für den Hesiods einführen wollen [1]. Wie dem auch sei, das hier ausgesprochene anerkennende Urteil des Silius über Ennius steht in scharfem Gegensatz zu den Stimmen der Geringschätzung, die sonst im 1. Jh. n.Chr. verbreitet sind, und es wird durch eine spätere Partie auch bei Silius (XIII 793 ff. ; vgl. III 9) etwas modifiziert.

Auch bei Petrarca ist die Erklärung, Ennius sei allen griechischen Dichtern — situationsgemäss konnten von Scipio maior keine lateinischen Dichter zum Vergleich herangezogen werden — überlegen, wohl kaum als sein

[1] Ruperti erwägt *Cumaeo* oder *Smyrnaeo* statt *Ascraeo*, was Homer an die Stelle Hesiods setzen würde ; Wesseling will durch *Homero* statt *honore* (eine Konjektur, der auch Ruperti zuneigt) und Barth durch *Smyrnaeue* statt *famaue* Homer neben Hesiod einführen. Möglicherweise ist der Name Hesiods einfach durch die Erwähnung des Helikon evoziert worden, mit dem sich eben nicht Homer, sondern Hesiod verbindet. Vielleicht liegt auch ein Einfluss des metrisch gleichwertigen *Ascraeo quos ante seni* aus der Gallus-Dichterweihe bei Verg. *Ecl.* VI 70 vor. Zur Rolle Hesiods in literarkritischen Partien vgl. meine *Untersuchungen*, S. 79, Anm. 245 und S. 315 f., zur Silius-Stelle dort auch S. 61 Anm. 188. Vgl. ferner oben S. 331, Anm. 4.

letztes Wort zu betrachten. Denn, wie wir in den folgenden Abschnitten III 8 und 9 noch hören werden und wie auch schon eingangs II 3 betont wurde, Petrarca hat die dichterische Leistung des Ennius für Scipio als unzureichend empfunden und den Ennius gerade von Homer distanziert, geschweige denn dass er ihn etwa über Homer gestellt hätte. Man muss diese Stelle (IX 65 ff.) innerhalb des Epos wohl als ein aus der Situation und aus der sprechenden Person zu erklärendes mehr oder weniger unverbindliches Kompliment für Ennius auffassen. Nach der Intention Petrarcas sollte die Äusserung Scipios wahrscheinlich dazu dienen, dessen huldvolle, geradezu noble Haltung gegenüber einem Dichter, der sein Bestes gab, auch wenn das Beste nur relativ sein konnte, zu zeigen. Petrarca selber hat sich nicht nur innerhalb der *Africa*, sondern auch in anderen Schriften von der künstlerischen Leistung des Ennius distanziert, wobei leitmotivisch der *rudis*-Begriff vorzukommen pflegt. Darüber wird gleich in Abschnitt III 8 zu reden sein. Nur einmal äussert er sich positiv über den Dichter Ennius. Petrarca führt nämlich *Rer. memor.* III 46, 19 ein längeres Ennius-Zitat mit einer Verspottung der Seher [1] mit den Worten ein: *uetusta illa et uenerabili facundia hos ipsos illos* (*sc. uaticinantes*) *eleganter irridet* (*sc. Ennius*). Bei dieser Anerkennung des Dichters und Künstlers spielt aber sicher mit, dass Petrarca den von Ennius inhaltlich vertretenen Standpunkt teilt.

III 8

Bereits im letzten Abschnitt hatte sich angekündigt, dass das Urteil Petrarcas über die künstlerische Qualität der Dichtung des Ennius negativ ist. Für ihn ist Ennius in der Regel der *p o e t a r u d i s*. Er charakterisiert ihn in der

[1] Vgl. oben S. 322, Anm. 1.

Africa zwar nie direkt so, wohl aber mit verwandten Begriffen. So spricht der Vater Scipios II 445 von dem *durum modulamen* und den *rudes Musae* des Ennius ; IV 38 ist Ennius nach den Worten des Laelius ein *rusticus* [1].

Die Urteile Petrarcas über Ennius ausserhalb der Africa sind womöglich noch schärfer formuliert und durchgängig auf den *poeta-rudis*-Tenor abgestimmt. Wenn Petrarca eine Einstufung des Ennius über Vergil, wie sie Kaiser Hadrian geübt hat, ablehnt [2] oder Ennius gegenüber Homer als *tanto inferior* bezeichnet [3], so klingt das noch verhältnismässig harmlos. Aufschlussreicher ist schon, dass Ennius in der üblicherweise gedruckten Redaktion des *Trionfo della fama* III (dem Abschnitt über die Schriftsteller) gar keine Stelle hat. In einer erst 1950 aus einem Londoner Kodex veröffentlichten anderen Redaktion, dem Ineditum *Weiss*, hat er zwar neben Lucilius, Pacuvius, Plautus, Accius und Naevius wenigstens eine namentliche Erwähnung gefunden, aber offenbar (es geht eine Lücke voraus) unter den Beispielen für solche Dichter, bei denen non è l'ingegno né lo stile equale | a la materia [4]. Hier hat

[1] Vgl. auch die Ennius selbst in den Mund gelegten Worte IX 45 ff. 60 (oben, S. 299, Anm. 3 zitiert).

[2] In einer Randnotiz seines Servius-Kodex mit Anspielung auf die bekannte Nachricht in der *Historia Augusta*, Spartian. *Vita Hadr.* 16, 5, die die archaistischen Neigungen des Kaisers zeigt (vgl. DE NOLHAC, *Pétrarque*, 140/168).

[3] In dem Brief an Homer, *Fam.* XXIV 12, 37, zitiert er, wie auch sonst mehrfach (vgl. oben S. 322, Anm. 1), das geflügelte Wort aus dem ennianischen Grabepigramm *uolito uiuos docta* (!) *per ora uirum* mit der Einleitung, dass Homer das mit viel grösserem Recht sagen könne als der *tanto inferior Ennius*.

[4] Zum (umstrittenen) chronologischen Verhältnis der verschiedenen Redaktionen des *Trionfo della Fama* und der X. *Ekloge* mit ihren Dichterkatalogen zueinander vgl. G. PONTE, Problemi petrarcheschi : La decima egloga e la composizione dei Trionfi, *Rassegna della letteratura ital.* Ser. VII, 69 (1965), 517-529, bes. S. 523 ff. Wenn PONTE (mit C. F. GOFFIS) recht hätte und die neu von R. WEISS entdeckte Fassung des *Trionfo della Fama* III die ältere Redaktion wäre, hätte also Petrarca bei der Überarbeitung u.a. auf den Namen Ennius verzichtet. Andere, wie G. MARTELLOTTI, halten aber die neuentdeckte Fassung für die jüngere, 1371 entstandene Redaktion.

Petrarca das folgenreiche Urteil Ovids *Ennius ingenio maximus, arte rudis* (*Trist.* II 424), in dem immerhin das *ingenium* des Ennius anerkannt worden war, noch verschärft zu einer Kritik sowohl des *ingenium* wie der *ars*. So einseitig urteilt Petrarca allerdings nicht immer. Die ausführlichste Ennius-Charakteristik ausserhalb der *Africa* bietet in « pastoral » verschlüsselter Sprache die X. *Ekloge* des *Carmen Bucolicum*. Nach der Erwähnung des Pacuvius, der bei Petrarca (nach Hieronymus) der Enkel des Ennius ist, heisst es dort:

Ecl. X 180 *maternumque ostendit auum per rura iacentis*
Apulie calabrumque nemus sub ualle Galesi,
182 *ingenio agricolam nulla tamen arte colentem*
plana uirum uideo ...

Dem bukolisch-ländlichen Milieu entsprechend, darf hier *agricola* nicht etwa als abwertender Begriff für den « Tarentiner » Ennius [1] verstanden werden (wohl aber das *rusticus* im Munde des Laelius, *Afr.* IV 38); die Übernahme des epigrammatischen Urteils Ovids, das an Ennius nur das *ingenium*, nicht die *ars* gelten lässt, ist jedoch unverkennbar.

Gerade im Hinblick auf die dichterische Leistung des Ennius für Scipio, also in einem für Petrarca, der darin mit seiner *Africa* als direkter Konkurrent des Ennius auftritt, besonders wichtigen Aspekt, kehrt die Bezeichnung des Ennius als *rudis* leitmotivisch wieder. In *Epist. metr.* II 9 [2] wird von der Liebe von Königen zu Dichtern gesprochen. Nach den Beispielen Augustus/Horaz und Vergil, Archelaos/Euripides und vor der Parallele Robert von Neapel/Petrarca wird am breitesten der Fall Scipio/Ennius vorgeführt:

[1] Tarent als Geburtsort des Ennius las Petrarca bei Hieronymus *Chron.*, ad a. Abraham 1777 = 239 v. Chr. Den Galaesus als Fluss bei Tarent kannte Petrarca aus Hor. *Carm.* II 6, 10 mit dem Kommentar Ps. Acros z.St. Vgl. MARTELLOTTIS Spezialkommentar *Laurea occidens* z.St.

[2] Edit. Basil. 1554, p. 1350 a.

hic (*sc. amor*) *olim Augusto Flaccum dedit atque Maronem,*
Euripidem Archilao, nec barbarus obstitit horror.
iussit et ut nostro rudis Ennius ille placeret
Scipiadae in partem lauri uenturus opimae
et uitae mortisque comes, custosque sepulchri.

Eben der Ennius also, der als *poeta laureatus* — in dieser 1344 geschriebenen Epistel liegt mit *in partem lauri uenturus opimae* die chronologisch offenbar erste Erwähnung einer Lorbeerkrönung des Ennius vor — Vorbild Petrarcas ist, wird in gleichem Atemzuge als *poeta rudis* abqualifiziert. Ennius, so scheint Petrarca andeuten zu wollen, war dieser vielfachen Ehrung (neben der Lorbeerkrönung wird auch auf die ständige Freundschaft Scipios und die Beisetzung im Grabe der Scipionen angespielt) gar nicht würdig.

Ganz deutlich ausgesprochen wird dieses Urteil in der jüngsten Redaktion der *Africanus-Vita*. Jene Erweiterung des Kapitels XI der *Vita Scipionis*, die uns schon (in III 1) beschäftigt hat, bringt in der Redaktion α nicht nur ein Claudian-Referat über den Triumph des lorbeergekrönten Ennius an der Seite Scipios, sondern schliesst daran ein abschätziges Urteil Petrarcas : auf den Bericht ... *laureatum secum illum* (*sc. Ennium*) *retulit* (*sc. Scipio*) folgt der Kommentar : *alta sors humilis poete* (XI 13). Auch die Fortsetzung dieses Kapitels [1] zeigt die gleiche Abfolge : Bericht

[1] Petrarca *Vita Scipionis* (Red. α) XI 13 ... *alta sors humilis poete ; quin et illius senis effigiem in sepulchro Scipionum iuxta suam ac fratris imaginem sculpi fecit, quod suum nomen illius ingenio ac literis illustratum extimaret : uir Homero Virgilioque precone dignior quam Ennio. Sed sic est : preterita ac futura optari possunt, sed presentibus uti oportet ; coluit ergo quos potuit.* Vgl. Val. Max. VIII 14, 1 *superior Africanus Ennii poetae effigiem in monumentis Corneliae gentis conlocari uoluit, quod ingenio eius opera sua inlustrata iudicaret, non quidem ignarus, quam diu Romanum imperium floreret et Africa Italiae pedibus esset subiecta totiusque terrarum orbis summum columen arx Capitolina possideret, eorum extingui memoriam non posse ; si tamen litterarum quoque illis lumen accessisset, magni aestimans, uir Homerico quam rudi atque inpolito praeconio dignior.* Wenn Petrarca präziser als Valerius

über eine Ehrung des Ennius / negative Charakterisierung des Ennius, die jene Ehrung als unverdient erscheinen lässt. Petrarca bringt nämlich anschliessend die aus Val. Max. VIII 14, 1 entnommene Nachricht, Scipio maior habe eine Statue des greisen Ennius in seinem Familiengrab aufstellen lassen. Schon Valerius Maximus hatte dazu den kritischen Kommentar gegeben, dass Scipio Africanus ein Mann war, der eher einen Homer als einen so rohen und ungebildeten Lobredner wie Ennius verdient habe : *uir Homerico quam rudi atque inpolito praeconio dignior*. Das hat Petrarca mit nur leichter Abwandlung (indem er zu Homer noch Vergil gesetzt und statt der Umschreibung *rude atque inpolitum praeconium* direkt den Namen des Ennius gebracht hat) übernommen : *vir Homero Vergilioque precone dignior quam Ennio*. Petrarca nennt hier in der *Scipio-Vita* nur Claudian als Quelle für die Vorstellung von Ennius als dem *poeta laureatus et triumphans*, nicht aber Valerius Maximus im Hinblick auf die Nachricht von der Statue im Scipionengrab und den zugehörigen negativen Kommentar. Das geschieht jedoch ausdrücklich in jenem Brief (*Fam.* X 4 ; aus dem Jahre 1348) an seinen Bruder Gherardo, der einen Kommentar zur I. *Ekloge* (aus d.J. 1346) darstellt [1]. Dort hatte es am Schluss über Scipio Africanus maior geheissen : *carmine fama sacro caret hactenus* (*Buc. carm.* I 120). Diese Aussage rechtfertigt Petrarca *Fam.* X 4, 34 folgendermassen:

Maximus von einer *senis effigies* redet, fusst er offenbar auf dem sog. Bildnis-Epigramm des Ennius (*Var.* 15), die Erwähnung auch der Statuen des Africanus maior und seines Bruders ist aus Livius XXXVIII 56, 4 ergänzt. Petrarca kennt auch die Tradition von der Beisetzung (nicht nur Statue) des Ennius im Scipionengrab : *Epist. metr.* II 9 (eben im Haupttext zitiert), wie Schol. Bob. Cic. *Arch.* 22 ; Ov. *Ars* III 410 ; Hieron. z.J. 1849 = 168 v.Chr. — Vgl. ferner S. 300, Anm. 1.

[1] Die Datierungen nach B. T. Sozzi, *Il ' Bucolicum carmen ' del Petrarca*, Parma 1968 (Università degli studi di Parma, Fac. di Magistero), S. 6 und 45. — Vgl. auch oben S. 310, Anm. 1.

sed de hoc tam laudato iuuene nemo canit; quod ideo dictum est, quoniam etsi omnis historia laudibus et rebus eius plena sit, et Ennium de eo multa scripsisse non sit dubium, ' rudi et impolito ' ut Valerius [*VIII* 14, 1] *ait ' stilo ', cultior tamen de illis rebus liber metricus non apparet. de hoc igitur utcumque canere institui, quia scilicet de eo liber meus est qui inscribitur Africa, utinam tam felici exitu claudendus seni quam magno animo coeptus est iuueni.*

Schliesslich sei für die stereotype *rudis*-Charakterisierung des Ennius bei Petrarca noch hingewiesen auf den Schluss der III. *Ekloge* (aus d.J. 1346), wo wieder der Triumph des lorbeergekrönten Ennius vorausgesetzt ist, wenn Daphne (die Personifizierung des Lorbeers) die Bedeutung des Kapitols folgendermassen rühmt:

Buc. carm. III
152 *haec iuga magnanimus ...*
154 *saltibus ex Libycis rediens puer ille reuisit*
155 *et secum rudis ille senex ...*

und auf *Sonett* 186, 12, wo die ungenügende Huldigung des Ennius für Scipio (Ennio di quel [sc. di Scipione] cantò ruvido carme) eine Parallele zur Dichtung Petrarcas darstellt — aber nicht etwa zur *Africa*, sondern zu seiner Dichtung zur Verherrlichung Lauras.

Die bei Petrarca so vielfach belegte Auffassung des Ennius als eines *poeta rudis* hat, weit über den als Quelle ausdrücklich genannten Valerius Maximus hinaus, eine feste antike Tradition. Wenn die hohe soziale Geltung des Ennius, wie sie sich konkret in den Nachrichten über seinen Umgang mit römischen Grossen und die von ihnen erfahrenen Ehrungen ausdrückt, die eine Konstante im Enniusbild der Antike ist, dann ist die *poeta-rudis*-Vorstellung seit der augusteischen Zeit die andere feste Grösse in der Beurteilung des Ennius. Unter den Belegen, die hier nicht vorgeführt

werden können [1], ist hervorzuheben das einprägsame Schlagwort Ovids *Ennius ingenio maximus, arte rudis* (*Trist.* II 424) [2]; denn es ist weithin zu d e m Urteil, wenn man so will, dem Todesurteil für Ennius, jedenfalls für die künstlerische Bedeutung des Ennius, geworden. Nicht nur in Antike und Mittelalter, auch auf Petrarca hat es seine Wirkung nicht verfehlt.

III 9

Zum Schluss sei noch eine besondere Methode der Wertung des Ennius betrachtet, die eng mit seiner Verurteilung als *poeta rudis* (III 8), aber auch mit seinem Messen an Homer und anderen Dichtern (III 7) zusammengehört. Die Leistung des Ennius für Scipio wird nämlich mit der Homers für Achill verglichen und auf diesem Hintergrund abgewertet. Als Motto für diesen Abschnitt kann die berühmte, für uns zuerst in der *Archias-Rede* Ciceros 24 belegte A l e x a n d e r - A n e k d o t e dienen, nach der Alexander den Achill glücklich gepriesen hat, weil er in Homer einen würdigen Herold seiner Taten gefunden habe. (Cicero bringt das Wort Alexanders mit jenem *praeco*-Begriff, den wir bereits III 2 betrachtet haben: *o fortunate adulescens, qui tuae uirtutis Homerum praeconem inueneris*). Zweimal in der *Africa* wird Ennius ausdrücklich mit Hinweis auf diese Alexander-Anekdote kritisiert: in der Rede des Laelius IV 37-41 und in der Selbstdarstellung des Ennius IX 51-60 [3].

[1] Die einschlägigen Ausführungen des Genfer Originalvortrags sollen bei anderer Gelegenheit publiziert werden.

[2] Es liegen hier dieselben Kriterien zugrunde wie in dem berühmten Urteil Ciceros über *Lucretii poemata*, *Qu.fr.* II 9 (11), 3 aus dem Jahre 54: *multis luminibus ingenii, multae tamen artis.*

[3] Die beiden Stellen sind oben S. 299, Anm. 2 bzw. S. 301, Anm. 3 zitiert. Vgl. ferner die beiden zusammengehörigen *Sonette* 186 und 187 (*Petrarca, Rime*, S. 252 f.). Der Alexander-Ausspruch wird auch, mit Hinweis auf die *Archias-Rede* Ciceros, in der *laureatio*-Rede Petrarcas p. 323 HORTIS angeführt,

In der *Archias-Rede* Ciceros dient der Alexander-Ausspruch als Beleg für die Wertschätzung der Dichter durch grosse Männer ; er wird — was bei der Verehrung Ciceros für Ennius selbstverständlich ist — nicht etwa verwendet, um Ennius als Parallele zu den ungenügenden Schriftstellern in der Umgebung Alexanders hinzustellen. Cicero will ja umgekehrt Ennius als einen Mann erweisen, der sich um die römischen Nobiles und die *res publica* verdient gemacht hat. In einer Zeit aber, die Ennius nicht mehr schätzte, ist die Anekdote gegen ihn ausgewertet worden. Das erste Zeugnis für eine solche Übertragung des Alexanderwortes mit dem Rühmen Homers und der implizierten Kritik an den Alexander-Panegyrikern auf das Verhältnis des Ennius zu Scipio findet sich bei Valerius Maximus VIII 14, 1, eine Stelle, die von Petrarca praktisch wörtlich übernommen worden ist [1].

Ein wenigstens impliziter Vergleich der panegyrischen Leistung Homers für Achill mit Ennius und seiner ungenügenden Scipio-Verherrlichung lässt sich auch bei Silius XIII 778 ff. finden, wo Silius den Scipio bedauernd ausrufen lässt, ein Homer würde seine Taten bei der Nachwelt wesentlich grösser erscheinen lassen — der Leser weiss : als Ennius es vermocht hat [2].

Und wieder einmal lässt sich dieses kritische Urteil der Nachwelt auf Ennius selber zurückführen. Ennius hat seinen Kritikern mindestens den Ansatz zu diesem für ihn ungünstigen Vergleich mit Homer geliefert. Diesmal ist nicht auf das *Somnium Ennii* mit der Homer-Metempsychose in den

allerdings ohne Bezug auf Ennius, obwohl unmittelbar vorher auch jene Claudian-Partie zitiert ist, in der Ennius erscheint.

[1] Vgl. oben S. 342 f. mit Anm. 1. — Umgekehrt hofft Petrarca natürlich, selber für Scipio die Homer-Rolle ausfüllen zu können. Dass er das erreicht hat, wird ihm in der Tat später von Boccaccio, *Geneal. deor.* VI 53 bestätigt : BERNARDO, *Petrarch*, 172 Anm. 11.

[2] Vgl. meine *Untersuchungen*, S. 318.

Annalen zu verweisen (vgl. III 4), sondern auf das Proömium des ennianischen *Scipio*; in diesem Proömium hat Ennius, wie uns durch Aelian in einer *Suda*-Partie (Vahlen S. 212, *var.* I) bezeugt ist, einleitend ausdrücklich betont, er sei nicht imstande, die Grosstaten Scipios hinreichend zu preisen; dazu bedürfe es eines Homers [1]. Das scheint mir eine (und zwar offenbar die älteste) Anspielung auf die Alexander-Anekdote zu sein; mindestens setzt sie die Auffassung Homers als Lobredners seiner Helden voraus. Es könnte nun sein — so arbeitet vor allem böswillige Kritik gern —, dass spätere Kritiker diese Äusserung des Ennius, die ja nur den auch sonst belegten Exordialtopos der fingierten Bescheidenheit [2] darstellt, für bare Münze genommen und geradezu behauptet haben: in der Tat war Ennius einer homerischen Aufgabe nicht gewachsen. Das ist eine Ironie der Literaturgeschichte, ähnlich der, dass Hieronymus den Anspruch des Ennius umdeutend ihn zwar als *alter Homerus* bezeichnet, aber über ihn noch Vergil stellt, den *primus Homerus apud Latinos* [3]. Das Bild, das Ennius von sich selber entworfen hat, ist von der Literarkritik der Folgezeit relativiert worden [4].

[1] Vgl. übrigens die elegante Variation des Historikers Livius (bei Sen. *Suas.* VI 22) in seinem Nachruf auf Cicero, ... *in cuius laudes exsequendas Cicerone laudatore opus fuerit.* Vgl. ferner Strabo XIV 5, 14 (Boethos/Antonius — Homer/Achill, Agamemnon, Odysseus).

[2] Einige spätantike Belege bringt T. Janson, *Latin prose prefaces*, Stockholm u.a. 1964 (Acta Univ. Stockh., Stud. Lat. Stockh. 13), 149 f.

[3] Hier. *In Mich.* II 7, 5/7.

[4] Für ihre Mithilfe, nicht immer nur in technischer Hinsicht, habe ich meinen Schülern D. Misslbeck und H. Sauer zu danken.

DISCUSSION

M. Skutsch : Mr. Suerbaum seemed to consider the modesty of Ennius in the *Scipio* a purely literary phenomenon. I would not deny that this is possible but should prefer to think that there was also an increase in self-confidence.

M. Suerbaum : Es ist aus verschiedenen Gründen wahrscheinlich, dass der *Scipio* chronologisch vor die *Annales* gehört. In der Tat kann darum bei der Steigerung der Homer-Konzeption vom *Scipio*-Proömium zum *Annales*-Eingang ein autobiographisches Moment wie das wachsende Selbstbewusstsein des Dichters Ennius mit im Spiel sein.

M. Waszink : Gibt es irgendwelche Indizien darüber, ob Petrarca Fragmente des Ennius für den eigenen Gebrauch gesammelt hat, wie z.B. Scaliger das mit den Fragmenten des Empedocles getan hat ?

M. Suerbaum : Es gibt zwar eine ganze Reihe von Ennius-Erwähnungen (und auch Ennius-Würdigungen) bei Petrarca, aber meines Wissens nur relativ wenige Ennius-Zitate, so das *Cunctator-Elogium*, das Grabepigramm, die Verspottung der Seher. (Darüber handle ich in einer Anmerkung meines Vortrags.) Diese Zitate konnte Petrarca leicht zugänglichen Schriften Ciceros (*Off. ; Tusc. ; Diu.*) entnehmen. Es ist nicht anzunehmen, dass er sich eigens eine Sammlung von Ennius-Zitaten angelegt hat.

Befremdlich ist, dass Petrarca *Fam.* XXII 2, 11 den Schriftstellern wie Vergil, Horaz, Boethius und Cicero, mit denen er ständig umgeht, eine andere Gruppe gegenüberstellt, die er nur einmal, eilig, gewissermassen wie auf fremdem Gebiet sich befindend gelesen hat, und zu dieser Gruppe an erster Stelle Ennius,

dann Plautus, Martianus Capella und Apuleius zählt (*legi semel apud Ennium, apud Plautum, apud Felicem Capellam, apud Apuleium, et legi raptim, propere, nullam nisi ut alienis in finibus moram trahens*). Das klingt so, als habe Petrarca genauso gut einen Ennius besessen wie eine Plautusausgabe, wenn er diese Autoren auch nicht besonders intensiv studiert habe. Doch kann kein Zweifel bestehen, dass er Ennius nicht — wie die anderen Genannten — im Original gelesen haben kann ; es wird die häufige Nennung und Zitierung des Ennius bei Cicero sein, die Petrarca den Eindruck vermittelt haben mochte, er habe auch Ennius gelesen. Als Bestätigung für diese Erklärung kann Petrarcas Betrachtung *Fam.* III 18, 4 dienen, dass ein Buch über sich selbst hinaus auf andere Autoren hinweisen kann. Unter den Beispielen nennt Petrarca als erstes, dass er Varro und Ennius durch Cicero als Mittelquelle kennengelernt hat: *Marcum mihi Varronem carum et amabilem Ciceronis Academicus fecit; Ennii nomen in Officiorum libris audiui.* (Vahlens Ausgabe bietet aus Ciceros *De officiis* 10 Ennius-Zitate, darunter eines, *Ann.* 194 sqq., im Umfang von 8 Versen).

Ich möchte noch die Behandlung einer allgemeinen überlieferungsgeschichtlichen Frage anregen. In meinen Betrachtungen zum Nachleben des Ennius brauchte ich methodisch gesehen nicht zu unterscheiden zwischen Autoren, die Ennius noch im Original gelesen haben, und solchen, die nur eine abgeleitete Kenntnis von ihm besassen. Aber unabhängig vom direkten Bezug auf meinen Vortrag wäre es eine für das Nachleben des Ennius aufschlussreiche Feststellung, wenn man die Zeit bestimmen könnte, bis zu der noch ein Ennius-Text nachweislich existierte und wenigstens von einzelnen gelesen wurde. Vahlen (p. CXXVII sqq.) setzt z.B. offenbar noch bei Isidor von Sevilla direkte Ennius-Lektüre voraus ; ein rätselhaftes Prager Bücherverzeichnis führt noch im 14. Jahrhundert einen Ennius auf (vgl. Barchiesi, *Nevio epico*, Padova 1962, Anm. 600, S. 118 f.). Wichtig zu wissen wäre nicht zuletzt, wann der Ennius-Text von der Papyrus-Rolle in den haltbareren und (gerade für Gramma-

tiker) leichter benutzbaren Pergament-Codex umgeschrieben worden ist.

M. Skutsch: Im allgemeinen gelten als letzte Zeugnisse eines Enniustextes die Fragmente, die Ekkehart der Vierte aus einer älteren Orosius-Handschrift in die St. Galler Handschrift eingetragen hat. Aber der Schluss, dass nach Orosius noch eine Enniushandschrift vorlag, aus der sich inhaltliche Zusammenhänge für mindestens einige Bücher erkennen liessen, scheint mir nicht zwingend. Es ist nämlich durchaus denkbar, dass solche Fragmente in eine viel ältere Liviusepitome eingetragen wurden und von dort sekundär ihren Weg in den Orosiustext fanden.

M. Jocelyn: There is a desire on the part of many scholars concerned with Ennius to extend as late as possible the period during which texts of his works were preserved and read. Students of late antiquity also like to exaggerate the learning and reliability of writers like Macrobius. Two important general considerations should be kept in mind.

Firstly, Ennius' poems were read and quoted extensively by all kinds of authors of the first century B.C. and the early first century A.D., most of whose works are now also lost but were still preserved in the fifth century. I have in mind particularly the antiquarian works of Varro. Second century A.D. authors, like Gellius who survives and Flavius Caper who does not, knew Ennius and other archaic poets well. Quotations of the *Annales* in works of the fifth and sixth centuries are theoretically as much capable of coming from such secondary sources as from the actual text.

Secondly, there are many particular cases in which late authors can be demonstrated beyond reasonable doubt as copying earlier quotations of the *Annales*, e.g. the account of Virgil's supposed dependence on Ennius in the sixth book of Macrobius' *Saturnalia*. It is accordingly reasonable to hold everything quoted during late antiquity in suspicion. The onus of proof is on the scholar

who wants to show that in a particular case Macrobius or Servius or Priscian actually consulted a text of the *Annales*.

M. Skutsch : I am convinced that Macrobius relied essentially on *furta Vergilii* but remember darkly that I once had reason to suspect that he also had access to a text.

M. Waszink : At all events it is certain that Lactantius still had access to the integral text of the *Euhemerus* ; cf. on this subject the well-known papers of Laughton and Ed. Fraenkel in *Eranos* 1951.

M. Jocelyn : I am not sure about Lactantius and the *Euhemerus*. There were, of course, argumentative treatises on θεολογία long before Lactantius. A man like Varro, steeped as he was in the archaic literature, might well quote Ennius' version of the Ἱερὰ ἀναγραφή. Somewhere about the time of Lactantius the African grammarian Nonius Marcellus had access to a big library of early Republican books. Ennius' *Hectoris lytra* and *Telephus* were there, but not, it would seem, the *Annales* and the *Euhemerus*.

M. Badian : Though I do not claim to be an expert on Macrobius and recognize Mr. Jocelyn's authority on this, I must warn against the 19th century German *Quellenkritik* which established the principle that no ancient author ever did the work he claims to have done, but that it was all done earlier, by a lost predecessor. This strange idea created havoc in source criticism (e.g. in the case of Plutarch) and is difficult to exorcize. It can be shown to be absurd in some cases : e.g. Plutarch and Gellius.

But obviously it is difficult — and sometimes impossible — to prove conclusively that an author used original texts and not merely handbooks. We all nowadays use handbooks and collections of sources, and it can be shown that we all make occasional mistakes due to this. But it by no means follows that those who use such works, and make such mistakes, never consult original

texts or should be described as habitual plagiarists. Nor does it follow that the onus of proof is on one who would maintain that they are not habitual plagiarists. It is easy to show by various criteria that the later grammarians on the whole use previous collections : their range is limited in certain ways, their texts are poor, their references often wrong, their actual interpretation sometimes faulty. Macrobius is not guilty of any of these errors, and the fact that he sometimes demonstrably uses (say) Gellius does not entitle us to presume him « guilty unless proved innocent » in the whole of his work. I must firmly reject the onus of this proof and transfer it where it belongs—to the *accuser*, who is not entitled to treat an intelligent and careful author like a hack grammarian, merely because he (like all of us) used his predecessors' work.

M. Jocelyn : I am arguing from grounds of common sense and common knowledge, not from authority. Mr. Badian's account of 19th century *Quellenkritik* is a grossly unfair parody. The writings of Wissowa and Linke on the *Saturnalia*, for example, seem to me models of how to approach the sort of question which Mr. Suerbaum raised. The question of the reliability of Macrobius' quotations is a different one, although related.

The case of Macrobius is very different from that of Gellius. Gellius used grammatical handbooks etc., and his own considered acquaintance with the archaic literature in order to construct the dialogues he presents in the *Noctes Atticae*. Macrobius was an outright plagiarist. The survival of Gellius' work enables us to see clearly the way Macrobius sometimes proceeded. Large slabs of the *Noctes Atticae* were simply copied out and put into the mouths of Macrobius' personages. A jury of tender-minded historians might presume Macrobius innocent elsewhere but a philologist, conscious of how much post-Ennian literature has been lost, will remain full of suspicion.

INDEX LOCORUM

A. Ennius *

* *Loci Enniani secundum editionem Vahlenianam tertiam laudantur.*

B. Auctores vetustiores

* * *

ANONYMA :

C. Auctores medii aevi et saec. XVI

D. Auctores recentiores

INDEX NOMINUM

N.B. *Deorum, heroum, virorum, feminarum gentiumque nomina minutis rectis, geographica minutis obliquiis scribuntur.*

PRINTED IN SWITZERLAND

Achevé d'imprimer
le 30 juin 1972 sur les presses
de l'Imprimerie du « Journal de Genève »,
à Genève, Suisse